William Tecumseh Sherman

and the

Settlement of the West

William Tecumseh Sherman
and the
Settlement of the West

—

by Robert G. Athearn

Foreword by
William M. Ferraro and J. Thomas Murphy

University of Oklahoma Press
Norman and London

FOR CLAIRE

Library of Congress Cataloging-in-Publication Data

Athearn, Robert G.
   William Tecumseh Sherman and the settlement of the West /
by Robert G. Athearn ; foreword by William M. Ferraro and J.
Thomas Murphy.
      p.   cm.
   Includes bibliographical references and index.
   ISBN 0–8061–2769–4 (alk. paper)
   1. Sherman,   William   T.   (William   Tecumseh),   1820–1891.
   2. West (U.S.)—History—1860–1890. I. Title.
   E467.1.S55A8   1995
   978'.02'092—dc20   95-11480
                                                           CIP

The paper in this book meets the guidelines for permanence and
durability of the Committee on Production Guidelines for Book
Longevity of the Council on Library Resources, Inc. ∞

2   3   4   5   6   7   8   9   10   11

CONTENTS

ILLUSTRATIONS

MAPS

FOREWORD

IN THE DECADE following World War II a new generation of
historians writing about the American West began to challenge
Frederick Jackson Turner's frontier hypothesis. For them the story
of western settlement could not be portrayed simply as a romantic
struggle between individual pioneers and an untamed wilderness.
Instead, they argued, it resulted from the interrelationship of
several factors, such as the development of transportation net-
works, financial investments from eastern and European sources,
and involvement by the federal government, particularly the army.
Among the scholars advancing this new interpretation was Robert
G. Athearn, a young Montana-born professor at the University of
Colorado, whose career as a teacher and writer would influence
both his and subsequent generations.

With the publication of *William Tecumseh Sherman and the Settle-*
ment of the West by the University of Oklahoma Press in 1956,
Athearn enhanced his reputation as one of the premier historians
of the American West. Earlier works, such as Frederic F. Van de
Water's *The Glory Hunter* (New York, 1934) and Fairfax Downey's
Indian-Fighting Army (New York, 1941), emphasize flamboyant cavalrymen, the isolation of frontier outposts, and marauding Indian
raiders. Athearn's book, by contrast, considers the role of the army
within a broader framework of railroad construction, experiments
with Indian policy, squabbling politicians, and the changing opinions of newspapers editors and the populace.

At the center of Athearn's study is William Tecumseh Sherman,
whose Civil War career overshadowed his eighteen years of postwar
military service. Sherman had been known primarily for cutting a
swath of destruction through Georgia and the Carolinas, but
Athearn portrays a man of greater depth and complexity. Sherman

appears as crusty and determined, as willing to punish recalcitrant and troublesome Kiowas as he had been to punish John Bell Hood's Confederate soldiers outside Atlanta. He is sharptongued when angered and is irritable with narrow-minded civilians, whether they be Indian-hating settlers or stingy congressmen. Sherman, who had lived in California and Kansas before the Civil War and who considered St. Louis his home, is also knowledgeable about the western landscape, uncomfortable with the intrigue found in eastern cities, unassuming, and a decisive leader. As Athearn states, Sherman was equal to the "ways of real western men" and, despite his position as a largely deskbound general, was a true western hero.

Sherman derived satisfaction from his constructive years of planning and executing the routine duties essential to western development. As commander of the Division of the Missouri from 1865 to 1869, Sherman exercised control over an expanse stretching from the Canadian border to New Mexico and from Montana and Utah to Missouri and Arkansas. When he was General of the Army, from 1869 to 1883, his command covered the entire United States, but the West received his special attention. As Athearn shows, Sherman promoted the completion of a continental rail system and made its protection a priority. Vast distances and difficult terrain slowed the deployment of troops and hindered the supply of scattered forts, but rail lines increased the mobility of Sherman's small western army. More important, the railroad operated as the "great civilizer" because it carried settlers into the West.

As these settlers crowded Indians from their homelands, confrontations and bloodshed became inevitable. Sherman knew that neither side held a monopoly on virtue, and despite a firm belief that the native inhabitants must give way to white encroachment, he maintained a stance that all wrongdoers deserved punishment. "The Indian question is a practical one," Sherman wrote, "and not one of mere feelings." But his plans for creating an effective policy were hampered at every turn. Unscrupulous or incompetent Indian agents angered Sherman; unrealistic but influential eastern philanthropists made him impatient; and the Interior Department frustrated him with its unwillingness to give the army complete jurisdiction over Indian affairs. At best, Athearn writes, "removing Indians to reservations and containing them" was "a thankless task." Sherman endured further exasperation after President Ulysses S. Grant rescinded an order giving the commanding general clear authority over the line and staff. As a result, secretaries of war either ignored Sherman or worked at cross purposes. He found it incomprehensible, too, that Congress reduced troop numbers and cut funds for the army despite its arduous duties in the West.

Athearn concludes that Sherman watched over the settlement of the West "like a father." With paternalistic concern he maintained a presence in the area through frequent inspection tours, traveling initially in mule-drawn ambulances known as Doughertys and later over rails behind iron horses. While on these tours, Sherman spoke to the settlers, counseling patience and good sense in dealing with Indians, encouraging efforts for economic self-sufficiency, denigrating all unnecessary clamor for military protection, and finally, as his retirement neared in early 1882, applauding his auditors for their role in the remarkable transformation of the recently raw and forbidding region. Their progress in developing the West, the general reported, was "simply prodigious." Sherman would readily admit that the process of western settlement left scars on the landscape and the national soul, but Athearn, like Sherman, does not allow these failings to overawe the magnificence of such an achievement.

In Sherman's mind the West held generative powers and offered opportunity to anyone willing to venture there. He expected, however, that by the 1880s the allure would subside, and he was fascinated when instead it persisted. This mythic appeal also attracted Athearn's interest, and it remained a focal point of his scholarship until his death in 1983. As a westerner himself, Athearn shared Sherman's enthusiasm for the region—it permeates his lively and cogent narrative. Relying on Sherman's correspondence and reports, Athearn takes advantage of his subject's ability to be acute and colorful, ironic and witty. At the same time, Athearn could draw on his own experience to describe a historical setting. He understood, for example, mornings in the Rocky Mountains cold enough "to produce ice in the camp water buckets," and the result is an evocative picture combining his own and Sherman's vision of the West.

To present his portrait, Athearn exploited manuscript collections, government archives, published primary sources, and many newspapers, and while this is an assumed practice among scholars today, his methodology helped set a new standard for writing histories of the American West. Missing from his account are reliable sources explaining the actions of Sherman's Indian antagonists. Their superficial voice mutes a dimension of the story. But Athearn laid the groundwork for further studies, and historians of the West have complemented his efforts by producing a number of works on U.S. Indian policy and the role of military leaders, including Philip H. Sheridan, Nelson A. Miles, and William B. Hazen, all of whom served under Sherman. Along with its scholarly influence, *William Tecumseh Sherman and the Settlement of the West* appeals to students and general readers. It is straightforward and entertaining, and we are pleased that the University of Oklahoma Press has again made Athearn's fine monograph available with this paperback edition.

WILLIAM M. FERRARO

Ulysses S. Grant Association
Southern Illinois University-Carbondale

J. THOMAS MURPHY

McLennan Community College

INTRODUCTION

ON A BRIGHT January day in 1847, the barnacled old warship *Lexington* nibbled at a fishhook-shaped bay on the California coast. The vessel's rails were crowded with blue-coated soldiers who jostled each other, anxious for a view of the curved, cream-colored outline of sand that spelled the end of a long and brine-spattered voyage. Beyond lay the whitewashed walls and red-tiled roofs of Monterey, palisaded by dark-green pines. It was a bright contrast to the drab New York sky line, now nearly two hundred pitching, rolling days behind the voyagers. As the anchor plunged into the water, excitement took command of everyone aboard.

It was a strange, new land that held out a promise to the young officers who commanded the newly arrived troops. The United States was at war with Mexico, and they were a part of the force sent out in a flanking attack on California. Fighting, bloodshed, and death meant that promotions normally gained in years could be had on the field of battle in weeks or months. The *Lexington's* passengers supposed that they would ply their trade immediately upon landing; and as the ship came to a halt, swords flashed and guns received a last minute oiling. A twenty-six-year-old lieutenant named William Tecumseh Sherman, acting as quartermaster and commissary, was particularly busy as the ship-to-shore movement commenced.

But there was no conflict. As the troops approached a small wharf, they were greeted by a handful of the inevitable marines and by the United States consul, Thomas Larkin, who filled in the two months' void of news. There had been no spectacular military events. Nor would there be. Young Sherman, who hauled ashore $28,000 in commissary and quartermaster funds, was to spend the next few years in a sprawling domain of ranches ruled by easygoing, not unfriendly, dons who seemed far less excited about international conflict than the newcomers. As he disbursed funds and scratched away at his reports, the conscientious officer wrote that he was ashamed to wear his epaulets. He passed through the war without even smelling gunpowder, while his Academy classmates won fame and promotion in Mexico.

Fate often defers fame, saving it for a time of maturity and full fruition in the man. Young John Frémont reached his peak and passed it during the war. Chesty little George McClellan, six years behind Sherman at West Point, gained a captaincy in battle, while Braxton Bragg became a major by serving up "a little more grape" for General Zachary Taylor at the Battle of Buena Vista. None of the youngsters fulfilled the promise of greatness in later years. Meanwhile, Sherman fretted in California, apparently locked indefinitely in rank, as peace returned in the fall of 1848. He would be nearly forty-five before fame reached out to knight him.

The early years, seemingly so barren, were golden in experience. While there were no decorations or sudden promotions, there developed in Sherman a thoughtfulness and a belief in the future of the land that would one day yield its dividends. His days in California planted a seed of interest in the development of the nation that continued to grow until his death. Fascinated, he watched the rush of miners come in 1849, and saw a community spring forth with the normal stress and strain of birth. While the attendant excitement was not that of shot and shell, it nevertheless provided a historic panorama of colorful movement and overnight change, the significance of which was not lost upon the studious officer who had come west to fight. A faraway and yet disconnected part of the nation was arising, and he was to write of it at length in his memoirs many years later.

Unable to stand aside, a disinterested army-officer spectator, Sherman himself fell victim to the speculative fever; and as the war ended, he became part owner of a store in the mining town of Coloma, California, the site of the original gold discovery. Later he turned his talents to surveying, and for his services took title to some lots at the mouth of the San Joaquin River on Sui-sun Bay, in a place the promoter bravely dubbed the "New York of the Pacific." Before long, he also owned three lots in Sacra-mento. Because of the small army salaries in a land of unbeliev-ably inflated prices, superior officers looked upon such extracur-ricular activities by their subordinates with approval. Leaves of absence were granted for these ventures, and in one two-month period, Sherman made $6,000. By January, 1850, he was trans-ferred back to New York, having spent three eventful years in California. He promptly applied for a leave of six months, during which time he married Ellen Boyle Ewing, daughter of the Sec-retary of the Interior.

The excitement of California and its myriad of economic pos-sibilities was to cost the army one of its promising young officers. After his marriage, Sherman was stationed at St. Louis, where from time to time he visited the land to the west. He was fasci-nated by the country around Fort Leavenworth and wrote of it as "a most beautiful spot, but in the midst of a wild Indian country." He could not keep his thoughts from the expanding country beyond, and with vivid memories of California con-stantly in his mind, he again applied for an extended leave and hastened back, leaving his wife and two small children. In Sep-tember of 1853, he resigned his commission and abandoned an army career.

The return to California was not successful, and by the spring of 1857, Sherman was back in his family home in Ohio. The panic of that year left him stranded financially; but still deter-mined to take part in the expanding economy of a frontier region, he joined his brothers-in-law in a law firm at Leavenworth, Kan-sas, the place that had so fascinated him earlier. "I did not pre-sume to be a lawyer," he later wrote, perhaps to explain why his new venture lasted less than a year. The beginning of the Civil War found him in Louisiana, the head of a small college, still groping towards a career that could both satisfy his restless imagi-nation and feed a rapidly growing family.

Until destiny plucked him out of the eddying backwaters of civil life and cast him headlong into the vortex of national conflict in 1861, Sherman was a man of unrealized potentialities. His deep and sensitive interest in the development of his country blended with his desire for personal accomplishment and security for his family, but chance and economic panic had so far prevented him from attaining even a small degree of success. His intense nationalism and abiding faith in the future of America had never had an audience outside the family circle until the Civil War cast him in a major role on the American scene. Even then he was to many men a dreamer and even a mystic, frequently misunderstood and sometimes scoffed at, but dazzling military renown lent his words so much weight that he could no longer be ignored.

At Bull Run, in 1861, he fumed at the disorderly mob he had to lead into battle, and his desire for military precision brought loud complaints from the volunteers he commanded. That fall, in Kentucky, he brought down upon his head the criticism of newsmen because he wanted more troops, refusing to believe that only a three months' war lay ahead. The next year, at bloody Shiloh, he came into his own, working at the side of another disgruntled West Pointer who, like himself, had left the army in prewar days. His association with Ulysses S. Grant, another tough and single-minded soldier, was probably the turning point in his career. Together they forged the victory at Vicksburg in the summer of 1863; and by the next year, Sherman, commanding the western armies, stood poised in Tennessee, ready for his fabled march to Atlanta, and beyond. Towards the end of December, he could offer the city of Savannah as a Christmas present to President Lincoln. The gesture signified that the South had crumbled, and in the thunder and dust of that collapse Sherman firmly established himself in the national hall of fame. Within a few months the fighting of the Civil War was over. As the guns became cool, the gaunt Sherman, more tired of war than anyone knew, once again glanced at the unfinished map of the United States and longed for an opportunity to return to the West and participate in the final hours of the building of his nation.

During the years 1865 to 1883, Sherman was successively in

command of the Military Division of the Missouri, comprising roughly the high plains area, and of the entire United States Army. In both capacities, he revealed a real concern with the progress of western settlement and an understanding of the many problems attendant upon that historic movement. As a high-ranking army officer, charged with the responsibility of protecting the ragged edge of settlement that rolled forward, he had a real part in the development of America's last frontier.

The postwar rush westward was the day of the forty-niner re-enacted on a large scale, and in it Sherman must have found many interesting parallels. The settlement of the Trans-Mississippi West was the most spectacular of all American frontier experiences. Its many props—horses, stagecoaches, railroads, steamboats, Indians, cowboys, mountain men, large cavalry units, bonanza villages, and six-shooters—have fascinated writers of fiction and nonfiction for nearly a century. Much of the writing about it has been episodic and isolated in approach because the land was so vast and the experience of the people who sought to subdue it so varied. Those who have attempted to record the leading events have frequently been attracted by their more spectacular aspects, leaving untold the less violent but equally important happenings.

Sherman saw the enormity and complexity of the development and understood fully that it would be carried out in the American tradition of a tumultuous, head-over-heels scramble for gain and individual ascendancy. The disorderly process ran counter to the grain of his military and personal background, and he strove, with only partial success, to control the forces at work. Against the exploiters he threw everything he had: his talent, his training, and his personal prestige. He called upon his brother John Sherman, a senator from Ohio, to use his influence in Congress. He pleaded his case with an old friend, Ulysses S. Grant, who became president in 1869. And they were all engulfed by a trite phrase called Manifest Destiny. The stampede would not abate until the land was overrun.

Sherman soon found that while his soldiers were fighting Indians, the nation was technically at peace. No longer were his calls for more troops heard. Members of Congress, and men on the street, convinced themselves that there was no war, and for picket duty in the West, the army's demands were exorbitant. When, on occasion, the Indians would strike hard enough to cause public indignation in the East, there would be a momentary murmur about a larger fighting force, but in general it was drowned out by the normal postwar lullaby of peace and prosperity.

Through these years Sherman guided the army, trying to preserve it from the scalping knives of Congressional braves who were out to make coups by cutting taxes through military reduction. At the same time, he tried to satisfy the Westerners who spread over the land and into the little valleys, in search of sudden wealth. They demanded absolute protection, and he could not give it. Frequently, for this deficiency, they damned him. But in general, and especially as time passed, they praised him. The tall, spare, hard-bitten officer had a good many characteristics of a Westerner about him, and beyond the Missouri, in particular, he was largely held in high esteem. Despite periodic expressions of impatience at his inability to furnish hordes of troops—something over which he had no control—frontiersmen looked to him as their leader and sponsor among the untutored denizens of eastern stone and mortar pueblos. It was a responsibility that gave him great pride.

Sherman's postwar assignment was the climax of his career. The brief years of fighting that preceded it merely brought into full bloom the latent talents of the man and rocketed him to an eminence from which he could implement a lifelong desire to build, not destroy. His story has been known to succeeding generations as one of daring marches and bold decisions in a time of national crisis. The heart of his story—the harvest years—has passed by, lost in the noisier events of Little Big Horns and bugles in the afternoon.

ACKNOWLEDGMENTS

CONTRARY TO the information carried on the title page, this book is not the work of one person. There are many hidden partners in such a project, and credit should go to them. First and foremost, thanks for assistance are due the Social Science Research Council. Without its financial support, the extensive travel required to gather material could not have been undertaken. The University of Colorado, through its Council on Research and Creative Work, rendered additional aid.

Criticizing and correcting the manuscripts of a fellow laborer in the field comprise yet another of the many additional duties loaded onto my colleagues in the profession. To William Newell Davis, Jr., California State Archives; Professor Earl Pomeroy, Department of History, University of Oregon; Professor Robert E. Riegel, Dartmouth College; and Professor Hal Bridges, Department of History, University of Colorado, I offer an expression of deep appreciation for their time, patience, and talent. The late Professor Carl Coke Rister, Department of History, Texas Technological College, Lubbock, Texas, gave valuable suggestions and pointed the way to additional materials. Wayne D. Overholser, of Boulder, Colorado, lent some of his knowledge gained through years of successful writing.

The willing and enthusiastic assistance rendered by staff members in a number of libraries and archives is gratefully acknowledged. C. Percy Powell, Division of Manuscripts, Library of Congress, and Richard G. Wood, War Records Branch, National Archives, both of Washington, D. C., were extremely helpful. Harry E. Pratt, Illinois State Historical Library, Springfield, Illinois; Colton Storm, William L. Clements Library, University of Michigan, Ann Arbor, Michigan; Watt P. Marchman, Hayes Memorial Library, Fremont, Ohio; and Elizabeth C. Biggert, Ohio State Archaeological and Historical Society, Columbus, Ohio, all provided extremely useful manuscript material that enriched the study considerably.

From the following directors, staff members, and libraries, I received the fullest co-operation: Nyle H. Miller, Kansas State Historical Society; Charles Van Ravenswaay, Missouri Historical Society (St. Louis); Margaret Rose, State Historical Society of North Dakota; James C. Olson, Nebraska State Historical Society; Claude R. Cooke, Iowa State Department of History and Archives; Arthur H. Parsons, Omaha Public Library; Gertrude McDevitt, Historical Department of Idaho; A. R. Mortensen, Utah State Historical Society; Lola M. Homsher and Henryetta Berry, Wyoming State Archives and Historical Department; Caroline Wenzel, California State Library; Elizabeth Tindall, St. Louis Mercantile Library; Edward B. Morrison, Division of Manuscripts, New York Public Library; Dorothy C. Barck, New York Historical Society; K. Ross Toole, Historical Society of Montana; Mulford Winsor, Arizona Department of Library and Archives; Ina T. Aulls, Alys Freeze, and Opal Harber, Denver Public Library; George P. Hammond, Bancroft Library, University of California; Agnes Wright Spring, State Historical Society of Colorado; Eugene H. Wilson, University of Colorado Library; Archibald Hanna, Western Americana Collection, Yale University; and the staff at Chicago's Newberry Library.

Others who lent their skills or materials for the volume are: Mr. Victor D. Spark of New York City; Burton Harris; Virginia Brasel Grieder; and Professor Isaac Bacon.

The maps were drawn by William A. Greig, Barbara Dumont Samsel, and Pamela Wilson, under the direction of Professor Albert W. Smith, Department of Geography, University of Colorado.

Some of the material used in writing this book has appeared in article form in *The Pacific Historical Review, The Mississippi Valley Historical Review,* and *Montana, The Magazine of Western History.*

Finally, some acknowledgment ought to be made to the au-

Acknowledgments

thor's children, who have finally become convinced that father's study is "off limits," and to their mother, who performed the meritorious service of holding them at bay while she read proof, suggested stylistic improvements, and in general performed tasks over and above the call of duty. The author, of course, provides the escape clause for all who helped him, by solemnly swearing that any and all errors are his own.

ROBERT G. ATHEARN

University of Colorado

August 30, 1956

William Tecumseh Sherman

and the

Settlement of the West

One

———

OUR PLAINS RESEMBLE YOUR SEAS

IT WAS NOT YET nine o'clock, but already the city streets reflected the heat of a bright morning sun. Pennsylvania Avenue stretched out like a dry river bed, stripped of its normal traffic, as thousands of milling people jostled one another at its edges. Normally sedate business houses were swathed in blankets of bunting, and as the swaying crowds waved bright bouquets, the scene was one of brilliant undulating color.

The military phase of the American Civil War had ended formally more than a month ago, at Appomattox, but that was a ceremony witnessed by only a few. Today, May 24, 1865, was the people's day. They had thronged into Washington from miles around, by train, by carriage, and on foot. After more than four taut years of waiting and watching from afar, they assembled now to see their victorious armies. On the previous day, General George Meade had led his resplendant Army of the Potomac, amidst thunderous cheers, down the cobblestone valley of flowers and flags. Today, the gnarled, flint-eyed William Tecumseh Sherman—almost Jacksonian in his rugged, plain appearance—would sweep before them, followed by his tough and often unruly Westerners. To the nervously expectant admirers it seemed fitting that he should climax the celebration. They had heard many complaints about the "Champagne and Oyster" armies of the East. But from Sherman they had heard of marching, fighting, and conquest. In him they saw their ideal soldier: resolute, single minded, and down to earth. Like Ulysses S. Grant, he was more interested in driving forward the machine of war than in promoting his own personal glory. Like Grant, he was the soldier's soldier. When nine o'clock drew near, the spectators restlessly awaited the booming of the cannon that would touch off the flood of blue before them.

3

As he sat erect on his horse, silent, hat in hand, the hero of Atlanta had reason to be satisfied. One of the newspapers had pointed out that this was his day, and for once he was forced to agree with the press. "Uncle Billy" had led his raw western farm boys on a slashing campaign through strange new lands in the South, and as they emerged from the Carolinas, headed for a juncture with Grant before Richmond, they had found themselves transformed into hardened, confident professional soldiers. For Sherman, too, it had been a time of maturing.

Looking down now, from the dizzy heights of sudden fame, he could view with content those kaleidoscopic months during which, after years of indecision and visionary dreams so frequently dashed to pieces by economic realities, he had at last found his true medium of expression. He regretted that the instrument of his success was the awful one of war, and that it had fixed upon him forever the opprobrium of a destroyer, but he would not now roll back the scroll of time if he could. He and Grant sparkled like twin jewels in the eyes of a hero-worshiping American public. He did not know what his taciturn friend's wishes might be for the future; for himself he hoped for something more than to live out his days in some army sinecure. He was only forty-five years old.

Fame and adulation, which he already found burdensome, could be turned perhaps to something more practical than a decade or so of testimonial banquets before retirement. Undoubtedly there were generals who would gravitate toward politics. That was one of the inevitable aftermaths of war, and there were those who would do well enough in the forensic arena. But not Sherman. Unlike his brother John, who was presently in Congress, he had no taste for the game. War-boom-rich America might offer something in the business world, but that field, too, lacked fascination for him. His banking days in California and New York had ended in disaster when the panic of 1857 inundated the country. The fleeting period as a lawyer out in Leavenworth, Kansas, had brought only memories of poverty. He had turned schoolmaster then; the war had found him running an academy at Baton Rouge, Louisiana; but it was doubtful that

the teaching profession could offer enough to support his growing family now. There seemed to be little choice but the army.
Even that would be a diminishing profession in the years ahead,
unless international complications occurred; however, the peacetime establishment might find work to do in the undeveloped
section of the country, and the thought attracted him powerfully.

If Sherman had closed his eyes for a moment and imagined a
map of the United States, he would have seen stretching westward to the Pacific, beyond the Missouri River and out over the
towering Rockies to the granite-like Sierras, a land in a virgin
state. True, its majestic sweeps were here and there dotted with
microscopic settlements of men who industriously, but often
vainly, scratched at the soil in search of mineral wealth. While
some had enjoyed splendid success, many others had not, and
as yet the over-all impression was not very deep. The larger work
of permanent settlement lay ahead. Even though much of the
West would long resist agricultural domestication, there would
be plenty of employment there for Uncle Billy's boys. The land
had minerals to be mined, timber to be cut, there were prairies as
big as oceans to be grazed, and limitless acres of rich sod waited
for the scalpel of the steel plow.

To supply these new legions of farmers and miners, railroads
and cities would have to be built. And there would be enemies
to combat—distance, drought, cold, and the angry, sullen Indians who had retreated to a point where they would contest
every remaining foot of land. Here indeed was the soldier's place.
Here the soldier could protect and shepherd the ever westward-
moving population as its cities and farms emerged. The man
who did this would have the satisfaction of seeing the American
Republic expand over lands to which it had title, but over which
it had no real control. The national structure was far from finished. Westward to the Mississippi, and a little beyond, the land
was sufficiently populated to be called settled; but to those who
viewed the nation from an international vantage point, this was
only a façade and as misleading as the false front on a western
business establishment. One-third of the nation lay as yet relatively untouched. While it contained a region long described as

5

a desert, much of it boasted of soil second to none in the country. Its only real curse was remoteness, but that could be no lasting limitation. Among man's greatest achievements had been the ability to shrink distances. With peace at hand the construction job could now continue, and the builders who had taken time out for a family quarrel could now resume their ever challenging task. The South lay in ruins; the East was settled and almost sophisticated. On the compass of destiny, the magnetic pull came from the West. It was the place of all-powerful attraction.

As Sherman sat astride his mount and listened to the impatient buzzing of the crowds along Pennsylvania Avenue, he stirred himself back into consciousness of the present. He was restless, too. Get all this over with. Hear out the accolades; then back to work. There was yet more marching to be done—westward.

A puff of smoke rose. The crack of a cannon's muzzle blast knifed down the avenue. Feet beat against pavement, and the last march began. A compact column, its muskets glittering like a coat of steel mail, lunged forward, and anxious admirers shouldered forward excitedly to look. All eyes were focused on the lean, rawhide-tough Sherman and the gentle, one-armed O. O. Howard who rode at his side. A small school girl was thrust forward self-consciously to hand the conqueror of Atlanta the appropriate wreath, and the avenue rocked with cheers. Before he could grasp the extended gift, his frightened horse began to shy and plunge. The crowd laughed nervously, and someone shouted out the rude jest, "Give it to Howard!" The crippled officer, busy with his own mount, smiled at Sherman and rode on.[1]

Down the avenue the procession moved, Sherman bowing and raising his hat repeatedly. As the cadence of his 65,000 veterans thundered behind him, almost drowning out the brassy melody of blaring bands, the General heard a song of victory and vindication in the echoes. He must have recalled, in his supreme moment, that December day back in 1861, when Murat Halstead's *Cincinnati Commercial* had appeared on the streets, its headlines shouting, "General William T. Sherman Insane." The charge had originated from nothing more than Secretary of War

1 *New York Times*, May 25, 1865.

6

Simon Cameron's complaint that Sherman's demand for 60,000, and ultimately 200,000, troops in Kentucky was "an insane request." Newsmen grasped at the remark and the term "Sherman the Crazy" was born.

Much had happened since that low ebb in his military fortunes. As "Sherman's bummers" laughingly told each other when they marched through the crumbling outskirts of Savannah, they hoped the General would have another one of his crazy spells and get the war over with. He had obliged them. Rather than ship his army northward from Georgia by sea, he had swung into the Carolinas by land, and as the military vise screwed relentlessly tighter, the life of the Confederacy was crushed out between Sherman's army and that of Grant's bearing down upon Richmond. Then it was over. And now, before he had the time to think much about it, here he was, leading his warriors down Washington's principal avenue with the crowd's frenzied cheers playing a gigantic symphony of victory. For "Sherman the Crazy," the hour of triumph was doubly rich. It was a time of personal vindication for which he had long waited.

The very prospect of the conqueror's return had caused nervousness in some circles. Every newspaper reader knew of the bitterness between Sherman and Secretary of War Edwin M. Stanton. The Secretary had brusquely refused to accept Sherman's recent surrender negotiations with Confederate General Joseph E. Johnston, charging interference in political matters, and the affair had started a buzz of rumor throughout the North. And now "the crazy" was back. What would he do? There were published predictions that Sherman's men would demonstrate, showing their anger toward Stanton, during the Grand Review.[2]

Sherman did not need his men to demonstrate for him. He had returned to Washington resolute and angry, and he had conspicuously avoided the War Department. When he passed the reviewing stand, he stiffened in his saddle and moved on. A moment later he left the line of march and entered the White House grounds, where he joined his wife and young son, Tom, in the presidential party. He shook hands with President John-

[2] *Ibid.,* May 24, 1865.

7

son, and then warmly greeted his old friend Ulysses S. Grant. Stanton thrust out his hand, but Sherman, his face scarlet and his mouth a straight line, ignored it and turned aside. It was a tense moment, one that neither man would soon forget.[3]

The *New York Times* scolded Sherman sharply a few days later, openly criticizing him for his studied rebuff.[4] Let them criticize, he must have told himself. He hated newspapermen anyway—they who had popularized the "crazy" appellation—and that dislike was no more secret than his feelings toward Stanton. He hated Washington, too, and the bureaucracy it represented to him. All he wanted now was to extricate himself from the political web that spread over the place and, if possible, to get back home. He had been given his day, and from it he had wrung grim satisfaction. Now let adulation, parades, and public fawning be done with.

As the excitement of the grand review subsided and demobilization became the word of the day, Sherman bade his beloved "bummers" farewell and returned to thoughts of his own future. Old problems again reared their heads, problems that the pressure of war had momentarily submerged. In the prewar years, since resigning his army commission in 1853, he had shifted from one venture to the next, trying to find security and sufficient means to support a growing family. Now, despite his high rank and his desire to serve in the West, he still had a lingering doubt about the ability of a military salary to cover his many domestic needs. He even considered resigning his commission once again to look around for a better-paying job. As he temporized during the summer of 1865, he wrote to his brother saying that it was probable some friends in St. Louis, his old home before the war, would give him a house. He hoped they would. As he told John, his army allowance for housing was only $48.00 a month. This would not be enough, for St. Louis prices were enormous. Almost "California prices," he called them. Despite rising costs, army allowances had not changed materially since the Revolutionary War.

3 Lloyd Lewis, *Sherman: Fighting Prophet,* 577.
4 May 29, 1865.

He continued to brood about the shape of things to come, while the temptation to resign still lurked in his mind. "I feel there is a desire to get rid of me," he rationalized to John. The first flush of victory had passed, and he was haunted once more by his natural moodiness and basic sense of insecurity. Stanton was unfriendly and persisted in issuing orders without even going through General Grant's office. He was fast gaining ascendancy in the councils of the Congressional radicals, and Sherman was bound to suffer from the dislike of so powerful a figure. Life under his control would be a hell on earth, and when Stanton had his chance, he would strike, and strike hard. Let him, Sherman growled defensively, stiffening at the threat of opposition. If he should try, "I will make his ears tingle with something he will like as little as the shouts that went up when I declined to recognize him personally at the Grand Review."

But then there was Grant. If Sherman should war openly with Stanton, it would simply start a controversy, and that would displease the General of the Army, who anxiously sought harmony. No, Sherman decided. If he chose to remain in the army, he would ignore Stanton's animosity. He would ignore Washington itself. "I shall not go near Washington this year," he promised his brother, "nor take part in the reorganization of the New Army, until ordered to do so officially."[5]

Neither as a soldier nor as a civilian did he want to live in the East—particularly in Washington. He had friends in St. Louis, the city which appealed to him because it was western in its atmosphere. And he was a Westerner at heart. Into the river town came traders, trappers, and now miners from the far-off mountains of Montana. Out beyond Missouri lay the endless plains, slanting slowly upward to meet the towering Rockies. From them came shaggy travelers telling tales of new Eldorados all up and down the mountain front. They mixed with the already diverse elements of the city and made it truly one of the most cosmopolitan towns in the nation. Sherman could take a

[5] Sherman to John Sherman. William T. Sherman Papers, Volume 17, Division of Manuscripts, Library of Congress, Washington, D. C. Letters of August 9, November 4, and December 28 cover his relationships with Stanton and his indecision about the future.

leaf from Brigham Young's book and say of St. Louis, "This is the place." It was a window opening out upon the great western veranda, and to it he must go.

He took his family to St. Louis and engaged rooms at the Lindell Hotel, hopeful that the promised gift of a house would be honored. School would open September 1, and he wanted to be there in time to enroll his children. Early in that month he wrote to one of Grant's staff officers, saying that he was still in the dark about his plans for the winter and was undecided whether to buy, rent, or simply board at the hotel all winter.[6] Within a few days, however, his problems were solved. The proposed gift materialized, and the Sherman family took up residence at 912 Garrison Avenue.

Meanwhile, Sherman had put off any thoughts of leaving the army, if he had not completely abandoned them. Despite his apprehensions over the future, there was really no other course to follow. His years of civilian life, during the fifties, had brought him very little success; he had no assurance that the days ahead would be any better.

Even as he was considering his future, he was assigned to the western area, then known as the Military Division of the Mississippi. It embraced a vast region west of the Mississippi River, out to the crest of the Rockies, and extended from the Canadian line southward to Mexico. Headquarters were at St. Louis. For a moment, the happy prospect of being stationed there appeared in doubt. A telegram from General John Pope, who preceded him in the western command, revealed that Pope was to be assigned to St. Louis, while Sherman's new headquarters would be in Cincinnati. Quickly, Sherman sent his objections to the Adjutant General's Office. "This change should not be made without my consent, and I do not consent."[7] He would not be shoved back into Ohio, even though it was his native state. He had his heart set on living at least so far west as St. Louis.

6 Sherman to Badeau, September 6, 1865. Division of the Mississippi, Letters and Telegrams Sent, 1863–65. Records of the War Department, U. S. Army Commands, National Archives, Washington, D. C.

7 Sherman to Bowers, July 15, 1865. Division of the Mississippi, Letters Sent, 1865–66. Records of the War Department, U. S. Army Commands, National Archives.

There were other annoyances. From the day he had returned to St. Louis there seemed to be some kind of an intangible conspiracy to keep him from acquainting himself with his new command. The problem of getting Ellen and the children settled had taken much of his time. When he managed to get away from house-hunting momentarily, hordes of hero-worshipers, hands extended in greeting, followed him, eager to identify themselves with greatness. He remembered the crowds in Washington the day of the Grand Review. "Damn you, get out of the way, damn you," he had snarled at them. He recalled how they had clamored, "How about going to Mexico, General?" suggesting that Sherman the terrible would make short work of Napoleon's puppet, Maximilian. He had snapped back, "You can go there if you like and you can go to hell if you want to!" But here it was different. These were St. Louis people. This was home, and somehow he would have to adjust himself to their jostling and inquisitive stares.

Hardly had he arrived at St. Louis before it began. He was serenaded at the Lindell Hotel and was given a banquet on the occasion of taking over his new command. At the serenade he tried to talk to his fellow citizens about the advantages of peacetime St. Louis, but he was almost unable to make himself heard amidst the shouting, the music, and cannon firing. He was thoroughly annoyed by the commotion and constant interruptions, but he told himself again that he must get used to it. He tried resolutely to hide his displeasure.[8] A few days later, en route to Ohio to take care of some family matters, he stopped off at Indianapolis and was subjected to the same noisy adulation. The irritation was even greater here, for in the excitement of the festivities a soldier was killed by the premature discharge of a cannon.[9] The needless death deeply disturbed him, but again he suppressed his feelings.

The banquets, the applause, the noisy demonstrations—all made him look longingly westward, and to his new command. He saw visions of a greasewood campfire on the prairies and

[8] *Daily Missouri Republican* (St. Louis), July 18 and 21, 1865.
[9] *Ibid.,* July 26, 1865.

11

roasted buffalo ribs—a place where he could hunker down on his heels and gnaw silently away, undisturbed by toastmasters and the dread of after-dinner speeches. He wanted to match his own solemnity with the eloquent silence of the western plainsmen; to see a land where the hand was raised in a hail and not extended clutchingly forward for that momentary sweaty clasp.

By September, the children were in school, his wife was busy organizing the new home on Garrison Avenue, and "Cump," as the family elders had always called him, could sit down to survey the extent of his new duties. He unrolled his maps and began to study the physiography of the vast empire that stretched westward to the mountains, his new field of endeavor. Here, along the little lines that were rivers, would one day be towns, and, where the rainfall was sufficient, farming communities would flourish. Over the now unmarked distances railroads would run. They would feed supplies into the new settlements and take away their produce.

He stepped back and viewed the larger picture. To the northwest lay the great Missouri River, winding from its headwaters in Montana down through Dakota, along the eastern edge of Nebraska, touching Kansas, and then flowing through Missouri to reach the Mississippi, just above St. Louis. It was a great avenue of travel across the barren waste of the northern plains and to the mining regions of Montana. The river had seen much travel in fur-trading days, and would see much more now that reports of rich mineral strikes had come from that distant country. How soon farmers would dot these regions was doubtful, but still the route would have to be made safe. How many troops would it take to guard the twenty-five hundred miles of winding, muddy waterway? He would have to find the answer to that question, and many more concerning the northern reaches of his vast command.

Looking down the map from the giant bow that was the Missouri River, Sherman studied next the overland routes of travel. Extending up the Platte River valley was the general route of the famed Overland Trail. Along the valley the Mormons, the Oregon settlers, and the forty-niners had gone westward. Now, long wagon trains toiled over it, loaded with goods for the scattered mining camps along the mountains. The trail forked off in western Nebraska and took both stagecoach and wagon travel into Colorado. To complicate matters further, a new road had recently branched northward and was now pouring emigrants into Montana over what was known as the Bozeman Trail or the Powder River Road. Its course angled northwestward from the Overland Trail beyond Fort Laramie and passed into Montana, around the northern spur of the Big Horn Mountains. It ran directly through the heart of the finest buffalo country of the Sioux. Certainly, troops and forts would have to be allotted to this area, which, sooner or later, was bound to be a trouble spot.

Paralleling the Overland Trail, to the south, lay the Smoky Hill route, leading to the Colorado mines. Yet farther south was the line of the old Santa Fé Trail into New Mexico and beyond. These were all familiar routes, used regularly, as are sea lanes, and if one stayed close to them, the chances were that there would be little trouble. But over the lines that fanned out to the West from Missouri and Nebraska, men and women were daily making their way to the outer reaches of the Division of the Mississippi. Not all of them could be depended upon to observe the necessary rules of safety. There were always the curious and the incautious, and many of them would become trail statistics. How could the army protect the whole empire that was suddenly crawling with ambitious, pushing settlers, seeking to explore and exploit every corner of the promised land? The size of the problem was appalling.

The new commander of the vast region explained the complications he faced in a letter to his old friend Admiral David Dixon Porter. "Next summer," he wrote, "I must look out on the Plains some distance and more and more each season. Our Plains resemble your seas and it will take some years of cruising for me to familiarise myself with all the interests and localities. I do not regret this for I naturally get tired of any single place."[10]

Ever restless, the General was anxious to be out on the rolling

[10] Sherman to Porter, November 24, 1865. David Dixon Porter Papers, Box 4: 1862–87. Division of Manuscripts, Library of Congress.

swells of grassy prairie where he could assess personally the problem of time and distance they posed. He wanted also to investigate some of the other complications of his vast command. For generations the American Indians had been shoved westward, and the line between them and civilization had been a fairly distinct one. Now, with a scattered mining population filtering eastward from California into Idaho, Montana, Colorado, Nevada, Arizona, and other western areas, the Indian was being pressed from all sides. For the first time in American history there was no place to which large bodies of Indians could be removed in order to keep them away from white settlements. The natives had no place of retreat, and they would have to make their last stand, regardless of the inevitability of the outcome. Sherman knew well the temper of a cornered enemy.

Years before, President Andrew Jackson had told Congress that the Indians could not live in contact with civilized communities and still prosper. This fact was more correct and more pressing now. The Indians knew it. The settlers knew it. Sherman knew it, too. But what would be done about it? Probably nothing. And the only explanation anybody had for the ceaseless white expansion was a lame, high-sounding phrase, an easy principle called "Manifest Destiny." If any people ever had a manifest destiny, it was the American Indians, and it was not as pleasant a prospect as that enjoyed by the empire builders who lived in the more settled regions of the country. Sherman could do little more than make the dismal retreat of the Indians as painless as possible; but even if he had this hope, it was to be denied him. He would discover before long that his forces were sadly undermanned, and the control of the enormous western region would at times be only tenuous. The scattered outposts, dotting the sea of grass like ocean atolls, would be completely out of touch with the army command from time to time. Weeks would go by, even months, with no report from them. Sherman's problem would be to keep them in existence; and during the next eighteen years he spent much of his time visiting these remote places. As he said to Admiral Porter, he was indeed to do a lot of cruising.

The problems of distance, time, Indians, and a lack of men were merely the apparent ones. There were endless intangibles that served to hamper and discourage even the patient. The most vicious of these was rumor, which spread by word of mouth and the nation's press. Some things could be denied; but others could not, simply because there was insufficient information either to confirm or deny. The cancer of rumor ate at the people's confidence and caused them to complain; but the irritation was not enough to persuade their elected representatives to provide more troops or more facilities to allay the causes of the rumor. There was also the constant carping by the newspapers—the medium of the story, during the war, that Sherman was insane. The eastern papers sympathized with the noble savage and counseled kindness, while the western press screamed, "Kill him." The army, in the middle, managed to please neither side. The Indian wars were local wars, involving no external threat to national security, and to the press there were no military secrets. The papers printed every bit of information they could get. When there was not enough actual information to work with, they attacked the army for holding out on them and, at the same time, published the wildest kind of hearsay.

Then there was the struggle with the taxpayers. As usual, after a war, the nation was eager to reduce the accumulated debt, and the armed forces were the most obvious subjects for economy. The magnificent armies that had stood before Vicksburg, Atlanta, and Richmond, now melted into history. Only a feeble, unrecognizable skeleton remained. Stretching out beyond the Mississippi for thousands of miles lay the vast, unsettled West, dominated by hard-riding, hard-fighting nomadic Indians, equipped with the finest horses on the continent and frequently the best arms. It was to be the job of the little postwar army to establish new forts and to maintain old ones; to keep open lines of communication, such as the stage and freight routes, and to protect new ones, like the railroads; and, finally, to keep the hostile Indians from pouncing upon widely scattered settlements that lay nestled in the mountains and strewn along the plains.

While the harried Sherman would seek frantically to patch

the leaking dikes against surging floods of Indians, congressmen would be making reputations for saving the taxpayers' money by reducing the army even further. Unfortunately for his cause, Sherman hated politics. When he succeeded, after Grant's inauguration, to the position of General of the Army, the grizzled veteran would have to face Congressional committees and explain to them as best he could why the army needed more men and more money. The grim, tight-lipped mouth, the scowling manner, and the cryptic comments would goad into fury those members of Congress who resented Sherman's aloofness and manner of superiority. His brutal frankness would alienate certain pressure groups, like the peace societies, which demanded lenient treatment for the Indians. Sherman was miserable in the public glare; and in trying to cope with those who could give him the things he needed—men and money—he showed his weakest side. How to fight politicians effectively, he was never able to learn.

In the summer of 1865, all these problems lay ahead, and if Sherman, not to mention many others in lower rank, had realized what was coming, he might have carried out his threat to leave the army. These were to be the years a historian would later call "the army's dark ages."[11] They were years that witnessed a shrinking and much-maligned force, struggling almost helplessly against problems that multiplied with each passing day. The men who served in that army were to share the public disdain heaped upon the heads of any peacetime army. Since there was no war, the man on the street told his neighbor the army was simply an unjustified public expense which must be reduced. True, there were some untutored savages out on the prairies, but surely, with all that had been learned in the Civil War, with all that modern military men knew, their subjugation ought to be no serious problem. If western residents like Red Cloud and his Sioux were merely biding their time to render a minority report to this dictum, Easterners did not seem to be aware of it. Even the soldiers, fresh from battles with the Confederates, often did

11 William Addleman Ganoe, *The History of the United States Army.* Chapter IX is entitled "The Army's Dark Ages."

not understand what they might face. The years before them would unfold a panorama of sweating troopers chasing small bands of Indians over great distances, only to see them divide and vanish before their very eyes. Only then would they begin to learn that Indian warfare was a singularly different kind of conflict from any they had known before.

As Sherman sat in his office at St. Louis that first summer after Appomattox and cast his eye over the domain that was his new command, he had reason to be discouraged. The jaunt from Atlanta to the sea would seem to him like a problem from some military primer before he had occupied himself long with the hell that was about to be raised on the High Plains. He would now fight enemies in front of him and enemies in back of him, none of whom he could see or touch. He was about to participate in a game of blindman's buff, and his was no disposition for that sort of play.

Two

━━━━━━━━

NEW ROUTES AND CIRCUMSTANCES

SHERMAN'S FIRST REACTION to his new assignment was to proceed slowly and to study his problem. He wanted time to reacquaint himself with western conditions before making any major changes. The summer of 1865 was too far advanced to introduce even the initial step of a long-range policy, and the campaigns already in progress against the hostiles would have to run their course. An old friend, General Grenville M. Dodge, was out in Indian country giving his personal attention to the matter of Indian control. Let him see what he could do.[1]

But as September came to a close and matters at St. Louis already seemed painfully routine, the restless Sherman decided upon a short western trip. Although the travel season was nearing its end for that year, he hoped to examine at least some of the localities for whose defense he was responsible. There would still be time to look over the first few completed miles of Union Pacific track and perhaps talk to some Westerners about the "new routes and circumstances" that had developed since he was last on the frontier.

The place of first interest was Omaha. Hardly a decade old, that city was now booming as thousands of railroad workers jammed its crowded facilities. The eastern terminus of the Union Pacific, Omaha had high hopes of being the plains metropolis. In July a little twenty-two-ton locomotive had arrived there, aboard a steamboat, from St. Joseph, Missouri, and to honor properly the first railroad engine on the new line, it had been named the "Major General Sherman." When Omaha residents sent word to its namesake that they would be proud to have him view the

1 Sherman to Rawlins, August 25, 1865. Division of the Mississippi, Letters and Telegrams Sent, 1863–65.

18

shiny black engine, Sherman could no longer resist the temptation to travel. Within a few days he was in Nebraska.

Sherman's arrival in Omaha was the occasion of an excursion out to the end of the railroad line, a distance of fifteen miles. As the General and his party set out, one of the local newspaper reporters noted that his interest in the road was particularly keen. Both he and railroad Vice President Thomas C. Durant clambered down muddy banks to inspect masonry culverts and gravely studied the various phases of construction at frequent intervals along the way. For those who were less interested in the technical aspects of the project, there were other amusements. Sherman's adjutant, for example, sat atop a boxcar and entertained himself by taking pot shots at partridges as the train moved along.

At the end of the road Sherman watched the tracklaying, amazed at the activity and fascinated by the piles of construction material strewn around on the prairie. When he had seen enough, the party settled down on the grassy sod for a picnic of cold roast goose, ducks, and other delicacies, washed down with excellent wine. The young reporter, enjoying it all immensely, wrote that the wine inspired "the highest state of social hilarity."

At the conclusion of the meal, the General, happy over what he had seen and warmed by the refreshments, made a speech. He described his long interest in railroading and told his listeners of his experiences in California a decade before, when he had been vice-president and a stockholder in a little road that jutted out hopefully from the small mining town of Folsom. It had been a brave beginning to what its promoters hoped would be a transcontinental line. Sherman recalled that he had lost $10,000 in the venture. Despite such an unhappy experience, he now urged upon his audience the importance of connecting the West to the rest of the country by rail, and he compared such a line with the Mississippi River, which had been the salvation of national unity and of major importance to the Union during the recent war. The reporter confessed that because it was such a good speech he wished he had recorded more of it, but the frequency with which the wine bottle had come around had somewhat numbed his reportorial facilities. He remembered later that on the way home, the train had stopped long enough for the engine to "take a drink," and with lingering pleasure he commented that the example was not lost upon members of the excursion party.[2]

Sherman was quite pleased by what he had seen on the short railroad trip. He wrote of it to General John A. Rawlins, in Grant's office, but cautioned him that the line would be of no immediate benefit to the army since there was a break of 159 miles between the Des Moines River and Omaha that isolated the latter place. He did not think this gap would be filled for at least a year. However, supplies could be carried to Omaha by river boat and then sent westward by rail. Even so, no real utility would be gained until tracks were laid as far as Fort Kearny.[3]

2 *Omaha Weekly Herald*, October 20, 1865.

3 The fort was named after General Stephen Watts Kearny, of Mexican War fame. Almost from the time of its establishment, in 1848, it was spelled both "Kearny" and "Kearney," even in official correspondence. Today the city of Kearney and county of the same name are spelled with the second "e." Sherman himself used both spellings. (J[ames] C. O [lson], "Along the Trail." *Nebraska History*, Vol. XXIX, No. 3 [September, 1948], 294.) Another explanation is found in the introduction to Alson B. Ostrander's *An Army Boy of the Sixties* (New York, 1924). The fort was named for S. W. Kearny. "Then a strange thing happened; an army engineer of English lineage, Lieutenant Colonel James Kearney, drew up the plans for the fort; and the English spelling was given to the new army post, though the army records plainly state that the post was to be named for the general."

Among the "minutia-men" of western history there is a difference of opinion about the spelling of Fort *Phil* Kearney. It revolves around the point of "to 'e' or not to 'e.' " This author has resolved to "e." Sherman used the "ey" spelling throughout his official and unofficial correspondence. While at Fort Laramie in August of 1866 (a month after Colonel Carrington established the near-by post), he referred to it in a letter to General Rawlins. (Sherman to Rawlins, August 31, 1866. Division of the Missouri, Letters Received, 1866–69, Special File.) Both the Secretary of War and the Secretary of the Interior used the "ey" spelling when referring to the massacre near there in December, 1866. (See Letter from the Secretary of the Interior, communicating, in obedience to a resolution of the Senate of the 30th of January, information in relation to the late massacre of United States troops by Indians at or near Fort Phil. Kearney, in Dakota Territory. 39 Cong., 2 sess., *Senate Exec. Doc. No. 16* [Serial 1277], 1867; Letter of the Secretary of War, in compliance with a resolution of the Senate of the 30th ultimo, the official reports, papers, and other facts in relation to the causes and extent of the late massacre of United States troops by Indians at Fort Phil. Kearney. 39 Cong., 2 sess., *Senate Exec. Doc. No. 15* [Serial 1277], 1867.) In Sherman's annual report for 1866 he thus referred to the fort. (See *Annual Report of the Secretary of War*, 39 Cong., 2 sess., *House Exec. Doc. No. 1* [Serial 1285], p. 21.) The investigation of the Fetterman massacre, held in 1867, is found in a 128-page printed document. All spellings of Kearney employ the "e," including those of War Department offi-

He was much pleased with the work already completed and noted that a heavy track-laying force was completing one-half mile of road each day and was using, with the exception of the soft cottonwood ties, the best of materials. Enough rails, ties, and bridge timbers were on hand to complete at least sixty more miles of road. There seemed to be no doubt that the company was working in good faith and with a large amount of capital. Fort Kearny, the immediate destination, would, for the time being, be a center of military operations. For nearly twenty years it had protected Platte Valley travel, and it was still important. All other posts east of it might now be abandoned; the new iron road had rendered them obsolete.[4]

Having satisfied himself that the Union Pacific line, which projected only fifteen miles west of Omaha, had already begun to alter the military situation, Sherman was now anxious to inspect the work on another western road. From Kansas City, out towards Fort Riley, a road known simply as the "Union Pacific, Eastern Division" was under construction. Its promoters were hard at work, trying to reach the 100th parallel ahead of the Omaha road, in the belief that they would then be awarded the subsidy to continue across the country.

After he had completed his inspection around Omaha, Sherman boarded the river steamer *Majors,* bound for Leavenworth and Kansas City. Any hope he had of enjoying a quiet river trip was shattered at every landing. At Plattsmouth, only a few miles along the way, he was dragged from his berth by a group of citizens eager to show off their new town. At Nebraska City, things were no better. Here a pale, gangling youth approached him, carrying a scroll that looked suspiciously like an oration. Sherman stood his ground well and listened patiently to the forensic bombardment until the young man, now emboldened by success, began to introduce the famed officer to all his friends.

cials, officers stationed at the fort (among them, Colonel Carrington, the commanding officer), and in the letters of the late Colonel W. J. Fetterman, as well as in a private letter written from the fort and reproduced in the document. (See 40 Cong., 1 sess., *Senate Exec. Doc. No. 13, 1867.*) Regardless of how the gallant Irishman, who lost his life in the Civil War, spelled his name, the fort honoring him carried the letter "e" in its name.

4 Sherman to Rawlins, October 23, 1865. Division of the Mississippi, Letters Sent, 1865–66.

"For God's sake, gentlemen, no more of this," the frustrated dignitary finally roared and then rushed for his stateroom in full retreat.[5]

By the time Leavenworth was reached, Sherman was tired of public demonstrations. He slipped into town before a bell could be rung or a cannon fired. The city council met in emergency session and produced a welcome resolution in record time. The lack of fanfare was disappointing to those who liked a show. They shrugged off the affair with the comment that the famed figure was just one of those men who did not like displays.[6] Nevertheless, they were determined that their famous quarry should not escape. Before he left town, Sherman had to submit to a reception at Laing's Hall and shake hands with those who remembered his earlier residence in the city. From the standpoint of numbers, the reception was a success. The daily paper reported proudly that the crowd was the largest ever assembled for such a ceremony. The visitor made a short speech, praising Kansans for their contributions in the recent war, and then turned over the rostrum to other speakers. Leavenworth was happy. "Uncle Billy" had seen some of his former soldiers and had performed for his fellow Westerners.

Sherman's immediate destination was Wyandotte, Kansas, the eastern terminus of the Union Pacific (Eastern Division). At the little river town he was met by the chief contractor of this section of railroad, and together they rode out to Lawrence in a private car. Ten miles beyond, they came upon crews at work. The fall air rang with the sound of mauls beating railroad spikes. Everywhere around were piles of ties and iron rails. Out of this scene of activity nearly one mile of new railroad track emerged daily. Already, trains clipped along at twenty miles an hour between the river and Lawrence, and if the weather held, they would be puffing into Topeka within a month. It would then be possible to go sixty-six miles beyond the Missouri by rail. Before long the road would reach Fort Riley, which would be a triumph for the army, because from that point a number of wagon roads

5 *Omaha Weekly Herald*, October 20, 1865.
6 *Daily Times* (Leavenworth), October 17, 1865.

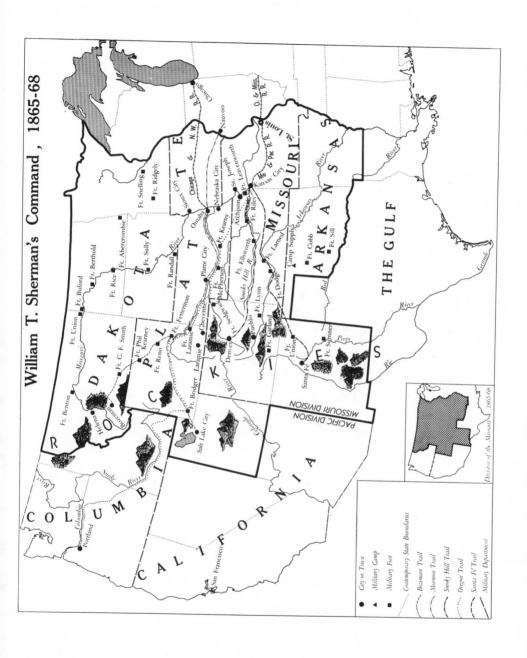

William T. Sherman's Command, 1865-68

fanned out to Fort Kearny, Denver, and New Mexico.[7] Sherman looked forward to this development eagerly, for each mile of rails simplified his own plans for western defense. Satisfied now that the road was progressing rapidly and was "being prepared right," he returned to St. Louis and reported what he had seen.

He had examined the railroads with especial care, he said, "because I see that each will enter large into our military calculations." When Omaha was connected to the East by rail, the frontier line would be thrown out as far as Fort Kearny. Supplying a large cavalry force far out on the plains would then be much easier; too, the extended rail lines would simplify the task of chasing down bands of raiding Indians that continually struck at travelers.

No less important was the Eastern Division road, running out across Kansas. "I regard this road as the most important element now in progress to facilitate the military interests of our Frontier," he wrote with great feeling. This road was connected to the Missouri Pacific Railroad, then nearly complete between St. Louis and Kansas City, and that meant a continuous rail link between central Kansas and any point east of the Mississippi River. He urged upon army headquarters the importance of federal encouragement to railroads and begged that there be no delay in granting it. Repeating himself, for emphasis, he maintained that this modern means of transportation would not only save the government a vast sum of money, but would immeasurably increase the efficiency of the military arm on the frontier. Meanwhile, he concluded, affairs on the frontier and beyond were going about as well as could be expected. His talks with General Dodge and others at Omaha had convinced him that for the moment there was no general danger from the West.[8]

If Sherman did not anticipate a major war on the plains, he, nevertheless, was aware of the multiplication of problems within his command. He had no illusions about the nature of the situation, knowing full well that even with the help of railroad lines

7 Sherman to Rawlins, October 23, 1865. Division of the Mississippi, Letters Sent, 1865–66.
8 *Ibid.*

his small force would have extreme difficulty in trying to protect thousands of settlers who were scattering out over the High Plains and into the Rocky Mountains. While the Indians might not strike in any great numbers, they would continue to make slashing attacks upon the flanks of settlement. This would not be fatal to the westward movement, but it would act as a deterrent. Sherman's most annoying job would be to persuade Westerners that he was doing all he could in their behalf and, at the same time, convince the growing group of eastern philanthropists that he was not bent upon destroying every last Indian who trod a prairie trail. It was in public relations that he was weakest.

During the fall of 1865, he carefully studied incoming reports, trying to acquaint himself with western matters as fully as possible. When spring came, he planned an extensive tour to examine personally the nature of his task. In November, he studied a report, forwarded by General Pope, written by two well-known Westerners: Kit Carson and William Bent. At Pope's request, they had given their estimate of the Indian danger and had offered suggestions with regard to it. Their first recommendation was that the control of Indian affairs be returned to the War Department, from whose hands it had been taken in 1849, with the formation of the Department of Interior. Both men sharply condemned the rapacity of the Indian agents and underscored their argument by citing the reaction of the Indians at a recent council. There, the Indians had lamented that the great father in Washington had given them many bales of goods, but foolishly entrusted them to the agents, who began rolling them westward, handing them on from agent to agent. The bales grew smaller and smaller as they moved along, the Indians said, "so that when they get out to us they are hardly worth receiving." Carson and Bent saw no alternative but to remove such matters from the hands of individual agents and let the army take over. Sherman agreed.

They also recommended that the reservation system be made effective. The buffalo herds were vanishing from the plains, diminishing the Indians' supply of food; the natives no longer had the alternative of moving on west, for "now emigration leaps forward from the West itself, its advance swarming over the Eastern slopes of the Sierra Nevada." The Indians were pressed from all sides, and their ancient hunting grounds were overrun by hordes of miners and settlers. It was the army's job to escort the Indians to reservations and keep them there. This would, of course, cause a certain amount of trouble, and to prepare for this trouble, the establishment of military posts at strategic western locations was urged. Use regular army officers, the men told Sherman. Use troops who would not act rashly at the first sign of Indian disturbance and thus precipitate a general war.[9] Both vividly recalled the murderous action of Colonel John Chivington, who, not so long since, had led his gun-crazy volunteers against a peaceful village of southern Cheyennes at Sand Creek, Colorado. In a matter of minutes, the parson, turned general, had set back the solution of Indian difficulties by years.

Sherman read the report with care and then sent it to Grant, with the thoughtful endorsement: "Probably no two men exist better acquainted with the Indians than Carson & Bent and their judgmt is entitled to great weight." That he fully agreed with them is seen in other correspondence. He told Grant that there had been, and would be, conflicts between western army officers and Indian agents, a situation that could readily be alleviated by giving the army control of Indian affairs. If Congress saw otherwise, then at least the army men should have copies of treaties made by the Indian agents, so that the army would know what agreements had been made.[10] It was the lack of such information that made him complain further to the Quartermaster General. How could he make plans for the disposition of his troops and supplies when he knew nothing about the government's plans for the Indians' future? "I am not yet even advised whether they are to be localized, whether they are to have their hunting grounds guaranteed to them or indeed anything that would enable me to prejudge now, for our plans for protecting the whites must be modified to conform to these treaties."[11]

9 Carson and Bent to Pope, October 27, 1865. Letters Received, 1865–69, Office of the Secretary of War, Records of the War Department, National Archives. Letter endorsed by Sherman on November 7.

10 Sherman to Grant, November 6, 1865. William T. Sherman Papers, Volume 17.

In the years ahead Sherman would continue his plea to have Indian affairs placed under army control, but without success. Requests for information and co-operation would go unheard. He would soon realize, if he did not in 1865, that he was fighting a new kind of war, with the enemy taking refuge from time to time with another branch of the federal government—the Department of the Interior.

But this was not to be the only novelty of his new assignment. The age-old military tactics, in which army men had been steeped, did not fit western conditions. Sherman admitted that no longer could his forces be massed "according to the systems of Europe." In the coming years the army would be forced "to adapt our conduct to the prevailing sentiment and necessities of the Frontier," and with the regulars scattered company by company over the plains, it would not be long before a four-company command would be a large unit. Recognizing the fluidity of the situation, he hoped to overcome the dispersion somewhat by grouping all the available cavalry units for major strikes in hostile country. Despite his recognition of new conditions that called for new methods, he could not shake off the effects of his earlier training and experience. When spring came, he planned to take his cavalry groups out on the grassy plains and see what they could do against a wily foe.[12] It was his notion that small army posts, used primarily for forage depots, could support the cavalry expeditions that would patrol the principal western routes during the travel season, protecting those emigrants and travelers who would follow regular roads and refrain from straggling.[13]

Sherman outlined his plans to Grant; in his opinion, if the plans were carried out, a general peace could be maintained upon the plains. He cautioned his superior that the situation would be one of touch and go, and only so long as travelers obeyed instructions could he promise protection. If they per-

[11] Sherman to Meigs, November 29, 1865. Division of the Mississippi, Letters Sent, 1865–66.

[12] Sherman to Price, Cavalry Bureau, November 16, 1865. Division of the Mississippi, Letters Sent, 1865–66.

[13] Sherman to Bowers, January 13, 1866. Division of the Mississippi, Letters Sent, 1865–66.

sisted in crossing Indian reservations or Indian hunting grounds, there would be trouble. "We must not be astonished if some of them lose their horses, cattle and scalps," he said bluntly.

Having made his calculations, the western commander sat back to await the coming of spring when he could put his plans into operation. Throughout the winter, he busied himself with correspondence, answering as best he could the letters of frantic requests for troops from excited territorial governors, making plans for the withdrawal of wartime volunteer troops from the plains, and plotting out strategic locations for the limited numbers of soldiers at hand.

Postwar events on the plains had been tumultuous, and there was no indication that another season would see any diminution in the clamor of various interested groups for favor. Army officers in the field were like leashed hounds, straining to break away for the hunt. During the summer of 1865, about the time Sherman was assuming his new duties, a young lieutenant named Caspar Collins and some of his men were killed while trying to protect a government wagon train against an attack by overwhelming numbers of Sioux along the Platte River west of Fort Laramie. General Patrick E. Connor, an ambitious officer under General Dodge's immediate command, lost no time in appropriate reprisal. His instructions to his men were unmistakably clear: "You will not receive overtures of peace or submission from Indians, but will attack and kill every male Indian over twelve years of age." Pope's reaction was prompt and equally clear. Any officer who chose to carry out such bloodthirsty orders would suffer the loss of his commission and perhaps more.[14]

Connor's vigorous proposals, highly popular in the Rocky Mountain region, at once touched off a controversy in the nation's press, and Sherman, whether he liked it or not, was involved. Editors, East and West, chose up sides and began throwing lead in the form of type. Literary shot and shell filled the air, and a journalistic battle of full-fledged proportions developed. If the Indians did not want peace, said the West, give them war; nonsense, replied the East hotly, this was only more of the stand-

14 Fred B. Rogers, *Soldiers of the Overland*, 168.

ard propaganda Westerners had been peddling for years. Irresponsible traders and adventurers who ranged the Indian country seemed to think that the only way to live in peace with the natives was to exterminate them; to Easterners this was ridiculous.

The suggestion that mass murder of the natives was frontier policy always irritated western newsmen. They indignantly explained to their naïve brethren, living in the sheltered East, that Indian warfare was expensive under any conditions. No businessman on the plains wanted a lengthy conflict, for even if it did generate a certain amount of trade with the army, it disrupted the normal lines of commerce and was fraught with all sorts of economic hazards. Such fighting as there had been was necessary; settlers could not stand by and be destroyed by red raiders. If the Indians understood only force, then force they would have. If a few of these kindhearted eastern sentimentalists could be chased around the plains by Indians in full cry and look upon the mutilated bodies of scalped victims, then, said the frontiersmen, they might have the proper qualifications for administering Indian policy.[15]

From New York came a sharp dissent. There were too many troops on the frontier, and their presence merely aggravated the native problem. Recall them, and ease the friction that resulted from their activity, or threatened activity.[16] These recommendations were in line with the course of events already under way; in the fall of 1865, Sherman's division had over 25,000 enlisted men; within a year, this figure would be cut in half. While such a diminution of force might please taxpayers living in the more settled regions of the land, it only aroused the men of the West. There were not enough troops on the plains, they said, and even those available were no good. A freighter, coming down from Fort Laramie to Fort Collins, Colorado, reported that the Sioux had just relieved him of $12,000 worth of his goods. "If you see anyone who wants to make peace with the Indians, just knock him down for me," he wrote hotly. "The troops in this country make a poor attempt at fighting Indians. More soldiers than In-

[15] *Montana Post* (Virginia City), October 7, 1865.
[16] *New York Times*, October 13, 1865.

dians are killed."[17] This brought agreement from the Montana press. Why spend millions equipping large armies of slow moving, unwieldy corps, "who know no more about their business than an old politician does about honesty," when there were plenty of mountain men ready to see action.[18] The notion that such a form of private enterprise could accomplish the task of "controlling" the Indians quickly and more cheaply was widespread in the West at this time. Papers all the way from Idaho to Arizona recommended the use of local volunteers. Local men, their senses sharpened by a bounty amounting to $100 a scalp, would make an Indian a curiosity in the West within five years.[19] And it would be the cheapest method. Some authorities estimated that it cost the government $10,000 for every Indian killed. Why not let the local boys contract for the job? In the interest of "efficiency" and "economy," men of the plains and Rockies recommended it.

Not all segments of the western press were optimistic about the outcome of Indian warfare. Nebraskans charged that the government simply did not care about them. Ever since the Minnesota outbreak in 1862, millions of dollars had been wasted in sending out military expeditions that accomplished nothing. The Indians were now taking more lives than ever. The frustration was too much for an Omaha editor who lost his temper completely. Charging that "this infamous imbecility, persistent, dogged, damnable disregard of the interests of the West" amounted to high crimes, he called upon the people of his section to unite in protest against Secretary Stanton, "the pestiferous, bull-headed potentate of the War Office, who sits in his cushioned chair . . . quietly planning his own unholy political ambitions, while the great interests of the West are neglected, spurned, and spit upon."[20]

It was outbursts like this that moved the *Army and Navy Journal* to comment that the reappearance of the American Indian in the press suggested his renewed assertion of himself

17 *Daily Times* (Leavenworth), November 8, 1865.
18 *Montana Post*, October 7, 1865.
19 *Owyhee Avalanche* (Ruby City, Idaho), November 11, 1865.
20 *Omaha Weekly Herald*, November 10, 1865.

on the High Plains.[21] Now that there was no war news from below the Mason-Dixon line, the public gaze shifted to the western prairies, and every man became a military expert, anxious to advise the nation how to solve the problems posed by the red men. Humanitarians, abolitionists, and crusaders in general turned from the cause of the black to that of the red, and quite suddenly the Cooperian Indian reappeared on the American scene. As these philosophers talked glibly about such worthy things as national honor and fair treatment for the nomadic owners of the soil, western men seethed. The historic frontier resentment against slow-moving, bureaucratic government, geared to eastern sympathies, boiled over. Plainsmen asked themselves if their part of the country was to be a mere colonial appendage, with Washington taking London's former position. If so, they hinted darkly, something would have to be done.

As Sherman watched the Indian thrust himself into print and saw the nation divide over the solution of the growing problem, he realized that there were days of bitterness and strife ahead. The coming years would see a struggle with the native that would dwarf anything Americans had known before. As time ticked by, as the railroad inched its way deeper into Indian country, the problem heightened. While the new roads would be of enormous military assistance, they aggravated the condition Sherman hoped they would ultimately alleviate. It was true that troops could be moved more rapidly by this more modern means, but the railroads were also more property that had to be guarded. In addition, about thirty-five hundred miles of stagecoach routes demanded protection. Those lines, under government contract, complained loudly at losses to Indians. As travel figures mushroomed with the coming of warm weather, the demand for troops would be universal. This might call for a tightening of the lines of defense; and when that happened, Sherman knew how small communities, temporarily cut off, would set up a din of accusation that the army was abandoning them to their fate. Then both East and West would be pointing the accusing finger at the military arm.

[21] *Army and Navy Journal,* September 9, 1865.

Viewing this future, Sherman grimly steeled himself for the time of crisis so near at hand. His love for the West had caused him to request his present assignment, but now he began to wonder if his position as mediator between the clamorous frontiersmen and the conservative Easterners was going to involve the kind of warfare he understood. Perhaps the peacetime army would prove to be an unenviable vocation. As he wrote to a young man who wanted a place in it, "I always advise my friends who have fair prospects in Civil Life not to enter the Regular Army."[22] Yet, as he told himself, he would be forty-six in February. It seemed too late, despite his threats, to turn to other pursuits. The army had brought him the only real success he had ever enjoyed, and, whether he liked it or not, he was now married to the military service.

Doggedly he fixed his attention upon his enormous command, which comprised nearly one-fourth of the area of the nation. It was his job to control this vast expanse. Despite his doubts and momentary fears, ahead lay one of the biggest challenges of his life. It was this thought that strengthened his resolve.

[22] Sherman to Warner, November 29, 1865. Letters of Major Willard Warner, Illinois State Historical Library, Springfield, Illinois.

Three

WE CANNOT AFFORD PERFECT PROTECTION

BEFORE HIS WESTERN ASSIGNMENT was six months old, Sherman had mentally sketched out plans for a general assault upon the complex problems facing him. Since his forces were small and the demands upon them large, he could not hope to guard every danger point. It would be hard indeed to guard even a few of the travel routes linking the settled eastern regions with the loosely connected chain of small settlements that were sprinkled along the slopes of the Rockies. There would be complaints about the lack of perfect protection, but it could not be helped. It was clear to him that he must employ the method of penetration, using well-guarded roads as wedges into the great block of territory he hoped to control. For the present, settlers would move along the rights of way granted them by previous treaties with the Indians. There would be time enough later for the whites to expand. Future negotiations with the tribes must provide that authorization. Early in 1866, with these views in mind, he made his recommendations to the War Department. Let the settlers move west as far as they could farm profitably. Beyond that line, travel through Indian country would have to be funneled into two, and perhaps three, principal routes. All other avenues should be temporarily closed.[1]

At the war's end, the United States was divided into five great military divisions. The one to which Sherman was assigned, the Military Division of the Mississippi, straddled the great river valley and sprawled westward beyond the Rocky Mountains. Two of its subdivisions, or departments, as they were called, were of little worry to him. The Department of Ohio, composed

[1] Sherman to Bowers, January 13, 1866. Division of the Mississippi, Letters Sent, 1865–66.

33

of the states north of the Ohio River, needed only enough troops to guard public property. It did not logically belong to the Division of the Mississippi, and before long it was to be separated. Nor was there much immediate concern over the Department of Arkansas, a fairly well-settled region requiring only a few troops. The third department, named the Missouri, posed the greatest challenge and would require all available forces for its defense. It was the largest section of the Division, stretching westward to Utah and northward to the Canadian boundary. Within it lay the main roadways over the plains as well as a rapidly growing series of mining communities along the mountains. No part of the nation was then undergoing greater change, and each day brought additional complexities in matters of defense. Sherman saw that a showdown with the Plains Indians was shaping up as a result of the white pressure, and he warned President Grant's office that clashes between the two races lay directly ahead. The once independent Indians were increasingly in need of the white man's cattle for food, and the emigrants' natural hostility to the natives would be only whetted by the persistent raids upon their settlements.[2]

Leading to the mountains were several well-traveled roads over which thousands of emigrants yearly moved westward. Sherman knew that the condition of peace prevailing in all other parts of the nation had no application along these roads, and with each passing day, as the volume of travel grew, the problem became more acute. The restless natives roamed the land, eyeing with increasing concern the invasion of their ancient hunting grounds, frequently asserting that treaties made long ago with the whites were for one reason or another no longer valid. Meanwhile, the ever pushing settlers edged forward, either oblivious of the natural conflict at hand or blissfully ignorant of the probability. If there were treaties delineating Indian lands, the settlers had not read them, or they, too, claimed that the other side had violated earlier agreements. Neither advice nor orders would

2 Sherman to Rawlins, February 17, 1866. Division of the Missouri, Letters Received, 1866–69, Special File. Records of the War Department, U. S. Army Commands, National Archives.

keep them from spreading in all directions as they anxiously sought new lands.[3] They confidently expected the government to furnish protection no matter where they might wander; it could establish posts to protect them as they plowed. No, Sherman answered. Not ever. Such attitudes were unreasonable.

He realized that a refusal of these demands would generate cries of anguish and stormy condemnation from territorial officials, but it had to be that way. Nor could he be sympathetic with the Westerners' desire for the establishment of forts as a market for their agricultural produce. He had little enough with which to work, and in his eyes, the maintenance of communication with all parts of his command took precedence. Even if Congress passed a bill, now before it, that proposed to furnish more troops, it was doubtful that the widespread demand for more army posts on the plains could be satisfied.[4] There was nothing to be done for the present but to abandon ruthlessly some of these remote little settlements and generally tighten the apparatus of defense. Even if more troops were allowed, their numbers would be offset by the steady discharge of wartime volunteers who clamored for release. It would be some time yet before he was prepared to expand his operations.[5]

The reason for Sherman's insistence upon maintaining communications with the mountain settlements lay in his belief that, for years to come, the belt of land lying in the western part of the present states of Kansas, Nebraska, and the Dakotas, long known as a desert, would defy ordinary agricultural settlement. He did not doubt that farmers would move closer to the desert's edge, nor that a considerable population would appear beyond it, but like most Americans of his time, he could not envisage changes in agrarian methods that would permit crops to be raised profitably in these arid regions.

Zebulon Pike, Stephen H. Long, G. K. Warren, and other army officers had thoroughly fixed in the public mind the desert theory.

[3] *Ibid.*

[4] Sherman to Brown, February 21, 1866. Division of the Missouri, Letters Received, 1866–69, Special File.

[5] Sherman to John Sherman, February 23, 1866. William T. Sherman Papers, Volume 18.

A host of travelers had confirmed their findings. Even the geographies of the day marked off the area as a void, and it would be some years before the myth would vanish. Thousands of settlers, who either did not read their geographies or chose to disbelieve them, would have to go forth and disprove the forebodings of the experts. Meanwhile, Sherman the conservative shared the caution of his predecessors. "In general terms," he wrote, "the settlements of Kansas, Dacotah and Iowa have nearly or quite reached the Western limit of land fit for cultivation, Parallel 99° of West Longitude. Then begin the Great Plains 600 miles wide, fit only for Nomadic tribes of Indians, Tartars, or Buffaloes. . . ."[6] Nor was this his private opinion. He stated publicly that the "vast and desert regions of our country between the 100th parallel and the Pacific basin" would be useless for agriculture as it was pursued in the Mississippi Valley. He admitted that while there were certainly precious metals in the region, "yet the great mass of the country seems utterly devoid of value in the future."[7]

Despite any disbelief that the desert would ultimately bloom, this vast area under the immediate command of General John Pope was of particular concern to Sherman. He wrote frequently to his department commander, urging him to do the best he could with his small number of troops and promising more when they could be found. From his vantage point at St. Louis, the division commander scrutinized the endless western stretches and, like the great tactician he was, tried to locate his military units in the places of greatest need. He suggested that a regiment of infantry should be placed in a position to cover Minnesota, remembering the Sioux outbreak in that state during the recent war. Patrols ranging westward to the Missouri River would give at least partial protection to the settled area and serve as watchdogs against sudden Indian thrusts. Meanwhile, the Missouri River itself, a main line of travel northwestward, had to be

6 Sherman to Rawlins, March 6, 1866. Division of the Mississippi, Letters Sent, 1865–66.
7 *Daily Missouri Republican,* March 28, 1866.

guarded to insure the safe passage of travelers bound for Montana and to guarantee additional security to the easterly areas.

The Platte route across Nebraska and the Smoky Hill road through Kansas were equally as important. Both these roads were heavily traveled, and their protection was an absolute necessity. During the preceding year, 1865, over 6,000 wagons, each carrying from one to four tons of freight, had passed Fort Kearny on the Platte within a period of six weeks.[8] Commerce from the Missouri River southwestward into New Mexico had been heavy for some years, and those arid reaches would require troops for a long time. Unfortunately, the defense of these lines of travel would immobilize a large part of his available forces. The only solution to this problem was the extensive use of cavalry, thrown out as a protective screen, to keep Indians from raiding wagon trains on such roads as became particularly hard-pressed.[9]

Such would have to be the disposition of forces for the moment. It might be only temporary, for in the next few months, as wartime volunteers continued to be discharged, the situation would be necessarily altered. If, during the coming travel season, relative security could be given to the scattered settlements and the host of emigrants who would cross the plains, the army would have done all that might be expected of it under the circumstances. At best, General Pope, commanding the important Department of Missouri, would have his hands full.[10]

Pope fully realized that great odds were against him. He could not possibly furnish an escort to every group of emigrants that wished to cross the plains. It would be difficult to keep lines of travel open generally, and individuals crossing the unprotected stretches westward would have to assume part of the burden of defense. Accordingly, on February 28, he issued an order defining the rules for travel and directed his officers to enforce them to the letter. Forts Ridgely and Abercrombie were designated as points for assembly for all trains of travelers leaving Minne-

[8] Charles F. Lummis, "Pioneer Transportation in America," Part II, *McClure's Magazine*, Vol. XXVI, No. 1 (November, 1905), 84.

[9] Sherman to Pope, March 5, 1866. Division of the Missouri, Letters Received, 1866–69, Special File.

[10] *Ibid.*

sota for the mining regions of the Northwest. Fort Kearny, in mid-Nebraska, was the rendezvous of those destined for Denver or Fort Laramie by way of the Platte Valley. Forts Riley and Larned were given a similar status, to accommodate those bound either to Denver or New Mexico via western Kansas. Emigrants going beyond these forts had to organize in a semimilitary fashion, electing a captain and other officers. Each man in the party would be required to carry a gun and to abide strictly by the orders of the train captain. No convoy of less than twenty wagons, or thirty armed men, could pass into Indian country; those who violated the rule would be arrested by the army. By means of such regulations, both Sherman and Pope hoped that emigrants would reach their respective destinations unharmed, thereby simplifying the many problems confronting the western army.[11]

As the prospect of unusually heavy traffic westward developed during the summer of 1866, Sherman understood the burden Pope would have to bear. The Department of Missouri was so large and unwieldy that no single department commander could handle adequately its rapidly emerging problems. Reports of rich strikes in Montana were daily reaching St. Louis, and as a result, all routes to the new bonanza were clogged. With the growing importance of his northern command in mind, Sherman appealed for more help. The traffic bound for Colorado, New Mexico, and Utah would be all that one commander could protect; another was needed in the north.[12] Grant recognized the necessity, and in March he authorized the reduction of the huge department, over the objections of Pope, who did not want his command diminished. The new department, named after the Platte River, lay between that waterway and the Canadian border. It was composed of the states of Minnesota, Iowa, and Nebraska, Montana Territory, and portions of Dakota Territory.

If the action annoyed Pope, neither was it carried out to the entire satisfaction of Sherman. The new subdivision was assigned

11 General Order No. 27, issued by General John Pope at St. Louis, February 28, 1866. In letter to the Secretary of War, 40 Cong., 1 sess., *Senate Exec. Doc. No. 2* (Serial 1308), pp. 2–4.

12 Sherman to Grant, March 7, 1866. Division of the Missouri, Letters Received, 1866–69, Special File.

to General Philip St. George Cooke, a veteran who had campaigned years earlier in the West. Sherman objected, arguing that Cooke was too old. "We need a young General who can travel and see with his own eyes, and if need be command both Whites and Indians to keep Peace," he told Grant. Why not use General W. S. Hancock, who was then wasting his talents at a quiet assignment in Baltimore? If Cooke were to go up the Missouri River, his lack of firmness might result in trouble; but if the younger and more resolute Hancock took over, security, and perhaps even peace, might result.[13]

Still hoping to change Grant's mind, Sherman urged Hancock to make application for the position. He related how Omaha, the departmental headquarters, would soon be connected by rail to both Chicago and St. Louis, and that it also had telegraphic facilities. The new command covered a region rich in minerals and was daily attracting thousands of people. Already more than fifty steamboats traded regularly in the Upper Missouri country, an area that appealed to Sherman as having more promise than any of the other territories. It would be an assignment of many opportunities, and Hancock should try for it.[14]

But Grant was deaf to the appeals of his old comrade-in-arms at St. Louis. General Cooke was given the assignment. The fifty-six-year-old officer was a veteran of the Black Hawk War, the Mexican War, and the recent Civil War. He had patrolled the plains with his dragoons when Sherman was still a boy. To those at Washington he seemed to be the right man.

Sherman accepted the decision without further complaint and within a few days wrote a long letter of instruction to Cooke. He enclosed a report made recently by Pope that outlined the existing military problems on the plains, and calling it the best compilation of facts he possessed, urged that it be used as a preliminary guide. "I do not intend to circumscribe your command by any conditions further than to point out the interests that in my judgment the military should guard and foster," Sherman explained. He then elaborated upon western conditions in general.

[13] Sherman to Grant, March 10, 1866. Division of the Mississippi, Letters Sent, 1865–66.

[14] Sherman to Hancock, March 12, 1866. Division of the Mississippi, Letters Sent, 1865–66.

Montana was a magnet, drawing thousands toward its gold, just as others had earlier been attracted to California. The northern Plains Indians would surely cause the army trouble in such a region, particularly since they were under the immediate control of the Interior Department's agents. With representatives of another arm of the government standing frequently between them and the Indians, army men would be on the defensive and must do everything possible to avoid an open conflict. Perhaps the best way to accomplish this for the present would be to control the whites, rather than the Indians, by sharply limiting the routes of travel. Emigrants from Wisconsin, Minnesota, and northern Iowa ought to be confined to the general line of the Missouri River. Those who chose to go to Montana by way of Nebraska would proceed up the Platte as far as Laramie; Pope, in the Department of Missouri, could then lend them some protection. This well-beaten roadway was of great importance, and Sherman underscored its significance to Cooke. Not only would it carry an immense amount of traffic west and northwest, but it was also the route of the Union Pacific Railroad, then under construction beyond Omaha. These facts made Omaha, the departmental headquarters, of great strategic importance, and its value to the army would grow when the railroads then being built across Iowa reached that thriving city. Give the construction crews all possible assistance, Sherman urged. Military success on the plains revolved around the problem of supply, and here the railroads were of primary importance.[15] Given the task of guarding a rapidly expanding railroad on his left flank and the protection of a long and busy Missouri River on his right, Cooke would, indeed, be a busy officer.

Sherman's decision to limit his efforts during the travel season of 1866 to protecting only the main western routes brought him the expected shower of complaints. Iowans thought the road up the Niobrara River across northern Nebraska was the shortest way to Montana, and they favored its development. So they might, Sherman agreed, but he could not offer it any protection

15 Sherman to Cooke, March 28, 1866. Division of the Missouri, Letters Received, 1866–69, Special File.

this year, and if emigrants persisted and disobeyed his orders, they would be doing a very foolish thing. Patiently he explained his position to the people of that state, as he had done to others many times in the past few weeks.

The regular army was extremely small, and it would be a major error to stretch its already limited resources too far. Iowans ought to go to Omaha, where they could use the Platte route out to Fort Laramie and then take the Bozeman Trail into Montana. This route already had military protection; when and if more soldiers were available, other roads might be opened. The Missouri River afforded an alternate means of getting to Montana, and it, too, was guarded. This was all the army could or should do in the matter of protection for the present. Use the routes afforded them, Sherman urged prospective emigrants; if they did not, trouble would surely result.[16] When Montanans saw a copy of Sherman's letter, they heartily agreed. Keep to the established routes, they advised eastern "tenderfeet," and preserve your scalps. Those who had "cut-off" on the brain might easily lose some hair, or even precipitate a general plains war, "for the Indian, like the wolf, knows neither rest nor truce when he has once tasted blood."[17]

Sherman did not publicize his inner convictions about such pressure for the Niobrara route. A letter from one of his inspectors general told him that not only was it impracticable, but a number of interested businessmen had paid a substantial amount of money to officers who had passed over it a year before, hoping to get a favorable report.[18] With this information at hand, Sherman's mind snapped shut to further pleas. That he would hear howls of dismay from Iowa legislators, he knew. Let them touch off their oratorical pyrotechnics; he was getting used to forensic fireworks.

Meanwhile, like jackals yapping at his heels, there were others to take up the cry. Senator Alexander Ramsey sent along a pe-

[16] Sherman to Wright, April 7, 1866. Division of the Mississippi, Letters Sent, 1865–66.

[17] *Montana Post*, May 26, 1866. Wright's letter is published in this issue.

[18] Sacket to Sherman, April 29, 1866, 39 Cong., 2 sess., *House Exec. Doc. No. 23* (Serial 1288), pp. 21–22.

tition signed by a number of prominent Minnesotans. Residents of St. Cloud wanted to be on the main line of travel to the Missouri River, and they felt that the army should give immediate protection to a route leading from that city. "We have not troops enough to guard and build a separate road of near sixteen hundred miles to accommodate every village and set of emigrants," Sherman fired back. Perhaps sometime in the future a suitable roadway from Minnesota to the West could be marked off and protected, but not now.[19] Clamorous citizens could bombard him with all the petitions they chose to sign; but for the present, he would stand pat. Nor could the knowledge that Ramsey would one day be his superior, as secretary of war, have influenced Sherman.

With Father Pierre Jean De Smet, the most widely known Catholic missionary in the West, Sherman was more gentle. The cleric, who was ready to leave for the mountains, had inquired about the plans of the military. For years, he had followed Indian relations closely and was eager to learn of any proposed developments. There were no elaborate plans for the coming summer, came the answer from St. Louis. The main routes would be guarded and further developed; little more could be done. Then Sherman revealed some of his thinking as it touched upon the final solution to western Indian affairs. Ultimately, the natives would have to be localized. So long as they ranged the land on buffalo hunts, there would be continual collisions and disputes over land rights. Perhaps the day would come when these people could raise their own food and build permanent homes. That alone would localize them and, ultimately, would end their nomadic tendencies.[20]

But all that was mere speculation and hopeful anticipation. For the moment, he knew full well that more practical measures faced the nation and the army. In the existing framework of things, persuading such Westerners as the Dakota Sioux that

---

[19] Sherman to Leet, April 17, 1866. Division of the Mississippi, Letters Sent, 1865–66.

[20] Sherman to Father Pierre De Smet, April 9, 1866. *Montana Post*, June 30, 1866.

following the plow was more interesting than pursuing buffalo would take much more than philanthropy and oratory.

Meanwhile, as signs of spring appeared in St. Louis, Sherman busied himself with final preparations for the coming summer. "We cannot afford perfect protection," he admitted. The cheapest, and only practical, method was the formation of a line of posts along emigrant roads. If the travelers followed Pope's regulations, they could make their way from fort to fort in relative safety. These military establishments would, of necessity, be small; to give them any sizable body of troops would mean placing them too far apart to be of much use. By spreading out the available men, outposts might be located as close as one hundred miles from each other.[21] Admittedly, these little posts were expensive to maintain and not very effective in the event of serious trouble, but the necessities of western travel dictated their locations. For the present, the western army could represent nothing more than a thin blue line on a vast tract of land. The soldiers would be mere policemen in a mob of swirling, tumultuous emigrants and Indians. Only by the rarest of luck would some kind of conflict be avoided.

But Sherman was cheerful about his prospects. So far, everything was working out well, he told Grant. "All I meet are engaged in useful work, or are preparing to migrate to one or other of the Frontier territories." Between Pope, in the Department of Missouri, and Cooke, in the Department of the Platte, order would probably be maintained along, at least, the main roads. Certainly, these major avenues would be teeming. Forty steamboats were already preparing to ascend the Missouri as far as Fort Benton, Montana. Aside from the protection of the great river, there were the three roads, of which he had already written, varying from twelve hundred to two thousand miles in length, stretching like fingers out to Montana, Utah, and New Mexico. All of them passed through Indian country. And over them, it was estimated, as many as one hundred thousand people would move during the summer months. There would be emigrants,

21 Sherman to Hunt at Fort Smith, March 12, 1866. Division of the Mississippi, Letters Sent, 1865–66.

with their wagons loaded with food and household goods, flanked by small herds of cattle. And there would be Indians, whose food supply was constantly diminishing, watching furtively, as the snakelike trains edged forward. In some cases the attraction would be too much, and the hungry natives would accost the trains; then there would be trouble. With the white advance, the military center of gravity in Sherman's Division would move westward. If things went right during the summer of 1866, the first step in the ultimate pacification of a prairie empire might be accomplished, and then it would be time to plan further moves in the grand strategy of settlement.

Like the director of a play, Sherman made a last-minute study of his actors and properties, hopeful that all would go well when the curtain went up. The stage was set; the players were in their places; the great drama of "Westward Ho!" was ready for its annual production. Nervously pacing back and forth in the wings—his office at St. Louis—Sherman watched the calendar as it ticked off the moments until curtain time. Then, he could stand the suspense no longer; he had to go out and investigate for himself.

Four

_____

AND I CAN SEE FOR MYSELF

THE HUM OF ACTIVITY around Division headquarters at St. Louis resulting from the General's preparations to travel may easily be imagined. The scurrying clerks, copyists working overtime on reports, and orderlies nervously moving around the outer offices must have lent an atmosphere of contagious excitement even to those who were not going along. A picture of Sherman himself would have revealed a spare-looking man dressed in a shabby uniform, his jaw tightened thoughtfully on a battered cigar stump, perhaps running his hand from time to time through a crop of unruly reddish hair that was beginning to fade under an invasion of gray. Hundreds of wartime soldiers had seen this high-strung, scowling officer, poorly dressed and almost unkempt-looking, pacing the floor on the eve of battle. Now, as the early spring sunshine thawed the frost-covered miles of rich western earth, he very much anticipated visiting the land he was supposed to protect. Four years of war and constant moving had left him restless and eager to be in the field. Nervous by nature and endowed with a burning curiosity, he could no more sit at St. Louis and direct operations than he could have remained behind a desk in Washington during the war. Every mark on the map had to be converted into a mental picture of what it really looked like as one stood on the actual ground. Until he went out to see for himself, the inked lines on paper would be meaningless. Grant, of course, had to approve the inspection tour. It was merely a matter of form, however, for that quiet officer, consigned to the political jungles of Washington, would only heave an envious sigh and give the necessary permission.

Taking a piece of ruled stationery, he scratched away in a fine, slanting hand, telling Grant of his plans and asking approval of them. By early May, travel on the plains would be feasible. First, he would go out along the new Kansas railroad, as far as Fort Riley, and after making an inspection there, he would take an army ambulance northward to the end of the Union Pacific line in Nebraska. Returning eastward to Omaha by rail, he would then take a boat up the Missouri to Sioux City and from there cross over by land to St. Paul. A trip down the lake to Detroit would give him an opportunity to see the northern portions of his command, and after that, he would return to St. Louis. While he confessed that the nature of the trip was partially personal, he justified its necessity by saying that it would make him "well acquainted with all the questions of the Frontier" and enable him to give official assurances of future peace and quiet out there. Later in the summer, perhaps in August, he wanted to go all the way out to the western part of his Division. He proposed to follow the same general route of the first trip, but to expand the loop to Denver, and perhaps Utah, returning by way of Fort Laramie and on eastward to Omaha.[1]

Having made a formal application for the inspection trip, he penned an enthusiastic letter to his brother John, inviting him to go along on the mountain trip in August. "Bring only the clothing you need and the essential personal articles," he advised the Senator. Transportation and subsistence would be Cump's problem. "Having command I can control all these things and therefore you need not give the subject your thoughts," he wrote generously.[2] He was eager to show his domain to John.

By early May, Sherman was off to Fort Riley. After examining the Kansas branch of the railroad with interest, he took to a two-horse spring-wagon ambulance and moved up the valley of the Republican River for over one hundred miles. These canvas-covered ambulances—"Doughertys," as Sherman called them—were a reasonably comfortable means of prairie travel, and he was to cover thousands of miles in them before he retired. Swinging northward from the Republican, he traveled over an inter-

[1] Sherman to Grant, April 13, 1866. Division of the Missouri, Letters Received, 1866–69, Special File.

[2] Sherman to John Sherman, April 24, 1866. William T. Sherman Papers, Volume 19.

vening high prairie ridge to the Little Blue and then followed the main road into Fort Kearny. As he had explained to Grant, "This route will carry me across all the emigrant roads, and I can see for myself the relative proportion on each road, and then form a judgment as to how much military protection we should extend."[3]

After six days of travel beyond Fort Riley, hampered somewhat by the lack of forage at that time of year, the party reached the old post of Fort Kearny. There was little of anything exciting to report about it. The dilapidated frame buildings, standing gauntly out on a vast, treeless plain, were desolate and lonely. Its location, at the junction of the roads leading west from Fort Leavenworth, Atchison, Nebraska City, and Omaha, had made it a place of importance, but before long, the railroad would change all that. Despite the barrenness of the country, there were a few farms dotting the landscape. The land to the east was more heavily settled and was generally considered safe from hostile Indians. Sherman wondered why there were any settlers around the place at all, for there was no stone, timber, or coal anywhere in the vicinity. The soil appeared to be fertile enough, and its grassy turf indicated that it could produce, but it seemed to him that the parched summers and violent winters ought to warn off the average settler.[4] The pressure of the westward movement puzzled him.

After a day or two at Fort Kearny, the General's party crossed the Platte River and went eastward to meet the steel tendrils that crept out across the prairie towards the mountains. Once the railroad was reached, the remaining seventy-five miles to Omaha evaporated like a spring snow. Sherman's interest in the new road quickened as he visited the machine shops and viewed the stockpile of materials at the booming river town. He talked at length with Grenville Dodge, who had recently given up his army commission to take a position as chief engineer of the Union Pacific's construction. Grinning at his old comrade-in-arms, now

[3] Sherman to Grant, April 30, 1866. Division of the Mississippi, Letters Sent, 1865–66.

[4] Sherman to Grant, May 14, 1866. Division of the Mississippi, Letters Sent, 1865–66.

dressed in rough working clothes, he told bystanders that Dodge looked like a mule driver. Together they inspected the railroad's headquarters and chatted with Vice-President Thomas Durant about prospects for the coming year.

Progress on the road had been wonderful, he wrote Grant. He had seen enough ties and iron to build at least 50 miles, and Durant had contracted for enough to lay an additional 150 miles. By the middle of June, the 100-mile marker should be passed, and by the end of the year, another 100 would be added, putting rails within 5 miles of Fort Kearny. With this completed, along with the parallel railroad through Kansas to Fort Riley, the problem of furnishing military supplies to the outposts along the mountains would be greatly simplified. Sherman hoped that the roads would not be brought together at the one hundredth meridian, as originally planned. He wanted to see the Eastern Division, or Kansas road, move straight west to Denver by the Smoky Hill route.[5] Two railroads in such a vast country were none too many.

As he prepared to leave for Sioux City, Sherman made an assessment of the travel situation on the western routes he had just examined. There was not very much movement over the road leading to Fort Riley. Much more heavily traveled was the old emigrant trail up the Platte to Fort Kearny and beyond. Hundreds of settlers were moving out of Missouri River towns to take the old military road on the south side of the Platte, and from what he had seen, Sherman concluded that it would be a very busy season, indeed.[6] So far, the travelers were proceeding to their new homes in the West in an orderly fashion and were generally following the roads defined for them by the military.

Perhaps the plans made for the protection of the High Plains would work. Sherman hoped so. His new assignment would be no Atlanta; in many ways it was much bigger and certainly more diverse. Compared to the number of troops he had once commanded, his men now were a mere handful. And the land he must control was as vast as the entire South. Also, since the

5 *Ibid.*
6 *Ibid.*

nation had been freed of the threat of destruction, there would be those who would try to curtail his activities. In fact, his enemies were already at work. During May, while Sherman was far out in Kansas, the radical congressman from Pennsylvania, Thaddeus Stevens, had maneuvered to block any possible promotion for the veteran soldier.[7] Although the move had failed, the action was a danger flag flying in the wind. Sherman had his critics, and they were powerful. When he finally heard of the plot against him, he probably grunted that Washington was a pestiferous place and chewed away at his cigar even more violently.

When he arrived at Sioux City a few days later, Sherman had additional reason to rage at officialdom in the Capital. Awaiting him was a letter signed by General S. R. Curtis and Henry W. Reed, relating that they had been appointed as Indian commissioners. They were bound for the upper Missouri River country to make treaties with the tribes in that area and fully expected the army to feed any natives with whom they might negotiate. Before they left Washington, the pair had been promised that such an arrangement would be suitable.

Sherman wrote an angry letter to Grant protesting such an assumption. He said that when troops were sent upriver, they were given a year's supply of food, and there was no anticipation that they would be called upon to share it. Look at such posts as Fort Berthold or Fort Union, high up on the Missouri. Curtis estimated that he might have as many as ten thousand Indians in council. Why, they would eat out one of these garrisons in a day. At places like Fort Rice or Fort Sully, four-company posts, a whole year's food supply would be gobbled up by the Indians at a sitting. The Interior Department was up to its old tricks, Sherman growled. Why could they not foresee their own needs and make adequate provision for them, instead of sending out an eleventh-hour appeal to the army? As an added vexation, Interior Department representatives never failed to suggest darkly that if the army did not produce some food, evil consequences might arise, since the Indians expected to be fed when invited to a parley, and they might react violently if neglected. On top of these

[7] *Congressional Globe,* 39 Cong., 1 sess., Part II, p. 2393.

unnecessary annoyances, Sherman wrote scoldingly, was piled the crowning one of ignorance. No one ever told him what agreements there were on such subjects between the secretaries of War and Interior. He could never be sure how he should treat these demands. If he tried to protect his own officers by backing their denial of the requests, he might well be running counter to Grant's orders without knowing it. It was perfectly senseless, anyway. The civilian agents assigned to Indian dealings could easily make their own preparations.[8] He'd be damned if he would "nursemaid" them.

As for such a place as Sioux City, where he had received the disturbing letter from Curtis and Reed, it was high time to realize that the frontier had moved on and left it behind. It had long been a depot for supplies, but now it was too far behind the firing line, and Sherman decided to clean house. "I gave orders to break it up absolutely," he told Grant bluntly. All supplies would be sent forward to Fort Randall, on the Missouri River, where there were adequate storehouses. Colonel J. V. D. Reeve, of the Thirteenth Infantry, whom Sherman found at Sioux City, was ordered to go to Fort Sully; supplies would follow him. As Reeve departed, the irascible redhead handed him orders relative to feeding any Indians who might be invited to dine with the commissioners. The answer was "no." Emphatically no. But then he softened somewhat and told Reeve that if it looked as if there would be any trouble over the refusal, he was authorized to turn over half the supplies at Rice and Sully for such purposes. Grumpily Sherman added the warning that if such a thing happened, the commissioners would have to give bond, assuring the replacement of any stores taken. The Interior people could have a loan; no handouts would be available.[9]

Having thus demolished an army installation nestled safely in settled country, Sherman snorted off to St. Paul, leaving behind consternation and confusion among those who had happily organized themselves for the defense of the Iowa farmers. Officers

---

[8] Sherman to Grant, May 26, 1866. Division of the Mississippi, Letters Sent, 1865–66.

[9] Sherman to Reeve, May 17, 1866. Division of the Mississippi, Letters Sent, 1865–66.

and men must have been content to retreat into Indian country to get away from the General's wrath.

At Fort Snelling, Sherman's temper was no better. He sat down and wrote a letter to John, telling of his trip and remarking grimly that he was then awaiting a deputation of citizens from near-by St. Paul who were bent on showing him the city, "where I am to undergo the infliction of a public reception, serenade in the evening and a public dinner at 9 o'clock, so I have before me a hard day's work." His mood warmed a little as he wrote on, telling of his plans for the trip west later that summer. Pick out four or five friends, he urged John, and he would invite a like number. They could all meet at St. Louis around August 20 and proceed to Omaha, where a Union Pacific car would be waiting. Then there would be Laramie, Denver, and some of the military posts in Colorado. The party would have horses and a cavalry escort with which to move along the base of the great mountain range. The trip would consume most of September and October, he wrote with contentment.[10] Thoughts of the High Plains and the vast spaces, free of reception committees, made him feel better. They were a tonic that helped to brace him for the ordeal of handshaking and the oratorical assaults of mayors and councilmen awaiting him in a matter of minutes.

When inspections in the Minnesota area were completed and the dignitaries had been faced, Sherman moved along on his tour, eager to get back to St. Louis. By the end of June he was again behind his office desk, writing to Grant about all the things he had seen. Aside from what he had personally observed, he was able to describe conditions along the upper Missouri, based upon reports from Inspector General Delos B. Sacket. At Fort Randall, in southern Dakota Territory, for example, the quarters for troops were simply uninhabitable. Men were obliged to live in log huts that were falling apart, and through whose every crack and crevice legions of bedbugs, fleas, spiders, mice, and rats paraded. Rather than face such company, the men had taken to

[10] Sherman to John Sherman, May 28, 1866. William T. Sherman Papers, Volume 19.

sleeping out of doors. It was better than the drafty hovels, whose only virtue, the men said jokingly, lay in their excellent ventilation. Sanitary conditions in the kitchens were not much better. Sacket called them low, dark, and unclean.[11] Farther upriver things were no better. The quarters at Fort Sully were just as uninhabitable. There, too, the buildings were in ruins; their rafters were broken and the floors consisted of mud. As elsewhere, fleas, bedbugs, and rats reigned supreme.[12] At Fort Rice, still deeper in the interior, the pattern was unchanged. As in the other posts, the men lived in unbelievable filth. The Indians stood around them, bold and defiant, "and some swore threats."[13]

It was a typical report, and it came from most of the western posts, Sherman told Quartermaster General Montgomery Meigs. Letters from Colonel Orville E. Babcock, who was inspecting posts out along the western land routes, described the new post at Big Laramie as intolerable. It was devoid of everything essential to the simplest comforts. Earth and cottonwood structures were unfit for his men, Sherman complained, for they bred vermin and drove the men into the cold. Even inside, keeping warm was a problem, for at such places as Fort Sedgwick, in Colorado, the cost of firewood "surpasses all decency."[14]

How could troops be worth anything if they had to winter in mere holes and fight rats, bedbugs, and fleas for their very existence, Sherman asked. At the time of their selection, the locations of the posts were probably the best available, but before long, the troops had stripped the surrounding lands of all their wood.[15] Then they froze or spent all their time hunting down elusive fagots. But it was hard to do much about it. Reports from the West varied so widely that it was difficult to know where the best locations for posts were. Moreover, each mile the railroad advanced westward changed the importance of these small out-

11 Report of Delos B. Sacket, May 8, 1866, 39 Cong., 2 sess., *House Exec. Doc. No. 23* (Serial 1288), p. 24.

12 *Ibid.*, 34.

13 *Ibid.*, 43.

14 Sherman to Meigs, July 3, 1866. Division of the Mississippi, Letters Sent, 1865–66.

15 Sherman to Grant, June 22, 1866. Division of the Mississippi, Letters Sent, 1865–66.

posts, and many of them would soon be abandoned. Bad as conditions seemed to be, it might be best to wait a little and make major changes, instead of a lot of minor ones. It was a perplexing problem, and Sherman was caught between the desire to make his men more comfortable and the demands for economy coming out of Washington. He would have to go out and see the picture for himself.

As he planned the coming trip to the Rockies, Sherman again urged John to accompany him. Ellen and the children were going to spend the summer at Lancaster, Ohio, and after he fulfilled a promise to attend the commencement exercises at Dartmouth in mid-July, he would be free to leave. Perhaps his brother could bring along several fellow senators, and by going out the Smoky Hill route and returning by way of the Platte, they could view both of the great western railroads then under construction. There was still some debate about the direction the Union Pacific would take after it reached the base of the mountains. He reminded John that here would be a fine opportunity to study the question firsthand and to see some of the possible routes available beyond the Rockies.[16]

In July, as he awaited John's final answer, Sherman left for the East, annoyed that he had to go. A few days later, he stood before a gathering of admiring Yale students and made some predictions that both puzzled and annoyed New York newsmen. "I tell you," he said to the boys, "that before you pass from the stage there will be fighting, in comparison with which mine will seem slight, and I have had enough." Whom are we going to fight? asked the press. Why did Sherman make such remarks? What did he mean? Was he withholding some secret information? Huffily the editor concluded that Sherman was a great fighter, but a poor prophet. He did not know what the great war hero was talking about, but still he refused to agree with him. Sherman made no comments on the buzz of speculation he had left behind him.[17] If the newsmen were perplexed, all the better.

---

[16] Sherman to John Sherman, June 30, 1866. William T. Sherman Papers, Volume 19.

[17] *New York Times*, July 16, 1866.

He moved on to Hanover, as he had promised, and stayed still long enough for Dartmouth's president to award him a Doctor of Laws degree at the commencement ceremony.[18] Then he started back for St. Louis.

Getting out of the East was not such a simple maneuver, however, and before he returned to his command, Sherman was obliged to report to Washington. Crowds at once gathered around his hotel, and when the clamor of the populace reached a crescendo, he submitted and reluctantly made one of his much-dreaded balcony speeches. "I have been told the less a man says in Washington, the more he is thought of," he told his listeners, with an eye cocked on Capitol Hill. The crowd roared with laughter and asked for more. "I am a stranger among you," he continued, almost proudly, "and shall depart tomorrow for St. Louis, where I should be very happy to have you call and see me, or on the plains where I soon expect to be." He wanted all Washington to hear that he would soon be far away, in his beloved western command. "A man is his own best friend when he don't make speeches," he concluded. "I now bid you good night."[19] With that crisp remark, he turned and disappeared into his quarters.

He was back at St. Louis within a few days, making final preparations for his inspection trip. He was anxious to see some of the land for whose defense he was responsible. He confessed to Grant that he did not yet have an "intelligent idea" of the troubles beyond Laramie. Apparently the Indians did not like the establishment of new posts in the direction of Montana. Inspector General Sacket, writing from Virginia City, Montana, was one of the sources of this information. He reported that, while there was no immediate danger in that new territory, the road leading from it to Fort Laramie would, without doubt, be a source of trouble, and he recommended more troops for the region.[20] The Sioux were angry at the rapid increase of travel over the short cut John Bozeman had marked off a couple of

18 See certificate in William T. Sherman Papers, July 25, 1866, Volume 19.
19 *Daily Missouri Republican,* August 2, 1866.
20 Sherman to Grant, August 9, 1866. Division of the Mississippi, Letters Sent, 1865–66.

years ago. Sherman made a mental note that here was one of the danger spots he must watch. He would make it a point to visit the neighborhood during his coming trip. While he worried about these points of contact between red and white, he was content that, in general, matters were reasonably well controlled. There would for years be a certain amount of conflict with the roving bands of Indians, but as the new postwar army shaped up, and the railroads pushed westward, the danger of any general outbreak would steadily diminish.[21]

Meanwhile, in order to contain the wandering Indians more effectually, as well as the droves of straying emigrants, the western commands were once again reshuffled. On August 6, the Division's name was changed from Mississippi to Missouri, and to make it an all-western unit, the Department of Ohio was dropped. Because of the surprising amount of travel up the Missouri River, the recently formed Department of the Platte was found too unwieldy, and from it, a new department, named Dakota, was formed, embracing Minnesota, Dakota, and Montana. General Alfred Terry, who had won Sherman's admiration with his brilliant action at Fort Fisher in the dying days of the war, was given the new command. Cooke's reduced Department of the Platte followed generally the main line of the old California Trail out toward Salt Lake. To the south of it, the Department of Missouri protected travel through Kansas westward to Colorado and New Mexico. To Sherman's satisfaction, General W. S. Hancock was now brought west and placed in command of this department. Finally, to the extreme south, lay the Department of Arkansas, headed by the old veteran E. O. C. Ord, who had been transferred from the Ohio Department. Sherman was now fairly well satisfied. With the exception of Cooke, whom he still hoped to replace, the departments were in capable hands, and he could expect the fullest co-operation in the days that lay ahead.[22] So far, 1866 had been a relatively calm year on the plains, but the

[21] Sherman to Townsend, August 10, 1866. Division of the Mississippi, Letters Sent, 1865–66.

[22] Report of W. T. Sherman, November 5, 1866. *Annual Report of the Secretary of War*, 39 Cong., 2 sess., *House Exec. Doc. No. 1* (Serial 1285), p. 19.

years ahead would be hazardous, for the flood of emigration showed no signs of diminishing. It would be well to be ready.

A few days after the changes were made, Sherman headed for Fort Leavenworth and the High Plains beyond. The local paper there complained of his rapid movements. When his presence in the city was discovered, admirers hastily organized to give him an appropriate welcome, but before they could accomplish their purpose, he was gone. It was one of Sherman's most annoying traits in the eyes of the hero-worshipers. But, as the editor sighed, "On duty, he never pauses. He looks to that and attends to that, and cares for nothing else." At the moment, Sherman's duty was to look after trade and travel westward, and Leavenworth readers were told that under the General's eagle eye, not only would it be done at once, but it would be done thoroughly.[23] Sherman had no pleasant memories of Leavenworth. If he rode down Main Street, he may have seen the old building on whose second floor he had once had a law office. That was back in the lean days of 1858, when, plunged in gloom, he had written Ellen, "I look upon myself as a dead cock in the pit, not worthy of further notice, and will take my chances as they come." Much had happened since then.

By August 17, Sherman was in Omaha, packing his effects into a Union Pacific train car. His aides, Colonel L. M. Dayton and J. C. Audenried, completed last-minute details for the trip, while Sherman enthusiastically showed John around the railroad headquarters. He was delighted that his brother had finally consented to come. Before the train left, Sherman wrote a long letter to headquarters. He wanted Grant to know what he had recently seen and something of his plans for the next few weeks. Once he left civilization behind, the matter of communication with Washington would not be so easy.

Addressing his remarks to John Rawlins, Grant's chief aide, Sherman dwelt upon the importance of the new railroads. The Eastern Division, or Kansas line, was completed as far as Manhattan, a distance of 115 miles, with branches feeding both Kansas City and Leavenworth. Barring delay, it would reach Fort

<hr />

23 *Leavenworth Daily Times*, August 15, 1866.

Riley by September. The railroad up the Platte Valley was progressing equally well. Omaha reflected the degree of activity to the west. It grew so fast between visits that Sherman always shook his head at it in wonderment. At the moment, there was probably no busier place beyond the Mississippi. Disbursements resulting from the construction work had made the city look like a bonanza mining camp. He had just talked with Grenville Dodge, who "as usual is possessed of every possible piece of information that is desirable"; the pair had carefully gone over plans for the future growth of the road. Already, Sherman revealed with pride, the line was carrying passengers 150 miles westward, and within a few days, another section would be opened, connecting Fort Kearny and making a total of 194 miles. Better than that, the company had enough iron and ties on hand to build an additional 100 miles, and Dodge was confident that it could be constructed at the rate of one mile or one and one-half miles a day. By the coming April, the railroad ought to be out in the neighborhood of Julesburg, Colorado. It would be an astounding achievement, but in the light of all that had recently transpired, it was perfectly possible. Beyond Julesburg there was some doubt about the direction the construction would take. Denver was applying strong pressure to bend it southward to the Colorado capital. Sherman hoped that it would go in the direction of Fort Laramie, but regardless of the decision, he was more than satisfied that the construction was in excellent hands, and he promised to give the company all the protection and encouragement he could.

Turning to the Indian situation, Sherman admitted that there had been recent depredations in Kansas. He had hoped to see Governor Samuel Crawford on this trip but had missed him. They had recently corresponded on the subject, and he had advised the Governor to discourage settlers from drifting too far from the more settled regions. He knew that this would be difficult to accomplish, but unless the whites could be somewhat contained, there would surely be trouble. While in Kansas that spring, Sherman had been surprised to see homesteaders far up the Republican Fork, making homes miles from any neighbors.

It was not surprising that they tempted Indian raiders. Such dispersion would certainly cause isolated attacks and possibly an Indian war. If large-scale fighting developed, he hoped that the frontier states could "be somewhat prepared by organized volunteer companies to help us . . . but it will not do to let the purpose of any one locality draw us all into such a war." Sherman distrusted some of the western governors and disliked their tendency to respond so readily to public clamor for war every time a small Indian raiding party struck some isolated outpost.

With regard to Indian problems on the northern plains, the commanding officer confessed that he knew little. It was his understanding that most of the difficulties had arisen out of raids and murders along the Powder River road into Montana. Not much could be done about that right now. It was all the troops could do to hold the long, thin lines that guided small parties of emigrants across the isolated stretches. Next year might be a different thing. The advance of the railroad would simplify defense along the eastern belt of his command and permit him to throw troops more rapidly and in greater numbers into more remote danger spots. If the Sioux continued to dispute the decision to make a road into Montana, the army would shortly be in a much better position to argue.[24]

With these comments, he concluded his business at Omaha and left for the troubled land beyond. Shortly he would pass Julesburg and be out of touch with the telegraph. He was a little like a sailor, setting sail for parts unknown and out of communication with the world. Here at last was his chance to cruise the endless miles of ocean-like prairie, as he had explained it to Admiral Porter. Ahead lay innumerable miles of space and solitude, and within a few days he would be in their midst. The thought appealed to him greatly.

24 Sherman to Rawlins, August 17, 1866. Division of the Missouri, Letters Received, 1866–69, Special File.

———

Five

THESE AWFUL DISTANCES

THE SHERMAN BROTHERS stretched their legs and relaxed. The steady movement of the car, swaying comfortably as it clicked over the rails, lent an air of luxury to western travel. Outside, the gray-brown prairie bottom, parched and uninviting, swirled by like a threatening sea. It would be like this for nearly two hundred miles, until Fort Kearny. Then they would board army ambulances for a jolting trip on to Laramie. But for the moment, it was better not to think of that. There were few places in the West where one could enjoy such travel as this, and each mile of it should be appreciated.

Within five miles of Fort Kearny the train ground to a stop, and the General's party alighted. The high-wheeled, canvas-topped ambulances were waiting, and as the men clambered into them, they could see construction crews laying the remaining few miles of track toward the fort. Whips cracked and the "Dougherty's" lurched forward, churning up the powdery road as they moved along. Up the north bank of the Platte a mile or so, the river had to be forded, and on the other side of "as mean a River as exists on earth" lay the military post that had become such a landmark for emigrants moving along the California trail.

In little over a year's time, that modern wonder, the railroad, had pronounced a death sentence on Fort Kearny. When Sherman had last seen it, only months before, the place had appeared to be strategically located. But now that the railroad was passing it by, leaving the fort isolated by "a miserable, dangerous and unbridgeable river," the picture had changed. It would have to be maintained for a while, because there was still wagon travel on the south side of the river, and all of that would not disappear, even with the coming of the railroad. Fort Kearny's growing uselessness would be no great loss to the government, for most of its buildings were in an advanced state of decay. In fact, two of the larger structures had become a positive menace, and they had been pulled down before they could fall and kill their occupants. Sherman decided that he would use the place during the coming winter to shelter some horses belonging to the army and next year "let it go to the Prairie dogs."[1]

Before moving on, the party was honored by the usual civic ceremonies. At near-by Kearney City, or "Dobytown," as it was better known, a salute was fired in honor of Sherman, whom the local editor proudly called the "Western Captain."[2] Despite such kindly sentiments, the visitors were eager to be on their way. Dobytown, consisting of a half-dozen drab sod houses, mostly saloons, was not a place of great beauty. However, it did have utility. The soldiers at the fort found solace at its bars, as did many a dust-covered bullwhacker, whose profane advice to his teams had parched his throat beyond endurance.[3] Sherman, who appreciated a social glass, must have acknowledged the courtesies of the citizens to the extent of joining them in a drink of "tanglefoot" before he left. For one sentenced to a trip westward in an army ambulance, no better anesthetic could be found.

The trip west of Fort Kearny was not entirely dangerous. Nor was it lonely. The road was well traveled, and the little caravan of five wagons met many other groups along the way. There was a surprising number of ranches, standing alone out in nowhere. Their means of existence seemed to be explained by the fact that each of them had large corrals and enormous piles of hay near by. It was unnecessary to post signs reading, "All travelers accommodated." Other than the monotony of sameness and the bleakness of the country, the journey seemed to be quite an ordinary one. Sherman noticed that no one he met had any apprehensions of danger. The telegraph line and stagecoach

---

1 Sherman to Rawlins, August 21, 1866. Division of the Missouri, Letters Received, 1866–69, Special File.

2 Kearney *Herald*, August 21, 1866, quoted by the *Daily Union Vedette* (Salt Lake City), September 1, 1866.

3 Frank A. Root and William C. Connelley, *The Overland Stage to California*, 207.

line, neither of which had ever been seriously molested, provided a constant contact with more populous regions. In addition, the traveler was rarely out of sight of a wagon train or a ranch.

For three days the men toiled along, covering only ninety-five miles. It was less than half the distance they had made in a single day on the railroad west of Omaha. Toward the end of the third day, Fort McPherson appeared in the hazy distance, and before long, the ambulances creaked into the post.[4] This place, better known to emigrants as Cottonwood Springs, had recently been renamed for General J. B. McPherson, who was killed in the Battle of Atlanta. It was a popular stop along the Overland Trail, and since the rush in 1849, thousands of wagons had paused there. While members of Sherman's party may have thought ambulance travel extremely slow, they had covered the distance from Fort Kearny in excellent time. Emigrants, especially those who drove herds of cattle with them, would require a week to cover the same distance.[5]

Here was another western post that would soon have to be abandoned. Once so desirable, by virtue of the fresh streams that flowed into the Platte from the near-by hills, it would be rendered useless shortly by the railroad. The great supply of cottonwood and cedar that had formerly made the place important was now nearly gone. Emigrants had scoured the valley thoroughly for firewood, and the railroad company had contributed to the depletion in its search for ties among the cedar groves. As in the case of Fort Kearny, this establishment would also be left isolated beyond a difficult river-crossing, since the railroad passed it on the north bank of the river. Sherman estimated that the place had until Christmas before iron rails would complete its obsolescence.[6]

[4] *Ibid.*

[5] Perry Burgess, who passed over the route two months before Sherman, took a week to cover the distance. He complained bitterly about the dust and the mosquitoes, both of which rose in great clouds around him. Robert G. Athearn (ed.), "From Illinois to Montana in 1866: The Diary of Perry A. Burgess," *The Pacific Northwest Quarterly*, Vol. XLI, No. 1 (January, 1950), 51–52.

[6] Sherman to Rawlins, August 21, 1866. Division of the Mississippi, Letters Sent, 1865–66.

There was not much to be seen at Fort McPherson, and Sherman learned all he wanted to know in a short time. The commanding officer of the post was dutifully carrying out General Pope's instructions, stopping small groups of emigrants and obliging them to wait until a sufficient number had gathered to make up the prescribed train of at least twenty wagons. This caused some complaint, and Sherman told himself that, without doubt, many a wagon train—most perhaps—would see no sign of Indians. But just let the emigrants scatter out, and there would be attacks. Then the army would be castigated for its carelessness.

Seeing that matters at McPherson were well in hand, Sherman ordered his drivers to harness up. The Rockies were beckoning, and he was impatient to be off. On up the valley the ambulances toiled, while the passengers watched the endless miles slowly evaporate. Sand lizards eyed them sleepily, and startled jack rabbits bolted through the prickly pears that dotted the gray soil. The otherwise drab landscape was here and there colored with the pale pink and yellow flowers of the thorny plants. They had a sweetness that faintly resembled hollyhocks. Now and then a prairie dog, sitting erect, would watch the party curiously as it passed. More interesting were the burrowing owls. These small birds, about the size of a quail, lived in mounds built by the prairie dogs. As the ambulances rolled by, the grave little owls beat their wings furiously and fled to mounds farther off the road, watching the strangers with profound respect.[7]

Sherman soon tired of such roadside attractions. More and more he kept his eye fastened on the horizon ahead, noticing how the pastels of nature blended so perfectly. By contrast, the immediate landscape repulsed him. "It is impossible to conceive of a more dreary waste than this whole road is—without a tree or a bush, grass thin, and the Platte running over its wide, shallow bottom with its rapid current; . . . nothing but the long dusty road, with its occasional ox team, and the everlasting line of telegraph poles." It was extremely tiresome, and he longed for that which lay ahead. "Oh, for the pine forests of the south,

7 Athearn (ed.), "From Illinois to Montana in 1866: The Diary of Perry A. Burgess," *The Pacific Northwest Quarterly*, Vol. XLI, No. 1 (January, 1950), 52–53.

or anything to hide the endless view," he wrote. "I shall feel an absolute sense of relief when I see the mountains, with their forests of timber, and shall henceforth urge with renewed energy the work on the Pacific Railroad." Although he might defend the value of his domain to others, for the moment he was a subscriber to the desert theory.

Timber would, indeed, be welcome. The prairie nights were cool, even cold, despite the fact that it was August. But the emigrants had scoured the land like locusts, and there was not a stick of wood with which to kindle a fire. Buffalo chips had to fill the bill, but even they were at a premium. Getting enough fuel for a pot of coffee was hard enough, let alone having sufficient fire to keep one's bones warm. A desert it was, indeed, where even a major general regarded a piece of dung as a prize.

After traveling for three days over the arid stretches of western Nebraska, the small caravan rolled into Fort Sedgwick, just across the Colorado territorial line. Like Forts Kearny and McPherson, this post was also located on the wrong side of the Platte. Although the railroad would run on the other side of the river, at least the stream could be forded at this point, which was more than could be said of the other locations. Sherman, unswerving in his prejudices, found no comfort in this fact. To him, the Platte "in its whole length, is a mean, ugly stream, shallow, but full of quicksand, never safe."

Nor was there much to be found at Fort Sedgwick, once the ford was crossed. The buildings were of sod and about as unattractive as any structures could be. Sherman called them "hovels in which a negro would hardly go," and allowed that if the southern planters had kept their slaves in such quarters, "a sample would, ere this, have been carried to Boston and exhibited as illustrative of the cruelty and inhumanity of the masters." He was angered to think his men had to exist in such dwellings. However, not all of the buildings were this bad. Some of the more recently constructed ones were made of neater-looking adobe and were equipped with good doors and windows, even if the floors and roofs were of earth. Lumber was a rarity in this country, and the prices were almost unbelievable. It was no wonder, Sherman admitted, that the quartermaster general was so shocked at the cost of constructing living quarters for the men out here. Still, the army had no business to put its men in these desolate regions if it did not propose to give them adequate food and shelter. When everything but sand and water had to be hauled from one to four hundred miles, it was not surprising that the troops became discouraged. Back at St. Louis, Sherman had read reports about such living conditions but had concluded that the army could not afford to make improvements on these temporary posts. Now that he had actually seen them, his impersonal judgment softened. Hang the cost, the men would have better quarters. He would order it.[8]

Having traveled unmolested from Omaha to the northeastern corner of Colorado, Sherman was struck by the fact that he had seen no dangerous Indians. There was something wrong here. According to the papers, if one could believe the infernal reporters, the countryside was simply crawling with redskins, all bent on the sudden demise of the white settlers and travelers. Where were the scourges of the prairies about whom one read so much? He had not seen any danger, so far, and concluded that "as usual I find the size of Indian stampedes and scares diminishes as I approach their location."[9] He noticed that the telegraph was unmolested and the roads were filled with travelers in wagons and stagecoaches. Ranches, located every few miles along the way, seemed undisturbed. While the land was quiet, "yet there is a general apprehension of danger, though no one seems to have a definite idea of whence it is to come. I have met a few straggling parties of Indians who seemed pure beggars, and poor devils, more pitied than dreaded."[10] That was the trouble with such a

8 Sherman to Rawlins, August 24, 1866. Found in "Protection Across the Continent," letter from the Secretary of War in answer to a resolution of the House of December 6, 1866, transmitting information respecting the protection of the routes across the continent to the Pacific from molestation by hostile Indians, 39 Cong., 2 sess., *House Exec. Doc. No. 23* (Serial 1288), pp. 6–8. Hereinafter referred to as "Protection Across the Continent."

9 Sherman to Rawlins, August 21, 1866. Division of the Mississippi, Letters Sent, 1865–66.

10 Sherman to Rawlins, August 24, 1866. Division of the Mississippi, Letters Sent, 1865–66.

vast command. Rumor, unfounded reports, and exaggerated stories hung wraithlike over the country. Vague accounts of danger broke into pieces and melted away as one approached the scene. A man had to go see for himself. Yet, how could he be everywhere at once? It was a vicious problem.

His annoyance at the situation grew when he learned that Hancock had established his headquarters at St. Louis. Why in thunder had he done this, Sherman wondered. In the Department of Missouri, which extended to the western extremity of the Division, the commanding officer ought to be at least as far west as Fort Leavenworth. If some of these commanders would place themselves nearer to their troops, perhaps they would get more accurate reports of what was actually going on. It cost money to support a headquarters, and with a staff and all its hangers-on to care for, the expense often mounted rapidly. If some of the departmental offices were located farther west, Sherman thought grimly, some of the leeches who clung to them would not be so much in evidence. He would have to look into this when he returned, but right now there was much to be seen, and he was eager to see it.

Accompanied by a ten-man escort, the ambulances forded the South Platte and headed up the shallow valley of Lodge Pole Creek, climbing slowly as they moved west. The terrain was smooth and level, but "bare of tree or bush as your hand." The going was not hard. After about thirty-five miles of pleasant traveling, the Laramie Road came into sight, and the little convoy moved abruptly to the right, swinging up onto a broad table plain, where nearly thirty miles of barren land lay ahead. This northerly leg of the journey ended when the North Platte River was reached, and once again they headed west. A little over one hundred miles up that well-known watercourse lay far-famed Fort Laramie, whose history dated back to the fur-trading days.

Five days out of Fort Sedgwick, the outline of Laramie's sprawling form came into view. Sherman was surprised when he saw it. He had imagined a fortress type of installation, complete with blockhouses and walled enclosures. Now it was nothing more than "a mixture of all sorts of houses of every conceivable pattern and promiscuously scattered about." The condition of even these was far from good. The two principal buildings, two stories in height, were so dilapidated that on windy nights the soldiers slept on the parade ground rather than risk their lives in them.

The condition of the buildings reflected the problem of the army on the wind-swept western plains. If anything but mud structures was erected, building costs soared out of reason, and even when wood was used, at great expense, it had a short life expectancy in the violent climate of the country. Frame buildings were in constant need of repair, and to give them the necessary attention was to divert the soldiers from their normal tasks. At Fort Laramie, Sherman saw the complexities in full array. Wood for fuel had to be hauled fifteen miles. A sawmill, erected for the post's use, was fifty miles away, and even then it was useless at the time of his visit. When the parts for the mill were unpacked, some necessary pipe was missing. A request for the proper size was sent to Fort Laramie and then relayed to St. Louis. After weeks of waiting, the pipe came—wrong size. More months would now elapse while the army struggled with its mail-order business. By the time the mill would be ready to operate, the grip of winter would be on the land.

Meanwhile, as the men toiled at a hundred and one tasks to insure their existence, small Indian raiding parties sniped at isolated settlements miles away. Their punishment would have to wait; preparations for a larger battle, the battle of survival against winter on the High Plains, had to come first. "With almost everything to do you can understand they have not much chance to hunt down horsethieving Indians whose lodges are in the Black Hills of the Cheyenne 400 miles off," Sherman explained to headquarters. "It is these awful distances that make our problem out here so difficult."

Despite such occasional small attacks, Sherman remained convinced that there would be no major threat from the northern tribes. Nothing he had seen between Fort Sedgwick and Fort Laramie changed his mind about the judgments he had made while traveling west. During the five-day trip from Sedgwick no hostile Indians had been seen. The few friendlies he met posed no serious threat to overland travel. The road would continue to be used, just as it had been during the California gold-rush days, and although larger numbers would traverse it, few would stop along the way to settle. Only irrigation could make the parched plains attractive to the average farmer, Sherman concluded, and he doubted that many would come so far for even that. They would come only when necessity forced them, but in the meantime, "the Government will have to pay a Bounty for people to live up here." Such harsh climatic facts did not mean that the Indian would be left undisturbed in this country. The Sioux were being driven steadily westward from Minnesota, and at the same time thousands of miners were sweeping in behind them to infest the Rockies all the way to the Canadian line. The noose of civilization was settling over the Indian, and no one saw it more clearly than Sherman. "The Indian agents over on the Missouri tell him to come over here for hunting and from here he is turned to some other quarter and so the poor devil naturally wriggles against his doom," he wrote with sympathetic understanding.[11]

In some cases the wriggling was going to develop into eruptions. For years, the Overland or California trail had been used as a white avenue to the West, and the Indians, who could have effectively stopped it at any time, let the travel pass. Treaties simply sealed the bargain. Nor had the Indians molested the thousands of individual miners who combed the mountains in search of gold. They resented the trespassing but usually failed to show it by violence. There was a point, however, where the Indians would draw the line against further aggression and fight. The Bozeman Trail was such a place. By August of 1866, when Sherman visited Fort Laramie, the Sioux had made their decision. And there was no better place than Laramie to hear about depredations along the Bozeman route, for it was at this point that travel branched off the main line westward and moved in a northwesterly direction towards the Montana mines. Between Laramie and the Yellowstone traveling was decidedly hazardous.

[11] Sherman to Rawlins, August 31, 1866. Division of the Missouri, Letters Received, 1866–69, Special File.

All summer small bands of Indians had lain hidden along the trail, just out of sight, and when the trains began to string out and travelers became confident—they struck. Most of the murders along western roads had been concentrated on this line of travel northwest of Fort Laramie. As Sherman explained it to headquarters, this new road was three or four hundred miles shorter than the Salt Lake and Fort Hall route, and its directness was irresistible to freighters and emigrants bound for the Yellowstone country and beyond. During the summer Colonel Henry B. Carrington had strengthened Fort Reno and had moved up the road to establish Fort Philip Kearney, a post that was almost at once referred to simply as Phil Kearney. By August, he had selected the site of Fort C. F. Smith still farther north, at the tip of the Big Horns, in Montana Territory. The army was ready to defend its line of communications.

There were some complaints on the part of the intruders that the Indians refused to come out and fight in the white man's style; instead, they carried on a harassing war. When Sherman was at Fort Laramie in August, he wrote that up to that time there had been no real opposition to the troops, but much horse stealing and sniping had been carried out. Twenty-five men had been killed, he said, but they were, true to his predictions, "mostly citizens belonging to trains who wandered off too far from their main parties." It was the most annoying kind of war to prosecute. The Indians would not attack the soldiers in their forts, of course, and they skillfully evaded them in the field. Depredations on civilian wagon trains went on, and complaints echoed across the country. While Sherman did not want a general war, this type of activity put the army in a bad light. No one in the East could be convinced that the soldiers were doing their duty on the plains so long as the pillaging continued.

While at Fort Laramie, Sherman spelled out his plan of operations to Grant's office. As always, he viewed the problem from a national standpoint and regarded his immediate task as one of preserving law and order. He repeated that he did not want a general war and underscored that fact in discussing affairs with the War Department. But if the Bozeman Trail was to be used with the sanction of the government, then it should be protected. That meant establishing strong posts along the way, manned by enough troops to punish marauding parties effectively.[12] On the other hand, he not only understood the Indians' problem but was sympathetic to it. They were doomed, in the long run, and he knew it. He could do nothing about that. They could either submit to the inevitable contraction of their holdings, or they could fight. If they chose to fight, it was his duty to oppose them, no matter how he might feel about it.

Meanwhile, at Fort Laramie he lost no opportunity to talk with the Indians. For those who professed friendship, he had advice. He told them to go to their local military commander and promise to settle down on a reservation in the vicinity of the post, where the commander could become acquainted with them and, in the future, could distinguish them from the hostiles. For those who temporized or equivocated, he had harsher words. If the Indians did not want to obey the laws of the United States, he would deal out punishment. Typically, some of the chiefs complained that they could not restrain their ardent young men, who were frequently rash and injudicious. It had been said many times before, and Sherman was tired of the excuse. When he heard it again, his well-known temper flared. Turning to the interpreters, he said he had heard much about the uncontrollable young braves. Nodding in the direction of the chiefs, he said, "Tell the rascals so are *mine;* and if another white man is scalped in all this region, it will be *impossible* to hold *mine* in."[13] This was strong language, and it would be a long time before he would be in a position to make it stick. Perhaps he knew it.

But what other kind of talk was there? Would anything else work with the Indians? The Indian Bureau and the philanthropists in the East set great store by the treaty system. And the Senate of the United States gravely ratified long agreements, bearing innumerable "X's" which purported to promise peace. Sherman took a dim view of the whole procedure. He had no faith

12 *Ibid.*

13 James F. Rusling, *Across America: or, the Great West and the Pacific Coast,* 115.

in either party, and the history of these dealings supported him. Of the Indians he said, "They will sign any treaty for the sake of the annuities, but can no more fill their part of the contract than if it were waste paper. There is a universal feeling of mistrust on both sides, and this will sooner or later result in a general outbreak." He by no means charged the Indians with the sole responsibility for treaty-breaking. The gold-hungry whites killed Indians as dispassionately as they hunted down animals and considered treaties a one-way street. Since the signatories on both sides regarded such transactions as binding upon them only to the degree that they were an advantage to their own individual interests, what good were they?[14] With the tribes sheltered by the protective skirts of the Interior Department and dignified as individual sovereignties, endowed by Congress with full treaty-making powers, the situation seemed hopeless. To an army man, military control of the Indian seemed to be the only solution, and Sherman felt that sooner or later it had to come.

While the nation debated the question of who should control the natives, the army would have to proceed as best it could and try to fight the kind of war the Indians dictated. Before he left Fort Laramie, Sherman wrote a personal letter to Grant, in which he tried to show how complex the problems of his command had become. He stressed the difficulty of extended communications in the West and urged that all available troops be sent in that direction. Various local pressures in some of the more settled regions kept men occupied who ought to be along the frontier. For example, Hancock, to his annoyance, wanted to hold back some of the soldiers in his department to deal with the local turbulence in Missouri, arising out of postwar hatreds. He had reversed these orders, maintaining that peace on the plains was the army's most important job for the present. Naturally, if Hancock wanted to appeal the decision, to Grant or to the President, he had Sherman's permission. In a like manner, General Cooke was showing a tendency to think defensively. He wanted to erect a rather elaborate headquarters establishment at

14 Sherman to Rawlins, August 31, 1866. Division of the Mississippi, Letters Sent, 1865–66.

Omaha. "Omaha is as safe as St. Louis," Sherman snapped. "I don't believe in conducting hostilities from the Rear." But, again, if Cooke persisted and Grant agreed with him, he could "remain at Omaha in hindquarters." He must, however, be ready at all times to send troops out promptly when needed.

Sherman's desire to get his men and commanders where the Indians lived was frequently misinterpreted. To have his troops nearer the enemy did not necessarily mean, as the philanthropists stridently alleged, that he advocated mass extermination. There probably would be no general war, but at the same time there would be for years "a kind of unpleasant state of hostilities." The continuance of such relations would ultimately result in the dispersion of the hostile bands, regardless of any sentiment towards the Indians, one way or the other. The abrasive of continuous pressure by the troops could have no other end. Regardless of the merits of the argument for peace and negotiation, the frontier had to be protected, and the only way it could be accomplished was to put troops all along the base of the Rocky Mountains.[15] Sherman hoped that Grant's military mind could appreciate the necessities of the situation.

With the laborious task of making official reports and answering correspondence behind him, Sherman renewed his inspection trip. Ahead lay the country he had been so eager to visit, and gladly he put aside his pen and paper. The dreary miles up the Platte, studded with sagebrush and cactus, had been monotonous and uninteresting. But the panorama of desolate distances had been informative, in that they dramatized some of the major problems of the western army. Now he wanted to turn to something more enjoyable. On the morning of September 1, his small train of five ambulances, flanked by an escort of twenty cavalrymen, moved out of Fort Laramie in the direction of Denver.

The clear, crisp air of the Fort Laramie country gave indications that a change of terrain and scenery was not far ahead, and Sherman's appetite for travel was whetted. To the southwest, mountains showed a dim and uneven outline. The character of

[15] Sherman to Grant, August 31, 1866. Division of the Missouri, Letters Received, 1866–69, Special File.

the streams predicted something more attractive, for instead of being wide and shallow, they gradually contracted into narrower and swifter channels, with gravel bottoms and clear, sparkling water. Here was the country Sherman had longed to see, and he was delighted. For nearly twenty miles out of Fort Laramie the ambulances followed a high ridge devoid of timber, but rich in grass. Then they came to the Chugwater and followed that little stream for nearly fifty miles through excellent grazing country, well supplied with water and yielding enough wood for camp purposes. Passing beyond its source and over a divide, they saw Horse Creek, which, Sherman explained, rose to the west in the Black Hills[16] and was as pretty as the stream they had just left. The ambulances splashed across Horse Creek and continued southward to Lodge Pole Creek. Here they joined the Salt Lake road they had left earlier on their side trip to Fort Laramie. Near the junction stood the gaunt ruins, stone and sod chimneys, of old Camp Walbach, long since abandoned and now a monument to the ever shifting requirements of the army in the West.

Ahead lay Cheyenne Pass, and as the ascent was made, Sherman noted that the whole character of the country gradually changed from treeless, rolling prairie to beautiful mountain scenery. "Pine trees begin with the Pass and become larger and more close up to the very summit where there is really the best body of timber I have seen yet," he wrote enthusiastically. The party now stopped long enough to visit with a small detachment of soldiers who were cutting timber for the construction of a new post, to be named John Buford, that lay nineteen miles beyond. They moved along again and reached the top of the pass, where Sherman called a halt. He had to stop for a few minutes and feast his eyes on the panorama before him. He called it magnificent. Below lay the Laramie plains, spread out like a huge stage, with the steel-blue Rockies, their peaks capped with snow, serving as a breath-taking backdrop. Both figuratively and literally, it was the high point of the trip thus far. Braking the wagons

16 He means the range presently called the Laramie Mountains, but known as the Black Hills to the many travelers who saw them during the years of the California gold rush and for some time afterward.

heavily, the drivers now guided the vehicles down a sharp grade nearly five miles long, and a few more miles brought them to the new post. It was located at the junction of the Salt Lake Road and the stage road leading to Denver.

Sherman thought the site of the post well chosen. It would cover operations of the two important roads and could readily be made into a supply depot for troops operating westward to Salt Lake or in the country to the northwest. Freshly trimmed poles lying near by told him that shortly the telegraph would connect the new establishment with both Denver and Salt Lake City. Learning that there had been no Indian troubles in the immediate vicinity for over a year, the General now dismissed his escort, sending it back to Fort Laramie, while he continued on toward Denver.

The days were crisp and the nights cold enough to produce ice in the camp water buckets. Early September showed the Rockies at their finest, since the autumn pageant of colors had begun to unfold. After a journey of thirty miles, the men arrived at Virginia Dale, a stage stop located in a place noted for both its beauty and a fine trout stream. Very shortly, they picked up the Cache la Poudre River and followed it down to a plain dotted with prosperous-looking farms. Colorado, indeed, looked welcome. Along the river was Camp Collins, where an officer and a handful of men were guarding military stores. Having observed the degree of settlement in the valley, Sherman decided at once that the post was of no further use and should be broken up. He ordered the officer in command to march the few wartime volunteers across to Fort Kearny, Nebraska, to be mustered out. The supplies would be moved up to the new post, John Buford. He was even willing to give up the military reservation, turning the land over to settlers, except for the possibility that the Pacific Railroad might conceivably be located up the Cache la Poudre valley.

The trip along the base of the mountains to Denver confirmed the Commanding General's opinion that this section no longer represented a portion of the undefended frontier. Crossing a number of small creeks that arose in the mountains, he studied with interest a section of the country already heavily under cultivation and fairly well populated. The importance of such agricultural development was not lost on him. By means of irrigation, crops equal or superior in quality to those grown farther east were being produced in quantity. Such volume meant a sharp decline in the high prices charged for goods that had formerly been hauled from the Missouri River. "I would not be surprised if these mountain streams would irrigate and make most fruitful one fourth of all the land from the base of the mountains out for fifty miles," he told General Rawlins, quickly adding "You will at once see how important this is to the military question."[17] Food for man and beast so many miles away from transportation was a vital question to the western command. It was so important that Sherman was willing to make a strong statement about its contribution. He felt that if supplies, in quantity, could be had at the base of the Rockies and in Utah, "then the Indian question and the Mormon question are easy of solution." Therefore, it was his announced intention to promote irrigation and cultivation all along the mountain front. He would write to commanding officers at all posts in the region, instructing them to encourage agriculture as much as possible. His enthusiasm was so great that he wrote at length on the subject to headquarters. "Nothing could be raised out here by the ordinary rains but these water courses, fed by snow are a better substitute, and the land lies exactly right for irrigation. Almost all of India, Egypt, South of Spain, Mexico, and Chile are cultivated in this way, and they have been at various epochs of the world history the granaries of the world." He pointed to the tremendous success of the Mormon farmers, who had in a very few years "converted an absolute desert into fruitful fields and gardens." Why could not the land along the Rocky Mountains be so utilized?

As the ambulances rolled along the well-used stagecoach road toward Denver, Sherman continued to view the land with delight. The rich soil, the flashing mountain streams, and the towering snow-capped mountains, captivated his imagination. It was a big land, a land of magnificent distances and limitless skies.

17 Sherman to Rawlins, September 12, 1866. Division of the Missouri, Letters Received, 1866–69, Special File.

He loved the solitude and the absence of handshaking public officials—people he had to treat pleasantly, despite his personal inclinations. For three weeks he had been free of dignitaries, receptions, and public addresses. This was an independence he cherished, and he reveled in every minute of it. As he mused, enjoying the bright sun and the crisp fall air, lulled by the gentle jolting of the ambulance, his freedom came to an end.

Across the slopes of the foothills a cloud of dust appeared, and, before long, an escort from Denver revealed itself. Here again were the familiar black broadcloth suits and "biled" shirts. Here, too, were extended hands and smiling nods of approval. The mayor of Denver and a number of important businessmen had come out to greet the hero of Atlanta and to extend to him the courtesies of the city. The past three weeks, filled with army uniforms or the rough clothing of emigrants, had caused him almost to forget "civilization." But here it was, in all its starched glory. He steeled himself for the ordeal.

It was the same as before. They arrived in Denver on September 10, and the next day a banquet was given at the Pacific House for the officers, followed by a ball at Dr. McClelland's new hall. A local paper announced that for the price of seven dollars residents could take in both events.[18] Two days later Sherman wrote of the attention paid him and confessed sadly that his period of trial was not yet at an end, for "today I must submit to two dinners—one at 3 P.M. and another at 7 P.M." But tomorrow would be better, he promised, because by then he would be off to Fort Garland and the San Luis Valley.[19] The thought of it helped him to bear up. Down at Fort Garland he would find Kit Carson. There would be no handshaking or admiring glances in Sherman's direction there. He would be treated as an equal, in the proud, yet friendly way of real western men. There would be no banquets, but there would be much food, strong drink, and long talks. The grim-countenanced officer swallowed his anxiety and forced a wrinkled smile for the adoring Denverites.

[18] *Daily Rocky Mountain News,* September 10, 1866; Frank Hall, *History of the State of Colorado,* I, 399.

[19] Sherman to Rawlins, September 12, 1866. Division of the Mississippi, Letters Sent, 1865–66.

Six

————

A RESTLESS PEOPLE BRANCHING OUT

SHERMAN WAS DISAPPOINTED in the people of Denver. All he heard during his stay was talk of "defense" and "protection." Every man, Jack, and boy in the city seemed to feel that red hordes were lurking in the very outskirts, ready to dispose of the whole population some dark night. He could put up with the handshakers and name-droppers if he had to, but those who crowded around him, begging for additional troops, frankly puzzled him. He could not understand this feeling of fear, especially since he had recently traveled hundreds of miles through unprotected country without being harmed.

Of course, business in Denver was bad. Production in the placer mines had begun to taper off; freight rates from the East remained high, keeping price levels of necessities from dropping. This was, perhaps, one of the reasons why businessmen pressed him so relentlessly for the establishment of a military post in the city, or, if not that, at least a large supply depot. They applied all kinds of pressure, including appeals to higher authority. The ever present petitioners had been sending the results of their work to Washington. Sherman realized that he would have to deal his cards right off the top of the deck when reporting on this matter to Grant. "The question of this as a Military Post I decide emphatically No," he wrote firmly. "Denver needs no protection. She should raise on an hours notice 1,000 men, and instead of protection she can and should protect the neighboring settlements that tend to give her support, and business." Nor was there any need for an elaborate quartermaster's depot. The clerks, stables, shops, and other paraphernalia would be superfluous. If materials could be purchased to any advantage in Denver, well and good, but "a single Q Mr & clerk with a cheap office

76

can do all this. It is folly to have here stores for distribution."[1] These people were unable to understand that the army was shrinking, not growing. Nor had they been listening, as had he, to the wails of the Quartermaster General about the high cost of military living on the western plains. There would be many places that in the near future would require protection and men. But not Denver. To all requests for men and money from such well-established cities, the answer was finally and brutally "no."

Saying good-bye to John, who was leaving from Denver for the East, Cump ordered out his ambulances and headed south along the foothills towards Colorado City. For the Denver businessmen, who had rubbed their hands in anticipation of army contracts and some federal money, the parting was less enthusiastic than the reception had been. No matter. Sherman was exasperated with crowds of people who wanted something from him. Now for the open road again.

Accompanied by General James F. Rusling, who was making an inspection tour of the West for the Quartermaster General's office, and Territorial Governor Alexander Cummings, the party left Denver on September 13. "We took a tent along, but seldom had occasion to use it," Rusling wrote later. "We had blankets and buffalo robes for the night; some stray books and magazines for the day, when weary of the scenery; pipes and tobacco for all; and other supplies, it seemed, *ad infinitum*."[2] Traveling again without escort and seeing only an occasional ranch house along the way, they seemed to be on more of an outing for sportsmen than anything resembling a military inspection. Sherman was glad to leave Denver, and all its supplicants for favor, behind. But ahead, near the present site of Colorado Springs, lay the little mining camp of Colorado City. Unfortunately, there would be more deputations of citizens and more requests for protection.

Wearily the General faced a committee, led by the Reverend William Howbert, and patiently he listened to a familiar story. Here was a little western town, said the Reverend Mr. Howbert,

[1] Sherman to Rawlins, September 12, 1866. Division of the Missouri, Letters Received, 1866–69, Special File.
[2] Rusling, *Across America*, 76.

77

exposed and defenseless. Who was to protect it? Could the army spare a few men? "General Sherman received the appeal with utter indifference, and replied that he thought we were unnecessarily alarmed, since there were no hostile Indians in this region," Mr. Howbert's son recalled years later. "He then sarcastically remarked that it probably would be a very profitable arrangement for this community could it have a force of Government troops located near here, to whom the farmers might sell their grain and other products at a high price. With this remark he dismissed the committee. . . ."[3] Indignantly the applicants marched from the room, convinced of the utter heartlessness of the far-famed General and perhaps muttering complaints about the neglect by the federal government of such colonial appendages as Colorado. Unmoved by their anger at his brusqueness, Sherman moved on, with what the younger Howbert erroneously called a "strong escort," bound for Fort Garland.

At Pueblo, another resolute band of petitioners lay in wait. Their request was the same: military protection. The proposition again nettled Sherman. He had seen no hostile Indians. "The Utes are harmless & peaceable, and the Cheyennes & Arapahoes are off after the Buffalo, God only knows where . . . ," he exclaimed. What did the civilians want? Extermination? "I don't see how we can make a decent excuse for an Indian war," he confessed. "I have travelled all the way from Laramie without a single soldier as Escort. I meet single men unarmed travelling along the road as in Missouri—cattle—horses—graze loose far from their owners, most tempting to a starving Indian, and though Indians might easily make a descent on these scattered Ranches yet they have not done so, and I see no external signs of fear of such an event, though all the people are clamorous for military protection." And yet, here was the inevitable petition again. He looked it over, amazed at its length, and crisply told his listeners that there were more signatures on the sheet than he had soldiers at any of his smaller garrisons in the area.[4] He

3 Irving Howbert, *Memories of a Lifetime in the Pike's Peak Region*, 211–12.
4 Sherman to Rawlins, September 30, 1866. Division of the Missouri, Letters Received, 1866–69, Special File.

was puzzled and annoyed. Here were the hardy pioneers, crowding around him, asking for personal protection. Scowlingly, his grizzled countenance a frozen mask, he handed back the document with the unmistakable inference that men on the frontier owed themselves something in the matter of self-preservation. How could the government furnish enough men to guard every isolated ranch, every village, every little mining camp? The land was large, and people filtered into the valleys and along the streams like blowing sand. To Sherman, their requests were unreasonable; to the people, he was a hard-hearted, unsympathetic military automaton.

Leaving another disgruntled group of civilians behind, he pushed his ambulances across the Arkansas River ford and headed for a stream called the St. Charles, traveling through a country of "ranches with corn and wheat fields." It all looked so pastoral, and so unwarlike. Where were the savages who were lying in wait for hapless travelers? All he saw was a prosperous-looking farming country. Soon the Huerfano River came into sight. The ambulances swung into line with it and followed the sparkling waters westward. It would lead to the crest of the Sangre de Cristo Mountains, and just beyond that lay Fort Garland. Wayside houses were less frequent now, and it was good to leave once again a more heavily populated region. As the horses tugged their vehicles to still higher elevations, the air became more brisk and the scenery breath-takingly beautiful. Sherman began to relax again, and the men noticed it. The grandeur of the country, its deathly stillness, broken only by the hard breathing of the horses, and the crump, crump, crump of the wagon wheels brought him out of the defensive silence he always assumed in more civilized parts. Camping at night by a cascading mountain stream, the men built huge fires and lay around them, feet towards the orange glow, on fragrant pine boughs or coarse army blankets. It was a time for smoking and the telling of tales. Every western man knew that, and Sherman was the West itself under such circumstances. "He was a prodigious talker and smoker, and stretched . . . before the fire, with a cigar between his teeth or fingers, often talked half the night away," wrote his friend Rusling, almost longingly, some years later. "As a rule, he was the last one to sleep and the first one to awaken, tending camp fires faithfully, and seemed literally to never tire of talking and smoking."[5]

Such gatherings around the fire inevitably brought on a yarn-spinning contest, and Sherman always joined in eagerly, forgetting his brusqueness and inherent shyness. No doubt the members of the inspection party heard some of his favorites on those fragrant Colorado nights, as the flames crackled and the pine nuts popped from the heat. He liked the broad exaggerations of western humor and was able to "spin a wide loop," as the natives said, with the utmost gravity and feigned veracity. For example, there was a story he liked to tell in defense of an extremely profane bullwhacker who had been ordered by his employers to stop cursing the oxen, and whose attempt to obey orders led to difficulty. The driver in question did his level best to follow instructions and managed to nurse his teams along for about 150 miles west of St. Louis, where the wagons became hopelessly stuck. Remembering the warnings about profane language, he dispatched a runner back to the firm, stating that the wagon was bogged down and the cattle would not pull it out unless they were cussed in the usual fashion. Permission was granted, the oaths flew like sparks, the cattle heaved at their yokes, and the wagon moved forward again. After this, said the storyteller, with a twinkle in his eye, Salt Lake City was reached in the usual good time.[6]

Another story he liked to recall concerned the time he visited the devout General O. O. Howard, late in the recent war, and was offered a freshly-filled glass by the gentle, one-armed officer. Sherman took a swig and spat it out vigorously, shouting, "What the devil is that?" The horrified Howard apologetically explained, much to his guest's amusement, that it was sherry.[7] Sometimes, the joke was on him, and Sherman would laugh at

[5] James F. Rusling, *Men and Things I Saw in the Civil War Days*, 119–20.
[6] Theodore R. Davis, "A Stage Ride to Colorado," *Harper's New Monthly Magazine*, Vol. XXXV (July, 1867), 139.
[7] W. F. G. Shanks, "Gossip About Our Generals," *Harper's New Monthly Magazine*, Vol. XXXV (July, 1867), 212.

that, too. No doubt his fireside companions heard about his experience at the Herndon House in Omaha, not long before. The Union Pacific Railroad Company had hired a Major Bent to manage the hotel, and the droll Major's prank on such a famous personage as Sherman was soon to be a legend. The guest, an omnivorous reader, had consumed everything in the house and, unable to find a fresh book, had asked for one. After making a brief search, the manager turned up with a volume that was seized eagerly by the prospective reader. The General took it to bed and read late into the night. Just as he had reached the climax of the story, he found he had been given the first volume of a two-volume work. When he asked for the rest of the set, his host replied carelessly, "Oh, we lost the second volume when we moved in. Anyway, you asked for a book to read." For a moment Sherman reddened and glared at Bent, his temper soaring. Then he realized that the joke was on him, and he joined the prankster in a good laugh.[8]

On into the night, as the stars twinkled back at the red-tongued campfire, the stories continued. There seemed to be no end to them. And as Sherman told his, he would get up from his resting place and walk back and forth, gesticulating freely at times, his wrinkled face suddenly expressive and meaningful. Moments later, he might have his hands buried deep in his pockets, with his brow furrowed in concentrated thought. Only at times like these did his men see him as he really was. And they made the most of such situations, enjoying them fully, for the next stop would be another post, and more problems. Then the General might revert to his stern, unbending self. Fort Garland was ahead now, and there would probably be hell raised there, too, if Sherman found things that displeased him.

When he reached the fort, he at once sought out Kit Carson. No other man in these parts knew more about Indian affairs, and his advice would be good. At present Kit was a brevet brigadier general of Volunteers and in command at Garland. "We found him in log quarters, rough but comfortable, and with his New Mexican wife and half-breed children around him," Rus-

[8] Levi O. Leonard and Jack T. Johnson, *A Railroad to the Sea*, 85.

ling noted. "I had expected to see a small wiry man, weather-beaten and reticent; but met a medium-sized, rather stoutish, florid, and quite talkative person instead. . . . In age he seemed to be about forty-five. . . . He talked and smoked homemade cigarettes (folding them himself as he talked) far into the night each evening we were there. . . ."[9] In the extended talks with Carson, Cump asked a thousand questions about Indian dangers, the sufficiency of military protection in the area, the best place for additional protection, and other related matters. He had heard that General Pope was contemplating the construction of a new post on the south fork of the Huerfano. Was it a good location? Was it needed? He talked it over at length with Kit and Colonel A. J. Alexander, Third United States Cavalry, who had been picked to command it. He asked the opinion of Governor Cummings. Then he made his decision. It was an unnecessary expense, and he would not have it. He dispatched word to General James H. Carleton at Santa Fé that the establishment would not be built. If the troops intended for it were divided between Fort Union, in New Mexico, and Fort Garland, the surrounding country could be adequately protected.

And by protection Sherman did not mean jumping the first band of Utes that came through the mountain passes. There was no need to go to war with them. "The Ute Indians, who have lived in this valley and the mountain country round about, have been reduced to a condition of absolute poverty that is painful to behold," he told Rawlins. "They are scattered, and not hostile further than a necessity compels them to steal occasionally a cow or a sheep to appease hunger. Of course the rangers, Americans and New Mexicans, want the troops to kill them all. . . . I will not permit them to be warred against as long as they are not banded together in parties large enough to carry on war. I have travelled myself through them without danger or form of danger. I have seen wagons hauling wood and hay and grain right through their country without molestation, and all the talk of war is to get troops sent here to make a market for the grain and stock the people have for sale at famine prices. Four companies here

9 Rusling, *Civil War Days*, 121.

will make it impossible for the Utes to combine, and if scattered hunting parties steal a cow or sheep now and then to keep from starving, I will not construe it war." If trouble arose, settlers could, themselves, help to put it down. There were plenty of men in the area. On any of the streams along the eastern slope of the mountains there were enough men, if gathered together, to cope with the Utes. "The settlers could in three hours assemble fifty men, ample for protection against any band of Ute warriors that has been seen for years," was his brusque assessment of the situation at that time.

Sherman had the feeling that this matter of constant complaint by the settlers was getting out of hand. It irritated him. Only recently a runner had come panting into Colonel Alexander's office with the report that Indians were running off the stock of a rancher named Doyle. Alexander immediately dispatched a detachment of men who made a forced march of seventy miles over rough country to save the beleaguered rancher, only to find a gathering of fifty frontiersmen at his place who collectively could claim the loss of only seven cattle. Unabashed, the men offered to sell corn at ten cents a pound to the troops, "and other things in proportion." To this generous offer Alexander replied that his men were stocked with food and did not need any corn. Doyle, apparently no longer worried about his cattle, contented himself with making the remark that soldiers were no good against Indians, anyway. "I propose to pass by Doyle's ranch on my return," Sherman wrote ominously, "and I will tell him plainly that our soldiers are not to be used against cattle thieves; but if they have occasion to visit him again, it shall be at his *cost*."

To the south, in New Mexico, affairs were little better. That territory presented a problem that would always be difficult of solution. "It is very large and thinly settled. The New Mexicans are a poor, miserable set as a whole, and white emigrants of our States will not go there unless to make a fortune out of the military expenses." There was a semblance of civil government there, admitted Sherman, but, letting his sarcasm get the better of him, he said it was "as useless as possible, and the military is expected to do all the dirty work." General Carleton apparently had gone security crazy along with the residents. He had the Third Cavalry, up to strength, the Fifteenth Infantry, and two Negro regiments, "and yet he thinks it necessary to retain a part of the New Mexican Volunteers." And Pope had approved it all!

Sherman sent a scorching order to Santa Fé, directing that the volunteers be mustered out and the military establishment brought down to the regular army only. Carleton had no business trying to guard Santa Fé, Albuquerque, and places of similar size. They were strong enough to guard themselves. And another thing, he had rounded up eight thousand Navajos and was holding them at the Bosque Redondo as prisoners of war. This meant that the Indians had to be fed, and it was extremely expensive. "I think we could better send them to the Fifth Avenue Hotel to board at the cost of the United States" was Sherman's caustic opinion.[10]

The annoyance at the situation in New Mexico would not leave him. One evening during his stay at Fort Garland, as the party sat around the fire, smoking and talking, he got on the subject again, to the amusement of his listeners. Pacing back and forth, his hands buried deep in his trousers pockets, as usual, and puffing furiously at the butt of a black cigar, he unburdened himself to his companions.

The Quartermaster General, he said, had been deviling him again about the high cost of maintaining posts on the plains, particularly in such a place as New Mexico. Could not expenses be reduced? How about a plan to save money out there? The questions kept coming from Washington.

"At first I paid no attention to these letters, because I could not help the matter," Sherman admitted ruefully. "The Posts were there—established by order of the Hon. Secretary of War—and he [the Quartermaster General] knew it. Moreover, the people would have them there, and I could not help it, if they did cost a 'heap.' Above all, I was *ordered* to keep them up, and I always obey orders; so what could I do?" He eyed his audience inquisitively.

10 Sherman to Rawlins, September 21, 1866. "Protection Across the Continent," 39 Cong., 2 sess., *House Exec. Doc. No. 23* (Serial 1288), p. 16.

"So, at first, I did not answer his letters, but let him write away! But finally they got to coming so thick and long, that one day I sat down and replied, that the Posts were all there, and ordered there, as he knew, and we were bound to supply them, no matter what the cost."

With a gleam in his eye, the grizzled redhead continued, "In my judgment, of the whole vast region there, the greater portion was not worth a Confederate note to us (I told him), and never would be; and if he wished my opinion as to the best way of reducing expenses, I would respectfully recommend, that the United States sell New Mexico, and all the region about, to Maximilian for $15,000,000, and lend him the greenbacks to pay with!"[11] One can visualize his crusty listeners rolling on the blankets, holding their sides in laughter, as the terrible-tempered Sherman spread himself on one of his pet peeves. Perhaps even the speaker could not help smiling at his own outburst.

On nights like these, with the day's paper work and a multitude of petty details put aside, Fort Garland's famous visitor was able to relax. General Rusling watched and was particularly impressed by the transformation. "He threw off all reserve . . . and entered fully into the life of the pioneer and Indian. He asked a thousand questions of everybody, and was never at a loss for a story or a joke, and added to the effect of these by the twinkle of his eye, the toss of his head, and the serio-comic twitch of his many-wrinkled features, in a way indescribable."[12] It was a release for the nervous officer, and it helped him to escape from the shell in which he lived. During most of his waking hours, he was on official duty, busy with the affairs of a large military division, and the responsibility never left him. Life was one decision after another, and lately, much of it had been "no" to some request. When there came rare evenings like these, with men like Kit Carson around—men who requested nothing, and let you know in their confident but quiet way that they were as good as you—it was a moment of escape from the days of unreality into a fleeting moment of reality.

[11] Rusling, *Across America*, 139–40.
[12] Rusling, *Civil War Days*, 122.

Before leaving Fort Garland, there was a parley with the Indians. Late on the afternoon of September 21, some of the chiefs gathered in a large room at the back of the post commandant's quarters. Most of them squatted on their haunches, looking somber but dignified, despite their grinding poverty. Facing them sat Sherman, in a loose and shabby uniform, looking very little more prosperous than the Indians. As he puffed at his ever present cigar, Governor Cummings and Kit Carson took their places on either side of him. Using Carson as his interpreter, Sherman urged the Utes to settle down on reservations. It was the only thing to do, he argued. The white man was closing in; the old days were gone. If the Indians were to preserve their tribal system and avoid destruction, they should consider his advice seriously. As Carson spat out a staccato of Mexican to them, the chiefs listened stoically. They thought over the words, grunting and nodding at each other, as if they agreed. After awhile they spoke. They were in general agreement, but there were the young men. . . . Sherman shook his head. Here were "the young men" again. He wondered how many times army officers had listened to that excuse from the Indians. The young men, said the chiefs, were opposed to such a policy. Of course, if their hereditary enemies, the Cheyennes and Comanches should adopt such a policy, perhaps it might be different.[13] Perhaps the young men would listen then.

Sherman sat and listened. Dealing with Indians took time and patience. A small brown child wandered through the door and watched the proceedings inquisitively. The General's face softened, and he reached out for the little boy, taking the startled youngster into his arms. A few minutes later, the anxious Indian mother, searching the grounds for her missing young one, glanced into the council room and saw him there, nestled comfortably in the visitor's lap.[14] Both seemed content.

The talk droned on, with Sherman advancing all the arguments he knew, using all the methods of reasoning he could

[13] Rusling, *Across America*, 113–14.
[14] A. B. Sanford, "Reminiscences of Kit Carson, Jr.," *The Colorado Magazine*, Vol. VI (September, 1929), 183.

muster. The faces of the chiefs were bleak and immobile. It was of no use. Abruptly he broke off the parley, and putting the little boy down, he stalked out of the room. As he and Rusling walked to their quarters, Sherman spoke out in his own blunt way, "They will have to freeze and starve a little more, I reckon, before they will listen to common sense."[15] For the moment, the matter was closed.

Later on, when all these strange men had gone, perhaps Carson could do something with the Utes. Time would tell. Kit had lived among them so long that he seemed to be a part of the tribe, and they trusted him. Sherman marveled at the relationship. "These Red Skins think Kit twice as big a man as me," he grinned at one of his companions. "Why his integrity is simply perfect. They know it, and they would believe him and trust him any day before me."[16] The impassivity of the Indians interested Sherman. He was somewhat that way himself at times, but here was one respect in which the natives bettered him. They could sit and stare at you for hours, with no change of facial expression. But it was better than handshaking and backslapping. At least they weren't begging for something that was impossible to deliver.

So the ambulances rolled again, leaving behind Fort Garland and the mute Indians. Over the mountains they went, eastward this time and down the slopes to a stream called the Cuchara. As they followed it, in a northeasterly direction, snow began to fall. It was only September 24. Members of the party may have told themselves that at such an early date it would be no more than a flurry. But as the day wore on, the snow became heavier and visibility poor. The wagons crunched along, the horses covered with white. Soon the Cuchara joined the Huerfano, "a beautiful stream fed by the springs and melting snows of the mountains." The next day, the Craig ranch was reached, and the party was glad for a chance to get out of the weather.

Craig was a former army man, "a gentleman of fine intelligence," who had built a small empire on the Colorado highlands.

15 Rusling, *Across America,* 114.
16 *Ibid.,* 137.

87

"He has brought round him about 50 families of New Mexicans who stand in the relation of Peons to him, cultivating his land on shares and buying all groceries and supplies of him which makes them absolutely dependent," Sherman remarked uncritically. Around the substantial home lay 2,300 acres of land, all under cultivation. The inspection party looked at his fine corn and other grains. They brushed aside the fresh snow, felt of the soil, and made complimentary remarks about the irrigation system. Craig had indeed accomplished much out here. "He has thoroughly proven the ability to produce," Sherman admitted, "but then comes the most difficult problem of consumption. Who is to buy his corn?" He answered his own question. The miners would take some. But they were two hundred miles away, in the mountains, and the cost of haulage was very high. Travelers and stage companies would also use part of the produce, but it would not amount to much. Actually, the army would be the best market, and men like Craig knew it. "That is the real pressure for Garrisons and an Indian war." Of that fact Sherman was absolutely convinced.

The next stop was near the mouth of the Huerfano, some twenty miles downstream from Craig's place. Here was the ranch of Colonel Boone, whom Sherman called a man of note in that part of the country. Boone had been on the plains for a long time, and the army men now listened carefully to what he had to say. He was an "Old Indian man," as Sherman respectfully put it; his time on the frontier dated back to his service with General William Ashley in 1825, "and [he had] been more or less connected with the Indians ever since." As recently as 1860, Boone had represented the federal government in treaties made with the Cheyennes and Arapahoes. The old gentleman talked freely of Indian matters and displayed no concern about any prospective hair-lifting in the neighborhood. It seemed to Sherman that most of the old hands in the region felt this way. They had managed to get along for years without federal troops standing by and probably felt that by now the place was getting downright civilized. There were no cries of help from Boone.

The Arkansas Valley lay ahead. The horse-drawn ambulances

clipped off the one hundred miles to Fort Lyon in three days. "I did not see or hear of an Indian the whole distance though we passed through the whole length of the Cheyenne & Arapaho Reservations." Sherman never lost an opportunity to underscore his thesis that the plains were peaceful. Fort Lyon, named after the little redheaded abolitionist General who had lost his life early in the Civil War, was located near the site of Bent's old trading post. The buildings were all of single-story construction, with flat, dirt-covered roofs and stone walls. In the officers' quarters were such luxuries as floors and window and door frames. The General looked around critically and was not pleased. The men were living in what amounted to pigpens, and this just was not good enough for Uncle Billy's boys. "The Post is about as good as could be expected under the circumstances," he admitted, "but it is not fit for troops. Anybody looking through them can see full reason for the desertions that have prevailed so much of late years. I believe it is now unanimously conceded that if the necessities of our Growing Empire demand that troops should be stationed in this barren country, they should have decent houses, and decent beds." The food and clothing were adequate, but that was not enough. On the spot, he resolved that a new two-company post must be built, and he would order it.

After he had reported to headquarters on his findings at Fort Lyon, Sherman ordered the horses hitched up once again. It was now the last day of September, and he was impatient to get back to St. Louis. Three weeks more of traveling should see him there. As he left Colorado, he looked back and made a judgment. For the moment, instead of more troops in the territory, there would be less. There were a number of wartime volunteers still serving, and they must be mustered out, leaving the defense of the West in the hands of the regulars. This would tighten the organization and, in the long run, amount to economy. It would result in cries from the western populace, but that could not be helped. "All the people west of the Missouri River look to the Army as their legitimate field of profit & support, and the quicker they are undeceived the better for all."[17] Colorado people had proved

[17] Sherman to Rawlins, September 30, 1866. Division of the Missouri, Letters Received, 1866–69, Special File.

to be no exception to this rule. He would certainly hear more complaints from them.

As the wagon train headed for Fort Ellsworth, in central Kansas, buffalo were in evidence, and the men unsheathed their rifles. The total score was eleven, and Sherman proudly wrote to his brother that "I killed two." From Ellsworth to Fort Riley the going was easy, and with that portion of the trip completed, the men left their ambulances. They had reached the end of the railroad, and from here the remainder of the trip was a much more enjoyable experience. Looking back on the long tour, Sherman was struck by the fact that he had traveled over a good part of the High Plains without experiencing Indian trouble of any kind, despite all the rumors which had circulated about the flaming frontier. Such reports, he decided, were "only accountable on the supposition that our people out west are resolved on trouble for the sake of profit resulting from military occupation." The idea was burned into his mind, and it would govern many decisions when he got back to his desk at St. Louis. By October 18, he was there, ready to write of these and other matters to the War Department.[18]

Hardly had he picked up his pen when reports of "Indian wars" again appeared out of the West. It must have been a moment of supreme frustration for him. On his desk lay a letter from Governor Cummings, dated October 12, quoting a dispatch to the Governor from Kit Carson. "We are now involved in a war with the Ute Indians," Kit had written, and "I can assure you, my Dear Governor this war will be no childs play." Cummings was obviously distressed and warned that things in southern Colorado looked serious, indeed, "utterly unlike what all hoped and believed when we parted would continue there for a long time." He advised that "a vigorous onslaught be made to close the difficulty at once."[19] It seemed hard to believe. If all this had come from a Denver businessman, it might be discounted

18 Sherman to John Sherman, October 20, 1866. William T. Sherman Papers, Volume 19.

19 Cummings to Sherman, October 12, 1866. William T. Sherman Papers, Volume 19.

readily, but here was a story of turbulence from such a man as Kit Carson. It shook Sherman's beliefs a little.

He turned to other correspondence. Here was a letter from General Carleton at Santa Fé. He was sounding warlike again. Why not round up all the Indians, as he had done with the Navajos at the Bosque Redondo, he challenged. "To spin out this war with Indians year after year is not a good policy. To have just troops enough scattered through the country to 'play hardly an even game' with the Indians, leads to no decisive results and is a 'penny wise and pound foolish' system." Then Carleton offered Sherman some gratuitous advice. "The true economy, in my opinion, is to put troops enough in the country to drive the Indians to the wall at once; to exterminate them if they won't give up; to put them on reservations if they do give up; and have done with it."[20] Sherman probably smiled wryly at this one. He could appreciate Carleton's position, and, in general, he agreed with it. But there were larger considerations. Carleton was sounding like one of the Westerners, viewing the situation from his own narrow vantage point. He did not have to listen to the humanitarians in the East, nor the congressmen who were impressed by their harangues about the *beau sauvage,* the children of the wilderness. Nor did he have to listen to cries of help from all other sections of the West, each convinced that it was about to be engulfed in a red tidal wave.

Of course, the newspaper editors were still declaring war with every issue. An accumulation of papers piled on his desk revealed the literary sharpshooters at their bloodthirsty best. Here was a copy of the *Idaho World.* "Treaties are just so many sugar plums; small whippings only ticklers, to the Indians," it shouted in bold print. "A sufficient force to whip them badly is needed. They should be followed up in the Winter, their stock taken and killed, their supplies and whole store of provisions destroyed, and themselves made to feel that life was contingent upon their own future good behavior." The editor was completely disgusted

[20] Carleton to Sherman, October 17, 1866. Letters and Telegrams Received, 1866–68, Headquarters of the Army, Records of the War Department, National Archives.

with the regular army. Only a while back, Major General Halleck —"Old Brains" of Civil War fame—had crawled out of the security of his division headquarters long enough to make a tour of inspection in the territory. It was a farce, snorted the western journalist. "He was accompanied by his aids, his black servants, and his wine and liquor cases. He rode in a covered wagon, so cleverly arranged that neither could he see any of the country through which he passed nor could anybody see him."[21] Sherman probably got grim amusement out of this blast. Things were no different in the Division of the Pacific, and Halleck was getting the normal frontier treatment accorded to visiting generals.

Less humorous to him were the attacks made by editors in his own Division. The Nebraska scribes were up in arms, too. Here was one, quoting a Colorado paper on the Ute "uprising," of which Cummings had written. "If the Utes do make a general outbreak, all we ask is that Col. Carson may have command of the troops sent against them; and not be hampered with orders from Washington or New England," the editor begged. All the mountain men wanted was the opportunity to "clean the Indians out."[22] More surprising was the attitude of the staid *Army and Navy Journal.* Its editorials complained that the problem under discussion was little understood, "except on our Western frontiers." Why not let the army control things? Turn the corrupt Indian Bureau over to the military. Let General Sherman take over completely. "We will guarantee that if he is intrusted with the full control of the whole matter, and is allowed the troops he needs, he will ensure a degree of protection to life and property on the Plains and in our mountain territories hitherto unknown."[23] While he agreed that the bureau ought to be transferred and could not help but approve of such counsel by the editor, Sherman undoubtedly wondered at the generosity of the man, in "guaranteeing" that in his hands all would be secure.

In general, eastern and western editors took divergent stands, reflecting the sentiment of the people in the two sections of the

21 *Idaho World,* October 13, 1866.
22 *Nebraska Republican,* October 26, 1866.
23 Vol. IV (October 13, 1866), 125.

country. For example, the *Omaha Weekly Herald* was highly critical of Sherman. Why, said the editor, the Indians were not only hostile and defiant, but actually held many western garrisons under a virtual state of siege. "This is a deplorable situation of affairs, and we think it is high time Gen. Sherman should recognize the fact of actual war with these Indians," he wrote sharply.[24] On the other hand, the *New York Times* had only praise for the present conduct of the army. It took encouragement from the words of Sherman, who had just returned from an extensive tour of the plains, that much of the rumor there was false and unfounded. Fortunately for the country, such a man was in command, and the editor could promise that "he will establish a policy with the Indians at once just and energetic." Without doubt, he would "deal severely" with the troublemakers.[25] The General must have been bewildered by the multitude of promises made by the editors for him. If he paid attention to what he read in the newspapers, he would, indeed, be busy in the months to come.

Shoving away from him all the newspaper accounts and gratuitous offers of his services by dozens of editors, the western commander set about summarizing the findings of his recent tour. Washington expected a formal report. Methodically, he described the vast region under his command, explaining that it stretched from the Mississippi River to the Rockies, an average of 1,350 miles in breadth, and was more than 1,000 miles long, between the Canadian and Mexican borders. The eastern tier of states— Minnesota, Iowa, Missouri, and Arkansas—represented a fertile area, "well adapted to settlement." Farther west lay the High Plains, well covered with grasses, but generally devoid of trees, or even minerals. These arid expanses had been well mapped and described by many earlier explorers, dating back to Pike and Lewis and Clark. However, they would never be of much use. "[They] can never be cultivated like Illinois, never be filled with inhabitants capable of self-government and self-defence as against Indians and marauders, but at best can become

24 October 19, 1866.
25 October 29, 1866.

93

a vast pasture-field, open and free to all for the rearing of herds of horses, mules, cattle and sheep." The sixty years that had elapsed since Pike's exploration had apparently effected little change in military opinion concerning the "great American desert." Even now, with the railroads creeping over the barren land and settlers beginning to think about agriculture in the region, the otherwise imaginative Sherman could see little prospect of tillage. The next few years were going to astound him.

In the mountain regions he saw more hope of immediate resource utilization. Enthusiastically penning words of praise for this remote country, he talked of its forests, its minerals, and its "numerous valleys susceptible of high cultivation, either by means of the ordinary rains, or the more certain system of irrigation...." Such territories, he thought, "present a most interesting feature in our future development as a nation," and certainly they were worthy of protection. Already the mines had grouped people sufficiently so that most communities could protect themselves against ordinary Indian war parties. Even so, they constituted something of a problem, since "they occupy at this time an isolated position, presenting a thinly settled frontier in every direction, with a restless people branching out in search of a better place, or of better mines. To defend them perfectly is an utter impossibility." Under such circumstances, all the army could do was to help the little settlements protect themselves and to keep open the lines of travel between them and "the States." It was important that such military encouragement be offered. "These [territories] are most important in a military sense," Sherman urged, "and they hold out the promise of a country that can now partially, and will soon be able to feed the men and horses needed in that hitherto desolate region at reasonable prices." Such a place as Denver was already a thriving city, and others near by were growing rapidly.

To the south of Colorado, however, there was little promise of healthy development. The General's prejudice against New Mexico was undisguised, and he made no attempt to keep it out of his official report. "It has been settled longer than Ohio, and yet remains poor and exposed, with but a thin line of fields along the banks of the Rio Grande, liable at all times to be swept by the inroads of the nomad Indians that surround it," he said, contrasting it with regions near by, such as Colorado. "The whole Territory seems a pastoral land, but not fit for cultivation. The mines undeveloped are supposed to be very valuable, but as yet remain mostly in a state of nature. We have held this Territory since 1846, twenty years, at a cost to the national treasury of full a hundred millions of dollars, and I doubt if it will ever reimburse to the country a little of that sum." He estimated that 2,500 men, mostly cavalry, would be required at once to afford any kind of protection. Food for both men and horses would have to be hauled one thousand miles, at the cost of approximately fifteen cents a pound. Each soldier supported in this fashion would require a thousand dollars a year of federal money. It was just too much.

The great distances, the high costs of transportation, and the scattered nature of settlement presented only part of the problem. The most dangerous barrier to western development was still the American Indian. To that matter Sherman next turned his attention. It was a twin-headed complication, knotty, and doubtful of reasonable solution. The frontiersmen, almost without exception, chose to regard all Indians as hostile, and the military, charged with the protection of long lines of travel, had no choice but to dispose troops in anticipation of hostilities. On the other hand, by the laws of Congress, the Indians were technically under the protection of the federal government and were being supervised by civilian agents who periodically called on the army for support. The dilemma was obvious, and Sherman flatly recommended that the management of the tribes be returned to the army so that the division of authority would end. "Indians do not read," he argued, "and only know of our power and strength by what they see, and they always look to the man who commands soldiers as the representatives of our government." Under military control there should be less corruption and fewer cries of short payments to the Indians. Army men, who were not serving under short-term appointments as were the civilian agents, ought not to be quite so tempted.

In any event, the Indians should be confined to reservations. Those already thus located offered little trouble; it was the roving, hunting bands that made the problem so difficult. Further restrictions had to be made, and Sherman proposed to make them during the coming year. The Sioux must be held back, north of the Platte River, west of the Missouri, and east of the Bozeman Road. "All Sioux found outside of these limits without a written pass from some military commander defining clearly their object, should be dealt with summarily." In a similar manner, the Arapahoes, Cheyennes, Comanches, Kiowas, Apaches, and Navajos should be kept south of the Arkansas River and east of Fort Union, New Mexico. "This would leave for our people exclusively the use of the wide belt, east and west, between the Platte and the Arkansas, in which lie the two great railroads, and over which passes the bulk of travel to the mountain Territories." If the Indians were allowed to roam along such routes, as they had during the summer of 1866, further difficulties were unavoidable. There would be depredations, "and worse yet, the exaggerations of danger raised by our own people, often for a very base purpose." It was the immediate task of the military to guard the new railroad lines, as well as the telegraph and stage lines. Their very length prohibited any thorough protection, and unless the government was willing to post "no trespassing" signs along the Arkansas and Platte valleys, and enforce the ruling, there would be scalps lifted just as surely as night followed day.

In conclusion, the division commander laid out his grand strategy for defending the plains during the coming year. In the Department of Dakota, General Alfred Terry would attempt to protect Missouri River travel. If possible, he would open and protect a wagon road from Minnesota to Montana. In the Department of the Platte, General Cooke would pay close attention to the defense of the railroads under construction and, at the same time, keep the Bozeman Road into Montana open, "which the Indians give notice they will resist." Further south, in the Department of Missouri, General W. S. Hancock must protect the Smoky Hill route to Colorado and New Mexico as well as give every assistance to the railroad, now out as far as Fort Riley.[26]

Sherman realized it would be, as he had said several times, an imperfect protection. The land was vast, and the problems it presented were thorny. Few people were more vocal than western editors, and they would, no doubt, keep up the drumfire of complaint against the army, to which he had listened all year. The Department of the Interior, jealous of its supervision over the tribes, would constitute still another annoyance. To top it all off, the philanthropists in the East had not abated their wails about the fate of "Poor Lo," and congressmen, always attentive, were listening to the cries of "reduce the army" with thoughtful expressions. With both whites and Indians raising general hell in both East and West, Sherman must have felt like the old woman who lived in a shoe. Certainly he had so many divergent responsibilities in his far-flung command that he didn't know what to do. But he would have all winter at St. Louis to mull over the matter.

[26] The foregoing material is found in report of W. T. Sherman, November 5, 1866, *Annual Report of the Secretary of War*, 39 Cong., 2 sess., *House Exec. Doc. No. 1* (Serial 1285), p. 18–23.

Seven

THE MOST DIFFICULT PROBLEM

LIFE IN ST. LOUIS proved to be far from quiet during the winter of 1866–67. In November, Sherman said in his annual report that the Sioux along the Bozeman Road had served notice that they would resist. Toward the end of the next month, the Indians carried out their threat, to the shocked surprise of the American public.

Since July of 1866, when Colonel Henry Carrington moved the Twenty-seventh Infantry into the Powder River country to construct a series of military posts, there had been trouble. While there were no encounters sufficient to make headlines in eastern papers, the Sioux had sniped at communications and threatened the Bozeman Road posts to such an extent that they were nearly isolated. By December, the Indians became quite bold and sortied within sight of Fort Phil Kearney, trying to lure out the troops. On the morning of the twenty-first word came that the wood train, which had been frequently attacked, was again fighting off Indians. A detachment of eighty-one officers and men, led by Captain William J. Fetterman, was sent out to relieve the wood-haulers. Fetterman, who had been in Indian country only a short time, was eager to "make coups" and had boasted frequently about what he would do against the natives when afforded an opportunity. Shortly before noon on a cold winter day, he got his chance.

Despite Colonel Carrington's warnings and positive prohibition against pursuing the Indians beyond near-by Lodge Pole Creek, Fetterman could not resist the sight of war-bonneted Sioux apparently fleeing across the countryside. He gave chase. When the trap was snapped, the entire army command was caught in an ambush that was perfect, and in less than an hour's work the struggle was over. The plains had witnessed a complete reverse for the army, which, according to contemporary terminology, was a "massacre." Ironically enough, as Fettermen and his men lay dying, the wagon train they had come to rescue made its way back to Fort Phil Kearney almost unnoticed.

Sherman's reaction to the tragedy was little different from that of the average American. "I do not yet understand how the massacre of [Brevet Lieutenant] Colonel [William J.] Fetterman's party could have been so complete," he confessed a day or so after the affair. But he did understand what had to be done about it. "We must act with vindictive earnestness against the Sioux, even to their extermination, men, women and children. Nothing else will reach the root of this case."[1] He was fighting mad, so much so that he said things he did not mean. Not now, nor ever, was he actually ready to order the killing of Indian women and children. It would have put him in the same class with the renegade preacher Chivington, who had committed such an atrocity at Sand Creek, Colorado, a couple of years before. But his feeling towards the Sioux braves would not soon abate. His patience with these raiding bands was exhausted, and he knew no course other than to strike and strike hard.

But the war would have to wait. Winter was no time to campaign in Dakota Territory, and, so far as Sherman was concerned, the Indians would be safe in their lodges until spring. Meanwhile, there was a shake-up in the western commands, partially arising out of the Fetterman affair. Carrington was relieved of duty at Fort Phil Kearney, and with this decision Sherman had no quarrel. "I know enough of Carrington to believe that he is better qualified for a safe place than one of danger," he told a fellow-officer. "The fact that he was a Colonel of the Regulars all the war, and yet never heard a hostile shot was enough, but last fall we had no choice."[2] When Philip St. George Cooke was

1 Sherman to Grant, December 28, 1866, in letter from the Secretary of the Interior, communicating, in obedience to a resolution of the Senate of the 30th of January, information in relation to the late massacre of United States troops by Indians at or near Fort Phil. Kearney in Dakota Territory, 39 Cong., 2 sess., *Senate Exec. Doc. No. 16* (Serial 1277), p. 4; Edgar I. Stewart, *Custer's Luck*, 38–46.

2 Sherman to Augur, February 28, 1867. C. C. Augur Papers, Division of Manuscripts, Illinois State Historical Library, Springfield, Illinois.

relieved of his command of the Department of the Platte, in which Fort Phil Kearney lay, Sherman was somewhat puzzled. He told his friend Dodge that he had not been consulted about this move, nor could he understand Grant's motives. He could not see how Cooke was personally responsible for the affair that had cost so many lives.[3] Regardless of any reasons for the change, Sherman could comfort himself with the fact that it might be all for the best. Cooke's replacement was General Christopher Columbus Augur, a classmate of Grant's at West Point, who had gained some experience with Indian affairs while campaigning in Oregon during the fifties. He was now forty-five years old, and this age appealed to Sherman, who liked his western generals young enough to be active in the field.

With Terry in the Department of Dakota and Augur commanding that of the Platte, a vigorous policy should not be hard to effect. There was Hancock, however, in the Department of Missouri. Sherman had wanted him for a western command and had earlier insisted that he was the "right man." But now he wondered. Hancock had not proved as aggressive as he had hoped, and his reluctance to move his headquarters farther out on the plains was annoying. If an opportunity for a change came, perhaps he could get fiery Phil Sheridan, the little cavalryman, for the job. Such an appointment would round out the team nicely, and some aggressive campaigning would surely follow.

As the spring of 1867 approached, Sheridan laid his plans for protecting the plains during the coming summer. The time had come for a "get tough" policy towards those Indians who would not stay on their reservations but persisted in ranging far off, making attacks on isolated groups of settlers or soldiers. The Sioux and the Cheyennes appeared to be the immediate targets. They were powerful tribes, now almost surrounded by fringes of settlement, and they were not yet ready to go the white man's way. "I expect to have two Indian wars on my hands," Sherman admitted to his brother. "The Sioux & Cheyennes are now so

[3] Sherman to Dodge, January 22, 1867. Grenville M. Dodge Papers, Volume 14, Iowa State Department of History and Archives, Des Moines, Iowa.

circumscribed that I suppose they must be exterminated, for they cannot & will not settle down, and our people will force us to it."[4]

Pressure against the Indians had increased sharply with the westward rush of population in the immediate postwar days. Now, with such a tragedy as the Fetterman affair on its record, the military began to feel increasing criticism from the press. Omaha papers moaned that the disaster along the Bozeman Road meant a diminution of business. One of them, calling Montana "a golden fact," stated sadly that after such events as the recent one near Fort Phil Kearney, no emigrant would feel safe in traveling the route, and trade between Omaha and Montana would certainly be curtailed.[5] From Leavenworth came the call to all western journalists to press for more military aid. All boards of trade in cities affected should officially address General Sherman on the subject, counseled one editor.[6] And up in frontier Montana the type was molten lead. Let there be "no such imbecility or cowardice as disgraced this route last summer. . . . It is high time the sickly sentimentalism about humane treatment and conciliatory measures should be consigned to novel writers, and if the Indians continue their barbarities, wipe them out."[7] The Montanans told one another that they were damned sick of it all. Any more temporizing on the part of the regular army might force them to take things into their own hands.

Sherman said nothing. He had made up his mind that the time for action had come. God, the Indian Bureau, and the peace societies willing, he would act. The success of the Sioux might so embolden them that the Union Pacific Railroad would be endangered. That alone provided sufficient grounds for attack. Don't worry about the road, he reassured the worried Dodge. The Fetterman affair was, of course, a matter of concern to the railroad builders. But they could rest easy, for "we shall persevere and push that [Bozeman] road to Virginia City and it will divert

[4] Sherman to John Sherman, December 30, 1866. William T. Sherman Papers, Volume 20.

[5] *Omaha Weekly Herald*, January 5, 1867.

[6] *Leavenworth Daily Times*, December 29, 1866.

[7] *Montana Post*, January 26, 1867.

the attention of the hostile Sioux from your road."[8] As he wrote, a letter was on its way from Dodge, advising him to get ten thousand men west of the Missouri as fast as possible. The engineer recalled his own recent campaigns in that country and warned Sherman, "Don't do as I had to—get well after the Indians, and then let the Interior at Washington stop you; but get after them early and follow them to Doomsday, without any let up. . . . They look upon us now as a lot of old women, who do not know whether we are for war, or peace, or both."[9]

The advice was sound, but easier to impart than to follow. The Interior Department was sometimes as formidable as the wild tribes in the West, and Sherman was finding out that it was as hard to come to grips with as the shifty Indians. But Dodge need not have worried. The railroads would go forward. The workers had accomplished a miracle in laying over three hundred miles of rails during 1866, and they would have every encouragement in matching that feat during the coming year. Sherman was convinced that "this coming year for better or worse is to be an important one to our country," and if only Dodge could, "by superhuman energy," reach the foot of the mountains, things would be simplified for the army. North and south, along the base of the Rockies, there was plenty of wood, and the grass was good. It was the parched distance that lay between the Mississippi Valley and those verdant slopes that posed the problem. The railroad could solve it. Sherman promised to do everything in his power to cover the working parties along the railroad against the Indians.[10]

During January, Dodge and Sherman frequently wrote to each other. The latter was amazed at the engineer's activity and found it hard to believe that the road builders actually hoped to get out as far as Fort Sanders (present Wyoming) during 1867. When he had written that if, by superhuman effort, the road could be

8 Sherman to Dodge, January 5, 1867. Grenville M. Dodge Papers, Volume 14.
9 This letter is found in Volume 6, page 564, of what are called the "Dodge Records," described as "Data, Chronologically Arranged for Ready Reference in the Preparation of a Biography of Grenville Mellen Dodge." Iowa State Department of History and Archives, Des Moines, Iowa.
10 Sherman to Dodge, January 5, 1867. Grenville M. Dodge Papers, Volume 14.

built to the foot of the mountains that year, he was only expressing a fond hope. Now, to his amazement, Dodge candidly admitted that such was his intention. Sherman wondered at such
optimism but confessed, "You have done so much that I mistrust
my own judgment and accept yours." He reassured Dodge that
if such wonders were accomplished, the army would be on hand
to lend every protection, because "I regard this road of yours
the solution of 'our Indian affairs. . . .' " The slender little life
line of rails fascinated Sherman, and he watched every report of
progress with interest. He promised Dodge, "I will surely be up
this year many times and will go over every rail more than once."
To him it was, as he told the chief engineer, a "great national
enterprise," and it must go forward without interruption.[11]

There would be resistance, of course. As the rails were laid,
the workmen would have the uncomfortable feeling that they
were being watched furtively from the near-by hills. Often, it
would be true. Not long ago, a Nebraska paper had warned that
the Sioux and Cheyennes were fairly gritting their teeth over the
progress of the Union Pacific. Two chiefs were reported to have
casually inspected the passenger and freight cars, taking measure-
ments of the thickness of their walls. "They want to make their
bows and arrows stout enough to go through the wood and
stick into the pale faces."[12] Never mind such rumors, Sherman
advised Dodge. Keep the men at work, and we will do our best
to protect them. Get the rails westward where the military can
employ them. When that was accomplished, "we can act so ener-
getically that both Sioux and Cheyennes must die or submit to
our dictation."[13]

Meanwhile, protection would have to be supplied by whatever
means the army had at hand. Pope's order of February 28, 1866,
regulating travel across the plains, had been effective during the
previous travel season. Why not use it again? This year four principal routes would be protected. The Minnesotans, who had complained so vigorously last year about having to use the Missouri

11 Sherman to Dodge, January 18, 1867. Grenville M. Dodge Papers, Volume 14.
12 Fort Kearny *Herald*, December 17, 1866, quoted by the *Montana Post*, December 22, 1866.
13 Sherman to Dodge, February 20, 1867. Grenville M. Dodge Papers, Volume 14.

River region in their travels west, would now be afforded a route of their own. Minneapolis and St. Paul merchants would now have their desired connection with the Montana mines, by direct overland road. The Platte Valley, "by which full 90 per cent. of the travel to Montana, Utah, California and Colorado have hitherto gone," of course, would be heavily defended, as would its new branch leading from Fort Laramie to the Yellowstone. Farther south, the Smoky Hill road to Colorado and New Mexico was of increased importance on account of the construction of the Union Pacific's Eastern Division out to Fort Riley. Also serving the southwest was the Arkansas route, by way of Forts Zara, Larned, Dodge, and Lyon to Fort Union, New Mexico. Wagon trains would, as before, be obliged to travel in force, with not less than twenty vehicles and thirty riflemen. This year, however, the post commanders along the way would be given a little more latitude in deciding when a train was strong enough to go out. In some cases the fixed minimum might be lowered. Last summer, some of them had been held up, resulting in delay and expense, when, actually, the Indian danger along some stretches of the road had not been serious.[14]

By March, final plans for the coming summer were rounded out. Perhaps something could be done during these dry months to widen the wedges driven into the plains country by the travel routes. Sherman hoped so. It appeared to him that in Hancock's department there should be no real trouble. The Cheyennes had been making all manner of friendly professions, but, even so, it might not be a bad idea to send the General there with a body of troops so that the Indians "may see that we are ready."[15] Hancock had assembled a special force of fifteen hundred men, composed largely of a new regiment known as the Seventh Cavalry. He would go out among the Cheyennes and Kiowas and "confer

14 Sherman to Grant, March 13, 1867. Letters and Telegrams Received, 1866–68, Headquarters of the Army.

15 Sherman to Leet, February 16, 1867. Division of the Missouri, Letters Received, 1866–69, Special File; letter of the Secretary of War, communicating, in compliance with a resolution of the Senate of the 11th instant, further information respecting armed expeditions against the western Indians, 40 Cong., 1 sess., *Senate Exec. Doc. No. 7* (Serial 1308).

with them to ascertain if they want to fight, in which case he will indulge them." At the same time, he would assure the Indians that so long as they maintained peace and minded their agents, they would not be disturbed. His principal mission would be to "impress on them the imprudence of assuming an insolent manner and tone when they visit our posts, and he will impress on them that it is to their interest to keep their hunting parties and their young warriors off our main lines of travel, where their presence gives the occasion for the many rumors which so disturb our people."[16] Sherman was ready to begin applying the pressure.

If Hancock moved among the Kiowas and Cheyennes, as planned, he would be busy. In addition, he would have the duty of looking after the great reservation known as "Indian Territory," spreading over present Oklahoma. Early in March, the state of Arkansas had been removed from Sherman's Division and transferred to the Fourth Military District, leaving an island of territory to the west without supervision. The region would now become a part of the Department of Missouri.[17]

North of Hancock's command, in the Department of the Platte, General Augur would also be ready for action. Together with the Second Cavalry and some infantry stationed at Fort Laramie, he could present a force of about two thousand men. These would be put under the immediate command of General John Gibbon and sent into the country at the head of the Powder and Yellowstone rivers to punish the Indians who had been raiding the Bozeman Road. The Sioux up there could be regarded as actively at war, and no mercy should be accorded them, for "they grant no quarter, nor ask for it." Already Augur had been instructed to send out runners to notify the Sioux that a state of war was now at hand, and those who wished to avoid destruc-

---

[16] Sherman to Leet, March 13, 1867. Letters and Telegrams Received, 1866–68, Headquarters of the Army; letter of the Secretary of War, communicating in compliance with a resolution of the Senate of the 11th instant, further information respecting armed expeditions against the western Indians, 40 Cong., 1 sess., *Senate Exec. Doc. No. 1* (Serial 1308).

[17] Report of W. T. Sherman, October 1, 1867, *Annual Report of the Secretary of War*, 40 Cong., 2 sess., *House Exec. Doc. No. 1* (Serial 1324), p. 31.

tion had only to come to one of the military posts along the Platte, where they would be fed and turned over to agents.

To Sherman's frustration, just as he was getting ready to level his guns, Congress intervened and announced that a peace commission would visit the Sioux. Already, in March, the members were at Omaha, ready to proceed. Sherman had no choice but to tell Augur to hold up. "I have instructed him to delay actual hostilities until these commissions have exhausted their efforts and reported to him their inability to influence the conduct of the hostile Sioux by pacific measures," he reported to headquarters.[18] Sooner or later, though, he growled, the Sioux must be taught a severe lesson.[19] He would let the peacemakers have their fling.

While he awaited further developments, he talked with Terry, who had come down for a few days from St. Paul. Reinforce the Missouri River posts, Sherman told him. Make them strong enough to withstand any attacks the Sioux might make, and at the same time, be ready to sally out for thrusts at any bands attempting to block river travel.[20] Defensive measures against the Indians were not enough now. In the task of protecting long routes of travel, the army detachments were so strung out that each unit was necessarily small and ineffective. It fully occupied most of the men available at an average post simply to gather firewood and build shelters. Construction materials had to be hauled hundreds of miles. Meanwhile, the Indians could move their whole camps—ponies, lodges, families, and all—hundreds of miles. While the troops were tied down at their posts, the ranging bands could strike at one point and be a great distance away within days. It was an impossible situation, and Sherman, now ready to go on the offensive, saw but one answer. "Our troops must get amongst them, and must kill enough of them to inspire fear, and then must conduct the remainder to places where Indian Agents can and will reside amongst them, and be

18 Sherman to Leet, March 13, 1867. Letters and Telegrams Received, 1866–68, Headquarters of the Army.
19 Sherman to Grant, March 13, 1867. Letters and Telegrams Received, 1866–68, Headquarters of the Army.
20 *Ibid.*

held responsible for their conduct."[21] No other course seemed practicable. But he would have to await permission for such action.

Meanwhile, the army was doing everything within its limited means to protect travelers on the plains, and while major attacks against warlike bands of Indians certainly would have to come, still, the immediate task lay in defending the roads. Sherman was satisfied that he had now done the best he could in distributing scattered resources, and if the emigrants would pay strict attention to the rules of the road, no trouble should occur. Tirelessly the army officers worked at the task of keeping the emigrants on the established trails, but it was as fruitless as telling a seven-year-old to come straight home from school. Short cuts or better-appearing grades tempted them. And often the new direction led them directly into small hunting parties of Indians who warmly welcomed such windfalls and promptly divided up the spoils. The army would have to fight against such things, and Sherman resolved to tighten up during the coming travel season. Local commanding officers were instructed to act vigorously against anyone ignoring military regulations in such a way as to endanger the life or property of these transient people. Transgressors would be dealt with, "be they white, black or copper colored. Where there are no courts or civil authorities to hold and punish such malefactors we must of necessity use the musket pretty freely, the only weapon with which the soldiers ought to deal." Those who kept the peace, Indians or whites, would have no trouble with the military authorities. Post commanders might modify the rules, with permission, but this was a privilege strictly denied to wagon masters.[22]

Congress was again talking about the "Mormon problem," and although these people in Utah did not reside in the Division of the Missouri, any action against them would call for troops much needed on the plains east of them. The army had its hands full now, and Sherman was busy enough, "without begging any new

---

[21] Sherman to Leet, March 13, 1867. Letters and Telegrams Received, 1866–68, Headquarters of the Army.

[22] *Ibid.*

causes of trouble."[23] If congressmen would just contain their impatience until the railroad could reach Utah, things would be much easier.

Then there was a rumor in the papers that Sherman would soon be transferred to the south to be detailed in military government. Although he usually discounted the speculations of the newspapermen, the story annoyed him. Sometimes they were right. By God, he wouldn't go, that was all there was to it. "I am perfectly willing to take a Regt of Cavalry and go out to fight Indians," he told Phil Ewing hotly, "but to hold an indescribable office of mixed jurisdiction impossible of logical execution and sure to result in curses from both sides would be a most ungracious task."[24] The task he had before him was controversial enough. But he preferred it to any duty connected with Reconstruction.

All day at the office he faced one complication after another. There were worries about the railroad, rumors to be denied about massacres on the plains, problems which arose when such rumors turned out to be true, as they had up near Fort Phil Kearney, and concerns about the vagaries of Congress and what it might do next to snarl further the affairs of the military. And then home for the night, to lie awake to the nerve-racking squalls of a newborn baby in the next room.[25] It must have recalled to him times like these during the early days of the Civil War, when he was faced by a multitude of problems, and his nervous system was stretched to fiddlestring tightness. They had called him crazy then.

But the pace did not slacken. More complications developed to multiply earlier ones. The Indian Bureau was becoming militant again, and it threatened to open another front in the wars Sherman had to fight. During the month of January, reports began to come into headquarters of the Division of the Missouri

---

23 Sherman to John Sherman, January 17, 1867. William T. Sherman Papers, Volume 20.

24 Sherman to Ewing, March 8, 1867. Sherman-Ewing Correspondence, Division of Manuscripts, Ohio State Archaeological and Historical Society, Columbus, Ohio.

25 Philemon Tecumseh Sherman arrived on January 9, 1867, making a total of six children in the Sherman family.

"The gnarled, flint-eyed William Tecumseh Sherman
—almost Jacksonian in his rugged, plain appearance. . . ."

Harper's Weekly, June 8, 1867
Courtesy Kansas State Historical Society

"The western army could represent nothing more than a thin blue line on a vast tract of land."

Above: Fort Larned, 1867.   Below: Interior of Fort Dodge, 1867.

Harper's Weekly, May 25, 1867
Courtesy Kansas State Historical Society

that the Indians were getting arms and ammunition in quantity from the traders. Sherman was furious when he read of it. The commanding officer at Fort Dodge complained that D. A. Butterfield, the former express company owner, was selling arms without let or hindrance. As a result, the Indians in that region were openly boasting that when spring came, they would have plenty of "smokepoles" to use on the whites.[26] From Fort Larned, also in Kansas, came the query, "Who are authorized persons?" General Order No. 70, dated July 30, 1866, had specified that only "authorized persons" could sell arms to the Indians. All the traders in that region seemed somehow to be authorized, for they were, without exception, doing a thriving business.[27]

How had all this happened, the thunderstruck Sherman asked of Grant? He had understood that only post commanders were permitted to make such transactions, and then for just enough ammunition for hunting purposes. "The thing seems to me so monstrous that I would not credit it, unless I had the papers well authenticated before me." The practice would stop at once. He told Grant that Hancock had been ordered to shut off all such supplies to the traders. This western assignment presented "the most difficult problem I have ever had to handle," Sherman told his superior officer, and it was being complicated unnecessarily by such actions as the unrestricted sale of arms to the Indians. If such sales were not stopped, the army had no recourse but to withdraw its men from the plains and give up. Even now, it was hard enough to carry out the almost impossible task of affording protection in the region. Take the matter up with the President, he urged. Tell him that these traders, with a profit of ten dollars a pistol, would involve the country in a war costing millions. Tell him, too, that when one department of the government was busy arming the Indians at the expense of life and money to another department of the same government, things had come to

[26] Major N. Douglas to the Assistant Adjutant General, Division of the Missouri, January 13, 1867. Division of the Missouri, Letters Received, 1866–69, Special File.

[27] Captain Henry Asbury, commanding Fort Larned, to the Assistant Adjutant General, Division of the Missouri, January 14, 1867. Division of the Missouri, Letters Received, 1866–69, Special File.

a pretty pass. Certainly it was bad enough to have the Sioux up in arms, but surely this meant that the Cheyennes and Arapahoes would hit the warpath, too.[28] The conduct of the Interior Department had been simply unbelievable.

Denial of gun-selling permits to the traders brought forth an immediate howl from the interested parties. The Indian Bureau vigorously defended its position and made no apologies for co-operating with the traders in the sale of arms. Lewis V. Bogy, commissioner of Indian affairs, called Sherman's move an "unwarranted interference of the military" and predicted openly that, unless such action was prohibited in the future, it would bring about the destruction of western settlements at the hands of the Indians. The greatest difficulty in administering affairs in the Bureau, Bogy charged, came from interference on the part of army officers. There was no doubt in his mind that the Fetterman affair was a direct outcome of such meddling. The Commissioner further took the view that arms were a necessity for the Indians in their hunt for subsistence, and to be denied them would result in starvation and a desperate struggle with the whites who were the cause.[29]

One answer seemed to be the transfer of the Indian Bureau to the Department of War where the problem might be put under a single jurisdiction. The Interior Department opposed the idea strongly, but many western papers talked of the "good old times" when such affairs were conducted by the army and strongly recommended a renewal of that system.[30] Sherman very much wanted such a transfer, and Grant supported him.[31] Early in the

28 Sherman to Grant, January 31, 1867. Division of the Missouri, Letters Received, 1866–69, Special File.

29 *Leavenworth Daily Times,* February 19, 1867; letter of Lewis Bogy to the *Philadelphia Press,* quoted by the *Daily Missouri Republican,* April 12, 1867; report of Lewis V. Bogy to O. H. Browning, secretary of the interior, January 23, 1867, in letter from the Secretary of the Interior, communicating, in obedience to a resolution of the Senate of the 30th of January, information in relation to the late massacre of United States troops by Indians at or near Fort Phil. Kearney in Dakota Territory, 39 Cong., 2 sess., *Senate Exec. Doc. No. 16* (Serial 1277).

30 *Helena Herald,* January 31, 1867; *Daily Union Vedette,* February 22, 1867.

31 *Washington Chronicle,* February 4, 1867, quoted in 39 Cong., 2 sess., *Senate Exec. Doc. No. 16* (Serial 1277); *Owyhee Avalanche* (Silver City, Idaho), February 16, 1867.

year, a bill providing for such a change was introduced into the
Senate, and Sherman expressed his conviction that it would become law. Jubilantly he wrote to John about how busy he soon
would be "in the transfer of the Indians to our management."[32]
He should have known better. The Indian Bureau and its parent,
the Department of the Interior, had powerful friends. By the
end of February, Sherman again wrote of the matter to his
brother; this time his pen dripped bitterness. "The defeat in
the Senate of the Bill to transfer to us the Indians relieves us of
all responsibility. . . . We surely cannot be held responsible
for the Peace of the Frontier if it is adjudged we are trespassers
everywhere in Indian Territory, and have no right to foresee
and prevent collision & trouble. After the Indians do mischief
is too late to apply the remedy." He promised John that he would
try not to let the matter distress him, but the blow was a hard
one to absorb cheerfully. It was a major victory for the Bureau;
no doubt about it. But, said the General, he would be hanged
if he would put his troops under the orders of the Indian agents
and traders to help them forward their own selfish ends.[33] They
could expect less generous response to their pleas for protection
in the future. An administrative battle had been fought, but the
war was not yet ended.

Hardly had the Secretary of the Interior decorated his coup-
stick before he was ready for another sortie against the army.
In March, he complained to the Secretary of War that troops
were gathering in Hancock's command to strike a mighty blow
at the Indians. The complaint was referred to Sherman, who
answered that no such thing was afoot. He explained that he had
recommended the removal of those who had ranged the area
between the Platte and the Arkansas because their presence was
dangerous to travel, but his suggestions so far had been ignored.
Hancock was merely in the region for a show of force. Waxing
impatient now, he continued. It was ridiculous to assume that
the Sioux were peaceful. They were at war, and it was idle to

[32] Sherman to John Sherman, February 1, 1867. William T. Sherman Papers, Volume 20.

[33] Sherman to John Sherman, February 24, 1867. William T. Sherman Papers, Volume 20.

shut one's eyes to such facts. He found himself defending Carrington, whom he did not privately defend, in that the attack on
the Fetterman party was the responsibility of no one officer. The
Sioux had hung around Fort Phil Kearney for months, and only
when the chance for an ambush came did they strike.

"I wish I could feel as confident as the Hon. Secretary of the
Interior of the peaceful disposition of the Indians, but he must
pardon me if I cannot, and accept the reports of our Military
Commanders who live in contact with these Indians," he continued icily. Facts were facts, and with an enormous public
pressure for action prevailing, it was hard to stand by and "hold
our hands" merely because a different opinion obtained in the
Interior Department. Certainly, he said, he did not argue that
the Indians, by act of Congress, were lawfully under the tutelage
of that department. He wished Congress would go even farther
and rule that any hostilities against the Indians should be conducted only after a formal declaration of war had been made.
Then Congress would have to provide by law the force which
was to end the conflict. "This state of quasi-war when we are
held to protect our vast frontiers and lines of travel measured by
thousands of miles with our troops forced to remain on the defensive to be dealt with in detail by Indians who say they are at
war and mean war of utter annihilation and no quarter shown,
is not a state of facts pleasing to the military mind."[34] Sherman
was at his trenchant best. When he let go on such occasions, he
fired from the hip.

But blasts from St. Louis had little effect in Washington, and
before long, it looked as though the advocates of negotiation
would knock all of Sherman's long-range plans into a cocked
hat. His natural impatience with delay was rasped into a deep-
seated anger as he watched civilian hands stay his actions. While
he was sympathetic to those Indians following a peaceful existence and was ready to chastise any whites who molested them, he
was eager to punish severely any Indians committing warlike acts.
However, thanks to the Indian Bureau, there seemed to be no

[34] Sherman to Leet, April 3, 1867. Letters and Telegrams Received, 1866–68,
Headquarters of the Army.

distinction, as there was in his mind, between good Indians and bad Indians. He had thirsted for a chance to strike back at the Sioux for their audacity at Fort Phil Kearney last winter, and now it was impossible to do anything conclusive.[35] Here was a spectacle of Indians actively at war with the army, with Secretary of the Interior Browning standing between the contestants, blissfully intoning the word "peace." "So we must keep our hands off till the Indians become utterly uncontrollable, and then it will be too late," Sherman wrote darkly. With the troops held in leash, the Indians were free to roam at will and to fall upon any detachment of soldiers they might choose. When tired of the chase, they could turn up at the nearest agency and draw their annuities. Under such circumstances, it seemed to Sherman that "soldiers are meant to be killed, and citizens are fools to expose themselves so far off." Well, if the whites wandered into trouble, somebody else would have to get them out. "I will not concern myself unnecessarily by these events as long as we are hampered and controlled by Law. We in fact legally have no more to do with the Indian wars than with Irish riots on the Railroads in New York."[36]

Sherman's famous temper had flared again, and this time it was no momentary pout. He was both angry and frustrated. It was bad enough to have to fight against unreasonable odds, but to have one's hands tied down—it was too much. The whole outfit at Washington could go to hell. He was going to Europe. An excursion was being organized—tickets were $1,250—and he had been offered free passage. His eldest daughter, Minnie, who was now sixteen, was anxious to go. John was alarmed at Cump's violence and once again sought to sooth his warlike brother's ruffled disposition. "I have been thinking about your trip to Europe," he wrote. "I do not like to influence you in a matter about which you can judge best but it does appear to me that with your extensive & responsible command and the important duties of the Army this summer that your absence would be

[35] Sherman to Dodge, April 15, 1867. "Dodge Records," Volume 6, 570–71.
[36] Sherman to John Sherman, April 3, 1867. William T. Sherman Papers, Volume 21.

noticed." Would the President approve of Sherman's running off like this? John asked. He was treading carefully, yet putting on all the pressure he could.[37]

Sherman answered a week later. By now, he had slept off some of his earlier violence, but he had not lost any of his stubbornness. Obliquely, he professed to have little real interest in Europe, but Minnie had now set her heart on the trip, and he must go.[38] The next day, he sat down and resolutely wrote to Captain C. C. Duncan of the *Quaker City* at New York. "You may . . . register my name and that of my daughter Minnie for your excursion," he instructed the Captain.[39] The deed was done; Secretary Browning could sugarplum his brown friends out West to death; Sherman would have no part of it.

[37] John Sherman to Sherman, March 20, 1867. William T. Sherman Papers, Volume 21.

[38] Sherman to John Sherman, March 27, 1867. William T. Sherman Papers, Volume 21.

[39] Sherman to Duncan, March 28, 1867. *Leavenworth Daily Times*, April 13, 1867.

Eight

▬▬▬▬▬

A CONCERTED AND MISCHIEVOUS DESIGN

IF JOHN SHERMAN worried about his brother's state of mind, he had good reason for it. The quick-tempered veteran was thoroughly disgusted, and he appeared determined to visit Europe, temporarily shelving his cares and responsibilities. The excursion promised to be an interesting one. Men like Alexander Stewart, Moses Taylor, Peter Cooper, William H. Aspinwall, and other well-known merchant princes were sponsoring the excursion, and they wanted to honor the General by providing his passage. It was a truly tempting offer, and Sherman had gone so far as to make reservations for the trip. But he couldn't go. He knew it when he weakened, telling John he would carry the thing through only because of Minnie and her determination to see the Continent. Even at that point he had begun his retreat. As sailing time drew near, he capitulated to the demands of duty. The prodding about responsibility that John had penned probably helped to crystallize the necessity of staying home and carrying out his assigned tasks.

"It will not be in my power to accept the proffered honor," Sherman wrote to his New York friends. They had been very kind, but he decided to remain at his post. He would tell them why. "You doubtless know that my military command embraces a vast region of wild country, which is being rapidly occupied by our people, and across which are being built two railways, destined in a few years to span the wide space between the Atlantic and Pacific states. This country has been from time immemorial the homes and hunting grounds of various tribes of Indians who still number some 300,000 souls, and who, being pressed from every quarter, have become nervous, excited, and in some cases positively hostile. At this moment there are fears that they may combine and do infinite mischief, and we have daily calls for protection at a hundred places, hundreds of miles from each other, and it requires our constant attention so to apportion our limited military force as to protect the most vital interests." Therefore, he said, concluding a rather simple explanation of a highly complicated set of problems, he would be obliged to forego the pleasures of ocean travel.[1]

As the spring of 1867 warmed into summer, Sherman must have wondered more than once if he had made the right decision. By July it would be two years since he took over his western command, and instead of gaining the upper hand, he seemed to be losing his battle to control the situation. Travel was on the increase, the Indians were correspondingly hostile, the Interior Department was loud in its demands for a greater control of the tribes, and Congress was reflecting the usual postwar pressure against army requests. All these things were intangibles. Fighting them was like wrestling with one's shadow; there seemed to be no way of coming to grips with the opponent. But in all such cases, there were at least identifiable people involved, and you at least knew who your enemy was, even if you couldn't seem to grapple with him. That characteristic set apart such problems from the one and most annoying irritant with which Sherman now had to contend. The whole country was buzzing with rumor concerning this tragedy or that mishap in the West. Only occasionally was there any basis for the talk. Here the crusty veteran was completely lost. He did not even know the people involved in this kind of warfare. To a man of action and one who knew only how to deal in a straightforward, direct manner, it was puzzlement combined with frustration.

The Fetterman affair had apparently touched off the powder keg of gossip. After the Sioux had rendered such a complete decision on that cold day near Fort Phil Kearney and the veracity of the report had been established, no account of similar happenings was too wild for the American public to accept. And once such stories were out, they could not be stopped. By word of mouth along the streets, through the smoky haze of tavern

[1] *New York Times*, May 31, 1867.

talk, and even in the newspapers, the most bizarre kind of tales drifted across the country. Nothing could stop their spreading, not even the truth.

During May, the story was current that a steamboat named the *Miner* had been attacked about five hundred miles west of Sioux City. The boat, according to the standard account, had tied up to take on wood when it was overcome by Indians. The Sioux were the criminals this time. In the best tradition of massacres, they "murdered every man, woman and child on board," after which the vessel was pillaged and burned.[2] Editors pondered over the report, discussing its merits, grasping for confirmation, and the public mind was hazily under the impression that perhaps it was all true.[3] Grenville Dodge wrote of the matter to Sherman,[4] and the latter had no official answer to the query. Like the public, he was also puzzled. On March 26, he had issued General Order No. 8, which provided that the Ordnance Department would arm any of the vessels going up the river beyond Sioux City.[5] Surely the *Miner* must have had sufficient fire power to protect itself. But he was at St. Louis, and the *Miner* far up the Missouri somewhere. He could neither confirm nor deny; he could only wait and see.[6]

One such rumor merely whetted the public appetite. During May and June, the newspapers served up more unconfirmed reports that were tossed around from column to column. This latest batch said that the regular troops had been severely defeated on the plains[7] and that General George A. Custer had been killed.[8] When the military authorities would not admit the truth of such

[2] *Nebraska Advertiser* (Brownsville), May 16, 1867.

[3] The *Nonpareil* (Council Bluffs, Iowa) seemed to think it was true; the *Nebraska Advertiser* thought it needed confirmation; the *New York Times* was doubtful.

[4] Dodge to Sherman, May 13, 1867. William T. Sherman Papers, Volume 21.

[5] General Order No. 8, March 26, 1867. General Orders, Division of the Missouri, 1865–82. Records of the War Department, U. S. Army Commands, National Archives.

[6] Portions of this chapter dealing with the rumors that circulated during the spring of 1867 have appeared in Robert G. Athearn, "The Fort Buford 'Massacre,'" *The Mississippi Valley Historical Review*, Vol. XLI, No. 4 (March, 1955), 675–84.

[7] *Leavenworth Daily Times*, May 9, 1867.

[8] *Ibid.*, June 28, 1867; *New York Times*, July 1, 1867.

tales, the editors pouted that information was being withheld by
the army. When these accounts of supposed military reverses
were proved untrue, the papers next took up the report that a
Catholic bishop and his party had been wiped out near Fort
Larned. Sherman had no such information and was bold enough
to say so. Then he was excoriated by a Leavenworth editor who
was furious at him for suggesting that such stories were fabricated to satisfy a purpose.[9] Nor did Sherman win any friends
in the newspaper world by making even so mild a statement as,
"I think journalists should endeavor to ascertain the truth before shocking the public with such terrible announcements."[10]

But all these gossipy tidbits were mere *hors d'oeuvres* for the
public's palate. The main course came during the spring of 1867,
and it was nearly two months before it could be thrown out as
unsavory. This time it was a rumor to the effect that a whole
military post had been wiped out high up on the Missouri River.
It was so far up the river that no one could battle the frozen
wastes to find out the truth. According to the Philadelphia *Inquirer,* "a private letter, dated Fort Sully, Dakota Territory, Feb.
25," just received, related how the tiny command at Fort Buford
had been annihilated. The details—printed appropriately on
All Fools' Day—described how the fort, situated at the confluence of the Missouri and Yellowstone rivers, had been heavily
attacked by Indians. All hands, of course, fought bravely until
they were overpowered and killed. The commanding officer,
Brevet Colonel William Galloway Rankin, and his wife were
said to have escaped bodily harm in the initial onslaught, only
to be reserved for the more legendary treatment so well known
to the readers of western adventure stories. "They then took
them a few yards from the post, having built a fire, tied the
Colonel's hands and feet and put him in the fire, while his wife
was compelled to see him burning. After that was done they
maltreated her in a shameful manner, and having rolled her
up in a buffalo robe, they fastened her on a wild horse and
turned him loose." By the time readers got this far in the news-

9 *Daily Missouri Republican,* July 25, 1867.
10 *New York Times,* July 24, 1867.

paper account, they must have been simply bug-eyed with suspense. But there was more; the reporter was just getting warmed up. "God only knows how long she was on the prairie," the story continued, "but it happened, very fortunately, that the mail carriers for that fort encountered her in that condition, and after they had heard who she was they took her in charge and returned her and the mails to Fort Rice." No further excitement seems to have occurred, and the journalist concluded his efforts, almost anti-climactically, by saying that the Indians had scalped all the dead, and "those who were officers they cut up into small pieces and ate them."[11]

A Washington, D. C., dispatch of April 1 gave the Colonel a little better billing. This story named the source of information as a letter from "the wife of a distinguished Army officer at St. Louis." Her information revealed that Rankin's force had fought off two or three thousand Indians, killing three hundred and wounding over one thousand before being overwhelmed. Before he was killed, he reportedly paid his wife the kindness of shooting her so that she would not fall into the hands of the Indians. The informant did not reveal just how the casualty report on the Indians' side came to hand.[12]

Even the *Army and Navy Journal* believed the rumor and devoted much of the front page of its April 6 issue to it. That weekly demanded an explanation and the fixing of responsibility for the atrocity. It also expressed the hope that such an affair would awaken the public to the army's almost impossible task on the frontier. "The currency-tinkers and dove-of-peace philosophers who have been accusing our officers of having cosy overpaid places, with nothing to do except to practice against an 'inoffensive' race of red men, ought now to keep quiet, for very shame," the editor clucked.[13] To the *New York Daily Tribune*, the affair was further evidenced that the western army was inadequate. It complained sharply about half-measures and charged

[11] The Philadelphia *Inquirer*, April 1, 1867, quoted in the *New York Times*, April 2, 1867.

[12] *New York Times*, April 2, 1867.

[13] April 6, 1867.

that the forces sent to deal with the Indians were "just large enough in every case . . . to secure their own slaughter."[14]

The original story in the *Inquirer* and the letter from the army officer's wife, which was said to confirm the report, were carried widely in the nation's newspapers. Anti-administration papers seized upon it as proof of failure on the part of those responsible at Washington. The *Chicago Daily Times,* for example, charged the radicals in Congress with a subversive plot to regain their slipping power by encouraging an Indian war. "It—congress—finds itself obligated to economize its resources. It sees the coveted Negro vote of the south slipping from its grasp; it is losing its hold upon the conservative element of its own party; it discovers that it is growing in *impuissance* as rapidly as it once grew in power. To preserve to itself such strength as may be contained in this border influence, and to avail itself to the powerful patronage arising from a state of war, congress will undoubtedly lend itself to aiding the grim politic-tragedy about to be enacted on our frontiers."[15] The Detroit *Free Press* joined the chorus and accused Secretary of War Stanton of being "closeted with his radical friends and intriguing with Congress against his official superior. He was just then arranging the details of the Southern military occupation programme and had no time to attend to the safety of the far western frontier posts."[16] Sherman must have smiled at the bombshells being hurled at Congress and Stanton. It was nice to have someone else as the target for a change.

For the man on the street, the reaction to such an affair probably was one of curiosity rather than violence against those who might be held culpable. Where was Fort Buford? How could such a tragedy have happened? Who was Colonel Rankin? Did he actually have a wife at that remote outpost? Was the rumor true? The average newspaper reader knew even less about Fort Buford than he did about most of the remote western posts, for it was not yet a year old when reports of its destruction reached the public. Back in April of 1866, Colonel Rankin had been

14 April 3, 1867.
15 April 3, 1867.
16 The Detroit *Free Press,* quoted by the *Cleveland Plain Dealer,* April 4, 1867.

ordered to proceed to the vicinity of Fort Union, a trading post on the Missouri River near the Montana line, to erect a small military establishment. By June 15, he had landed his command, consisting of seventy men from the Thirteenth U. S. Infantry (Sherman's old outfit), about eight or ten miles downriver from Fort Union. Here he laid out the ground plan of the new fort. Within a week the troops had a sawmill running and were turning out boards for the construction of the post, which was to be named after Major General John Buford, of Civil War fame.[17]

To Colonel Rankin's intense annoyance, his labors were halted early in August by the arrival of an Indian peace commission which requested a guard. "That 'Peace Commission' which by its energetic endeavors in the wrong direction, by its extraordinary promises and measures, totally at variance and sometimes in direct opposition to the published and established rules and regulations of the War Department . . . succeeded in creating more disturbance, dissatisfaction and finally outright hostilities, than all the alleged depredations and outrages by the whites since Gen. Sully's expedition," Rankin wrote bitterly. Sherman must have read these words with a smile. They fitted his impression of peace commissioners exactly; the words could well have come from his own pen. Further along in his report, Rankin wrote that he had complied with the request for soldiers to accompany the commissioners and some traders who were along. With grim satisfaction he told how, despite the presence of the troops, the Indians had helped themselves to several times the quantity of goods agreed upon, as the unhappy whites, vastly outnumbered, glumly looked on. "Finally, their barter being over, by way of ratification of their trade, and to evince their adherence to, and compliance with their peaceful contracts and agreements with the aforesaid 'Peace Commission,' they (the Indians) let fly a

[17] The best account of the founding of Fort Buford is found in the report of Brevet Colonel W. G. Rankin, December 31, 1866. Letters and Telegrams Received, 1866–68, Headquarters of the Army. Other works that deal with the early days of the post are: Joseph Mills Hanson, *The Conquest of the Missouri;* Theo. F. Rodenbough and William L. Haskin, *The Army of the United States;* Joseph Henry Taylor, *Sketches of Frontier and Indian Life on the Upper Missouri and Great Plains;* James P. Kimball, *A Soldier-Doctor of Our Army* (ed. by Maria Brace Kimball); and Lucile M. Kane (ed.), *Military Life in Dakota.*

volley of arrows among the traders wounding one man and a boy, and then departed on their ways."[18]

From that time on, the Indians struck the new fort periodically, running off cattle, killing unprotected woodchoppers, and putting continuous pressure on the troops in general. In November, Crow's Breast, a Gros Ventre chief, passed on the information that large bodies of Sioux were gathering in the vicinity, determined that the new post must not survive. During December, six miners, en route to "the States," were obliged to seek shelter at the fort, and Rankin put them to work "without compensation, being only furnished one ration per day."[19] Despite Rankin's inhospitable attitude, the men were probably glad enough to stay behind the protective walls of the fort. On December 20, the seriousness of their plight was demonstrated to any who doubted the Indians' intentions, for on that day a civilian coming over from Fort Union was attacked and his horse killed within five hundred yards of the post. The next day the Indians swooped in and struck at the sawmill, Rankin's pride and joy. They were driven off, but on the twenty-third they returned, this time capturing the sawmill and the icehouse. "A few shots from my 12 pdrs soon drove them skulking away to the cover of the gullies, willows and woods," the commander reported. The Indians came back on the following day, however, and this time tried to burn the haystacks. When this project failed, they once more captured the sawmill, and it was with difficulty that the troops, aided by the twelve-pounders, drove them out.

The Indians now called for a talk. They explained that they felt no resentment toward the traders, but that the Peace Commission had promised them plenty of ammunition, and now "the military" would not let them have it. Unless the commanding officer at Fort Buford gave them ammunition or allowed them to trade for it, the Sioux promised to "wipe every soldier on the Missouri River out of existence"; and if they could not take the

18 Report of Brevet Colonel W. G. Rankin, December 31, 1866. Letters and Telegrams Received, 1866–68, Headquarters of the Army.

19 Post Returns, Fort Buford, February, 1867. Office of the Adjutant General, Records of the War Department, National Archives.

fort, they would prevent its occupants from getting wood, which would soon freeze them out.

On January 1, 1867, the fort was again threatened by a large force, but when a single shot was fired from one of the twelve-pounders, the Indians moved out of range and retreated to Fort Union, where they made a number of threats to the traders against the soldiers.[20] During February, a very heavy attack occurred in which one of the civilian employees was killed.[21] From that time on there were no more sorties against the little post, although in March, Rankin wrote that he had not been able to send out any mail since January 17.[22]

While the Sioux and Rankin's men were exchanging compliments and shots on the Missouri, the press throughout "the States" continued to fret about the "massacre" which was said to have occurred. The report had appeared in most of the nation's papers on April 2, and in the next few issues there was some wrangling about its veracity. By the sixth, Chicago papers carried a dispatch from St. Louis to the effect that a gentleman from that city had received a letter from Fort Sully, carrying a date later than the one upon which the story was based, which stated that all was well in the Upper Missouri country. In addition, it was pointed out that General Sherman, with headquarters at St. Louis, knew nothing of any such massacre, and he was not inclined to believe the rumor. As early as March 29—two days before the story appeared in print—Sherman had heard the disturbing story and at that time had written, "I cannot deny the report but hardly believe it possible."[23] He made no further comment on his feelings in the matter other than an ominous note directed to headquarters, asking that office to "find out for me the name of the wife of the distinguished officer at St. Louis who confirmed the report of the massacre at Fort Buford."[24] When and if he found out, heads would surely roll.

[20] Post Returns, Fort Buford, January, 1867.
[21] *Ibid.*, February, March, and April, 1867.
[22] *Ibid.*, March, 1867.
[23] Sherman to Augur, March 29, 1867. C. C. Augur Papers.
[24] Sherman to the Assistant Adjutant General, April 6, 1867. Division of the Missouri, Letters Received, 1866–69, Special File. Early in May, Sherman told

The press would not let the affair alone. Although the New York papers told of a letter Sherman was said to have received from Rankin, carrying a date subsequent to that of the supposed disaster, the *Times* seemed to take this as fresh proof of slaughter in far-off Dakota. "We fear this denial is of doubtful authenticity. It is vague in its terms and without any responsible name." The paper insisted that without official word to the contrary, it would have to stick by its earlier position. Certainly, said the editors, if such a catastrophe had happened, it was due to the "incapacity, ignorance or willful blindness" of army men who had charge of the frontier, and it was "but natural" for them to try to divert the public mind by concealing the facts.[25] Papers from New England to the Ohio Valley took much the same point of view, complaining that nothing official, confirming or denying, had yet come forward.[26] Even the *Army and Navy Journal* refused to discard such an interesting story completely. In its issue of April 13, that journal surmised that the movements of the Indians in the vicinity of Fort Buford were "so well known as to add probability to the rumor of disaster."

Toward the middle of May, rumors of the fort's destruction began to die out. By the eighth of May, Sherman had written to Grant that citizens who had left Buford on April 16 had arrived at Omaha with the news that "Col. Rankin and garrison were all well. The report of the massacre originated in Chicago."[27] Newspapers now rushed to the position of denial, each trying to be the first to give the new version. In the Far West, a California paper explained to its readers that the story was a hoax which had been fabricated in Chicago and accused papers of that city of trading in rumor to hurt the commercial life of its rivals.[28] The *New York Times* now took the same position, at last confess-

Stanton that "if . . . this cruel rumor was started by interested parties, we should hunt them up, and no fate would be too hard for them." Sherman to Stanton, May 5, 1867. Division of the Missouri, Letters Received, 1866–69, Special File.

25 April 10, 1867.

26 Boston *Herald,* quoted by the *New York Times,* April 12, 1867; *Cleveland Plain Dealer,* April 12, 1867.

27 *Leavenworth Daily Times,* May 10, 1867.

28 *Sacramento Daily Union,* May 19, 1867.

ing that it had been taken in this time. "The story probably had its origin among emigrants' agents, who were interested in turning the tide of emigration from the Northwest to points further South . . . ," the editor speculated. And then, with righteous indignation for also having been a victim of the hoax, the management lamented that "it is almost impossible to conceive a mind base enough to invent so malicious a falsehood, one so calculated to wring the feelings of those who had friends in that isolated garrison."[29]

Sherman was probably amused at the paper's embarrassment, but without doubt he found some satisfaction in its dilemma. Maybe those editors would think twice before being swindled again by such stories. It was only a fond hope. Like disappointed lovers, they would recover from the reverse in sufficient time to be taken in by the charms of another and more attractive rumor as it flirted by. It was in the nature of things. But it was the army officers in command who had to pay for all this misspent printer's ink. So often they had no immediate answer, since the subject of the rumor might be hundreds of miles away, beyond communication facilities, in some remote place like Fort Buford. And while they waited for information, they were subjected to scathing comments from indignant citizens who railed at them for not even knowing what was happening on the plains. As in the case of the Buford incident, most of the reports were pure figments of someone's misguided imagination and contained not one shred of truth.

Towards the end of the year, when Sherman wrote his annual report, he turned to the subject and patiently outlined the problems it involved. "During the past year we have been infinitely embarrassed by many causes that I trust will not occur again. In the early part of the year there seemed to be a concerted and mischievous design to precipitate hostilities by a series of false reports almost without parallel, such as that referred to at Fort Buford, and the subsequent report of massacre of all the people on board the steamboat *Miner,* both of which were manufactured out of whole cloth." Nor were these all, he wrote wearily. They

[29] May 19, 1867.

"were followed by exaggerations of similar nature on the other travelled roads, such as that of Moore's ranch, on the Platte, and of Bishop Lamy's party on the Arkansas. These may have originated in a natural rivalry for business of the others by these inventions and exaggerations; but the truth is, that all the roads have been seriously damaged thereby, and worse, yet, emigration to the mountain Territories has been seriously checked by them. There is and can be no remedy for such things until the people in general learn to measure such reports by the experience of the past."[30]

But the avaricious, ever pushing merchants, fearful of missing out on this bonanza rush westward, were little concerned about the army's problems. Soldiers were merely the government's "hired hands," whose job it was to protect the citizens wherever they went and in whatever they wanted to do. The taxpayers footed the bill, didn't they? And so, with difficulties like extended communication lines, hundreds of dusty miles served only by a rude trace etched through unpeopled areas, an ever diminishing army, loud cries for help from the scattered settlements in the West, and persistent attacks at widely distant points by a cunning and skillful enemy, men like Sherman slogged along in what gave every appearance of being a losing battle. Piled atop all these physical problems was the unnecessary and insidious enemy of rumor, darting back and forth across the plains, a tantalizing apparition, impossible to anticipate and wraithlike in substance. Small wonder that Sherman thirsted for the name of "the wife of the distinguished army officer" who had fanned the blaze of rumor about Fort Buford. To be struck from behind, as it were, by a member of the army family was the final aggression. As he contemplated this piece of treachery, he probably wondered how the gentlemen from New York were enjoying the sea breezes from the cabin deck of the *Quaker City*. Hang it all, Minnie had been right!

30 Report of W. T. Sherman, October 1, 1867, *Annual Report of the Secretary of War*, 40 Cong., 2 sess., *House Exec. Doc. No. 1* (Serial 1324), pp. 36–37.

Nine

EVERYBODY IS SCARED

As the summer of 1867 approached, Sherman realized that he was being forced into a dilemma. Despite all the careful planning and the skillful husbanding of meager resources, it began to appear that forces beyond his control would intervene to frustrate the whole scheme of things. The Indian Bureau was demonstrating its power at Washington by clucking angrily at the army every time a soldier leveled his carbine at one of the wandering tribesmen. At the same time, the press was increasingly militant. The Fetterman affair, followed so closely by the Buford "massacre," had inflamed the public mind to an almost hysterical pitch, and western newspapers daily demanded the demise of every Indian in sight. Between the two camps stood Sherman, at leash. He was ready and willing to act, but the yelps of the humanitarians were forcing the War Department, for the moment, to say to him, "At heel."

The influence of the peace faction infuriated those who lived beyond the Missouri. From Omaha came the demand that the government stop its "damnable twaddling and trifling with the interests of millions of people." The issue must be clarified, and it was relatively simple. "Give us peace or give us war."[1] To the businessman of that Missouri River town, it was imperative that the lines of western traffic be kept open. The Union Pacific was its most recent prize, and any danger to the rails brought immediate complaints. Augur would keep travel moving, Omaha people told each other, and he would do it despite the "ridiculous bungling of the civil authorities." Even attempts to protect the Platte Valley brought complaints from other western sections. From the Northwest came bitter talk that the moneyed

[1] *Omaha Weekly Herald,* March 15, 1867.

interests, represented by the Union Pacific, were getting the lion's share of military attention, while less fortunate souls, living in more remote regions, were neglected.[2] Already the West was experiencing growing pains, and its very development revealed fissures of sectional splits. With the coming of steel rails— the hallmark of the eastern industrial giant—such a place as Omaha soon would be viewed by those farther west as "East."

The cries for action did not diminish. Kansans hooted at the "Utopian, humanitarian ideas that largely prevail in the East" and too heavily influenced Washington. They demanded that the Indian be "subjugated and not bought and pampered."[3] Still farther west, the sentiment was stronger. A warlike letter writer from Denver said bluntly that "vigorous war is what the people of the frontier demand" and called for "more powder and lead and less 'talk.' "[4] A Utah paper spoke freely of the prospect of a general Indian war on the plains during the next few months and recommended changing "our ridiculous tactics" of Interior Department control.[5] The editor struck a familiar theme when he recommended the use of two or three frontier regiments, "men led by determined officers conversant with Indian warfare."[6] West of Utah, the feeling seemed stronger yet. A bill was introduced into the Nevada legislature recommending the withdrawal of federal troops and the payment of cash for each scalp brought in by white volunteers.[7]

Such violent use of the pen upset the staid *New York Times*. "What shall be done with the Indians?" asked the editor helplessly. And then fussing like an old lady on the subject of sin, he tried to answer his own question. He complained that between the belligerent army officers and corrupt traders working with the Indian Bureau, it was almost impossible to get the true story. The only solution seemed to be force, the paper ruefully admitted, but cautioned that the Indians must not be extermi-

[2] *Owyhee Avalanche* (Silver City, Idaho), February 9, 1867.

[3] *Junction City Weekly Union* (Junction City, Kansas), May 4, 1867.

[4] Letter signed "Colorado" in the *Daily Missouri Republican*, May 9, 1867.

[5] *Daily Union Vedette*, March 13, 1867.

[6] *Ibid.*, April 11, 1867. The same sentiment was expressed by a writer identified as "Veritas" in the *Army and Navy Journal*, Vol. IV (April 20, 1867), 553.

[7] *Daily Union Vedette*, March 13, 1867.

nated.[8] To follow this advice would pose problems of campaigning that would cause the most experienced Indian fighter to
pause and think. But the journalist had to talk in generalities,
because he was obliged to say something on a subject so current,
while not knowing what to say. A few issues later, he became
a little bolder and asked that the coming summer campaign be
"short, sharp and decisive" in the interest of "justice and humanity to the Indian as well as the white man."[9] Westerners probably smiled at this and allowed as how the *Times* editor was
getting plumb hostile.

While the newspaper poured out advice as colorfully as an old
sergeant instructing his recruits, Sherman gave no indication
that he was listening. Instead of entering the free-for-all, he
talked quietly with his departmental commanders, outlining the
discipline that would be necessary in the trying months ahead.
While he admitted to Augur that he would "like to have those
Sioux about the Big Horn & Yellowstone taken down a good
many notches," he said such action would have to wait until the
peace commissioners were through "making medicine" with the
tribes. "Still if they molest travel or intercourse along the Road
from [Forts] Reno, Phil Kearney and C. F. Smith to Virginia
City, I want them attacked, commissioners or no commissioners.
Those Indians are emboldened by past success and we must take
the conceit out of them, else there is no telling to what extent they
may go." If the Sioux kept the peace, treat them as peaceful
people, and above all, advise them that they were now dealing
with regular officers. With regulars on the job, they would have
no reason to fear such an event as the Chivington affair, which
was being used by the Indians as the supreme example of bad
faith on the part of the army.[10]

Augur's task would be the same as Cooke's had been the preceding summer. Sherman outlined his duties carefully so that
there would be no doubt about procedure. He was to guard the
mail and telegraph lines westward, as far as Utah, and, at the

[8] *New York Times,* April 23, 1867.
[9] *Ibid.,* April 30, 1867.
[10] Sherman to Augur, March 12, 1867. C. C. Augur Papers.

same time, protect the railroad construction crews. The settlements in Nebraska, northern Colorado, and southern Montana were to be aided as much as possible, under the circumstances.

Aside from these more or less routine duties of protection, Augur was advised to "enforce and command that respect to our military power which alone enables us to fulfil our office." Sherman did not let the generality stand; he explained to his subordinate just what he meant. The Sioux along the road to Montana had thrown down the gauntlet, and, as he had written earlier, they had to be punished. They had shamed the army, and Sherman could not rest until the act had been avenged. The success the Sioux had enjoyed along the road during the preceding summer, reaching a climax in December near Fort Phil Kearney, had caused them to become "bold and insolent in the highest degree." If this situation were ignored, the war parties would next swoop down on the thin lines of communication and strike at isolated settlements. Provide for the safety of the main roads, Sherman wrote, and then get your forces together and head for the Powder River country. Ignore departmental lines if hostile bands are being pursued and follow the Indians until they are caught and punished.

Earlier in the spring, Sherman had cautioned Augur that the peace commissioners had prior rights with the Sioux, but now, as summer neared, he threw all caution to the winds and boldly tipped his hand. "If the Peace Commissioners . . . promise any substantial results, you should of course defer to them, but the season allowed us in that latitude for military operations is too short for us to await their action. Therefore you may go ahead with your preparations, as though they were sure to fail. The question of whether the Indians mean peace or war will be simple enough by the time you can have your troops on the spot."[11] Nor did he make any attempt to mask his plans when writing headquarters. He explained that the peace commissioners were down along the Platte, talking with Indians that were now, and had been, peaceable. "I don't see what is the use of treating with

11 Sherman to Augur, April 14, 1867. Division of the Missouri, Letters Received, 1866–69, Special File.

them," he complained. The hostile Sioux were ranging just to the north, and it was with them that the government really had to deal. He revealed that Augur had been instructed to get among them and to press his attack. They were now "boastful and insolent," and perhaps in that mood they might accept battle, "which will be the best thing to hope for." In any event, a circle tour, from Phil Kearney to the mouth of the Yellowstone and back around to the north, would have a good effect. "In that district of country there are no peaceful Indians, and General Augur can hardly go amiss."[12] The Indian Bureau be damned; this was his command. The people needed protection, and they would get it.

To Hancock, in the Department of Missouri, went much the same kind of advice. Sherman pointed out again that the Indians, by law, were under the Interior Department's management. This "deprives us of a legal right to control them and prevents our adopting preventive measures." However, it was the duty of the army to protect "our own people," and that included settlers on lawful locations, mail routes, and lines of travel. In view of the fact that the Cheyennes, Arapahoes, and Kiowas were reported to have been concentrating along the Smoky Hill route and were defying their agents, the army necessarily would be involved in protecting the whites. Should there be any depredations, Hancock was to strike at once and "punish on the spot." Sherman counseled caution in the matter of indiscriminate killing. "I have no fear that you or any officer under you will kill or injure unresisting people of any race or kind," he wrote, but confessed that such an impression was abroad concerning Hancock's projected sally into hostile country. He would reassure the War Department of the General's peaceful intentions.[13]

[12] Sherman to Leet, April 20, 1867. Division of the Missouri, Letters Received, 1866–69, Special File.

[13] Sherman to Hancock, March 14, 1867. Letters and Telegrams Received, 1866–68, Headquarters of the Army. Two days earlier Sherman had written to Augur that he had recently talked with Hancock and that the latter was merely going among the Cheyennes and Arapahoes "to show them that he is ready and willing to fight them, but will not attack them unless they require chastisement." Sherman to Augur, March 12, 1867. C. C. Augur Papers. Early in April Sherman reassured headquarters that Hancock was not operating against Indians in the

Sherman was smoking cigars in the powder house. He may have been aware of it and was simply willing to gamble. Hancock was ambitious and had under his command some hot-blooded young officers. One of them was George Armstrong Custer, whom Sherman himself called "young, very brave even to rashness, a good trait for a Cavalry officer," but admitted that "he has not too much sense" and he had "no excuses to offer for his attempt to act a political part."[14] Hancock himself complained that he could not go after the Indians the way he wanted and "settle things definitely." Even when he forced himself to be co-operative with the Indian agents and let them go along with him in the field, they complicated matters by advising the Indians on how much they should talk and what they should say.[15] The situation was explosive, and with his command set on hair trigger, Sherman would indeed be lucky if his readiness to fight did not get him into more trouble than he wanted. And then the humanitarians would follow him in wolf packs, crying "murder."

As the western prairies began to take on a hint of pale green and cottonwoods along the streams threatened to leaf out, the entire West grew increasingly tense. A Leavenworth paper nervously predicted trouble as it told of letters it had received from the various territories. They all coincided in the belief that an Indian war was at hand.[16] Omaha echoed the apprehension and bravely expressed confidence in General Sherman's notion of punishing Indians but pointed out that it was a big order, and to do it, he must first catch them.[17] Sherman stood pat and said nothing, much to the annoyance of editors who constantly accused the army of withholding information. He had made his plans. When the opportunity came, he would act. Meanwhile, the Indians were getting restive. The weather was warmer and the

---

Platte Region, but against Cheyennes, Arapahoes, Kiowas, and Comanches south of the Arkansas, where disturbances had been reported. Sherman to Leet, April 2, 1867. Letters and Telegrams Received, 1866–68, Headquarters of the Army.

14 Sherman to John Sherman, February 24, 1867. William T. Sherman Papers, Volume 20.

15 Hancock to Sherman, May 1, 1867. Letters and Telegrams Received, 1866–68, Headquarters of the Army.

16 *Leavenworth Daily Times*, April 11, 1867.

17 *Omaha Weekly Herald*, May 3, 1867.

hunting season was near. The young bucks were uneasy, after a winter's confinement, and they were impatient to get out and range the trails. As they limbered their short hunting bows or tinkered with brand-new Indian Bureau rifles, they thought about targets and cared little whether they were four-legged or two-legged. Time ticked stealthily on, and both sides waited quietly, reflexes taut, ready to spring.

And then some fool civilian in Montana fired off a wild shot.

With his mind filled with problems of military planning, his path blocked by the Indian Bureau and Washington's nervousness that he might do something violent, Sherman hardly expected trouble in the quarter from which it came. The first hint of difficulty appeared when he picked up a telegram dated April 9, forwarded by Grant, from Virginia City, Montana. That country was threatened by the Sioux, the dispatch said. "The greatest alarm reasonably prevails. . . . Danger is imminent & will overpower unless measures for defense are instantly taken." Volunteers, to be hired by the federal government, were needed at once, the message urged. Sherman ran his eye down the telegram. It was signed "Thomas Francis Meagher, Actg. Govr."[18]

The name brought back old memories. It was a well-known name. Meagher, a brilliant young Irishman, had come to the world's attention back in 1848 when he participated in an abortive rebellion against England. He had been tried, along with other revolutionaries, and shipped off to Tasmania. After a few years he had escaped, and soon turned up in New York, where he became the darling of the American Irish. When the war broke out, he joined the Sixty-Ninth Regiment, New York State Militia, as a captain. The regiment was a part of Sherman's command at the Battle of Bull Run, and here the eager young captain and the acid colonel locked horns. Sherman did not conduct the movement to suit Meagher, and after the battle the latter rushed back to New York and published the opinion that the Colonel was "a rude and envenomed martinet" who was "hated by the regiment."[19] Sherman, the subject of so much abuse from

[18] Meagher to Grant, April 9, 1867. Letters and Telegrams Received, 1866–68, Headquarters of the Army.

[19] Robert G. Athearn, *Thomas Francis Meagher: An Irish Revolutionary in America*, 96.

the press at the time, never forgot the young man who had taken to the inkstand to hurl insults.

After the war, Meagher cast about for a position. By ingratiating himself with President Johnson, he succeeded in getting an appointment as secretary to the new territory of Montana. When he arrived at his post, he was met by Governor Sidney Edgerton, who hastily thrust the few official documents he possessed into Meagher's hands and headed for "the States," leaving the startled secretary as acting governor. The ambitious Irishman, who envisaged himself as the first senator from what he hoped would soon be the state of Montana, at once set about making a name for himself. As a "war hero" who had led the fabled Irish Brigade during the recent hostilities, it seemed only natural that he now apply his military talents to the solution of Montana's Indian problem. It was a ready-made opportunity, and he lost no time in grasping it. There were Indians around. The gold panning was getting light, and the miners were anxious to spread out in their search for treasure. Driving off the Indians would serve the dual purpose of opening up new prospecting areas and committing the currently popular act of "killin' Injuns." All that was needed was a man who would take hold of the situation and act. For the role, Meagher was a natural.[20]

Sherman was annoyed. Back in February of 1866, Meagher had demanded a whole regiment of cavalry to protect his territory. It was absurd. "You ask for a Regiment of Cavalry," he had answered the Acting Governor. "I now have one Regiment of Regular Cavalry (the 2nd) for Montana, Dakota, Nebraska, Colorado, Kansas and New Mexico." It was unreasonable to expect that protection should be given one remote territory while the others were left unprotected. He had told Meagher so. Nothing more had been heard from the mercurial executive until now. Like all western territories, however, Montana displayed an unusual nervousness in the spring of 1867. During the winter reports had filtered into settlements like Helena and Virginia

20 For a further discussion of the Montana Indian situation, see Merrill Burlingame, *The Montana Frontier*, or Athearn, *Meagher*, chap. XI; Robert G. Athearn, "General Sherman and the Montana Frontier," *The Montana Magazine of History*, Vol. III, No. 1 (January, 1953), 55-65.

City that when the grass grew in the spring, Red Cloud and his Sioux warriors would sweep into the exposed Gallatin Valley and wipe out such places as Bozeman. These Indians had retreated westward after the great Sioux uprising in Minnesota during 1862. Now there was pressure from the south since the Arapahoes and Cheyennes were being shoved away from the railroad as it nudged along the Platte Valley. Reports had it that Red Cloud was trying to organize a confederation of these Indians, along with his own, to drive the white man forever from the rich buffalo country that was Montana.

Meagher's telegram of April 9 to Grant brought him very little comfort. The General had simply noted on it, for Sherman's guidance, that if Montanans were in danger, they ought to organize to defend themselves, "and if the services rendered by them warrant it, they should afterward look to Congress for compensation." Meagher knew, if Sherman and Grant did not, that this would not work. The merchants had no interest in long and drawn-out negotiations with Congress to regain such monies expended. The only thing Meagher could do, to induce action, was to find some Indians and get a war going. That he had thought of it earlier is suggested in a letter of the Commissioner of Indian Affairs, who said the Acting Governor "had not acted prudently toward the Indians" and had warned that it might involve the government in a large expense if he persisted.[21]

Then, in the spring of 1867, Meagher's chance presented itself. During April, John Bozeman and Thomas Cover were stopped by some Indians while en route to a government fort where they hoped to get a contract for the sale of some flour. Bozeman was killed; Cover, slightly wounded, returned to the Gallatin Valley with a tale of murder at the hands of the Indians. As a resident of Helena disgustedly wrote, "And now the cry is War to the Knife. The most that possibly can be made out of all this cry about Indians is, that two men foolishly start to travel through an Indian country without protection, and meet with the fate

[21] D. N. Cooley to James Harlan, secretary of the interior, April 10, 1866. Territorial Papers of Montana, Volume 1, Department of State Archives, National Archives.

before mentioned. There is a bare possibility that the Indians might come to the Gallatin Valley, but the prospects or evidences up to this time certainly do not warrant the warlike movements that are being made by our officials."[22]

The warlike movements mentioned by the writer came principally from Thomas Francis Meagher, known by less enthusiastic Montanans as "the Acting One." On April 24, in response to the excitement arising out of Bozeman's murder, he called a war meeting in Helena. He told a group of excited miners that there was no militia in the territory and that any military action had to be spontaneous and voluntary. According to a local newspaper, he dramatically related that "the passes of the mountains were the ramparts of Montana; blood had been shed, life sacrificed; the exigencies of the case demanded action, and he, for one, would leave immediately for the threatened quarter, with whoever would bear him company."[23] He called for six hundred volunteers that night, and before long, Montana had an "army" of its own, bent on saving the territory.

Not everyone looked with enthusiasm upon Meagher's efforts to reduce the Indians "to friendly and reliable relations with the whites." A. H. Chapman, an Indian agent in Montana, denounced the proceedings vehemently.[24] "Acting Governor Meagher's Indian war in Montana is the biggest humbug of the age, got up to advance his political interest, and to enable a lot of bummers who surround and hang onto him to make a big raid on the United States treasury. . . . When volunteers are sent out and told by the commander, as General Meagher told those under his command in a general order *that they shall have all the property they capture*, such as robes, horses, etc. it would be strange indeed if they did not create unnecessary trouble with the Indians."[25]

22 Nowland to Sherman, May 14, 1867. Division of the Missouri, Letters Received, 1866–69, Special File.

23 *Montana Post*, April 27, 1867.

24 The foregoing paragraphs have been previously published by the author in "Early Territorial Montana: A Problem in Colonial Administration," *The Montana Magazine of History*, Vol. I, No. 3 (July, 1951), 15–22.

25 Report of A. H. Chapman, *Annual Report of the Secretary of the Interior*, 1867, 40 Cong., 2 sess., *House Exec. Docs.* (Serial 1326), pp. 259–60.

For once, Sherman agreed with a representative of the Indian Bureau. He had been caught in a cross fire between public opinion that demanded annihilation and the peacemakers, who represented the Indian Bureau and humanitarians in general, and now here was a new adversary for him to consider. The territorial governors were also representatives of the federal government, and as chief executives of their own political divisions, they had to be handled by the army with care. Meagher's action in Montana caused an outcry from both War and Interior departments, each of which charged an invasion of its field of operations. They were united, momentarily, in common defense.

After Meagher's request for aid had been considered by President Johnson, General Grant, and War Department officials, Stanton telegraphed Sherman the decision which would be henceforth considered official policy. It was the undivided opinion of those at Washington that to confer upon territorial officers the power of raising troops was a dangerous thing. They even doubted whether it was possible. However, if troops were seriously needed in Montana, Sherman was authorized to call out militia, provided it was under his command. In such an emergency, the army would equip and subsist such a force until the immediate danger was past.[26]

Sherman agreed immediately with the substance of Stanton's telegram. "You are perfectly right that discretion to call out the militia in Montana, or any of our Territories, cannot safely be lodged with their Governors, for, to be candid, each has an interest antagonistic to that of the United States. Meagher, in Montana, is a stampeder, and can always with a fair show of truth raise a clamor, and would have in pay the maximum number of men allowed." Nor was Montana unique. Sherman now considered the whole problem of territorial defense. In Utah, for example, the population was so scattered that it would be almost impossible to arm enough volunteers to answer every call for aid. In Colorado, federal troops were placed at strategic locations

[26] Stanton to Sherman, May 3, 1867. Telegrams Sent, 1866–67, Office of the Secretary of War, Volume 36, 207. Records of the War Department, National Archives.

and afforded adequate protection, but "as the people do not see the soldiers in their midst, they do not realize the fact that they are protected at all." Here, as in Montana, the people would "force any Governor to keep in pay their stay-at-home militia." To the south, in New Mexico, it was the same. In that territory there had been for some time "and will forever continue to be" an agitation for troops. If the people were so anxious to join up for their own defense, why didn't they enlist in the cavalry or infantry units assigned to that area?

The problem was a real one, and it would not easily be solved. Sherman confessed that he could not be everywhere at once to judge the necessity of calling out extra troops, and he would have to entrust one of his subordinates with that responsibility. A move of this kind, he admitted, would "be attended with risk," but it could not be avoided. It would be necessary, now that the problem had come up, to work out a general plan to be applied in such contingencies during the years to come. He complained sharply about emigrants who pushed into regions like Colorado or Montana, where the Indians must be hostile "from the nature of things," and then cried loudly for help. To protect them all was a sheer impossibility, particularly where they scattered so widely. The Westerners had some responsibility for their own safety, and they ought to conform somewhat to army plans rather than expect military protection wherever they might want to go. "Instead of extending thin settlements, and putting their horses and stock in tempting proximity to the Indians, they should make their settlements in groups and colonies capable of self-defence, and when the Indians combine against them, the white people must combine against the Indians."[27] Sherman's theory of planned settlement sounded sensible enough, from a purely military standpoint, but it did not indicate that he thoroughly understood the nature of the settlers who were demanding much more from the central government than their forefathers had ever expected. By the 1860's, some of the traditional independence and self-reliance attributed to the frontiersmen was beginning to

27 Sherman to Stanton, May 4, 1867. Division of the Missouri, Letters Received, 1866–69, Special File.

fade as the field became crowded with amateurs. Before offering their services, even those who appeared willing to join the territorial volunteers had to be assured that they would receive what they considered the "right price."

With regard to Stanton's authorization to call out the militia, Sherman demurred, and said, "I think I shall not use it now." Montanans would have to take care of themselves. The regulars would be used only to guard roads leading out to such remote settlements and for fighting those Indians who were actively at war. If the situation in Montana actually got out of hand, he would allow Terry, commanding the Department of Dakota, to organize a battalion of not more than eight hundred men. Governor Green Clay Smith, en route to Montana to replace Acting Governor Meagher, visited Sherman at his office in St. Louis early in May. The two talked over the alarming news coming out of the Northwest and agreed that Meagher was "liable to stampedes" and that "the dangers that beset Montana are the necessary incidents to its remote position." About all the help the regular army could offer at the moment was to send twenty-five hundred muskets up the river. They would be on the first boat that cast off for Fort Benton.[28]

On May 5, the day after Stanton had authorized Sherman to raise troops if necessary, the Secretary of War forwarded a telegram to St. Louis that had been received from Mayor Castner of Virginia City, Montana. It seemed that the Mayor also wanted to raise troops and was quarreling with territorial officials about who had the right to organize forces for local protection. As Stanton correctly explained, this argument alone was sufficient to show the necessity of turning such matters over to the regular army.[29] Sherman at once advised Castner that there was no need of mustering in any volunteers. "You should render this service in self-defence and so help your neighbor without the formality of muster in or muster out."[30] At the same time, he got off a tele-

28 *Ibid.*

29 Stanton to Sherman, May 5, 1867. Letters and Telegrams Received, 1866–68, Headquarters of the Army.

30 Sherman to Stanton, quoting his telegram to Castner, May 6, 1867. Letters and Telegrams Received, 1866–68, Headquarters of the Army.

gram to Augur, at Omaha, telling him that Meagher and Castner were stampeded by reports of an Indian invasion and were demanding the right to raise troops. "I am authorized to call out Volunteers if the case demands it. I don't think the case demands it as I have no faith in the parties who want to raise and command Volunteers." Admitting that the Indians had it "in their power to do mischief in that quarter," he advised Augur to push his operations in the direction of Montana, as they had planned earlier, with even greater haste.[31]

During the next twenty-four hours Sherman must have given much of his time to weighing the probabilities of danger in Montana. Perhaps there was real danger. The regulars might not get there in time. Then there would be the devil to pay in Washington. Sometime during the day of the seventh, he sent a terse telegram to Meagher that reflected his anxiety. "If Indians enter the valley of the Gallatin organize eight hundred volunteers and drive them out. Those troops should only be used until the regulars reach the Yellowstone."[32] Nothing was said about the central government's footing the bill; that it was to be an emergency measure only was understood. To Sherman, the sense of the telegram was direct and unmistakable. And in case of real trouble, he was covered.

For Thomas Francis Meagher, the recipient, the message was heaven-sent. All it needed was a little editing and it would do handily for his purpose. By the time the *Montana Post* got hold of the telegram, its first sentence read, "If Indians *threaten* the valley of the Gallatin, organize (800) eight hundred volunteers, and drive them out."[33] The degree of emergency indicated in the original dispatch had been altered for local consumption.[34]

31 Sherman to Augur, May 6, 1867. Division of the Missouri, Letters Received, 1866–69, Special File.

32 Sherman to Meagher, May 7, 1867. Testimony in relation to Indian war claims of the territory of Montana, 42 Cong., 2 sess., *Misc. Doc. No. 215* (Serial 1527), p. 1.

33 May 11, 1867. The italics are mine.

34 William H. Claggett, who testified later in the Montana war claims hearings, said, "I have heard it stated that General Sherman's telegram was charged by him to have been changed by Governor Meagher so as to read 'threatened invasion' instead of 'invasion' of the Gallatin Valley." Testimony in relation to Indian war claims of the territory of Montana, 42 Cong., 2 sess., *House Misc. Doc. No. 215* (Serial 1527), p. 5.

Harper's Weekly, May 25, 1867
Courtesy Kansas State Historical Society

Sutler's store at Fort Dodge, 1867

"The Pacific Railroad was more than parallel strips of steel;
it was a 'link in the chain which binds all mankind together.' "
Section men at Salina, 1867. Gardner photograph.

There were still no promises of future reimbursement for expenses incurred, but to some of the Montana journals, like the Helena *Herald,* the mandate was clear. The editor stated flatly that the War Department "has commanded us to muster, arm, equip, and place in the field at once 800 efficient citizen soldiery."[35] Between the editor on one hand and the governor on the other there was an undisguised attempt to encourage the merchants who were carefully watching their supplies. During this time, Sherman again refused to equip Meagher's volunteers, and on May 14, he repeated that there was "no law authorizing the enrolling of troops in a territory subject to the governor." He suggested that the emergency be met without formal organization if at all possible. These warnings did not alter the case for the Montanans.[36] In fact, no one bothered to publish them.

Happily the territorial militia organized for war. Helena newspapers carried stories about events "at the front," and printed Meagher's reports on the numbers of Indians lurking in the mountain passes near the city of Bozeman.[37] During May, the small army began to materialize, and merchants offered supplies somewhat more liberally, in the belief that the militia now had the blessing of the central government. When some difficulty developed in obtaining the desired number of horses for one of the companies, it was explained by the comments of a Helena paper: "If the dispatches from the Secretary of War and the Adjutant-General had arrived a day or two earlier the movement would have undoubtedly resulted in a success."[38] No hint was given concerning the contents of the dispatches; the inference simply was left that they also sanctioned the volunteer organization.

Sherman saw that things were now rapidly getting out of hand. He ordered Augur to send "a discreet officer" to Virginia City to assess the real necessity of calling out volunteers. Major William H. Lewis was selected for the assignment, and he reached Virginia City on May 19. A few days later, on the twenty-fourth,

[35] May 14, 1867.
[36] Report of W. T. Sherman, October 1, 1867, *Annual Report of the Secretary of War,* 40 Cong., 2 sess., *House Exec. Doc. No. 1* (Serial 1324), p. 33.
[37] *Helena Herald,* May 14, 1867.
[38] *Montana Post,* May 18, 1867, quoting the *Tri-Weekly Republican* of Helena.

he received permission from his superior at St. Louis to muster in a battalion of eight hundred men for two months' service if absolutely necessary, letting the men furnish their own arms and horses at forty cents a day, the government to provide rations, forage, and supplies.[39] Sherman the realist was dreaming; or he sought to give permission under impossible conditions so that he could later argue that he had tried to co-operate with the Governor. No troops could be raised in a mining area on those terms. It wasn't even tobacco money. Lewis immediately reported that fact. However, in the telegraphic communications between the two officers, which seem to have been made public by Lewis, the impression was left in Virginia City that once again Sherman had given permission to muster in volunteers led by territorial officers. One of the Montanans asserted that he had seen such a telegram and that the Major had waved it before some of the residents with the remark, "There, gentlemen, is authority for you; that is sufficient."[40] Another later testified that such a dispatch had reached Lewis, "and when that dispatch was made known the question was settled in the mind of the people as to the authority, and they began to get the men."[41]

During June the Montana Volunteers continued to recruit, despite the fact that Lewis decided there was no danger and so informed Sherman. By now the merchants were convinced that the federal government would pay for any supplies advanced for the cause, and they lost no time in selling their stores, at war prices, in return for vouchers signed by Thomas Francis Meagher. Lewis, having made his report to Sherman, apparently did nothing to stop the local organization. After about a month in Virginia City, he returned to Salt Lake City.[42] The Montanans

39 Sherman to Lewis, May 24, 1867. Letter from the Secretary of War, 41 Cong., 2 sess., *House Exec. Doc. No. 121* (Serial 1417), p. 2; Sherman to Grant, April 27, 1867. Telegrams Received, 1866–67, Office of the Secretary of War. Records of the War Department, National Archives.

40 Testimony of M. H. Insely, May 10, 1872. Testimony in relation to Indian war claims of the territory of Montana, 42 Cong., 2 sess., *House Misc. Doc. No. 215* (Serial 1527), p. 2.

41 Testimony of William H. Claggett, May 10, 1872. Testimony in relation to Indian war claims of the territory of Montana, 42 Cong., 2 sess., *House Misc. Doc. No. 215* (Serial 1527), p. 4.

were unabashed by this lack of interest on the part of the regular army. They continued to organize, drill, and make warlike dashes into the near-by hills. The only pall on the whole affair was that they found no Indians to fight. The Sioux did not invade the Gallatin Valley as had peen predicted. This was discouraging in view of the Governor's promise that loot would result from the expected clash. Despite the limitation of having no adversaries, or possibly because of it, the organization grew from an original 80 to around 250. From the beginning there were at least 50 line or staff officers on the rolls, and most of these carried alarmingly high rank.

On July 1, an event occurred that temporarily disrupted the rush to arms in Montana. Acting Governor Meagher made a trip to Fort Benton to receive some of the expected guns from St. Louis, and while spending the night aboard one of the river steamers, he wandered to the stern in an alcoholic haze and fell into the swift Missouri. Sherman must have received the news of Meagher's demise with mixed feelings. Governor Green Clay Smith, en route to Montana to take over executive responsibilities, was still somewhere along the river and would shortly arrive at Fort Benton. Meagher, the political opportunist, over whom Sherman had no legal control, was gone. Perhaps Smith, who agreed that the eloquent Irishman in Montana was a stampeder, would stop this nonsense. These territorial officials were as difficult to cope with as the Indian Bureau or the tribes themselves, Sherman thought. He hoped that Smith was not also imbued with notions of political grandeur.

The "volunteer virus" was not peculiar to Montana. During the spring of 1867 there was a general outbreak of the malady, and Sherman's office was the sounding board for cries echoing off the Rockies from Canada to Mexico. During May, Governor William K. Marshall of Minnesota complained to Stanton that his state must not be exposed. Couldn't he call out some volunteers? The federal government could send the money for sup-

[42] The account of the altered telegram and events following its publication have been previously published by the author in "The Montana Volunteers of 1867," *The Pacific Historical Review*, Vol. XIX, No. 2 (May, 1950), 127–37.

plies and arms. Minnesota had the men. Patiently Sherman explained to the Secretary of War that the whole Sioux Nation was not likely to rise up and strike. If such a thing should possibly happen, he would send the Tenth Infantry, and other units, out to the line of the Missouri River. In an extreme emergency it might be possible for Marshall to raise "a few Companies, say four or five," to protect public property in the state while the regulars were gone.[43]

During the same month, at a time when Acting Governor Meagher was bombarding Sherman and Stanton with telegrams from Montana, another voice chimed in. Governor Alexander C. Hunt of Colorado decided that his territory was also about to be wiped out. "Depredations from Indians on our Eastern and Western borders are of daily occurrence," he wrote, giving the impression that his people were being encircled. "The present military being mostly Infantry are entirely inadequate for the protection of settlers and the great thoroughfares. I would most respectfully ask, as in Montana, authority to organize mounted volunteers for a campaign against the savages. Three hundred friendly Utes will join the expedition with your permission."[44] The plea was addressed to Stanton. He referred it to Sherman, who agreed to take up the matter with Hunt. There was no danger in Colorado, he told the Secretary of War. The mails had not been disturbed by the Indians. It was, in his judgment, nothing more than a "conspiracy to produce trouble." Lately he had heard nothing but wild stories of alleged violence on the frontier, and the situation was steadily getting worse. "The Indian rumors unattended by fighting now extend systematically from the Arkansas clear round to Minnesota."[45]

To the Governor of Colorado went the familiar message, "There is no law to pay volunteers." If that executive wanted to raise a regiment of five hundred men to protect his own terri-

43 Sherman's endorsement of May 22 on a letter of May 3 from Marshall to Stanton. Letters and Telegrams Received, 1866–68, Headquarters of the Army.

44 Hunt to Stanton, May 27, 1867. Letters and Telegrams Received, 1866–68, Headquarters of the Army; *New York Times*, June 7, 1867.

45 Sherman to Stanton, May 29, 1867. Telegrams Received, 1866–67, Office of the Secretary of War.

tory, he could go ahead and do it.[46] When the danger had passed, the men could seek any remuneration, above that of saving their own hides, from the central government.

Hunt seemed to be of the same breed as Meagher. He was bent on saving somebody from something. And he employed the usual pressures. Alexander H. McClure, the Pennsylvania politician, was pleading with Stanton to support Hunt's application. "I have been detained here two weeks," he roared indignantly from Colorado, "because the Indians presumably raid on the Western route at pleasure, and there is no pretense of adequate military protection."[47] Politicians, Indian Bureau agents, newspaper editors, territorial governors, and ambitious young braves —they seemed allied in a conspiracy to frustrate a dwindling, much-maligned, and discouraged army. It was a Donnybrook Fair. When you saw a head, you hit it. Sherman paused and wondered once again about tilting his forces against windmills. It would have been some satisfaction to know who the enemy was and to have the chance to hit him. This kind of warfare was simply flailing at ghosts.

The matter of volunteers was one that had to be dealt with here and now, Sherman decided. There was some indecision at Washington about how to treat the requests coming in from the territorial governors. Resolutely he set about trying to formulate a policy that would accord equitable treatment. There simply were not enough funds available to glut the governors into silence. Nor would he have used them, had there been plenty. As long as the regular army was assigned the task of protecting the frontier, it would work at the task as best it knew, despite its limitations. All others who wanted to get into the act would find the doors closed to them. Meanwhile, the problem cried out for an answer.

Addressing his remarks to the governors of all the states and territories in his Division, he now outlined the situation, as it appeared to him. He asked for co-operation between western citizens and his soldiers and suggested that increased security might

[46] *New York Herald,* June 11, 1867.
[47] *New York Times,* June 7, 1867.

result if local militia worked in concert with the regulars. The governors were reminded that the army, because of its diminished forces and expanded duties, could do little more than maintain certain outposts and try to keep main-traveled roads open. It would be of assistance if each governor could organize a regiment of volunteers composed of ten companies with sixty men each. They should stand ready, and if called into service for over thirty days, they would be regularly mustered in and paid by the federal government. "I believe your young men will do this cheerfully, and that this mere precaution may ward off the danger altogether," Sherman wrote, with undue optimism.

Warn the people not to scatter so much, he asked the territorial officers. They made it impossible for any kind of defense by so doing. It would take a half-million men to protect them "as they are, and running off after every cock and bull story of new mines and new country." If the territorial people would offer their co-operation and try to work more closely with the regular army, a "universal war, which is unnecessary and cruel," could be averted.[48]

Having made his rough draft, Sherman sent the document to Stanton and Grant for their suggestions. He told Grant that there was little probability of having to call out any such volunteer regiments, but their existence, "when known will give confidence to the people." Here would at least be tangible evidence that there were men available, organized and ready to fight. It would comfort the homefolks and quiet them. It would also help to counteract the effect of "the newspapers [which] so mingle the little truth with so much falsehood, that everybody is scared, though the plains are as safe now as ever."[49]

Stanton approved of the idea but fretted over legal technicalities. There was no act of Congress in force to provide for any such action. He knew of no state or territorial laws dealing with

48 Sherman to the governors, May, 1867. Letters and Telegrams Received, 1866–68, Headquarters of the Army.

49 Sherman to Grant, May 5, 1867. Letters and Telegrams Received, 1866–68, Headquarters of the Army. He wrote to Stanton the same day, saying that he wanted to send the circular to the governors because "I think if it does no other good, it will enable them to meet the pressure on them." Sherman to Stanton, May 5, 1867. Division of the Missouri, Letters Received, 1866–69, Special File.

such subjects. However, the matter was of sufficient urgency to justify some "provisional measures" in the hope that Congress would sanction the plan. With regard to the particulars, Stanton cautioned that the army must watch the purse strings. No money for pay or supplies should be expended until such volunteers were actually mustered into service. Nor should officers be commissioned without approval of the regular army, unless territorial laws adequately provided for their selection. Not a penny would be forthcoming for any officer whose appointment was not recognized by the War Department. Stanton was concerned also because it might encourage the idea of raising volunteers in places where they were not needed. Would it be wise to advertise the fact that the government in any way recognized such organizations? Might not some of the governors in states not directly threatened leap to the conclusion that the government was requesting them? "Past experience shows how such pretenses may be used to fasten a claim upon the Public Treasury," he warned.[50]

Sherman agreed to restrict the use of his plan, as Stanton had suggested. Only those governors applying for help, on cause, would receive authorization to proceed with their volunteer organizations. It would be clearly understood in such instances that the central government was liable for no expense of any kind until Sherman called for troops. "On this point I will exercise great caution," he promised, "as I think I comprehend the motives of some of the Governors whom I would not entrust with a picket post of fifty men, much less with the discretionary power to call out troops at the national cost."[51]

The time and effort spent on the plan went for nought. The Westerners had no intention of hiring out at regular army pay. They weren't *that* hard up. Even then, the United States Treasury was looked upon as fair game, and territorial residents saw no reason why they should not have a shot at the target. After all, they told one another, they were wards of the central government, and to it they must look for protection. If the army

[50] Stanton to Grant, May 10, 1867. Letters and Telegrams Received, 1866–68, Headquarters of the Army.

[51] Sherman to Grant (forwarded to Stanton), May 22, 1867. Division of the Missouri, Letters Received, 1866–69, Special File.

could not provide the men, they would do it, but, naturally, their services would cost something. Sherman's plan was unworkable from the start. He may have known it and possibly used it as a method of saying "no" to the western demands. At any rate, no one paid it any attention. Meagher went ahead, during his last few dipsomaniacal days on earth, with the organization of the Montana Volunteers. Before that affair had ended, the federal government was billed for over one million dollars, as angry merchants tried to cash the vouchers he had so generously signed. In Colorado, Governor Hunt suddenly made the disconcerting discovery that no one wanted to take to the field with him under Sherman's terms. Unwilling to take things into his own hands, as Meagher had done, Hunt had to give up his venture. But it was not without violent complaint.

As the din kept up, with letters pouring into the office at St. Louis and across editors' desks, it seemed to Sherman that everybody in the West—both red and white—had gone crazy. He had traveled thousands of miles through that country only a year ago. Everything seemed peaceable enough then. He guessed he would have to go again. Wearily he stuffed a few wrinkled clothes into a carpetbag and made ready to leave.

Ten

███████

POPULAR IDOLS FALL

"I THINK THIS YEAR is our crisis on the Plains," Sherman confided to Dodge during May.[1] Certainly all evidence pointed in that direction in the spring of 1867. By May, things had reached a crescendo pitch. Ironically, the Indian situation became so tense that Sherman could not put into motion his earlier plan to send Augur's forces against the hostile Sioux along the Bozeman Road. Occasional Indian raids on the railroads and hysterical demands from the various territories for soldiers forced a retreat to the main-traveled routes. Because of the general fear expressed by Westerners, Sherman was obliged to defend only the lines he had set up during the previous year.

Grenville Dodge, an old Indian campaigner himself, agreed that the situation was tight. He warned Sherman that Augur's forces were too limited for the projected campaign. It would strip the Union Pacific of its protection and "play h——l with our completed road."[2] Augur also expressed doubt about going through with the original plan. Toward the end of May, he explained that when they had talked things over at Omaha, during April, there was quiet along the Republican River, but now the Sioux were ranging that country daily, committing depredations at scattered points. The railroad crews were frightened and were calling for help. Wasn't the season too late now for an effective northern campaign? Disgruntled, Sherman sent the letter to Grant with his endorsement. "If we assume the pure defensive as suggested here, the Sioux will be free to roam at will, and attack any point of our defensive line," he argued. The weather

---

[1] Sherman to Dodge, May 7, 1867. Grenville M. Dodge Papers, Volume 14.
[2] Dodge to Sherman, May 20, 1867, from Council Bluffs. "Dodge Records," Volume 6, 513–17.

ahead would be good for campaigning. The Sioux had insultingly placed their camps within sight of such forts as Phil Kearney and C. F. Smith. They could be struck; why not do it? What if Augur's horses were jaded from extended patrol duty? Surely they must be in as good condition as those of the Sioux after such a severe winter. Sherman was not to be denied. "I have ordered Gen. Augur to go ahead, and take the chances."[3]

To Dodge went the same answer. The Sioux along the Bozeman Road must be punished severely, for if they were not, they would soon be down along the railroad. The place to hit them was at home, and not after they were strung out in scattered bands picking off working parties laying rails. Apologizing for his insistence, he said, "You know that the same call [for help] comes from every other quarter and it is very hard to say which is of most importance." Then, softening the refusal somewhat, he explained that if "worst comes to worst," it was possible to call on Nebraska for some temporary help. He did not want to do it unless things were desperate, because it would set off a clamor for a similar favor from other states and territories. "I have the same appeals from Minnesota, Montana & Dacotah, as well as from Kansas, New Mexico & Colorado. Each wants enough of the army to guard them against all the Indians."[4]

On the same day, Sherman turned to Grant for more troops. The Indians, he said, were "restless and mischievous everywhere." Every little settlement demanded protection. That, of course, tended to divide up his forces badly. "I have now by me a long letter from General Dodge which is a fair sample of what I get from every quarter, each party as a matter of course, exaggerating their difficulties and necessities and underrating that of others." More troopers were needed to guard the railroad because Augur had only the Second Cavalry "and will need it all up about Phil Kearney all summer and fall." He was reluctant to call for volunteers," as it would stampede the whole country."[5]

3 Augur to Sherman, May 22, 1867, forwarded with Sherman's endorsement. Letters and Telegrams Received, 1866–68, Headquarters of the Army.

4 Sherman to Dodge, May 27, 1867. Grenville M. Dodge Papers, Volume 14.

5 Sherman to Grant, May 27, 1867. Letters and Telegrams Received, 1866–68, Headquarters of the Army.

The regulars would have to do the job, and he was still determined to send part of the Second Cavalry after the saucy Sioux.

But the Powder River campaign did not take place. The forces against the militant redhead from St. Louis were too great. A Colorado newspaper announced that war had now opened along the Platte, and the government was sleeping, doing nothing.[6] An Omaha editor almost weepingly lamented that he could not "beat into the brain" of Grant or Sherman the seriousness of the situation west of that river town. Send more troops![7] Even the *New York Times,* for its own strange reasons, agreed. That authority on Indian affairs felt the red man was "naturally a coward" when faced by equal numbers and would not fight under such circumstances. Why not send out soldiers in sufficient quantity to equal the number of Indians. This would "save the Indians as well as the whites."[8]

This journalistic drumfire was normal, and Sherman tried to ignore it. But the clatter of type became louder and louder. From all over the West came warnings of doom. Idaho sounded a doleful hope that perhaps the army could keep the main roadways open during the coming summer. There was no talk of "To the attack."[9] Yes, even the freighters were becoming chary, nodded the *Omaha Weekly Republican.* They did not want to risk their trains and were turning down business offered them.[10] Rumors were flying thick and fast in the streets of the river town. There was no doubt about it; war was at hand. There was going to be a bloody struggle along the Platte, and officials in Washington were sitting on their hands.[11]

Leavenworth was gloomy too. Travel seemed no longer safe along the principal western routes. A better year had been hoped for, but "from all the tribes, west and north of us, through both national railroad lines, we hear only of depredations and murders."[12] Kansans in general were disturbed about events which

[6] *Central City Register,* quoted by the *Leavenworth Daily Times,* May 16, 1867.
[7] *Omaha Weekly Herald,* May 24, 1867.
[8] May 19, 1867.
[9] *Idaho Weekly Statesman,* May 23, 1867.
[10] *Omaha Weekly Republican,* May 24, 1867.
[11] *Ibid.,* May 31, 1867.
[12] *Leavenworth Daily Times,* May 30, 1867.

had taken place on the Pawnee Fork of the Arkansas River in April. Hancock, as previously ordered, had proceeded to that country where he had talked with some of the chiefs. The Arapahoes had been threatening to close off the stagecoach roads when the grass was green again. Some of the Oglala and Brûlé Sioux had come down from the north and were in an ugly mood. They were rumored to have joined with some of the Cheyennes in a projected strike against white settlements. Hancock held interviews with a number of the Indians but had no apparent success. Then, on April 19, he struck. His men burned one of the Cheyenne villages on the Pawnee River as punishment for, as Sherman put it, "depredations and murders previously committed."[13] With that action, a thrill of terror rippled across Kansas. The whites knew that from then on, every stagecoach driver had better clasp tightly to his scalp and lay on with the blacksnake. The Indians would never forget April 19. And the press renewed its howl that disaster was just around the corner.[14]

The pressure was too great. Sherman had to yield. With all this talk and hysteria, he could not send his forces away from the paths of commerce to strike the threatening enemy elsewhere. Public clamor for protection had kept him from giving it in the manner he thought best—the attack. Bitterly he realized he would have to give in. In deep anger he wrote to Grant that all these reports of damage to the railroads and mail lines were exaggerations arising from "natural fear & a good deal by interested parties." Well, he would have a look at it. Hancock would go in person up the Smoky Hill route and make a careful survey. Meanwhile, "I will go up the Platte & find out how the Indians can be so *universal*."[15]

In this bitter mood he set out for Omaha. He would meet Augur, and they would go along the railroad together. To his dismay, he found a party of senators, who were about to make an excursion over the new road, waiting for him. Now he would

13 Report of W. T. Sherman, October 1, 1867, *Annual Report of the Secretary of War*, 40 Cong., 2 sess., *House Exec. Doc. No. 1* (Serial 1324), p. 34.

14 *Leavenworth Daily Times*, April 26, 1867.

15 Sherman to Grant, May 28, 1867. Telegrams Received 1866–67, Office of the Secretary of War.

have to get over his rage. There would be handshakings, nod-
dings, smiles, and forced pleasantries. Well, maybe it was all for
the best. If the situation along the road had been painted too
vividly, as he thought it had, it would be well for the lawmakers
to see it with their own eyes. There were some powerful men
in the group, too. B. F. ("Bluff Ben") Wade of Ohio and tough
Zach Chandler of Michigan were along. John Covode of Pennsylvania and Lyman Trumbull of Illinois were there too. Here
were some of the most widely talked-of men in the Senate. Perhaps this would be a useful trip after all. He would have to suffer
the presence of the ambitious T. C. Durant of the Union Pacific,
who was padding around, shaking hands.[16] Durant and Dodge
had been quarreling about the route the road should take. He
would bear watching.

On Monday, June 3, the train clicked toward the West, with
Sherman in the role of host. Smilingly he explained the advantages of the railroad and dwelt upon the safety of western
travel in these modern times. Wouldn't the ladies in the party
like to go through to Denver? It would be perfectly safe. The
ladies shrank back and said no. They had been reading the newspapers. Well, said the General, at least they could enjoy themselves to the end of the track. That portion of the trip would
be one of complete comfort. A whole car of the train had been
set aside for provisions and cooking facilities. One of Mr. Pull-
man's fine new sleepers was attached. There was even a special
car. It had been built at Alexandria, Virginia, in 1865, and de-
signed especially for the use of President Lincoln, whose only
ride in it came when his body was taken back to Illinois for
burial.[17]

The train hurtled along at twenty-five miles an hour. In no
time at all it was three hundred miles beyond Omaha. Stops
were made along the Platte River, where the senators unlimbered
their guns and fired away at startled antelope. Then back to the
train again. Past Fort Kearny they rolled, and on west to the
little village of North Platte. Sherman looked wonderingly back

16 *New York Times,* June 7, 1867.
17 *Ibid.,* June 11, 1867.

over the road and said that it would have taken an ox team thirty days to make the journey the train had covered in the past twelve hours. It was almost magic to him. He was annoyed at some eager citizens here, who. anxious to impress the dignitaries, went out to dig up the bodies of some men recently slain by the Indians. The corpses were too badly decomposed to make good specimens, however, and the project was given up. As a witness to the affair said, the Westerners wanted to give the members of the party "ocular proof that the Indians were murdering the whites—that the high road across America was no longer considered safe, and that it was absolutely necessary that the Indians should be driven off."[18] Sherman needed no such ghoulish evidence. He had never denied that men were being killed on the frontier, but he was sure that the extent of the slaughter was much exaggerated. In any event, he was doing all he could, and the Nebraskans could keep their skeletons under the sod. He would believe them.

About three hours beyond North Platte the railroad ended. Here Sherman left the party and made his way, twenty-two and one-half miles, to Fort Sedgwick, Colorado. Before bidding the excursionists farewell, he submitted to the usual ceremonies. There were the expected speeches, and Sherman said a few words, expressing his delight with the new road and reminding the senators that he had helped to start the western end of it, in California, back in 1855. Some of the others made brief comments about "progress" and "destiny." Then the eccentric George Francis Train, who was later to identify himself as "the Champion Crank," sounded off, while Sherman scowled and clenched his teeth.

"Most of the frontier towns like war," said Train, who knew nothing about frontier towns. "It makes good trade; hence traders and military men become active. . . . Help me cheat the Indians and I will give you one half! The officer on small salary says 'extermination' and the war bugle is sounded."[19] The half-baked idiot! Was he trying to tell the lawmakers that the army men and Indian traders were in cahoots? Did he think the army

18 *Omaha Weekly Herald*, June 14, 1867.
19 *Ibid.*, June 7, 1867.

was to blame for all this turmoil? Sherman let a few of his best swearwords carom off his brain, but he kept still. The wealthy Train was sufficiently known as an unstable character to make his mouthings questionable. He was along only because he was a railroad stockholder. Let him babble. The annoyed general said "good-bye" and then headed for Sedgwick.

If he had hoped to escape the supplications of frightened men by taking refuge in the little adobe fort, he was to be disappointed. Governor A. C. Hunt of Colorado kept the telegraph wire between there and Denver buzzing like an angry bee during the next few days. He had bombarded Sherman with demands for aid before the inspection party had left Omaha. He wanted to go out and fight Indians. Would the General approve of volunteers now? Patiently Sherman told him that there were certainly bands of Indians "at mischief everywhere," but getting at them was something else. He wondered "when and against what Indians" would the Governor campaign?[20] The answer awaited him at Fort Sedgwick. Hunt sent word that he had three hundred carbines but no money or credit with which to equip the five hundred men he said were ready to fight. He did have a plan. He wanted to send separate columns down the Smoky Hill and Platte rivers to search for the Indian villages. The Governor promised to war against hostiles only—Sherman need not fear another Sand Creek fiasco.[21]

The volunteer problem persisted. Here were more demands for money and authority. The territorial officials were wild with desire to do something spectacular against the Indians to satisfy their people. But Sherman refused to delegate the power. It would spell disaster. Following the policy established as a result of Meagher's applications, he answered Hunt's request. The Indians involved were probably Cheyennes who had been set off by Hancock's raid along the Pawnee a month ago. Custer was scouring the country for them now, but if the Governor would get three hundred men out at once—tomorrow—and head them for the Republican River country, they could be mustered

[20] Sherman to Hunt, June 2, 1867. *Daily Rocky Mountain News*, June 4, 1867.
[21] *Daily Rocky Mountain News*, June 4, 1867.

into the army for two months. The arrangement really should not be necessary, "because it is for your own safety," but if it was imperative, he would agree to it. The volunteers would be paid for their services when Congress could appropriate the money. If Hunt wanted to go to war under these stipulations, it was agreeable. But it must be at once. They would, in the main, be out after small scattered bands of raiding Indians, because most of the dangerous Sioux were not within five hundred miles of Sedgwick.[22] The outcries from stage stations and travelers were caused largely by the attacks of horse-stealing parties led by young bucks out to make a reputation.

When he later wrote his annual report, Sherman alluded to his correspondence with Hunt while at Fort Sedgwick. The whole plan fell through, he revealed, because the Governor was unable to buy horses for his men, "and I had no right to buy them, so that the project was dropped."[23] But it was not abandoned as quietly as Sherman's crisp official phraseology might suggest. Western papers went into a rage so violent that before long their eastern relatives were parroting them in sheer admiration. Dark words about the General were heard in Denver. The feeling was "very bitter" because of his failure to appreciate the danger. Tempers flared at him for the "cool, offhanded dubious pieces of advice he is in the habit of dealing out to the frontiersmen." One scribe guessed that he had fallen "fifty per cent at least in the estimation of our population," and said that if the great man who had gone smashing to the sea in Georgia were to appear on the streets of Denver, he would meet anything but a cordial reception. "So do popular idols fall from their high pedestals."[24] Denver's *Daily Rocky Mountain News* snarled at him for sitting safely at Fort Sedgwick while men were being robbed and murdered all around him. Meanwhile, he "rubs his hands with the utmost indifferent composure, assures everybody that there is no

---

[22] Sherman to Hunt, June 6, 1867. *Daily Rocky Mountain News*, June 7, 1867.

[23] Report of W. T. Sherman, October 1, 1867, *Annual Report of the Secretary of War*, 40 Cong., 2 sess., *House Exec. Doc. No. 1* (Serial 1324), pp. 33–34; Letters Received, 1866–69, Special File.

[24] Denver correspondent to the *New York Times*, June 3, 1867, published in the *Times* of June 17, 1867.

danger. Few men are greater than Sherman—in their own conceit."[25]

The blast brought an apology from the mayor of Denver. He explained that while there was no immediate danger to people in his city, the Indian depredations had so reduced the flow of supplies from the East that prices had soared to a starvation level, immigration had ceased, and business conditions in general were very bad. "We . . . look upon ourselves as a very unfortunate and almost 'used up community.'" It was unfortunate, however, that the journalists of his city had indulged in such personal abuse. They somehow, along with the people, imagined that the famous officer could put down the Indians with a single blow. The mayor had to admit that part of the anger stemmed from Sherman's report of conditions at Denver as he had assessed them a year ago. Business men were offended at the intimation that they had wanted a military depot as a means of making money for themselves. The writer strayed from the softness of tone at this point and came to the defense of the merchants. Stepping into his best chamber of commerce stance, he opened his literary guns with words of praise for Colorado. "We have traversed a trackless desert of seven hundred miles to establish in the heart of the continent an Empire which must grow in importance until we shall be known and acknowledged by all the world," he said proudly. Colorado had done more than its part in saving that region for the Union during the late unpleasantness. Meanwhile, it had contributed disproportionately in riches from its golden mountains. Why should it not expect protection and even patronage? Relaxing his patriotic reflexes, he concluded in a friendly vein with the hope that if Sherman planned to visit Denver this time, he would "drive directly to my house and remain our guest during your stay here."[26]

The journalistic howls of anguish amused the Omaha newspapermen who were now satisfied that the precious Union Pacific was being ably defended. The *Herald* editor chided Hunt for thinking that he and his volunteers could teach Sherman—

[25] *Daily Rocky Mountain News*, June 15, 1867.
[26] DeLano to Sherman, June 14, 1867. William T. Sherman Papers, Volume 21.

"that stupid military novice"—how to solve the Indian problem. Go ahead, Sherman had said—organize volunteers. "Something less than five hundred patriotic men instantly tendered their services as colonels, majors, captains, &c., and more than a thousand quartermasters," scoffed the paper, while praising Sherman. And when it was revealed that such duty would bring in forty cents a day, enthusiasm plummeted. All Hunt could produce was 150 men, mostly officers, and no horses. It had been a huge practical joke on Sherman's part, and the *Herald* office rocked with laughter at the clever General's triumph. Before long, the same journal would be saying that Chivington was a wretch and that Indian difficulties were the fault of the whites. It would insist that there was no "Indian war" in the West; that the hostiles did not number over five hundred; and that the raiding bands numbered only from five to twenty-five and were dangerous to those who were merely careless.[27] Omaha was moving East.

Coloradans were apoplectic at the *Herald's* barbs. From Blackhawk came the charge that the editor was a coward, a Democrat, and a president maker. He was merely trying to boom Sherman politically. All the Colorado complainant could see was that the General's conduct had been one of "stubbornness and imbecility," and it had done nothing but arouse "the anger of the great West."[28] New York papers were forced to admit that Sherman was indeed "rapidly losing the good opinion of the border settlers," but they insisted that the fault did not lie with him. If more troops were needed, and Sherman had said so time and time again, the responsibility for providing them rested in Washington. The papers held no brief for "the bellicose Governor of Montana" or the "equally blood-thirsty" executive of Colorado. Because Sherman had not acceded to their demands, the frontiersmen were now telling each other that he was not the man for the plains.[29] New York cast its vote for Sherman.

As the editors lobbed literary mortar shells at each other, the object of their quarrels sat down at Fort Sedgwick and tried to

27 *Omaha Weekly Herald*, June 28, July 25, and August 8, 1867.
28 T. R. Tannatt, of Blackhawk, in the Blackhawk *Register*. Quoted by the *Daily Rocky Mountain News*, July 3, 1867.
29 *New York Times*, June 16, 1867.

think the whole thing through. At a rude plank table in a squat adobe room, he scratched away, trying to tell Grant of western matters in his own forthright and hardheaded way. "You know the map," he wrote simply. Few places fifty miles beyond Omaha actually felt strong enough to protect themselves against a dozen Indians. All the way to the Pacific the situation was much the same. A single steel span, with board station houses every ten or twenty miles, crossed country "incapable of maintaining inhabitants." It had to be protected. Over this parched land also went a telegraph line and some blurred ruts that were wagon roads. They, too, had to be kept open. The task was almost impossible, with distance, drought, and desolation as the immutable enemies to be faced. Add to this the wily, ranging bands of Indians, who could strike and run, and the enormity of the army's task was obvious. "To defend my old line of 300 miles to Atlanta against Forest [General Nathan Bedford Forrest] and the guerillas was easy as compared with this," Grant read. Every stage station, telegraph hut, and party of travelers demanded guards. All this in an enemy's country "as big as the whole settled United States [where] one may travel weeks, months, years, without seeing an Indian, a pony, bush, tree, or anything."

There was no desire to produce a general war, Sherman continued. Even if he had the necessary armies, they could not be maintained in such a land. Right now his small and scattered forces could hardly get enough food for the men and horses, and both were worn out from pursuing "the faint tracks of some little thieving band that comes from no one knows where, and have gone in like manner." The planned expedition against the Sioux, up along the Yellowstone, had to be abandoned for supply reasons. That was why the railroad was of such importance. When corn and stores could be accumulated along the base of the mountains, expeditions could move—not before.

He knew it was hard for Grant, sitting in Washington, to understand all this. But to appreciate it, he ought to at least see the Platte River. "It is now running about 7 miles an hour, half a mile wide, so shallow in parts that a skiff drawing 4 inches has to be hauled over its quick moving sandy bottom at other points deep enough to swim a horse. To cross a boat with a load they have to put in the water from 30 to 50 men. Some wade ahead pulling at a rope and have of course to swim at the deep places. Others cling to the boat, pushing and swimming as they go. Already two men have been drowned, and two men escaped within one inch of their lives yesterday. It is about the meanest river I ever saw." Even a bridge would be difficult, for there was no foundation firm enough to hold it, and a pile bridge would cost as much as one laid over the Mississippi.

Nor was the countryside along the river any better. "The valley is flat, wide and absolutely devoid of bush or plant higher than ordinary grass, so that an object may be seen as far as on water. The hills that bound the valley are rounding and not high, so that you can gallop a horse up them anywhere, but instead of being a plain it is a high plateau with unnumerable ravines in which the bands of Indians conceal themselves absolutely, and from some high point they see every train, horse & man pass." From these hills, he explained, small groups of Indians dashed out and pounced upon horses and cattle they saw grazing. Before any pursuit could be organized, they were gone, and the gray, lifeless hills stared unspeakingly back at the panting soldiers. The only evidence that usually remained were scalped corpses, stiffening in the sun. "It is this that enrages the people of Denver, Montana and elsewhere, that depend on these Roads for all they buy. They are clamorous for extermination, which is easier said than done, and they have an idea that we are moved by more human sentiments." The outcry for what Sherman called "the Chivington process" was not the answer. Extermination of guilty Indians was not reprehensible to him, but so often innocents died under the blaze of rifles too.

Dealing with these people was another and most perplexing difficulty, Sherman told his old wartime friend. Hunt, of Colorado, had asked permission to make a campaign, but this was absurd, for he could range the Smoky Hill and Platte routes all summer and would probably never see an Indian. The whole idea had blown over anyway, because the Governor had been unable to raise troops under existing army terms. To make matters worse, Hunt had published one of Sherman's communications in a Denver paper, and when the latter saw it, he lost his temper. "I notified the Governor that I considered the publication of one of my dispatches without my consent a breach of honor. He is very much hurt thereat but it is true." It was all very annoying that members of the two branches of government did not understand each other's methods. "These civilians cannot appreciate what we do unless they appeal to the people of their neighborhood," Sherman explained. "Like Meagher in Montana, and Hunt in Colorado they must use events of this kind as a means to secure local popularity. They cannot forget themselves in an occasion that demands personal sacrifice." Why couldn't these people understand that they must "lend their aid unbought"? Was it not enough to save their own lives and property? Sherman shook his head over them.

In fact, the whole thing puzzled him. The country was large, and at the risk of their lives men insisted upon crossing it. The Indians were powerfully attracted by the prospects of such loot on wheels, and they found it laughably easy to capture. The military was perfectly willing to punish such thievery, but ferreting out the criminals was like looking for fleas in a field uniform. At the same time the Indian Bureau was chanting a song of peace and complaining of the army's violence toward its charges. "If this condition of affairs indicates peaceable Indians, I would like Mr. Browning to define to us, what war and peace means," Sherman wrote angrily. "This whole state of things cannot be traced to any single cause, and we should not charge it solely to Indian Agents or Traders. Nor should they charge it on us. It is an inevitable conflict of races, one that must occur when a stronger is gradually displacing a weaker. The Indians are poor and proud. They are tempted beyond the power of resistance to steal of the herds and flocks they see grazing so peacefully in this valley. To steal they sometimes kill. We in our turn cannot discriminate—all look alike and to get the rascals, we are forced to include all." It was an apparently insoluble problem. Even more men and horses would probably not help, although he had been asking for them because he knew no other answers. The cavalry horses that were out on the plains now did not seem to thrive on the fare given the Indian ponies, of which "the Ghosts of horses I see here are good proof." More horses would complicate an already large forage difficulty. He had seen enough to change his mind about sending Augur's jaded horses in pursuit of Sioux riders. Meanwhile, the war—such as it was—would have to go on between the two races "till the Indians are all killed or taken to a country where they can be watched." Sherman knew the problem; he did not know its solution.[30] Neither did anyone else, but, as always in such cases, there were many people who were willing to cry out "incompetent" at those who were not omniscient. He had heard it all before—during the war. And now he would have to listen to it again.

As he made his way back to the end of the railroad and then eastward to Omaha, he turned the recent developments over in his mind. The immediate decision seemed obvious. Before branching out to strike the hostiles further north, he must clear out all Indians between the two railroads—peaceful or warlike. At Fort McPherson he sent a dispatch to Stanton, expressing the opinion that "if fifty Indians are allowed to remain between the Arkansas and the Platte, we will have to guard every stage station, every train, and all railroad working parties. In other words, fifty hostile Indians will checkmate three thousand soldiers. Rather get them out as soon as possible and it makes little difference whether they be coaxed out by Indian Commissioners or killed."[31] From North Platte, he requested permission to give civilians any stock not already claimed between the two roads. The Indians had been given ample time and warning to get out; now let the whites take over.[32] He was ready to close the vise.

30 Sherman to Grant, June 11, 1867. Letters Received, 1865–69, Office of the Secretary of War. He had written Grant on the day before, saying, "The only course is for us to destroy the hostile, and to segregate the peaceful and maintain them." Sherman to Grant, June 10, 1867. Letters Received, 1865–69, Office of the Secretary of War.

31 Quoted by N. G. Taylor, Indian commissioner, in a letter read to the United States Senate, July 13, 1867, at the behest of Senators John B. Henderson (Missouri) and Samuel C. Pomeroy (Kansas). *Congressional Globe*, July 13, 1867, 40 Cong., 1 sess., p. 624; Sherman to Stanton, June 17, 1867. Records of the Bureau of Indian Affairs, Letters Received, 1865–70, Central Superintendency, I, 294. Department of the Interior Archives, National Archives.

Upon reaching St. Louis, Sherman made a formal report to Stanton in which he explained his position on the whole question of territorial volunteers. He reminded the Secretary of the clamor in Montana and said that the fever had spread to Colorado and now to Kansas. If he answered every call for help, it would require one hundred thousand men—mostly cavalry—on the plains. "Each spot of every road, and each little settlement along our five thousand miles of frontier, wants its regiment of cavalry or infantry to protect it against the combined power of all Indians, because of the bare possibility of their being attacked by the combined force of all these Indians." It was not within his province to call for an unlimited number of troops to meet these requirements, and he would not assume such responsibility by calling out an unlimited number of volunteers "and compromising those who in their ignorance would respond, and learn too late that Congress alone can pay the bill."[33]

In order that his ideas about protection of the West be made perfectly clear to all, and not subject to any misinterpretations, he decided to issue a public proclamation clarifying the status of volunteer organizations. He had discussed the matter with Stanton and Grant in May, and plans for local protection had been tentatively decided upon. At that time Stanton had suggested as little advertising as possible, giving details only to those governors who requested aid, because he feared a general rush to arms and consequent raids on the Treasury. During June, developments on the plains told Sherman that he must make his plans public. There was so much misunderstanding and rumor afloat that the military was obliged to show its hand.

On June 21, with Stanton's approval, he issued a circular that was widely published in western newspapers. A prefatory paragraph explained that the purpose of the document was to work toward uniformity of practice in the Division of the Missouri. Next, as he had done many times before, Sherman carefully pointed out that the Indians were under the jurisdiction of the

[32] Sherman to Grant. Telegrams of June 18 and 19, 1867. Letters and Telegrams, 1866–68, Headquarters of the Army.

[33] Report of W. T. Sherman, July 1, 1867, *Annual Report of the Secretary of War*, 40 Cong., 2 sess., *House Exec. Doc. No. 1* (Serial 1324), pp. 67–68.

Interior Department and protected by law. When they left the reservations assigned them and committed crimes, they then came under military surveillance. The great expanse of land toward the mountains, over which the Indians ranged, was divided into states and territories; it was also divided into military departments, or subunits of his division. This dual authority sometimes led to misunderstandings since there was "great diversity of opinion and practice" existing with regard to procedure against these warlike bands of Indians.

Co-operation between civilian and military authorities was needed, and Sherman now proposed it. "If each State and Territory will organize a battalion of mounted men *ready to be called into the service of the United States,*[34] it will be called for by the department commander, and used in connection with the regular troops, if an emergency should arise, in his judgment, to make it necessary." What he had written Meagher and Hunt, he now stated again: Each man must provide his own horse, for which the allowance of forty cents a day would be paid. Pay, food, and allowances for the men would be at the regular army rate. "But it must be clearly understood that it will require an appropriation by Congress to make the actual payment of everything except rations, forage and supplies needed by such volunteers during the time they are in the service of the United States. . . ."

The small, horse-thieving bands, whose operations fell under the classification of "nuisance," Sherman decided to put into the hands of local authority. County sheriffs and their deputies should keep small posses at hand, ready to run down these little groups that sifted through the fingers of larger military units. Capture them and lodge them in the county jails, he advised; they could be tried like white thieves.

The document closed with the solicitation to any state or territorial governor interested to "communicate freely" with departmental commanders on all subjects touched within it.[35]

---

34 The italics are mine.

35 General Orders, Division of the Missouri, 1865–82. Published in the *Daily Missouri Republican,* June 29, 1867; republished in the *Montana Post,* July 20, 1867.

Governor Hunt received his pamphlet copy of the General Order with little enthusiasm. He thanked Sherman for it and said, a little sadly, "I suppose it is all you can do." He saw no possibility of raising any troops on the terms advanced. The men would not volunteer for such wages, and the territory could not supply any funds, for it was already in debt. At the same time it would be hard to restrain his people, many of whom had lost friends and property at the hands of the Indians. As governor, he had to try to understand their feelings, and he explained that in so doing it might appear to such people as Sherman that from time to time he overacted his part in calming the public mind.[36]

The army's apparent condescension toward territorial military efforts was not received so politely by some of Hunt's fellow citizens. The Denver *News*, in an article headed "Murderous Stupidity," confessed it lacked a vocabulary "severe enough to express our condemnation of General Sherman or to picture the contempt in which he will be held by our people. His conduct is both obstinate, stupid and criminal." The *Tribune* had less trouble with its vocabulary. Not only did Coloradans have to fight Indians, but they were "over-lain by that self-conceited and rickety-headed General whose peculiar glory was in marching a great army over a country where there was no opposition. The government has no interest in her children, and has handed us over to that man whose tastes every way, as well as his capacities, better fit him to take sides with the savages than to fight against them."[37]

Montanans found comfort in Colorado's attitude. It was the same with them. Sherman's order caused a howl of protest in Virginia City, the territorial capital. It was "an elaborate piece of nonsense." What miner would leave six dollars a day to go out, furnishing his own horse at forty cents a day, to campaign—perhaps months later—"if the commander of the military department, cut off from all communications, should, in his infinite sagacity and unerring judgment, determine that an emergency had arisen . . . ?"[38]

---

[36] Hunt to Sherman, July 1, 1867. William T. Sherman Papers, Volume 21.
[37] Quoted by the *Montana Post,* June 22, 1867.
[38] *Montana Post,* July 20, 1867.

Westerners found some strange allies in their attacks upon Sherman. Alexander McClure, who had been born thirty-nine years earlier at a place called Sherman's Valley, Pennsylvania, now joined the attack. A great admirer of the General in wartime days, he now threw in with the plains people. The politician had recently crossed the Indian country, and from Salt Lake City he offered his wisdom. He knew the West; he had just seen it. And he had noticed that there had been some military bungling out here. He also knew the culprit. "General Sherman has wasted fully two months in petty quibbling with the western people, and in disgraceful submission to the systematic deception of the hostile Indian leaders," the writer trumpeted. All the while, settlers and emigrants were being sacrificed to Indian savagery. Without doubt the General was harrassed by speculators and contractors who were eager for a real Indian war, but "had he covered his glittering stars" and spent a few hours with the "intelligent stage drivers and ranchmen," he could have learned the true situation. The regular troops, McClure confided, did not want to fight. Their desertions were numerous, and their horses were no good for Indian fighting. A thousand men from the western plains would be worth double the number of regulars.[39] Another traveler had "seen the elephant."

As the month of June ran out, Sherman sat in his office at St. Louis and watched the show from the wings. The tumult up and down the Platte seemed to be subsiding, with only the echoes of the perennial letter writers ricocheting around the columns of local newspapers. Even verbal bombast seemed to be on the wane, and an Omaha paper noted that "rumors are getting scarce on the market."[40] Troops patrolled the Union Pacific and its connecting stagecoach routes daily. Travel was uninterrupted, and the Indians seemed to have wearied of their raids for the moment. Every day of such calm sent the rails plunging deeper into the hostile country, and Sherman proudly told Phil Ewing that "we *now today* ship clothing, arms, and stores from Saint

[39] Written as a correspondent for the *New York Tribune* from Salt Lake City, June 20. *Daily Rocky Mountain News*, July 18, 1867; *Sacramento Daily Union*, August 5, 1867.

[40] *Omaha Weekly Herald*, June 28, 1867.

Louis and *Leavenworth* to the Plains *via* Chicago."[41] This was more alarming than comforting to St. Louis merchants, but Sherman found no interest in their worries. Goods were going west by the fastest means; from a military standpoint, that was the salient fact.

As the days went on, the army was gradually tightening its organization. Most of the wartime volunteers had now been mustered out, and although it was within his power to call out temporary troops from the states or territories, Sherman planned to use this authority grudgingly. He was refining the quality of his forces, not diluting it. As he earlier cautioned Augur, only the most reliable men were being kept on as officers. He had told the Platte Department's commander to take nothing but the best. "We know of course that clean fellows sometimes take a drink and we are apt to make full allowance, but we must have sober officers and if they drink so as to be 'muddled' they must be dismissed. I feel less and less patience with drunkards as I get older. Their promises of reform are so rarely realized."[42] There would be enough problems without others within the commands. John Pope, now commanding the Third Military District of the South, in Atlanta, Georgia, recognized the difficulty of the situation. He had been taken from a plains command and assigned to one in the Reconstruction program—a post that Sherman had so abhorred. But even in those complexities, Pope could extend sympathy to his old friend at St. Louis. "I know no task more hopeless than the attempt to keep the peace in Indian country under the operations of the organized system of fraud & rascality known as the Indian system & administered by the Indian Bureau," he wrote. ". . . I can understand perfectly your situation and its trials & consequences & I assure you I sympathize with you."[43]

It was good to hear from one of the "old hands" in the army, and Sherman read the letter with pleasure. Given his choice of dealing with Indians and an irate western citizenry or the snarl

[41] Sherman to Ewing, June 28, 1867. Sherman-Ewing Correspondence.
[42] Sherman to Augur, February 28, 1867. C. C. Augur Papers.
[43] Pope to Sherman, June 26, 1867. William T. Sherman Papers, Volume 21.

of problems surrounding the freedmen of the South, he would have instantly chosen the former. In either case the matter was bound to become a political and public battleground. Better to be out on the plains than in the shattered South. One was new and undeveloped, the other a scene of desolate former glory. Both problems had been snatched up by amateur reformers, each of whom was sure he knew the answer. Sherman must have had a chuckle over the proposed solution to his problems said to have been advanced by Mark Twain. The story was going the rounds that the writer had advised the Secretary of War to get all the Indians together and stage a giant massacre.

"I said there was nothing so convincing to an Indian as a general massacre," the humorist was supposed to have propounded. "I said the next surest thing for an Indian was soap and education. Soap and education are not as sudden as a massacre, but they are more deadly in the long run; because a half-massacred Indian may recover; but if you educate him and wash him it is bound to finish him sometime or other. It undermines his constitution; it strikes at the foundation of his being."

" 'Sir,' I said, 'the time has come when blood-curdling cruelty has become unnecessary. Inflict soap and a spelling book on every Indian that ravages the plains, and let them die!' "[44]

As good a solution as any, Sherman probably concluded. It would satisfy the "rosewater" philanthropists of the East and accomplish the end sought by the extermination-minded Westerners. In the problem confronting him, nothing appeared to make sense anyway.

[44] *Cheyenne Daily Leader,* July 28, 1876.

━━━━━━━━

Eleven

THE EARNEST WISH OF THE GOVERNMENT

WHILE MONTANANS muttered that the Indian policy of the government was "the most stupendous humbug of the century," and Coloradans talked of stopping federal tax payments, Sherman went ahead with his plans. He was eager to inspect the Union Pacific's Eastern Division, which had now crawled out the Smoky Hill route beyond Fort Riley and was groping toward Denver. On July 4, he passed through Leavenworth, and the next night he stopped at Fort Harker, where he visited with General A. J. Smith, in command of the troops during Hancock's absence. Smith, whom Sherman had characterized during the war as an officer "who will fight all the time," expressed deep concern at attacks upon the work trains. Could Sherman recall the Seventh Cavalry, which had been ordered across the Platte? The answer was negative, but the need for more troops had to be answered. The Division commander was forced to call for volunteers—an act he had opposed vigorously.

Governor S. J. Crawford, of Kansas, had recently made lengthy appeals to Washington for permission to send his volunteers into the field,[1] and the requests echoed from the walls of the Senate chamber, while the Kansas solons took up the war chant. Sherman also had heard from Crawford. Reluctantly he answered, "You may call out a volunteer batallion of six or eight com-

---

[1] S. J. Crawford to Senator E. G. Ross, June 29, 1867. Read to the United States Senate by Senator Ross, July 17, 1867. *Congressional Globe*, 40 Cong., 1 sess., pp. 705–706. The Senator told his colleagues that volunteers were essential. "An interdiction is laid upon travel and traffic of the Plains; the great United States mails are stopped; the great interior States and Territories of the Union are more effectually cut off from the capital of the nation than though the ocean rolled between. There are vacant seats in these Halls which could not be filled by reason of an intervening hostile people. . . ."

panies mounted."[2] As he admitted to Stanton, this would be necessary because of the attacks along the railroads, and if the Indians were to be followed into their own camps, he would have to find more troops.[3] As soon as permission was granted, Crawford sent out the call for men. They were to be mustered in on July 14 at Fort Harker, but when that day arrived, there appeared only enough volunteers to form four companies. Old Captain F. H. Bates, mustering officer for the Department of Missouri, signed them on, and even though the men would serve during the summer, the West had at last seen the realization of one of its fond hopes.[4] Everyone seemed happy, except, of course, Sherman's gadfly, the *New York Herald*. That paper had deviled him all during the war; now it pouted that the governors should run their own show and accused the army of being jealous of its prerogatives.[5] Sherman shrugged off the pettiness and headed back home.

He wrote to Grant of his delight with the progress of the railroad in Kansas. It was finished as far as Fort Harker; before the year was out, another hundred miles might be completed. Beyond the rails, the Santa Fé stage line seemed to be operating without interruption. For some unaccountable reason, the Smoky Hill line into Denver had suspended operations. Hancock, who had just passed along the whole route, had sworn that the stations were unharmed and that ample guards were available for

2 *Junction City Union* (Junction City, Kansas), January 25, 1868.

3 Sherman to Stanton, July 2, 1867. Letters Received, 1865–69, Office of the Secretary of War.

4 Report of W. T. Sherman, October 1, 1867, *Annual Report of the Secretary of War*, 40 Cong., 2 sess., *House Exec. Doc. No. 1* (Serial 1324), p. 35. While Sherman gives the date July 14, both Governor Crawford and one of the men who participated say that the mustering in occurred on July 15. The Eighteenth Kansas Volunteer Cavalry was armed, uniformed, and equipped by the federal government. It campaigned for four months (July 15 to November 15), after which it was disbanded. During that summer the Eighteenth served with the Seventh and Tenth U. S. Cavalry and was part of the time attached to Custer's Seventh in northwestern Kansas. See Samuel J. Crawford, *Kansas in the Sixties*, 260 and 281; Henderson L. Burgess, "The Eighteenth Kansas Volunteer Cavalry, and Some Incidents Connected with Its Service on the Plains," *Collections of the Kansas State Historical Society*, Vol. XIII (1913–14), 534–38.

5 *Leavenworth Daily Times*, July 10, quoting the *New York Herald*. During the war Sherman had court-martialed Thomas W. Knox, the *Herald's* star reporter, as a spy.

the coaches. Sherman suspected that the company had taken advantage of the Indian scare to cease running, in the hope that it could make claims for damage and loss of property. He recommended that the postmaster general withhold compensation until the matter could be investigated.[6]

He repeated the railroad news to John and further described progress along the Platte route. Remember where they had left Lodge Pole Creek to cross over to the North Platte on their trip last year? Cump asked. The new railroad was nearly that far west. And those mud chimneys they had seen on the way to Denver—the ruins of old Camp Walbach? A new town called Cheyenne was being laid off about fifteen miles south of that point. Dodge had promised to push the Union Pacific out there this year.

"You have doubtless heard much of the war," he went on. It was only the natural skirmishing that took place when two races collided. Actually, there was no war yet. There had been so much clamor for protection among the settlements that he had been unable to get at the Sioux up along the Yellowstone. "I see it stated that the Indian War is costing a million a week." That was all poppycock. Only regular troops had been employed, except for the Kansas Volunteers, and even the combined force could cost no such figure. Congress had called a halt—for the time being. Peace commissioners were negotiating on the plains, and until they got out of the way, there would be no fighting. Any treaties they might make could not last twenty-four hours. When the commissioners got through with their piddling projects, the Indians would have to be rounded up, put on reservations, and made to stay there. If they did not comply, then it was time to fight in earnest.[7] These commissioners were a nuisance and a public expense. He disdained and scorned them. Fortunately, he had nothing to do with such creatures, and when they were through with their interference, the army could act, unhindered.

Four days later, Congress provided for a new board of com-

[6] Sherman to Grant, July 16, 1867. Division of the Missouri, Letters Received, 1866–69, Special File.

[7] Sherman to John Sherman, July 16, 1867. William T. Sherman Papers, Volume 21.

missioners and charged it with making a general settlement with the Plains Indians. To Sherman's horror, his name was on the list of appointments. The whole action meant a complete road block to his plans. He realized at once that until the board had come to a conclusion, the army would be checked and held to the defensive. Sherman had hoped that the settlers in close contact with the tribes could also be prevailed upon to await the outcome of this new move. About this, he had some doubts.[8]

Unhappily he contemplated his new assignment. Congress had authorized the President to appoint a commission consisting of three army officers, none below the rank of brigadier general, along with four civilians.[9] He examined the list and found that he would have to deal with N. G. Taylor, the commissioner of Indian affairs, Senator John B. Henderson (Missouri), who was the chairman of the Senate Committee on Indian Affairs, Samuel F. Tappan, and John B. Sanborn. The army officers—in the minority, he noticed—were chosen by President Johnson. Besides himself, there were Alfred Terry and old W. S. Harney, brought out of retirement for the assignment. It was quite a mixed crowd.

Senator Henderson, a fellow Missourian, was the author of the bill creating the commission. A scholarly, hard-working lawyer who had now served five years in the Senate, he would soon be tagged as the student of the commission. Sherman thought that the wealthy bachelor, an outspoken peace advocate, would surely oppose the military. So would Taylor, the Indian commissioner. He was a preacher by profession and had also served in Congress. Another negative stand would come from Samuel Tappan. Although he had lived in Colorado before the war, he was a Bostonian who had come west to Lawrence, Kansas, in 1856. Despite his frontier experiences, he had spoken loudly about the warlike policy of the government against the Indians.

[8] Report of W. T. Sherman, October 1, 1867, *Annual Report of the Secretary of War*, 40 Cong., 2 sess., *House Exec. Doc. No. 1* (Serial 1324), p. 37.
[9] The act of July 20, 1867, found in General Order No. 72, July 30, 1867. William T. Sherman Papers, Volume 21; report of Charles E. Mix, acting commissioner of Indian affairs, November 15, 1867, *Annual Report of the Secretary of the Interior*, 40 Cong., 2 sess., *House Exec. Doc. No. 1*, Part II (Serial 1326).

"At the end of the road Sherman watched the tracklaying,
amazed at the activity and fascinated by the piles of construction
material strewn around on the prairie."

Above: Laying track 600 miles west of St. Louis, 1867.
Below: A section of the train.

Courtesy Harper's New Monthly Magazine, June, 1867

Denver in 1867

Omaha in 1867

Courtesy Harper's New Monthly Magazine, June, 1867

About the others, there was some doubt. Sanborn, now a rich Minnesota lawyer, had risen to the rank of major general in the Volunteer army during the war. Beside him would sit General Harney, now nearly seventy, also something of a question mark. Once a well-known Indian fighter, he was now recognized as an Indian sympathizer. He had been inactive in recent years; his Southern leanings had kept him out of any major role during the war. Sherman thought the old gentleman would vote on the army's side.

About Terry, there were no doubts. The Commander of the Department of Dakota, still a bachelor at forty, was known for his ability to co-operate with equals or superiors. He and Sherman had sat over their maps on many occasions, and they agreed on Indian policy. The former Yale law student was a fine scholar who had pursued his intellectual interests while many fellow officers had gone to seed at some quiet post. The handsome six-footer was one of the few volunteer officers of the war who had succeeded in getting a berth in the shrinking postwar regular army, and Sherman was very fond of him. He would do.

But the army men stood to be outvoted, and Sherman thought they could "hardly expect to influence the Board from the settled conviction that Indians can best be managed by traders and agents." So be it. "I shall make but little effort to change the court but leave it work out its own solutions." Let the peacemakers carry the burden this year; the plains army was still small, and it could use a little time to prepare for the inevitable war that would follow their failure.[10]

With the exception of Terry, who was still up the Missouri River, and Senator Henderson, who had agreed to join the group at St. Joseph, the commission gathered on August 6 at St. Louis to lay its plans. As the men discussed possible procedures and routes of travel to visit the Indians, western papers jeered at the whole scheme. Predictions of failure came from Leavenworth; Nevada rocked with cries of "no confidence"; and Montanans railed at "the host of vampirian commissioners, agents

[10] Sherman to John Sherman, August 3, 1867. William T. Sherman Papers, Volume 21.

and speculators who are under their wing, sucking treasures from the Government and blood from the people."[11] Coloradans continued to scorn Sherman, who had now joined the rose-water crowd. "The Indians say that Sherman is 'heap big tall, but no good fight, squaw chase them with a stick.' " And the Indians were not far from right, nodded a Denver editor.[12] Westerners raged at the commission when they read of Indian raids. As it meditated in quiet St. Louis, Spotted Tail's band struck a Union Pacific freight train at Plum Creek, scalping and pillaging before slipping back into the Nebraska wastes. The very act was certainly an appropriate way to "commemorate and to show the utter fallacy of all such commissions," said the *Rocky Mountain News*. "No doubt but in a cool parlor, over a little ice and ——— in cut glass, the indian question was disposed of in time for dinner at the Southern [Hotel], and another day was occupied in devising ways and means to appropriate the $450,000."[13] Nebraskans, who had just felt the stinging attack, were beyond sarcasm. "For God's sake send us men for protection, and we will discuss Peace Commissioners afterwards," came the plea from Nebraska City.[14] The West smoldered with resentment and cried out in frustration, while at St. Louis, in the American tradition, a committee studied the matter.

As the gentlemen deliberated, Sherman stayed the military arm. Hancock and Augur were instructed to limit their operations to the two main routes of travel. "Do not invade the country south of the Arkansas river, except in pursuit of parties guilty of hostile acts," he warned Hancock. "I want the deliberation of the Commissioners to be as little disturbed by acts of our troops as possible; so that the effort to settle the Indian question peaceably may have a fair chance of success."[15] This brought hoots from Omaha, now concerned over attacks on its own child,

---

11 *Leavenworth Daily Times*, August 11, and 13, 1867; *Helena Herald*, quoting the *Territorial Enterprise* (Virginia City, Nevada), August 14, 1867; *Montana Post*, August 10, 1867.

12 *Daily Rocky Mountain News*, August 9, 1867.

13 *Ibid.*, August 12, 1867.

14 *Nebraska City News*, August 9, 1867.

15 *Leavenworth Daily Times*, August 9, 1867; *Montana Post*, September 14, 1867.

the Union Pacific. How could Sherman return to the defensive when he had never left it? All the available federal troops were busy answering demands of "the sainted negroes in Virginia and Tennessee," anyway.[16] The western army was nothing. Personally, Sherman agreed with this sentiment; publicly, he did not reveal it.

There had been pressure on him a year or two before to serve on a commission, but he had refused on the ground that it was incompatible with his other duties.[17] This time he felt obliged to accede. Johnson had asked him to participate, and Grant had approved. Peace must be kept in the official family. Much to his annoyance, Congress had answered the Fetterman massacre with a special peace commission, and the legislators apparently were still convinced of their own wisdom. "I would have preferred to have followed the savages to their own country and to have avenged the massacre in such a way that it would not have invited a repetition," Sherman muttered.[18] Now he would have to wait out the advocates of peace.

From the General's point of view, his civilian associates had at least one virtue; they wanted to go out and talk with the Indians. That was more than could be said for some of the Easterners who were safe along the Atlantic seaboard, offering gratuitous advice from lecture stands and printed columns. At least going into hostile country to study the situation made sense. They wanted to go up the Missouri. Fine, so did he.

Amid cries that "the West has no faith in it," the group started out. At Leavenworth its members boarded the *St. Johns,* ready for the ascent. It was August 14. As the steamer cast off, Sherman chatted with Colonel J. H. Leavenworth, the agent for the Kiowas and Comanches. He was the son of General Henry Leavenworth, so well known to the Westerners of an earlier day. A reporter, pad in hand, edged in and inquired eagerly about the mission. It was a humbug, said Sherman, glaring at the young man. It

16 *Omaha Weekly Herald,* August 22, 1867.

17 Remarks by Senator James Harlan of Iowa to the Senate, July 18, 1867. *Congressional Globe,* 40 Cong., 1 sess., p. 709.

18 Report of W. T. Sherman, July 1, 1867, *Annual Report of the Secretary of War,* 40 Cong., 2 sess., *House Exec. Doc. No. 1* (Serial 1324), pp. 65–66.

would accomplish nothing.[19] Then he turned to more pleasant conversation.

A stop was made at St. Joseph to pick up Senator Henderson, who years later would urge the presidency upon Sherman. Crowds of curious spectators came down to the steamer to look at the distinguished gathering. Two German bands serenaded them simultaneously, each playing a different tune. Amid the uproar, visitors gathered around to chat with the famous soldier, seated on the forward part of the boiler deck between two huge piles of boxed goods. Sherman sat relaxed, hat and coat off; he seemed unusually voluble. When the boat pulled away for the next leg of the journey, it was discovered that one of the towns-men had taken the General's hat. However, when the theft was revealed, Sherman did not show his famous temper; unper-turbed, he laughed and remarked that it was much more easily parted with than his scalp.[20]

It was good to be on the move, and even the annoyance of having one's hat stolen could not mar the occasion. During the days afloat, the men sat around on deck, chatting, smoking, and reading. Those who had never seen the dull, gray banks of the Missouri looked at its drab scenery and the twisting course ahead. Members of the press hung around, hoping to pick up a word of news. Before long, they grew bored. "We smoked, sipped poor cock-tails for twenty five cents apiece at the bar, stole the *Herald* man's Bourbon, got shaved, shampooed and dressed," wrote one of the brethren. Sunday was no different. Although there were two chaplains aboard, Sherman, whose prerogative it was to order services, remained silent, and the reporters went back to the bar.[21]

By August 23, the *St. Johns* had splashed its way up to Fort Randall, 1,288 miles above St. Louis. Sherman visited with the Indians who flocked around the boat, and his colleagues put numerous questions to their leaders. Farther on, at Fort Thomp-

19 Remarks made to correspondent of the *Cincinnati Gazette; New York Times,* August 27, 1867.
20 *Daily Missouri Republican,* August 21, 1867.
21 *Omaha Weekly Herald,* September 12, 1867, quoting the correspondent of the *Chicago Times.*

son, General Terry was welcomed aboard. At Fort Sully, the steamer tied up for a few days; here extensive talks were held. In all, nine small groups of Sioux were interviewed during the stay. To impress the Indians, as well as to please the General, a military review was held, and an artillery display of six-pounders was offered.

Sherman had dressed for the occasion, donning white silk gloves and a long military cloak. The inevitable cigar stump, badly chewed, stuck out of the corner of his mouth. The Indians put on their finest, too. One of them, wearing a blue shirt, red pantaloons, and a black silk handkerchief tied around his head, wagged his blackened chin happily at Sherman. Appropriately, his name was Burnt Face.[22] Another, named Long Mandan, representing the small Two Kettles band of around 160 lodges, complained that few goods reached the Upper Missouri country. Sherman explained that the army usually supplied only its soldiers; the Indian Bureau was supposed to feed the Indians. The Chief then charged that in any event, his people were afraid to come near the forts. Sherman denied that any soldier in that neighborhood would hurt an Indian, but they could not be blamed for being on guard at all times. Why did not the Sioux build their own houses and walk the white man's road? the General countered. Had they heard about the Cherokees who owned homes and farms? Long Mandan promised that his people would follow the same course if furnished with materials and instruction. Would they chop wood for the river steamers? Yes, said the Chief. Did the Indians object to the river boats? Personally, he admitted that he had no objection; other tribesmen might resent them.[23] On and on the interviews went. Questions and answers and an occasional mute silence. The commissioners jotted down information for future reference.

As the days went on, the men came to know each other better. Sherman's colleagues watched him with interest. They saw a man tall and thin, without an ounce of spare flesh on his frame. When they asked his opinion, he would turn up his eyes in

[22] *Junction City Weekly Union*, September 28, 1867.
[23] *Daily Missouri Republican*, September 12, 1867.

thought for a moment and then render a positive decision. His bitter opposition to newsmen was displayed frequently; he even made efforts to get the reporters sent home. Despite his dislike for the profession, he read the work of its members with care, and one of them called him a "walking dictionary," claiming that he knew "by name every man who ever disobeyed him." Everyone was impressed by his interest in geography. While the studious Henderson pored over Indian treaties, Sherman seemed never to be without a map in his hand. Now he would be seen in the salon, quietly puffing a cigar, running his long forefinger over a map spread upon the marble-topped table. Later, someone would pass the open door of his cabin and notice his lanky frame stretched out on a bunk, with a large map stretched across it, almost hiding his body. He knew the name of every river and creek mouth passed, of every hamlet or town, of every geographical location. The captain and crew, subjected to constant questioning, were often hard put to produce some of the answers.[24]

As the *St. Johns* slid back down the river, complaints about the commission's activities began to be heard. Particularly annoyed were those interested in exploiting mineral possibilities in the Black Hills. During the spring of 1867, about one hundred former Union soldiers gathered at Yankton and laid plans to invade the hills when the snows melted. Sherman, knowing that the Sioux valued the region and would fight for it, proposed to the commissioners that a reservation covering the area be laid off, and reserved for the Sioux.[25] Businessmen in such river towns as Sioux City, Iowa, saw that possible trade was being nipped in the bud, and their cries were loud and long. Editors, sensitive to the wants of their own communities, flew to the attack. "Gen. Sherman, by a high handed and extraordinary use of his power, as military commander, has for the past two years prevented the opening up and development of this region," accused one journal. A reporter from another paper picked up the war club and

24 *Army and Navy Journal*, Vol. V (December 7, 1867), 241, quoting correspondent of the Philadelphia *Press*.
25 George W. Kingsbury, *History of Dakota Territory*, I, 864.

swung wildly. "May God deliver us from the visitation of any more Peace Commissioners, especially those headed by a semi-lunatic and full blown knave," he lashed out. Sherman was called a "brainless and peaky-headed vagrant, who is known in the Paymaster's Department as Lieutenant General, and who knows as much about Indians, the wants and interests of the people of the frontier as a Missouri shovel fish."[26]

This was too strong for Omaha editors. They scolded Sioux City sharply and refused to quote the scurrilities. A St. Louis paper expressed pleasure that the writer of the article had been fired. Sherman was no more than grimly amused; he was used to it. He was actually getting better! During the war he had been called insane; now he was only half-crazy.

At Omaha, the commission boarded a train and headed for North Platte, Nebraska, to meet with the Oglala and Brûlé Sioux. Some of the Cheyennes had also promised to come in. On September 19, white and red leaders faced one another in what Henry M. Stanley, who was later to find Dr. Livingstone and fame, reported to be a "grand pow-wow." At the front of the commission group stood the slender Sherman; behind him were Terry, Henderson, and the others. Farther to the rear, reporters and civilian spectators looked on. When the Indians discovered a warm friendliness on the part of the "big chiefs" of the whites, they became quite amiable. So jovial were they, wrote Stanley, that they "laughed with a reckless glee as they threw themselves on the ground."

Facing the peacemakers were such well-known Westerners as Spotted Tail, Man-Afraid-of-His-Horses, and Man-that-walks-under-the-Ground. The notorious Pawnee Killer, in whom Sherman had told Custer he had no faith, was there. So was Standing Elk, Swift Bear, Turkey Foot, Cut Nose, Whistler, Big Mouth, Cold Face, and Crazy Lodge. And everybody was sober. Sherman had seen to that. As soon as he arrived, he had placed North Platte under martial law. Guards were stationed in front of the saloons so that "neither white, red, nor black man could get liquor of any kind."

[26] *Daily Missouri Republican*, September 18, 1867, quoting the Sioux City papers.

As the talks proceeded, it became obvious that the Indians were there in the belief that they would get guns and ammunition; by such promises Swift Bear had persuaded some of them to come. There were other requests. Whites were disturbing the hunting along the Smoky Hill and Powder River roads. The whites would have to abandon that region. As the Indians stated their case, they became grave, and their earlier cordiality disappeared. Sherman listened quietly to all they had to say, and on the next day he answered them.

Speaking in what Stanley called "his own peculiar and pointed manner," he told them that the roads had to be maintained. The Smoky Hill line to Colorado and New Mexico was important to those territories, and it must not be blocked by the Indians. The Powder River road was marked off to get the whites to their settlements to the north. There were no towns along it, and travel did not destroy the buffalo. The Great White Father understood that last spring, at Laramie, consent had been given for this route. He would be at Laramie in November, and if it was found that the so-called Bozeman Trail was hurting the Indians, they would be paid, or it would be given up.

About the powder and ball—he would give some to his friends. But not much. White men had been killed and trains were being attacked. Such friends as Spotted Tail, Standing Elk, Two Strike, and Swift Bear would receive "almost anything they want." They had remained at peace all summer. The rest could work with their bows and arrows until they had proved themselves friends to the whites. This news infuriated Pawnee Killer, and he glared fiercely at the speaker. Perhaps he recalled that the favored Spotted Tail had been accused of the Plum Creek raid earlier in the year, and now Sherman chose to overlook that act. Staring back coldly at Pawnee Killer, Sherman, his voice thin and icy, continued: "We now give you advice. We know well that the red and white men are not brought up alike. You depend upon game for a living, and you get hats and clothes from the whites. All that you see white men wear they have to work for. But you see they have plenty to eat, that they have fine houses and fine clothes. You can have the same. . . ." He described the herds of cattle and horses owned by the Cherokees and Choctaws, and the cornfields of the Poncas and Pottawatomies. Why did not the Sioux and Cheyennes settle down before all the good land was gone? If the Sioux acted now, they could have the land along the Missouri River between the White Earth and Cheyenne rivers. Go there, he urged, and live like white men, "and we will help you all you want."

But time was short. They must decide. The railroads were coming, and "you cannot stop the locomotive any more than you can stop the sun or moon, and you must submit. . . ." If the young Indians attacked the roads, "the Great Father, who, out of love for you, withheld his soldiers, will let loose his young men, and you will be swept away." This commission was not only a peace commission, it was also a war commission, he warned. The whites in the East had paid little attention to what the Indians had called war on the plains, "but if they make up their minds to fight you they will come out as thick as a herd of buffalo, and if you continue fighting you will all be killed." With this solemn injunction, Sherman looked hard at the stoic countenances and said, "We shall be here again in November." A decision would be necessary then.[27] He did not explain that the real reason for this period of contemplation was that the northern Sioux, with whom the commissioners very much wanted to talk, had sent word they were too busy fighting in the Powder River country. They would try to come later for talks.

The efforts of the group, so far, had brought small success. As the members made their proposals, the Indians, in beady-eyed taciturnity, responded with a series of blank looks. The only conclusions reached were offered by the press. The West doubted whether the offering of "Harney austerity, . . . Sherman sharp talk, Sanborn shallowness, and Sam Tappan sentimentality" would achieve much.[28] The *Rocky Mountain News* said flatly that the North Platte council was a failure, which surprised that journal very little. The Indian was still defiant, and all that had

[27] Henry Morton Stanley, *My Early Travels and Adventures in America and Asia*, I, 208–11; *Daily Rocky Mountain News*, September 23, 1867; *New York Times*, September 27, 1867.

[28] *Junction City Weekly Union*, September 28, 1867.

been achieved was a further humiliation of the government.[29] "Words but not deeds," echoed Montana writers. A whole summer had passed, and nothing had been accomplished. "The commanding Generals rush furiously from one point to another, issuing portentous orders and presiding at councils [while the Indians raid].... On the impulse of the moment, Sherman declares he will protect the roads, and the next day he relents." Now he proposed another meeting in November. That would give the Indians time to pillage until the frosts came; they could then take time off to parley again. "It is not natural that the hero of the march from Atlanta should thus demean himself when the enemy are defiant," a Montana editor lamented. "It looks very much as though the Presidential aspirations of Sherman were hampering his movements in view of the morbid sentimentalism on the Indian question pervading the Eastern States." Send out Sheridan, a fighter. Sherman had "fully demonstrated his incapacity as an Indian fighter" and would be better off in the White House than on the plains.[30]

Toward the end of September, Sherman was back in St. Louis, where he made some judgments of the commission's accomplishments. After nearly two months on the commission, he thought he could "pretty closely judge of the Result." There was no doubt that such work could be neither complete nor final, for it was a large assignment and would be years in consummation. Henderson, whom he otherwise admired, had the notion the government was violating treaties by building western railroads. This seemed to him an impractical view. "Whether right or wrong, those Roads will be built, and everybody knows that Congress, after granting the charters, and fixing the Routes, cannot now back out and surrender the country to a few bands of roving Indians." The Senator also thought that railroads, stage lines, and telegraph companies took their franchises in full knowledge of the dangers they faced and should not now ask for military protection. Sherman, however, thought permission granted for such public carriers did involve an implied promise of protection, and

29 *Daily Rocky Mountain News*, September 23, 1867.
30 *Montana Post*, September 28, 1867.

he had always proceeded on that theory. Perhaps by the time Congress met, some workable plan could be devised. He was beginning to be optimistic. Even the commission, which at first voted against the military, had shifted. "Henderson and Sanborn now vote with me," Cump told John with satisfaction.[31] For the moment, things were looking up.

Within a few days after their return from North Platte, the commissioners set off again, this time for Fort Harker at the end of the railroad in Kansas. They were bound for Medicine Lodge, seventy miles south of Fort Larned on the South Arkansas River, to rendezvous with the southern tribes. About two thousand Arapahoes, Kiowas, and Comanches awaited them and the $10,-000 worth of presents they carried. Sherman, who had been called back to Washington, did not go along, and the treaty of Medicine Lodge, signed October 21, was concluded without him. At that meeting the Comanches and Kiowas relinquished their lands between the railroads and were assigned a small reservation in the southwestern part of present Oklahoma. The Southern Cheyennes and Arapahoes were located north of them. The area was too small and did not allow ample room for the hunt, which was so vital; therefore, the commissioners did little more than create an unworkable arrangement.

When the treaty makers returned to St. Louis, they found Sherman, just returned from Washington. The administration had again pressed him to accept the position of secretary of war. Secretary of the Interior Orville H. Browning wrote in his diary that "he is willing to remain here in a subordinate position to Grant, but not otherwise—Would not take the War Department but would go into the Genls office. Sherman is fully conservative and utterly opposed to the unconstitutional and revolutionary measures of the radicals." Rawlins had been arguing for such a move for more than a year. He regarded Sherman as both a soldier and a statesman, while Grant was a soldier only.[32] But Sherman refused to budge. He said "no thanks" to the gentlemen and hurried back to St. Louis.

[31] Sherman to John Sherman, September 28, 1867. William T. Sherman Papers, Volume 21.

[32] *The Diary of Orville Hickman Browning*, II, 104 (October 25, 1866), and 163 (October 9, 1867).

When his colleagues on the commission urged him to keep his bag packed—they were ready to go on to Fort Laramie—he begged off. The Army of the Tennessee was to have a reunion in St. Louis on November 13, and he wanted to be present. Would it be all right, he asked, if Augur took his place this time?[33] It was agreed that if Sherman would go as far as North Platte, where some of the Sioux bands had promised to meet again, he might return in time for the meetings.

The commissioners arrived at North Platte on November 6, expecting to find the chiefs with whom they had talked in September, but only Swift Bear of the Brûlé Sioux was on hand. At Laramie the picture was equally discouraging. Neither Red Cloud nor any others from the North had come down. They sent a message saying they were too busy right now. At this point, Sanborn and Harney lost their tempers and shocked Taylor by asking Sherman's office how many troops it would take to thrash the Powder River Sioux soundly. Sherman replied, after feeling out Augur and Terry, that such a force—whatever its size might be—was not now available.[34] Discouraged, the commissioners headed for home, to stop again at North Platte if more Indians had arrived. But only a few were on hand; these glumly received blankets as gifts and hurled insults back in payment. They complained to Taylor that they liked neither the quality nor the color of the blankets, and that while they might be good enough for soldiers, the Indians regarded them as strictly inferior goods.[35] Sherman, meeting with his old comrades in St. Louis, had missed nothing except the enviable opportunity of seeing his associates embarrassed and insulted by the Indians for whom they had so much affection.

Meanwhile, he had given the necessary orders to his troops, according to the decisions at Medicine Lodge. Hostilities against the Kiowas, Comanches, and Apaches, who had signed, would cease. For the moment, those Indians were to be allowed hunting

33 Sherman to John Sherman, October 28, 1867. William T. Sherman Papers, Volume 21.

34 George E. Hyde, *Red Cloud's Folk: A History of the Oglala Sioux Indians*, 157.

35 *Daily Missouri Republican*, November 25, 1867.

privileges beyond their reservations, and the troops must be vigilant. Some of the natives might forget the object of their hunt and commence to admire wagon trains again. Under the circumstances, troops must do their best to preserve order and to treat the Indians as friendly until crimes were committed, "because it is the earnest wish of the government of the United States that war be avoided and the civil agents of the government have a full and fair chance to reduce them to a state of comparative civilization."[36]

In his annual report for 1867, Sherman summed up the accomplishments of the year and looked into the future. There had been a general apprehension of war that caused an extreme nervousness on the part of the Westerners. At one time, the Indians had openly threatened violence, and in April, Hancock had struck, burning a Cheyenne village on Pawnee Fork. There had been an outcry from the Indian sympathizers and talk of indemnification. Sherman begged that this not be done, "for it would encourage them to believe themselves warranted to commit any number of murders and thefts, and they would necessarily infer that we feared to strike them in their most vulnerable points, viz., their property and families." It was extremely difficult to catch the mobile braves, and the only way of restraining them was to hit at their families and property. Hancock's position was defended on the ground that he had been better able to judge than anyone else, and had he failed to act, surely travel along the Smoky Hill would have been cut off, leaving Colorado and New Mexico isolated.

During the coming year more troops must be found for western service. The matter was equal in importance to that of Reconstruction, and he had told his senator-brother so. There was never enough cavalry. He had been obliged to shift his regiments back and forth, wearing out the horses and tiring the men. There was also a need for clarification of authority on the plains. Stanton was urged to study the problem. There was no law there, except the Indian Intercourse Act of 1834, which was "utterly in-

[36] General Order No. 10 issued at St. Louis, November 2, 1867. *General Orders, Division of the Missouri, 1865–82.*

applicable to the case." By this law the military could be called upon at any moment to eject by force the white population, "which embrace more or less of Indian lands." There were stage roads, telegraph lines, and railroads established in country where Indian titles had not been extinguished. Towns and settlements were "daily 'occurring' in western Dakota without any civil government." Murders and robberies were frequent. The military had no authority to intervene in these cases, and the situation would deteriorate more as people poured into these lands.

The railroads—the "Omaha Pacific" and "Kansas Pacific," as Sherman differentiated them—were, of course, the prime objects of protection. Not only did they aid the army by rapidly transporting troops and stores over a desolate land, but the states and territories to the west were increasingly dependent upon them. "When these two great thoroughfares reach the base of the Rocky Mountains, and when the Indian title to roam at will over the country lying between them is extinguished, then the solution of this most complicated question of Indian hostilities will be comparatively easy, for this belt of country will naturally fill up with our own people, who will permanently separate the hostile Indians of the north from those of the south, and allow us to direct our military forces one or the other at pleasure if thereafter they continue their acts of hostility." But until that time, the army, representing the government, which was "largely interested pecuniarily," would have to offer sufficient protection to allow unhampered progress in construction.[37]

Although Westerners bitterly criticized Sherman for not acting with sufficient vigor, there was basic agreement with his policy. What he hoped to accomplish in years, they, of course, wanted done immediately. He was impatient too, but he knew he had to restrain his feelings. If they hooted at the peace commission, so did he; but it was his duty to give the other side a chance to fail before he became too caustic. He frequently saw matters in the same light as the armchair strategists in western newspaper offices, but his official checkrein constantly tugged at

[37] Report of W. T. Sherman, October 1, 1867, *Annual Report of the Secretary of War*, 40 Cong., 2 sess., *House Exec. Doc. No. 1* (Serial 1324).

him, warning caution and prudence. While he patiently plotted his moves on his beloved maps, journalists painted their pictures with figurative blood and purple prose. When they ran out of violent phrases, biting sarcasm, and wild statements, they tried poetry. From Denver came one effort, entitled "Ode Onto the Friendlies."

> *Noble red man of the plains,*
> *Pouncing on unguarded trains,*
> *Where you come and where you go,*
> *Sherman's scouts would like to know.*
> *Burning here and scalping there,*
> *East and West and everywhere,*
> *Prowling like a tiger cat,*
> *Night and day along the Platte.*
> *Stealing boldly at your will,*
> *All along the Smoky Hill,*
> *First you come in parties small,*
> *Now in numbers that appal,*
> *Spreading death and devastation,*
> *Robbing ranches, burning stations,*
> *Such persistent visitation,*
> *Does not claim our admiration.*
> *Mr. Lo, now quit your tricks,*
> *Surely you'll get in a fix;*
> *Now just stop these ugly capers,*
> *Or we'll send you to the Quakers,*
> *If our boys start on the scout,*
> *Surely they will wipe you out;*
> *Go, bold red man of the West,*
> *Here your stay is short at best,*
> *Go and hunt the buffalo,*
> *We can spare you, Mr. Lo.*"[38]

Ignoring the growing volume of prose and poetry on the subject of Indian relations, Sherman tightened his resolve to move

[38] *Omaha Daily Herald,* August 8, 1867, quoting a Denver paper.

ahead methodically, step by step, until he was ready to snap the trap of military steel shut on these warlike nomads of the plains. He wished that he had only Indians to fight in the great campaign ahead; it would be much more simple that way.

Twelve

TIME IS HELPING US

As the year 1867 died, Sherman took inventory of his stock and noted that the past twelve months had provided both satisfactions and disappointments. The crop of rumors, especially the nasty one about Fort Buford, had left a bad taste in his mouth, but he tried to forget it. The persistence of the Interior Department in its cry for continued custody of that problem child—Indian affairs—meant future difficulties. Here was a matter of policy; it could not be ignored. It was fundamental to the completion of his task, and that disturbed him. Then there were the buzzings of western complaint and the snappings of the press. They were like cockleburs under the saddle blanket, annoying and distracting, but only superficial.

On the positive side of the ledger, he could smile over the progress of the railroads. The Union Pacific—Kansas and Nebraska branches—had crept forward, with only minor delays chargeable to Indian depredations. Soon the "Omaha Pacific" would reach the base of the Rockies; so would the "Kansas Pacific" that was now headed up the Smoky Hill route toward Denver, instead of in the direction of Fort Kearny, as originally planned. That would make two lines, all the way to the Rocky Mountains. They would revolutionize travel and go far toward a solution of the military problem in his Division. Already such places as Omaha and Fort Leavenworth were being left behind. A Leavenworth editor publicly admitted that already he missed those miles of canvas-topped schooners he used to watch churning up dust along Main Street. Now a railroad train snaked by the town, its whistle moaning progress at the residents, and then it was gone. Leavenworth was just another Kansas town.[1]

[1] *Leavenworth Daily Times,* July 27, 1867.

189

Nor had travel been disrupted as much as Westerners claimed. Missouri River steamers carried record cargoes in 1867, and wagon trains lined out beyond the railroads in greater numbers than ever before. No general war had ensued, despite the dark predictions earlier in the year. And since it failed to materialize, some of the fearful began to breath more easily. The *Army and Navy Journal* noted that the Indians were dividing, to the north and south, as the railroads knifed ahead. To Sherman's determination and insistence upon protection of the vital links went the credit.[2] New York called him another Andy Jackson and asked that people understand his genius. He was erratic, passionate, hasty, extreme in his likes and dislikes, even foolish sometimes. So was Jackson. But like Old Hickory, he always repented.[3]

As winter settled over the plains and the Indians stayed close to their camps, gnawing jerky and eyeing the deep snows, a white mantle quieted summer fears. It was time for the white men to quarrel with each other now, and Washington rang with echoes of oratorical frenzy. The main show was provided by the radicals, whose war against Andrew Johnson over Reconstruction was reaching bloody proportions. Next to the center ring, smaller performances were seen, as the Interior Department put on spectacular maneuvers to retain control of Indian affairs. Sherman wrote of it to Phil Sheridan, who in September, had replaced Hancock in the Department of Missouri. "The Peace men have been busy and have called into requisition every species of misrepresentation to impose on the Senate to prevent a transfer of the Indians to the War Department." He suspected that the Senate committee stood against the army. Senator Ross of Kansas already had predicted the outcome when he wrote Sherman, asking him to submit gracefully to an adverse decision. "I emphatically declined," the General told his fellow officer. But the game seemed lost. Even though the House had expressed its willingness, the conservative Senate appeared to be standing pat.[4]

2 Vol. V (June 29, 1867), 709.
3 *New York Herald*, July 16, 1867, quoted by the *Daily Missouri Republican*, July 21, 1867.

The peace commissioners submitted a report in early January that talked piously of its desire to see a speedy settlement of the western territories by "an industrious, thrifty, and enlightened population," and condemned the whites for violating Indian treaties. In its search for a plan to eliminate the causes of Indian wars, the commission had vaguely recommended that by February 1, 1869, all superintendents and agents should vacate their offices, so that they could be filled by men who were known competents. This did not bar men already in service who had demonstrated ability. Against Sherman's vote, it had decided to push for the establishment of an independent department for Indian affairs, taking the matter away from both War and Interior departments. The report also expressed disapproval of the system of territorial volunteers where the governors had any control. It was regarded as a war breeder.[5]

At the new and brawling village of Cheyenne, frontiersmen jeered in derision and said that since the treaties were made at Fort Laramie last fall, seven white men had been killed in the area. Bitingly the *Cheyenne Leader* explained that the natives were innocent. They were merely trying out the guns given them by the commissioners to see that they were in working order and that no swindle had taken place.[6]

There were other worries for Sherman. He had been called back to Washington, much to his dislike, to sit with the commissioners. Red Cloud had sent word that when the grass grew again, he would come to Laramie and "make talk." In the meantime, the peacemakers mulled over the results of their recent excursions into hostile country. Taylor fussed about the prospects of an Indian Bureau transfer, fearful that it would legislate him out of a job.[7] Sherman paid little attention to it; his mind was preoccupied with things more personal. President Johnson had

---

[4] Sherman to Sheridan, January 4, 1868. Sherman-Sheridan Correspondence, Volume 1. Division of Manuscripts, Library of Congress.

[5] Report of the Indian commissioners, January 7, 1868, *Annual Report of the Secretary of the Interior*, 40 Cong., 3 sess., *House Exec. Doc. No. 1* (Serial 1366), p. 492.

[6] January 28, 1868.

[7] Tappan to Sherman, February 8, 1868. William T. Sherman Papers, Volume 22.

quarreled with Grant, and his alienation now turned him anew toward Sherman, who received the presidential attentions with great discomfort. In an attempt to build up the hero of Atlanta to an equal status with Grant, who was General of the Army and in supreme command, Johnson was promoting the idea of creating a new military rank. Since there was provision for only one full general, the President hit upon the idea of making Sherman a brevet general and assigning him to a new military command to be known as the Department of the Atlantic, with headquarters at Washington, D. C. It would include all of the East, the Great Lakes, and the Capital itself.

Desperately Sherman pleaded with Johnson. He did not want to leave St. Louis; he could not afford to live in Washington and properly educate his children; it was an awful place anyway—it had been "fatal" to both Zachary Taylor and Winfield Scott.[8] "For eleven years I have been tossed about so much that I do really want to rest, study and make the acquaintance of my family," he wrote in anguish. "I do not think since 1857 I have arranged 30 days out of 365 at home." His command demanded much time, too. Soon he would have to go out West again and talk to the Sioux. Couldn't he have a little time with Ellen and the children?[9]

During February the struggle went on. After voicing all the the personal arguments he could muster, Sherman told Johnson that he doubted the legality of the move and asked him to recall the nomination. There was no provision for it in law, he said. It was inexpedient.[10] He did not approve of the brevet system. It had been badly misused. On and on he pleaded with Johnson, begging him to relent. Privately he knew it was embarrassing to all concerned, and he wanted no part of any struggles involving his old friend Grant. The political tentacles that enmeshed Washington had always terrified him. On his way back to St. Louis, Cump wrote plaintively to John, "I wish people would let me

8 Sherman to Johnson, January 31, 1868. William T. Sherman Papers, Volume 22.

9 Sherman to Johnson, January 27, 1868. William T. Sherman Papers, Volume 22.

10 *New York Times,* February 16, 1868; *Daily Missouri Republican,* February 18, 1868.

alone on politics which are more and more offensive to me...."[11] As winter began to weaken its grip, and the cold, gray period of dirty snow and occasional signs of spring appeared, he continued to fret. From Washington there was only silence. He was not yet sure that he could avoid the place, and his gloom deepened. "I don't care so much about St. Louis—any place out West is more to my family than Washington," he confided to John. Summers were hot in St. Louis, and the family usually left there during those months anyway. As a result, he felt "half disposed to move farther West."[12] St. Louis had originally attracted him because of his old friends there. In 1865 it had also been the most logical place for his headquarters and residence while commanding the great Division of the Missouri. But now there were railroads where only prairie sod had been at that time. What had been a raw frontier in 1865 was already being tamed with strips of steel in 1868.

Back again at St. Louis, Sherman tried to shove aside his concerns about Johnson and the horrible prospect of Washington. He had been forced to neglect his Division long enough, and plans must be laid for the coming summer. The most pressing item was the Bozeman Road. The Sioux had struck at it repeatedly during the past year, while the army, pressed by cries for help along the Union Pacific, had watched helplessly. The garrisons at Forts Reno, Phil Kearney, and C. F. Smith had been under a virtual state of siege, and although Sherman thirsted for revenge on Red Cloud, he could not spare the men to launch an all-out attack. In August, 1867, Grant had asked him, "What is the necessity of keeping up the posts...? No emigrants or trains seem to pass over. Let me have your views on this subject & if you deem it advisable break up these posts and remove the troops at once."[13] Sherman must have winced at Grant's naïveté. "No emigrants or trains *seem* to pass over!" Good Lord—there was reason enough for that. The simple fact was that the Sioux had

[11] Sherman to John Sherman, February 10, 1868. William T. Sherman Papers, Volume 22.

[12] Sherman to John Sherman, March 14, 1868. William T. Sherman Papers, Volume 22.

[13] Grant to Sherman, August 26, 1867. William T. Sherman Papers, Volume 21.

made good their threat to close that trail. To back out of the fight would be an admission of weakness and an invitation to further trouble, Sherman had then thought.[14]

By the spring of 1868 matters began to take on a different light. The railroad had passed Cheyenne and would before long be laid out as far as the Great Salt Lake. Its existence changed the military situation, and the first dividend to be declared was the ability to abandon the Bozeman Road in favor of one farther west. Sherman turned the problem over in his mind. Would it not be just as easy to use some other side road off the main line of travel? The rapidity and economy of the railroad reduced the earlier necessity of the Bozeman short cut into Montana. Why not cross the mountains, and then go north? If the Indians took the move to be a sign of weakness, the railroad could shuttle men back and forth along its line and offer ample protection. He thought that by now he could "with just propriety" consider the matter of vacating the war-torn road. "I would like to have your views as to the time, mode, & manner of making the change and what use you can make of the troops thus set free," he wrote Augur.[15] The railroad, which he had predicted would work toward the solution of the Indian problem, was now about to give him some much needed troopers. And time was working on the white man's side.

It looked as though additional men would be quickly put to use. Correspondence and newspapers at Division headquarters indicated that spring must be just around the corner, for cries of "help" were beginning to be heard from various western points. It was no different from last year. During the winter Arizona had been muttering about raising volunteers and had pointed out that in 1866 one company of them had killed one hundred Indians in three months, while the Fourteenth Regular Infantry companies stationed there had not accounted for a single one in twice that time.[16] W. A. Carter, the post trader at Fort Bridger, called for help too. Miners along the Sweetwater, near South Pass,

14 Report of W. T. Sherman, July 1, 1867, *Annual Report of the Secretary of War*, 40 Cong., 2 sess., *House Exec. Doc. No. 1* (Serial 1324), p. 65.

15 Sherman to Augur, February 28, 1868. C. C. Augur Papers.

16 *Omaha Weekly Herald*, November 7, 1867, quoting a San Francisco item.

were complaining that they were not safe and had asked him to intercede for them. The men, through Carter, forwarded the interesting idea that under the Treaty of Guadalupe Hidalgo in 1848, which ceded part of the country involved to the United States, no title to the land had been transferred to the Indians. The Mexican government had never recognized their ownership of the land, so why should not the United States put the Indians off it?[17] Young Cheyenne picked up the cry and bugled the song of danger from its infant newspaper. The inevitable "old settlers" had sounded off again with warnings that an Indian league was forming and would soon wipe out the white settlements. The paper collected such gossip and handed it along, with the judgment that surely this would be a bloody year on the plains.[18] In Kansas there were nods of assent. This would surely be a year of unparalleled turmoil. The journalistic drum-ruffling burst into a roll as it worked eastward. By the time it reached New York, papers there were sold on the certainty of war. The *Times* solemnly predicted an uprising when the grass grew in the West but offered the pious hope that this year's conflict would be less severe than the preceding one. Doggedly, the journal maintained, if only in a whisper, that the peace commission was on the right track when it proposed to place the Indians upon reservations.[19]

Cump wrote to John about the Indians. Everyone, East and West, seemed to be holding his breath, waiting for the war whoop, except the man in command of western forces. He rated the situation "quiet." If there should be any trouble during the coming season, he would "leave the agents to manage it until they confess an inability to manage their Indians when we would have to step in."[20] There was no talk this year about launching a mighty attack against the Sioux. The railroad was across the worst part of the plains; he could get supplies and men to danger

[17] W. A. Carter to Colonel W. A. Morrow, commanding officer at Fort Bridger, December 14, 1867. Division of the Missouri, Letters Received, 1866–69, Special File.

[18] *Cheyenne Leader,* March 30, 1868.

[19] April 19, 1868.

[20] Sherman to John Sherman, March 14, 1868. William T. Sherman Papers, Volume 22.

spots in good time if he had to; therefore, let the other side play a card now.

For the time being, Sherman allowed himself to go along with the peacemakers—literally and figuratively. They wanted to hold a council at Fort Laramie and talk with the Sioux again. Fine. He welcomed a chance to be in the West, in any capacity. Any time the gentlemen were ready. . . . Dodge was talking of locating what Sherman called "a dirty little town" (to be called Laramie) near Fort Sanders. Here would be a good chance to look into the matter.[21] He was eager to inspect the railroad again. It figured so largely in his plans.

On April 1, Sherman arrived at Omaha, where he joined his fellow commissioners. His pleasure at the prospect of another trip over the new rails was extinguished when he received orders to return at once to Washington. Henderson had been kept there because of the impeachment trial involving President Johnson. Now the managers called for Sherman, who was to testify in Grant's behalf. They expected him to be before them at 11:00 A.M. on April 14. Dutifully, if reluctantly, he turned back eastward after saying good-bye to the others, who went on to Fort Laramie. By the twenty-first he had completed his unpleasant task in the Capital and was once again bound for the West. Augur had telegraphed his hope that Sherman could get to the council. It appeared that all the Indians they wanted to talk with would be there, and "your presence is regarded as important."[22]

On his way back, Sherman stopped at St. Louis, where he wrote of his desire to meet with the gentlemen who had gone on ahead. "I notice the Indians are getting restless. This is natural for the Department has been unable to fulfil any of the promises we held out to them of ploughs, seed, cattle etc. to begin their new life of peace." At Fort Laramie there would be more parleys and more promises. He wanted to be there, but he was reluctant to be a party to any more promises. It meant more misunderstandings, more trouble. The government was getting "very venture-

21 Sherman to Dodge, March 10, 1868. Grenville M. Dodge Papers, Volume 15.
22 Augur to Sherman, April 17, 1868. William T. Sherman Papers, Volume 22.

some" in "these naked promises." The Indians must be made to understand that the commission's work was preliminary and in no way conclusive.[23] He would tell them that.

On April 29, a treaty was signed at Fort Laramie. Sanborn had telegraphed to Sherman the day before, "You need not hurry," explaining that the northern Brûlés and some of the Oglalas were ready to sign. Red Cloud had not yet arrived, and Sherman would be there in plenty of time to talk with him. "Everything looks most favorable for peace with the exception of the small war parties," Sanborn concluded.[24] By the treaty most of the Sioux agreed to accept reservations along the Missouri, but they insisted upon a clause giving them the right to hunt in the region of the North Platte and the Republican and Smoky Hill rivers, "so long as the buffalo may range thereon, in such numbers as to justify the chase." Sherman objected strongly to this concession, but the other commissioners argued that it was only a temporary thing because soon the buffalo in the area would be gone, and the Indians would move out. He shook his head over their optimism and, in his own hardheaded way, wrote Sheridan about it. "I think it would be wise to invite all the sportsmen of England & America there this fall for a Grand Buffalo hunt, and make one grand sweep of them all. Until the Buffaloes & consequent[ly] Indians are out from between the Roads we will have collisions & trouble."[25]

With the Brûlé Sioux agreeing to move to a reservation near Fort Randall, and the Crows pledged to occupy lands along the Yellowstone, the commissioners tried to persuade the Northern Cheyennes and Arapahoes to locate with the Sioux or to go with some of the tribes located, as Sherman put it, "back of Arkansas." The Oglalas and Miniconjou, meanwhile, remained to be dealt with. They were the terrors of the Powder River country and could not be brought to any agreement. The commissioners

23 Sherman to John Sherman, April 26, 1868. William T. Sherman Papers, Volume 22.

24 Sanborn to Sherman, April 28, 1868. William T. Sherman Papers, Volume 23.

25 Sherman to Sheridan, from Fort Laramie, May 10, 1868. Sherman-Sheridan Correspondence, Volume 1.

heard that the young bucks were holding out to see if the Bozeman Road would be closed, as promised, before signing.[26]

Sherman told Grant that he had "long since" given orders for the Powder River (or Bozeman Road) posts to be closed, but the matter would have to wait until summer. On June 1, all stores at Fort C. F. Smith that could not be moved to Omaha would be sold at auction to the Montanans. The garrison would then drop back to Fort Phil Kearney. That post would, in turn, be abandoned and everything portable removed to Fort Reno, farther south. Shortly, Reno would be broken up, and the withdrawal to Fort Laramie would complete the abandonment of the Montana road. Fort Fetterman, begun last year, would not be finished. A projected post, at the head of the Wind River, would not be built. The retreat to the railroad would then be fully accomplished; that should certainly satisfy the Oglalas and Minniconjou.

It satisfied Sherman. The railroad had changed things sufficiently that, from now on, troops could be wintered at such places as Omaha, and during the summer they would live in tents, out in the field. "We have never had reserves in hand for the clamors that always open with spring, and instead of pushing our troops out so far, I am convinced we should have a Regm't at Omaha in winter to send out on the Railroad to meet these cases," he explained to Grant. The government could save money by discontinuing the expensive small posts scattered over the prairies. Citizens of Omaha had offered to donate the land. Why not build cheap barracks there for winter use? "I am satisfied this will prove more economical and more efficient than to rebuild one or more new Posts only to have to replace those to be abandoned."

As for the treaties, they were about to be concluded, and that would terminate business in the Fort Laramie region. Sherman was discouraged by the progress so far. Congress was engaged in a death struggle with the executive, and impeachment proceed-

26 Sherman to Grant, May 8, 1868, in letter from the Secretary of War, transmitting a communication of Lieutenant General Sherman, relative to the subsistence of certain Indian tribes by the War Department, etc. 40 Cong., 2 sess., *House Exec. Doc. No. 239* (Serial 1341), XV.

ings occupied the center of the stage. Meanwhile, promises to the Indians were not being carried out, and the natives were convinced that the Great White Father's word was no better than it had ever been. Even though Congress seemed unwilling to take action on the commission's recommendation of last fall, the peacemakers would continue their efforts. From Fort Laramie, Augur, Terry, Tappan, and Sherman would go to Cheyenne, leaving Harney and Sanborn to await Red Cloud and Man-Afraid-of-His-Horses, who had promised to come in. From Cheyenne, Sherman and Tappan planned to go to Denver and then to New Mexico, to treat with the Navajos. Augur would proceed to Fort Bridger, where the Shoshones and Snakes were reported to be willing and waiting. Terry, meanwhile, would head for Forts Randall and Sully to prepare for the coming of the Sioux, who had promised to take up their reservations in that region. Harney and Sanborn hoped to join him later and make treaties with other Missouri River Indians. "Thus you will see we have cut out work for all summer," Sherman concluded.

With regard to the reports of war on the plains, he expressed confidence that there would be only scattered raiding and marauding. "In time we must take these wild Indians in hand, and give them a devil of a thrashing. They deserve it now, but they are so scattered and so mixed up that even if we were prepared we would hardly know which way to strike." For the time being, Sherman promised, he would try to give the railroads every protection, but he simply could not run down every horse thief and protect every ranch in the vast expanse under his command. The railroads alone provided a big enough problem. There were stations every twenty miles or so, which were not really settlements, and they were sufficiently dispersed "that they are a weakness instead of a strength. They are all clamoring for protection and Genl. Augur has been forced to place soldiers at nearly every station outside of Omaha." Despite this, the railroad was of great value because it lent mobility and rapid communication, "and cannot be stolen like horses and mules of trains of old." If only the friendly Indians who gathered along the line could be moved, it would be a big help, for the whites regarded all of them as hostile and were willing to pull the trigger on sight. Why not move them at once? he asked Grant. "I deem it essential . . . even at our own Military expense, without awaiting the lawful but slow action of Congress."[27]

With the business at hand concluded, most of the commissioners left Fort Laramie for further Indian negotiations throughout the West. Sherman and Tappan arrived on May 13 at Cheyenne, from where the latter entrained for Omaha on private business, promising to overtake his traveling companion at Denver. After a day or two, Sherman himself headed for the Colorado capital. Meanwhile, he looked at the progress of the railroad and reported to John that it had now gone seventeen miles beyond Fort Sanders. The "dirty little town" he had warned Dodge about was now mushrooming two miles north of the Fort. "[It is] called Laramie City but it is of the temporary kind which takes up its boards and moves on as the Railroad progresses," Cump wrote his brother. He hoped it would move; its fleshpots that disturbed discipline at the post would not be missed by him. Officials of the road told him that rail service as far as Fort Bridger could be expected during 1868, and there was even talk of reaching the Salt Lake valley. The proposed route would take the rails north of the lake, leaving Salt Lake City to the south, but, as Sherman said, "Brigham Young will build him a branch."[28] Cheyenne was delighted by its recent connection with "the States," and boasted that railroads would soon dispel the "Great American Desert" theory. The infant village with a full-grown chamber of commerce spirit shouted the prediction that "the greatness of America's future will be found in the West. . . . The ocean steamers, the river steamers and the railways, are all crowded to overflowing with the multitudes who form the Star

27 Sherman to Grant, May 8, 1868. Division of the Missouri, Letters Received, 1866–69, Special File.

28 Sherman to John Sherman from Denver, May [?] 17, 1868. William T. Sherman Papers, Volume 23. The date given on this letter, in manuscript form, and printed in Rachel Sherman Thorndike (ed.), *The Sherman Letters*, 320, seems in error. It is dated June 17, 1868. Other evidence shows that Sherman was en route, by coach from Santa Fé, via Fort Lyon and the Smoky Hill route, back to St. Louis at this time. He did go from Cheyenne to Denver on May 16 and was in that city May 17. The letter itself suggests that May 17 is the correct date.

of Empire."[29] Thomas Hart Benton would have been proud of Cheyenne.

Sherman was probably interested in another little station lying between Cheyenne and Laramie. It had recently sprung up as an "end of the track" settlement, and it bore his name. He later explained the circumstances of its christening. When he was out along the line in 1867, Herbert M. Hoxie, chief of the surveying corps for the railroad, had shown him a map of the road and remarked that one of its stations would be called Sherman.

"Where is it?" the interested General had inquired.

"Down here in Nebraska."

"Oh, I don't want a water station named for me," Sherman replied. "Why, nobody will live there. Where is the highest point on the road?"

Hoxie ran his finger over to a place labelled "Altimont."

"Just scratch out that name, and put down mine," Sherman told him, and it was done.

Some years later when he was asked what name had been given to the place in Nebraska, he replied, "Oh, God only knows. But I've heard that it contains only a water tank and a section house."[30] Sherman's pride in his namesake would be somewhat wounded if he were to see the place today that lost its name of Altimont. It is little more than a signpost between that "dirty little town" and "hell on wheels"—both "temporary" towns that refused to take up their boards and move with the railroad.

Shortly after the middle of May, Cump was in Denver, telling John of dining with A. C. Hunt and the DeLano family. "They are very friendly and have made full inquiries about you and speak most affectionately of our former visit." Denver had not changed much since the brothers saw it in 1866. It was "even duller by reason that the Rail Road carries travel past, and nobody comes here unless on business pertaining to Colorado."[31] Western papers reported less friendly relations and talked of a "charivari" in which he was burned in effigy at the mile-high city.

[29] *Cheyenne Leader,* April 20, 1868.

[30] *Cheyenne Daily Leader,* September 8, 1880.

[31] Sherman to John Sherman, May 17, 1868. William T. Sherman Papers, Volume 23.

"Such is popularity! Not long since he was, perhaps, the most popular man in the United States."[32] Sherman shrugged it off and explained to John that "I am of course held responsible by the Frontier people for not rushing to war because of occasional depredations some of which have undoubtedly been committed by white men. Yet as I don't ask their votes I can stand their personal abuse."[33] While in Denver he freely answered all questions put to him about Indian affairs. "He was cordial and animated in conversation," admitted the town's leading newspaper. With an air of resignation, the editor concluded that if it was the "settled and determined policy" of the government, "which is high over all," to carry forward its peace plans, the territorial residents would have to submit gracefully, even if they had "ever so little faith in it."[34]

A few days later he was bound for Fort Sumner, in eastern New Mexico, ready to talk with the Navajos. Tappan had returned from Omaha, and together they went south into the country Sherman so disdained. As he traveled, a letter from his old West Point crony and close personal friend, General Stewart Van Vliet, felt its way toward him. "Van," as Sherman called him, hoped that the letter would find him back in St. Louis, safe. "I want to see you out of that Indian country, for you expose yourself so unnecessarily with insufficient escort, that I am always afraid that you will 'go under' on some of your trips. As you are now about to scoop the rewards for all your services to the country [the prospects of being made General of the Army if Grant became President] I don't want you to lose the chance through the instrumentality of some rugged Indian."[35] If Sherman received the letter before returning to his office, he must have smiled at it because, as he said to Grant, four armed men could go safely anywhere in New Mexico.

32 *Deseret News* (Salt Lake City), June 3, 1868. The *Omaha Weekly Herald* of May 13 said it was reported that Sherman had been "publicly insulted" at Cheyenne.
33 Sherman to John Sherman, May 17, 1868. William T. Sherman Papers, Volume 23.
34 *Daily Rocky Mountain News*, May 16, 1868.
35 Van Vliet to Sherman, from Baltimore, May 29, 1868. William T. Sherman Papers, Volume 23.

On May 28, Sherman and Tappan began their talks with the Navajos. They were without the services of the veteran Westerner Kit Carson this time. He had died quietly at his home only a few days before, while Sherman was at Fort Laramie. The Indian reservation near Fort Sumner, called the Bosque Redondo (round forest), lay along the Pecos River not far from the Texas border. It was, in Sherman's words, "a mere spot of green grass in the midst of a wild desert," where the Navajos had been collected by General Carleton four years before. Looking at the miserable, starving Indians before him, Sherman spoke, reviewing the causes for their removal to that spot. He said that the government had provided tools, seeds, and protection. Why had they not made farms, as it had been intended? Barboncito, their recognized leader, spoke for the Indians. They had done their very best. The first year, worms had eaten the corn; the second year, the same; the third year, hail had wiped out the crop; now, in the fourth year, they had given up. The Navajo probably wondered why the observing General had asked such a question.

"I have listened to all you have said of your people and believe you have told us the truth," Sherman answered. "You are right, the world is big enough for all the people it contains and all should live at peace with their neighbors. All people love the country where they were born and raised, but the Navajos are very few indeed compared with all the people of the world, they are not more than seven leaves to all the leaves you have ever seen. Still we want to do to you what is right—right to you—and right to us as a people. If you will live in peace with your neighbors, we will see that your neighbors will be at peace with you." He then explained to them the reservation system and promised that representatives of the tribe could go east to Indian Territory and see it. If they moved there, the army would guarantee protection.

Barboncito countered with the argument that the Bosque Redondo had been described to them as a good place. It was not. Nor did the Navajos want to go east; they wanted to go home. Sherman thought it over, and on the next day he promised the Indians that they might go back to their old haunts in northwestern New Mexico. There the Navajos would be given a one-hundred-mile-square reservation as their own. Barboncito expressed pleasure at the arrangement and agreed to sign a treaty to that effect on the following day, Monday, June 1.[36]

Sherman faithfully reported his negotiations to Grant and asked approval of his decision. The Navajos, he said, had sunk into a condition of absolute poverty and despair at the Bosque Redondo. They did not want to move farther east and he did not blame them. The Plains Indians there would make life perilous indeed for such a weak tribe. Meanwhile, something had to be done. John, who had been listening to Senator Henderson discuss the question on the Senate floor, also learned from brother Cump that the present Navajo situation was untenable. There were 7,200 of them, huddled together, starving. The first year of their residence at the reservation had cost the government $700,-000. The next year, the expense had been $500,000. Although the Indians were reported to have worked hard, they had raised no crops in that period and were totally dependent upon outside support. Now there was only about $300,000 left for them, which would buy only one pound of beef and one pound of corn a day for each Indian. It was a situation with no future. The wood was gone and the water was foul. If left, the Indians would be forced to scatter, and that would mean more trouble. "So of course we concluded to move them, after debating all the country at our option we have chosen a small part of their old country, which is as far out of the way of the whites, and of our future probable wants, as possible. . . ."

Nobody in eastern New Mexico was happy about the decision. Sherman promised Grant that he would come home "fortified by facts that will satisfy most people," but confessed that Carleton and the New Mexicans were "half-crazy" on the question. The rancheros in the region were displeased because the reservation "consuming so much public money was of profit and advantage to them." Only those around the proposed western location, hungry for federal largess, were happy. "Now if the Navajos were

36 Council proceedings of May 28, 29, and 30, 1868. William T. Sherman Papers, Volume 23.

"From talk of war and campaigns—things he knew—Sherman was now obliged to turn his thoughts to talk of peace."

Above: Indian peace commissioners in council with Arapahoes and Cheyennes, 1868. Sherman is third from the left, next to white-bearded General Harney.

Below: Peace commissioners at Fort Laramie, 1868. Left to right: Generals Terry, Harney, and Sherman, a Sioux woman, N. G. Taylor, S. F. Tappan, and General C. C. Augur.

Satanta, the Kiowa chief whom Sherman returned to Texas
to be tried for the fatal attack
on Henry Warren's wagon train near Fort Richardson, Texas.

a hostile or dangerous tribe of Indians the very reverse would be the case," he rasped. It was the same wherever he went in the West. He found scattered settlements, with no transportation and no market for agricultural goods, all nuzzling at the nearest Treasury teat. And New Mexico was the worst of them all.

"This whole country is a desert," Sherman bluntly wrote. ". . . One county of Ohio will maintain a larger population than all New Mexico. Nor do I see any hope in the future. This Territory has cost over a hundred millions of dollars already, and will always cost from three to five millions a year, and never by any process can it ever contribute one cent to the national income. The population is a mixed band of Mexican, indian, & negro, inferior to either race if pure. A few Americans from the U.S. are here holding office, having stores or farms, entirely dependent for maintenance & profit on the Government disbursements. . . . We are spending annually more than all the country with its houses, land, cattle, sheep and people would sell for, but I suppose it cannot be helped." He had made similar remarks to Grant a few days before and had written that "the only profitable mines in New Mexico have their base in the U.S. Treasury in Washington."

As he wrote on, Sherman grew more bitter. If a sheep or a steer was stolen in this country, the owner would ride one hundred miles to report it at some post. Consequently, the troops were running all over the territory, hunting for common thieves. This was not "soldiering" to Sherman and he promised that he would put a stop to it, even though "you will hear me abused terrifically." But to the devil with all of them. They could bleat about it as much as they liked. He would have Congress know the truth —that millions were being spent that "a few miserable people may live and thrive." It was "an outrage on human nature." These people could easily defend themselves if they wanted to. Instead, they set up a clamor that reverberated all the way to Washington and came echoing back in dollar signs. All the frontier people had a right to ask for was ordinary protection for their main roads and principal towns, or places where Indian concentrations called for more than usual defensive measures.

The New Mexicans were the most vocal with the least cause. He was reminded of a story about "that Hypochondriac Doctor, who was delivered of the Woodchuck baby. 'Well you are a d——d ugly looking thing, but as you are mine I suppose I must support you.' So of New Mexico. It is a d——d ugly elephant on our hands, but as we were fools enough to buy it of Mexico we must feed and maintain its mongrel population forever."

On June 11, Sherman and Tappan headed north of Fort Union to deal with some of the Utes in New Mexico. "They are like the Navajos fed by the Government in absolute idleness, in the theory that it is cheaper to feed than fight them," he explained to his brother. He didn't object to the principle; it was all right in a place like "the borders of Kansas, where there is some hope of land being rendered to use, but out here, where there is no human probability of anybody settling, I think those Indians should also be located." They would be well out of the way, for even then they were eating government beef, and at the same time stealing out for a raid or two, making sure to get back in time "to let the Navajos or Apaches get the blame." Why could they not be put with the rest of the Utes, in southwestern Colorado, beyond the Rockies? Of course the philanthropists wanted to chrisitanize them. "I wish they would come & undertake it," Sherman snorted. The best that could be done with them was to protect and keep them quiet "till time and events settle this, one of the most vexatious things I have ever had to deal with. ... Time is helping us & killing the Indians fast, so that every year the task is less."[37]

After talking with the Utes, Sherman headed for home. Moving north again, into Colorado, he passed through Trinidad and then went down the Arkansas River to Fort Lyon, retracing his steps of 1866. Much of the way he traveled by ordinary stage line and noted that although he read all kinds of accounts of Indian outrages, he found none. The trip had been perfectly safe, and

---

[37] Sherman's attitude toward the Navajos and Utes and details of the treaty can be found at length in two letters: Sherman to Grant, from Santa Fé, June 7, 1868. Division of the Missouri, Letters Received, 1866–69, Special File; Sherman to John Sherman, from Fort Union, New Mexico, June 11, 1868. William T. Sherman Papers, Volume 23.

at no point had he asked for an escort of more than ten men. Most of the time he had no escort at all. From Fort Lyon he rode north to Cheyenne Wells, then on down the Smoky Hill route to Fort Wallace. At that point he was only thirty-two miles from the terminus of the Union Pacific's Kansas branch.[38]

Homecoming at St. Louis was in every way normal. Requests for reports, back correspondence to answer, and complaints about his management of the Division from the western press—all stared at him from his desk. He did not mind the reports; they were as inevitable as the red tape that bound them together. The correspondence was sometimes enjoyable; it kept him informed on affairs in his command. But the newspapers nettled him. While they were nothing more than a surface irritant, their insistent clamor on the subject of Indians got tiresome. He had just made a circle tour to Fort Laramie, the end of the main railroad track, Denver, Santa Fé, Fort Sumner, Fort Lyon, and back up the Smoky Hill through Fort Riley and Leavenworth. At no point had he seen a single threatening Indian. But editorials reflected complaints of alleged depredations and the army's apparent inability to prevent them. They talked darkly about "the new war on the frontier" and predicted awful things for the West. And while this was going on, a bill appeared on the floor of Congress recommending a reduction of the army to 25,000 men. Eastern papers, smelling economy in the measure, had backed it, saying, "We have no need whatever for an army of fifty thousand men. It subserves no valuable purpose, no public security."[39] Here would be a new front to combat. With a population fanning out all over the West, demanding more and more protection, the army was to be cut to mere squads of men. Sherman had a right to be discouraged.

Writing to a friend of Mexican War days, he expressed his concern. "Very few men appreciate the vast extent of these Territories, and when I travel days & weeks & months and then on the map see how little I traveled, as compared with the whole,

---

[38] Sherman to Townsend, June 24, 1868. Division of the Missouri, Letters Received, 1866–69, Special File.
[39] *New York Times*, July 10, 1868.

I feel almost in despair at ever bringing all that country into any sort of order or subjugation. Little by little however it will be done. . . ."[40] The problem would certainly be one of tortuously slow solution. Much of the land was arid; the Indians, in small bands, had the tactical advantage; the distances were such that few Easterners understood them. But the land was shrinking as the railroads revolutionized transportation. Perhaps the distances would diminish faster than his dwindling army, giving him relatively more strength.

Reporting on his trip to headquarters, he said that his travels in the West had convinced him that the "true military policy will be for many years to keep small but well supplied posts along the great lines of travel east and west, marked by the two Pacific Railroads." As he had said at Fort Laramie, reserves could be kept at such points as Omaha and Leavenworth during the winter and shuttled back and forth across the plains in the fighting season.[41] If the Indian ponies could outrun and outlast the jaded cavalry stock, perhaps the panting iron horse might be brought into use against them. Both time and money could be saved. During one year, 1867, the cost of transporting military supplies on just one branch of the railroad—the Kansas—was $511,908.24. If they had been hauled by wagon, and the mails carried by stage, and if the troops transported had marched instead, the cost would have run to $1,358,291.06. The government had saved $846,382.82 on a part of the Union Pacific Railroad in a single year.[42]

The year 1868 marked the turning point in western defense. From that time on, until the Indians were submerged to a point of being subjects for a Congressional investigation, the army would flank the advancing rails as they sliced the land into submissive segments. It was the beginning of the end, and the ring of sledges on railroad spikes ticked off the time for a condemned race. Even before the Union Pacific was linked with the Central

40 Sherman to Bailey, July 14, 1868. Rutherford B. Hayes Papers, Hayes Memorial Library, Fremont, Ohio.

41 Sherman to Townsend, June 25, 1868. Division of the Missouri, Letters Received, 1866–69, Special File.

42 *Cheyenne Leader*, July 1, 1868.

Pacific at Promontory, the West Coast was beginning to feel as secure as the Atlantic seaboard. The Sacramento *Union* was now lecturing the hinterlanders about their wrongs against the Indians and accusing the whites of being the aggressors in nine cases out of ten. Montana, still remote and isolated, was driven into a fury by this attack "from the rear." A Virginia City editor shouted that "if the author of the above would take a small dose of personal experience and retire nights with a poultice of brains inside his head, he would not write such stuff."[43] In a few years rails would infiltrate the wild reaches of Montana, and such editorial outbursts would be passé. The Indian problem diminished in direct proportion to the extension of the railroads, and Sherman knew it. He would stick to his present plans.

For the moment, the delay in hostilities occasioned by the peace commission's efforts seemed to be working in the army's favor. Terry wrote Sherman a personal letter from Fort Rice, Dakota Territory, saying that the disposition of the Indians in that sector seemed good. "Many of them at least, if not all, are I think, sincerely desirous of peace & I look forward hopefully to the result of our efforts to conclude a treaty."[44] Tappan, with whom Sherman was later to quarrel, wrote glowingly of the General's efforts. Congress was confused about Indian matters, he said, and surely no bill ordering the removal of the Navajos from the Bosque Redondo could have passed that body in its existing state of indecision. "But now it is done, and well done, all except a few from New Mexico are gratified and most heartily endorse the movement. No objection is made. What you do will be approved." He praised Sherman lavishly, expressing his conviction that "Congress and the people are glad to leave it to you. . . . You are in a fortunate position. Your march to the sea and your settlement of our Indian Affairs so far, gives you a prestige no one else has or ever will have in this country."[45] There were others who recognized such genius too, Tappan went on in another letter. He had talked with Ben Butler, notorious in the

[43] *Montana Post*, June 12, 1868, quoting the Sacramento *Union*.
[44] Terry to Sherman, June 13, 1868. William T. Sherman Papers, Volume 23.
[45] Tappan to Sherman, July 8, 1868. William T. Sherman Papers, Volume 23.

recent war for his "woman order" at New Orleans, when he had insulted the belles of that city in demanding their respect for his troops. Butler was now in Congress and would for some years be a noisy participant on the political scene.

"Tappan," Butler was reported to have said, "now tell me upon your honor, who in this country is the best man to disburse this money [to the Indians]?" Tappan, who swore he had long since made up his mind on the subject, answered, "General Sherman."

"That is so," replied Butler, "and he shall have it."

Tappan wrote on, saying that Butler seemed determined that not a cent of money should be expended in Indian country except by Sherman. However, some inconvenient treaties in the past had specified that the commissioner of Indian affairs should be the purchasing officer in such cases. Well, continued Tappan, Sherman should not be bothered with such details anyway, "so it was not done." As military commander, he at least could regulate their distribution "in such a manner as you may consider for the interest of the public service."[46]

Sherman was deeply suspicious of both Tappan and Butler, and he paid little attention to the flattering remarks, but it did seem, in view of mounting evidence, that the waiting game was going to pay off. Aside from the splutterings coming from more remote parts of the West, the nation seemed to have settled down somewhat on the Indian question. Happier sounds were coming from the main body of the press, and Congress, in its recent preoccupation with impeachment and the excitement resulting from Grant's nomination, was sufficiently disorganized to prevent anything positive, one way or the other, from happening. It was a period of waiting. As time passed, and the Indians admired the "gewgaws" dangled before them by the treaty makers, shrill Chinese voices drifted nearer to rich Irish brogues, revealing that railroad workers were closing the gap in the West. Sherman had echoed Grant's sentiment in a recent letter when he wrote, "I agree with you that the chief use of the Peace Commission is to kill time which will do more to settle Indians than anything we

46 Tappan to Sherman, July 20, 1868. William T. Sherman Papers, Volume 23.

can do."[47] As he sat in his office at St. Louis and scanned the ever present maps, he knew it was all that could be accomplished for the present. Kill time now; kill Indians later.

[47] Sherman to Grant, June 7, 1868. Division of the Missouri, Letters Received, 1866–69, Special File.

Thirteen

WITH VINDICTIVE EARNESTNESS

SHERMAN'S ENTHUSIASM for the West was so infectious that his reports to Grant, both official and unofficial, must have aroused the latter's curiosity about the vast reaches of land stretching toward the Rockies. While many of the letters reaching Washington talked gravely of military problems and possible solutions, there was an overtone that revealed delight with the region concerned. The stark grandeur of the blue-gray peaks, their lower elevations clothed in rich green and the jagged spires shrouded by fluffy clouds, had appealed mightily to Sherman. So had the cascading streams that mixed clear blue water with occasional white, boiling spume as they dropped breath-takingly down precipitous slopes. To lie beside one of these sparkling watercourses, in a world screened off by a mighty granite backdrop that seemed to reach the heavens and lit up by a roaring fire of snarling pine knots, was worth the many parched days it took to reach such a land. And now it was simple; anybody could do it. Just get on a railroad car. Sherman was happy when Grant had said that he wanted to go.

There was no objection to retracing his steps so soon after returning to St. Louis. The Mississippi Valley was hot and humid in July, while Colorado was high, crisp, and much cooler. It would be a pleasant trip, and Grant could see some of the problems with his own eyes. It was even more important now because the Republicans had nominated Grant for the presidency, and in Sherman's mind he was sure to win. With an army man in the White House, many snarls that tangled the military could be quickly straightened out. Grant's campaign managers were also happy about his decision to go West in 1868. They wanted to elect a legend and were satisfied to have the man out of public view and unavailable for the political turmoil that was sure to ensue. The idea suited Grant, who was no politician, and it positively delighted Sherman.

In the middle of July, Sherman and Grant picked up "Little Phil" Sheridan, the dashing cavalryman who had come to fame by his spectacular ride at the Battle of Winchester during the war, and started over the Kansas Pacific Railroad. Sheridan, who commanded the Department of Missouri,[1] and Sherman, his immediate superior, were both eager to take the presidential candidate over the Smoky Hill route to Denver. Much of the rumor and excitement in the West had come from this region during the past two years. At that very moment, Hancock, whose place Sheridan now held, was writing angry letters to Sherman about the commotion arising out of the Pawnee-village burning on April 19, 1867. The peace commission, of which Sherman was a member, had suggested that the troubles of that summer had stemmed from Hancock's raid, and Senator Henderson had recently made such an inference on the floor of the Senate. Sherman had defended the action at Pawnee Fork thoroughly in his reports to headquarters and had vindicated Hancock completely, but the sensitive officer was not yet satisfied.[2] It would be well, Sherman thought, for Grant to see some of this country; he would be better able to appreciate the many complicated problems involved. The Hancock case demonstrated perfectly the dilemma of the military.

By July 17 they were at Leavenworth, where admiring reporters visited with them. Seldom had that city seen so much high brass at one time. Grant looked a little careworn, but "Sherman looks remarkably well all over. He is a soldier and a gentleman without fear and without reproach."[3] There now seemed

[1] Sheridan was assigned to command the Department of Missouri in September, 1867. He asked for a few months' leave, "as I was much run down in health from the Louisiana climate," and did not go on duty at his new assignment until March, 1868. Philip H. Sheridan, *Personal Memoirs of P. H. Sheridan,* II, 283.

[2] Hancock had asked Sherman for "an explanation" on May 27. See Hancock to Sherman, May 27, 1868. William T. Sherman Papers, Volume 23. Henderson assured Hancock that Sherman, while on the peace commission, had always defended him. Henderson to Hancock, June 24, 1868. William T. Sherman Papers, Volume 23.

[3] *Leavenworth Daily Times,* July 18, 1868, quoted by the *New York Times,* July 22, 1868.

to be peace, even with the press. Such accolades! This was too good to last. Correspondents who traveled with the officers were surprised at the air of joviality. Was it because of Grant's political aspirations? Or did it arise from the pleasure of three fighting generals who were glad to be together again in a kind of traveling reunion. There were frequent stops and the inescapable speeches from the rear platform. Grant was affable and full of stories. The onlookers were fascinated. Even Sherman dropped the mask he usually presented to the press and opened up. "[He] did most of the talking—he never stops." Sheridan was reported to be "full of life, fun and fire." And it all seemed to come naturally, for, as one correspondent wrote in near disappointment, no liquor was seen on the train.[4] Grant was not living up to his reputation. He was voluble and sober.

At Cheyenne Wells the men left the railroad and boarded a stagecoach for Denver. Twenty-four hours and 170 miles later they were in what residents proudly called "The Queen City of the Plains." They moved on into the mountains as far as the mining camp of Georgetown, where they relaxed for a week. Although there were "numerous toadies" around, as usual, they were left to themselves most of the time. Dressed in ordinary civilian clothing, they attracted little attention. "This may be one of the reasons why they stayed so long," concluded one of the townsmen.[5] It was the same at Cheyenne a few days later. During the short stay there, while waiting for a train to take them to the end of the track, they appeared on the streets "with so much of an unassuming and quiet air that, had not everyone been on the *qui vive* to see the renowned visitors, they would not have been distinguished from any ordinary gentlemen strolling around the town."[6]

But pleasure was not to be undisturbed by responsibility. At Fort Sanders, near Laramie, a major decision was thrust at Grant. Thomas Durant, first vice president of the Union Pacific and one of the heaviest stockholders in the road, chose this time to have

---

4 *New York Times*, July 24, 1868, quoting the *Leavenworth Bulletin*.
5 Mason Bradford Shelton, *Rocky Mountain Adventures*, 100.
6 *Cheyenne Leader*, July 25, 1868.

a showdown with General Dodge. The two had quarreled over possible routes to the west, and now Durant decided it was a strategic time to play his hand. He charged Dodge with selecting impossible terrain over which to build, of wasting money, and of ignoring the judgment of others in the company. Grant, leaning back in his cane-bottomed chair, puffed thoughtfully at a cigar and said, "What about it, Dodge?"

"Just this," Dodge said evenly, "If Durant, or anybody connected with the Union Pacific, or anybody connected with the government changes my lines I'll quit the road."

There was a tense silence as Grant puffed away, squinting at Dodge and glancing at Sherman, whose wrinkled face revealed nothing. The three men had been very close friends all during the war, and Dodge knew he held some high cards in the game. As Grant set his jaw on a black cigar stub, Durant's delicate fingers nervously stroked his Vandyke beard. Dodge was frozen in silence; he had called Durant and had raised him. Finally Grant spoke.

"The government expects this railroad to be finished. The government expects the railroad company to meet its obligations. And the government expects General Dodge to remain with the road as its chief engineer until it is completed."[7] Sherman said nothing, but his faith in Grant was further strengthened. He would have said the same thing in the same even tones.

Durant withdrew his objections, and with the impasse broken, the Generals continued their inspection of the road as if nothing had happened. When they returned to Cheyenne, a reception was held for Grant, and the same pleasant atmosphere prevailed as before. The *Cheyenne Leader,* so caustic in its remarks about Sherman's military policies during the past year, reported that the three notables talked "quite freely upon a variety of subjects with mutual pleasure to all." Before long, they boarded a train and headed east on the Union Pacific's main line, completing a circle tour of the High Plains. During the time they had been out, papers in general praised Sherman's recent efforts with the

[7] Jacob Randolph Perkins, *Trails, Rails and War; Life of General G. M. Dodge,* 221–22.

Indians. From the Atlantic seaboard came expressions of delight with the decision to put the disbursement of Indian money into his hands. "This kills completely what is known as the Indian ring," said one paper.[8] Meanwhile, Sanborn had written that although no general Indian legislation had come out of Congress, there was now appropriated a reasonable amount to carry forward the commission's work and policy. For example, $500,000 would be available to move and feed the Sioux and other Plains Indians.[9] Things were looking better all the time. Senator James Nye's recent defense of Sherman and the commission on the Senate floor was heartening. Here was Nevada patting him on the back. How long could the love feast last?

As the train carried the men eastward again, such interesting things as railroad-building in the rugged mountains disappeared in the distance. Back now to the more settled sections of the country and inescapable politics. There would be speeches, handshaking, and public displays. Sherman dreaded them all. He recalled his anger recently in St. Louis when jostling crowds had surrounded him as he got out of a streetcar, asking what he thought of the Democrats' choice of Seymour as a candidate to oppose Grant. When he said, "Bad nomination; will be beaten all to pieces; Grant will be elected," the crowd roared its disapproval. Harsh voices replied, "We don't want the support of house burners," alluding to the desolation his "bummers" had wrought between Atlanta and Savannah during the war. "You wanted the nomination yourself," another shouted. "You want Grant elected so as to get his place at the head of the army," came a taunting call. Sherman had stormed off in a rage, leaving the muttering mob.[10]

Now, on the return from Cheyenne, there was more of such turbulence. When Sherman tried to help the taciturn Grant in St. Joseph, Missouri, he ran into raucous cheers for Seymour and Blair. "I do not desire to advise violence, but if I was a resident of St. Joseph I would duck that fellow in the Missouri River,"

8 *New York Daily Tribune,* July 22, 1868.
9 Sanborn to Sherman, July 27, 1868. William T. Sherman Papers, Volume 23.
10 *Omaha Weekly Republican,* July 15, 1868.

Sherman shouted at the crowd, pointing at a particularly loud detractor. No one moved to disturb the heckler, and the groans from the gathering grew louder.

"There was a time when people who wanted to fight could be accommodated; we gave them all they wanted," snarled the angry General. "When you learn to behave yourself, I'll continue my speech." Another outburst of catcalls and groans followed this remark.

"Well, I'll eat my supper and go to bed; you can do what you please," Sherman said tersely, ending his attempt at speech-making.[11] His efforts to help Grant had been a miserable failure here. Probably he wondered why anyone in his right mind ever thought he would be interested in politics. If he should enter that sordid arena, he would agree with Murat Halstead's earlier charge that he was indeed crazy.

The western trip had been otherwise enjoyable, but it was with a sense of relief that Sherman bade Grant and other members of his party good-bye at Omaha. He was perfectly willing to give the monosyllabic candidate any help he could in fending off crowds of eager listeners, but he found it hard to hold his temper when dealing with the shoving, clamorous, rude mobs. The commission had now made provision for a large Indian reservation on each side of the belt of land bordered by the two Pacific Railroad branches, and he was anxious to start moving the tribes onto them. He hastened back to St. Louis to put his plans into motion.

On August 10, General Order No. 4 was published at Division headquarters. Sherman directed his subordinates to conduct the Indians to the recently assigned reservations, using the money appropriated and given to him for locating them.[12] When the tribes were settled in their new homes, and civilian agents properly appointed to care for them, the army's authority would cease, and the Department of the Interior would take charge. The northern reservation, in Terry's department, was assigned ex-

11 *Cheyenne Leader,* August 3, 1868.
12 General Order No. 4, August 10, 1868. General Orders, Division of the Missouri, 1865–82.

clusively to the Sioux. Roughly it covered the western half of present South Dakota. The other reservation was in Sheridan's command and was set aside for the Cheyennes, Arapahoes, Kiowas, and Comanches. It was located in the present state of Oklahoma. General Harney was placed in charge of the Sioux, and General W. B. Hazen, a younger officer, was given supervision of the southern tribes.[13]

No forceful means had been provided for getting the Indians to come in. It had to be done, as Sherman told Hazen, "by gradual process." The Indians were to be persuaded that they could cultivate the land and rear stock successfully in the new locations. During the period of transition the army would give encouragement in the form of supplies. Sherman turned $50,000 over to Hazen as a starter, advising him to allow the Indians as much latitude as he saw fit in allowing them to stray beyond their boundaries to hunt.[14] Determined to make the peace plan work, if at all possible, he wanted to avoid trouble. At the same time, all necessary precautions would be taken. If the Indians complied with their agreements, there would be no shooting. If they did not, he was ready to use force.

There was complaint from the press about the fact that Sherman's Order No. 4 made persuasion the only means of getting the Indians corralled. Before the criticism became very widespread, the Indians rectified that deficiency themselves. Just after the middle of August, some of the Cheyenne and Arapaho bands attacked settlers between the Solomon and Saline rivers in northwestern Kansas. The Treaty of Medicine Lodge was broken. Sheridan notified Sherman that for once the barbarities committed were even bloodier than reported in the press. It was at this point that the fiery Sherman's patience ran out. He ordered Sheridan to herd the Indians south of the Kansas line at once, killing those who resisted. "This amounts to war," he reported to headquarters. "If the President does not approve, notify me promptly, for I deem further forbearance with these

13 *Army and Navy Journal*, Vol. VI (August 22, 1868), 9.
14 George Ward Nichols, "The Indian: What We Should Do With Him," *Harper's New Monthly Magazine*, Vol. XL (April, 1870), 735.

Indians impossible. In this case they are purely the aggressors."[15]

As usual, sharp reactions followed the outbreak. The *Army and Navy Journal* complained that the recent attacks were simply "one more chapter in the old volume." Depredations were followed by the chase, and the Indians, as always, eluded their pursuers. This, said the editor, resulted from a policy of alternately feeding and fighting the tribes. "We go to them Janus-faced. One of our hands hold the rifle and the other the peace-pipe, and we blaze away with both instruments at the same time. The chief consequence is a great *smoke*—and there it ends." Perhaps Sherman's order to punish the offenders would be followed up this time. As a helpful suggestion, a recommendation by General W. H. Brown, "late U.S. Vols.," was included. He seriously proposed the use of velocipedes for the infantry as a means of rapid transit in their pursuit of hostiles, not to mention the huge saving in forage and consequent diminution of graft in its supply that would result.[16] Meanwhile, other representatives of the press were less concerned with such modern methods. They asked merely that the military action, which must follow, be "short, sharp and decisive."[17] C. E. Mix, acting commissioner of Indian affairs, also expressed concern. What Indians did Sherman propose to attack? Indeed, murderers ought to be punished, but what assurance was there that he would strike only the guilty when he lashed out with his troopers.[18]

As the uproar over activities of Cheyenne and Arapaho raiders grew in intensity, Sherman took his usual course of action. He went to Fort Leavenworth, where he talked matters over with Sheridan and his aide, Colonel George A. Forsyth. He then moved up the river to Omaha to consult with Augur, after which they both went to the end of the Union Pacific, carefully examining the military situation. At Cheyenne he found that a com-

[15] Telegram from Sherman to Townsend, August 21, 1868. Report of the Commissioner of Indian Affairs, *Annual Report of the Secretary of the Interior*, 40 Cong., 3 sess., *House Exec. Doc. No. 1* (Serial 1366), p. 534.

[16] *Army and Navy Journal*, Vol. VI (August 22, 1868).

[17] *Daily Missouri Republican*, August 25, 1868.

[18] C. E. Mix to O. H. Browning, August 22, 1868. Report of the Commissioner of Indian Affairs, *Annual Report of the Secretary of the Interior*, 40 Cong., 3 sess., *House Exec. Doc. No. 1* (Serial 1366).

pany of volunteers had been organized in that city for the protection of near-by Fort D. A. Russell. It was Cheyenne's answer to the existing panic over prospects of a new Indian war, as well as a dramatic protest against recalling federal troops to Omaha for reasons of economy. The *Cheyenne Leader,* its hackles rising, caustically suggested that if the Twenty-seventh Cavalry, which had recently been sent back to Omaha, was there because of expense, the logical thing to do was to board the troops in China "where they could be subsisted on rice for a penny a day."[19]

On his return to St. Louis, Sherman wrote to a resident of Cheyenne, trying once again to explain his position. The peace commission had been composed of both military men and civilians, and although he had disagreed with some of its decisions, he had concurred in the main. Congress had recently designated him for the task of getting the Indians on reservations, assigned by treaty, and he intended to accomplish that task. As always, he was careful to point out that the Department of the Interior had control of the Indians, and because "that Department is extremely jealous of any interference by the military," army men had no right to anticipate hostilities with military action. It could act only after depredations had been committed. Now, however, the Arapahoes and Cheyennes had broken the peace, and "I have ordered the military to renew their efforts to remove to their proper reservations all Indians who have not been drawn into war, and to kill, destroy and capture all who have been concerned in the recent acts of hostility."

He was annoyed at the governors of western states and territories who thought he could make war and peace at his pleasure. They seemed to think he had a right "to call out volunteers, and pay them, and to do more in this connection than any monarch of a constitutional kingdom. I possess none of these powers." The regular army was provided by Congress, and only a small portion of it was in his command. With it he had to protect two railroads, the Missouri River, and the various stage routes—an aggregate of over eight thousand miles of traveled roads. In addition to this, he was expected to answer calls from every little

19 *Cheyenne Leader,* September 1, 1868.

community over thousands upon thousands of miles of frontier settlement. "With this small force, in the last two years, I have done as much as any reasonable man could hope for, and if any man be incredulous, let him enlist in any company, and he will soon find out if he don't earn his pay." He concluded by urging upon all Westerners the thought that the army could no more run down the many small bands of marauders than it could catch all the pickpockets and thieves in the cities. There was, of course, clamor against him, as well as against Sheridan and Augur. That attitude was "simply folly." For once, Sherman gave permission for the publication of his opinions, saying, "If you think this will be of service to the border people, I have no objection to its use."[20]

Patiently he told Governor A. C. Hunt, of Colorado, much the same thing, advising him to "make no concession to clamor," but assuring him that if the people out there wanted to fight Indians, "they can have all they want." Sheridan, he added, was after the Cheyennes, and Grant had promised more troops. The regular army would be able to handle the main bodies of hostiles. Nevertheless, "now that the Indians are clearly in the wrong I will not prevent your people from chastising them if they are really in earnest, but it is more than our small army can do to defend every ranch in Colorado, Montana, Nebraska and Kansas. The settlers should collect and defend their own property, leaving the regular troops to go after the Indians."[21]

Turning to his correspondence with Secretary of War J. M. Schofield and General Grant, he explained the whole situation as he saw it developing and outlined what he proposed to do. The Indians, he told Grant, had broken out again, committing murders in Kansas and Colorado "without one particle of reason." He was still inclined to think that most of the trouble was coming from the young bloods, who did not exceed three hundred in number, but who, by their rapid movements, appeared to the settlers to be thousands. The Governor of Kansas was

[20] Sherman to Williams, September 6, 1868. *Army and Navy Journal*, Vol. VI (September 26, 1868), 85, quoting the Cheyenne *Star*.
[21] Sherman to Hunt, September 7, 1868. *Cheyenne Leader*, September 10, 1868.

"dreadfully exercised" over it all and had refused, he said, to sit by and see his people murdered. The Governor did not have to sit still. Sherman was willing for him to help his people protect themselves, but the offer of two regiments of Kansas Volunteers would not be accepted until Sheridan requested it, and "Little Phil" had made no such request to date. The same clamor was coming out of Colorado, he went on to say, and Hunt had prevailed upon Schuyler Colfax, Grant's running mate, to put pressure on Sherman for more troops. It just could not be done, he explained. He had only four regiments of cavalry in his whole division. Sheridan had three, and Augur one. One of Sheridan's regiments was scattered all over New Mexico and was not available for an immediate campaign. Phil was meanwhile using the Seventh and the Tenth to chase the Cheyennes, and "I hope he may get hold of them and obliterate them."[22]

The attack was the only way to get the Indians on the two big reservations, Sherman told both Schofield and Grant. The Treaty of Medicine Lodge had been broken, he told the Secretary. All the Cheyennes and Arapahoes were at open war. Perhaps it was just as well; now the southern tribes could be hastened to their new homes. "No better time could possibly be chosen than the present for destroying or humbling those bands that have so outrageously violated their treaties." The innocent would have a reasonable time to clear out of the land between the two railroads, and then all who stayed would be labeled outlaws. The recent treaties providing for reservations had some beneficial aspects, for up to now the army could not point out to the friendlies where they might go to escape the consequences of hostile acts by others within the tribes. According to the treaties, also, the Indians had been given the right to hunt off the reservation, but this privilege, in Sherman's mind, was now lost to them as a result of their hostilities.[23]

22 Sherman to Grant, September 9, 1868. Division of the Missouri, Letters Received, 1866–69, Special File. In a letter from Colfax to Hunt, September 21, 1868, the former assured the Governor that upon his return to Washington he had, through Rawlins, interceded with Grant, who had ordered more cavalry into western Kansas. *New York Times,* October 13, 1868.
23 Sherman to Schofield, September 17, 1868. Report of the Commission of

Despite the reservations, and a consequent clarification of policy, there would be "a sort of predatory war for years," Sherman wrote to John. Every now and then there would be shocking murders, but the size of the country was just too great for one huge war to end it all. The Indians, "from the nature of things," would have to be cleaned out as they were encountered. The Indians would want a truce again when winter came, as they always did. They could not have it this winter, "unless the Civil influence compels me again as it did last winter." Surely Grant would be elected in November, and then the "old Indian system will be broken up." But the expectation of that political result was no reason to relax. "The more we can kill this year, the less will have to be killed the next war, for the more I see of these Indians the more convinced I am that they all have to be killed or be maintained as a species of paupers. Their attempts at civilization are simply ridiculous."[24]

Even though he anticipated scattered hostilities in the years to come, Sherman was convinced that his long-range strategy was paying off. It was now the fall of 1868, and the railroads were nearing completion. The last steps in laying the main Pacific Railroad were now under way, and before long California would be connected with Omaha. Shortly, also, the "Eastern Division," now better known as the "Kansas Pacific," would reach Denver. With the two great lines cutting across Kansas and Nebraska to the mountains, a steel fence would shut the Indians out of a great strip of land reserved for the whites. The Indians, now assigned by law to reservations on either side of the white preserve, could be herded on their reservations by force, if necessary. After that, the remaining lands, north and south of the roads, could be developed and protected, step by step. Roads would later be built into such places as Montana and Idaho, but for the moment they were, as he wrote Dodge, "all side issues." The Indians had signed treaties, and now they had broken them. That justified action on the part of the military, and it was shortly to come.

Indian Affairs, *Annual Report of the Secretary of the Interior*, 40 Cong., 3 sess., *House Exec. Doc. No. 1* (Serial 1366), pp. 536–37.

[24] Sherman to John Sherman, September 23, 1868. William T. Sherman Papers, Volume 23.

It was interesting to Sherman that the recent outrages by the Cheyennes and Arapahoes had been on isolated farms; they had stayed strictly away from the troops and the railroad lines. Each day of road-building and each hostile move by the raiding bands strengthened the hand of the military. Sherman had wanted to strike for a long time, and he was nearly ready. Sheridan and Augur were preparing their men, and Sherman promised Dodge that "we propose not to let up all winter & before spring comes I hope not an Indian will be left in that belt of country through which the two railroads pass."[25]

In September, Sherman wrote of his resolve to move against the treaty-breaking bands. "Spite of Indian Peace Commissions, and all our efforts to keep the rascals quiet, they have broke out simply because they can make more by war than Peace. We must not let up this time, but keep it going till they are killed or humbled."[26] Forecasting the shape of things to come, he advised the Secretary of War that the hostiles should have no annuities or supplies of any kind. They had asked for war, and "I propose to give them enough of it to satisfy them to their hearts' content." Sheridan would push ahead. He had already tallied seventy dead Indians and would continue the pressure, even into the winter.[27] Forsyth, in Sheridan's command, was praised for his "good execution" of strikes against the Cheyennes and Sioux on the Arikaree branch of the Republican River. "We have tried kindness, till it is construed as weakness," Sherman told Augur. Now let men of Forsyth's stripe offer punishment along the Solomon and Saline rivers.[28] With this Sheridan agreed, saying, "We ought to do much damage before January. The Indians will have no resting place this side of Texas. They have not yet put up their Buffalo meat which will also be an inconvenience to them." He also was pleased with his officers and their work. All had done

25 Sherman to Dodge, September 24, 1868. Grenville M. Dodge Papers, Volume 15.

26 Sherman to John Sherman, September 25, 1868. William T. Sherman Papers, Volume 24.

27 Sherman to Schofield, September 26, 1868. Report of the Commissioner of Indian Affairs, *Annual Report of the Secretary of the Interior,* 40 Cong., 3 sess., *House Exec. Doc. No. 1* (Serial 1366), p. 539.

28 Sherman to Augur, September 28, 1868. C. C. Augur Papers.

well, except Alfred Sully who had unwisely given arms to the Indians, and now that they were using them freely against the soldiers, he "appears to be a little stampeded." Perhaps he had better replace him with a younger officer. Custer, who was always eager to fight, would do.[29]

From talk of war and campaigns—things he knew—Sherman was now obliged to turn his thoughts to talk of peace. On October 7, the peace commission would convene in Chicago, and there surely would be verbal warfare before it adjourned. He made up his mind that the kid-glove policy urged by some of the members would have to be set aside, and he was ready to fight for his views. Already there were indications of what would take place in Chicago. Tappan, who had kept up a chatter of correspondence all year, now wrote Sherman another piece of advice. "It is evident that we do not agree on this Indian question," he commenced. Then he renewed his earlier defense of the Indians. Why should Black Kettle and his family be "hung for the Sand Creek Massacre and Chivington promoted to the command of our army, which is the logical result of this policy of extermination?" Hancock had burned the Cheyenne village on Pawnee Fork unnecessarily, he charged. And now Sherman proposed to condone the action by allowing more of the same. Such action "will secure you eternal infamy, and [your enemies] are ready to perjure themselves to get you into such a trap."[30] Tappan had written to Sheridan a month earlier with the same gratuitous advice. "Beware of the conspiracy to involve the country in an Indian war, the purpose being to engage our prominent generals and our army in the West to withdraw them from the South to the West, to incur enormous expense, compromise the generals of the Army & carry the South against Grant." He was sure that Browning, of the Interior, and McCullough, of the Treasury, "will do all they can to carry out this scheme. . . . They are determined to ruin the Members of the Peace Commission."[31] Sher-

[29] Sherman to John Sherman, September 28, 1868. William T. Sherman Papers, Volume 24; Sheridan, *Personal Memoirs*, II, chap. XII.

[30] Tappan to Sherman, September 29, 1868. William T. Sherman Papers, Volume 24.

[31] Tappan to Sheridan, August 26, 1868. William T. Sherman Papers, Volume 23.

man was annoyed by this constant advice. He didn't like Tappan and had told him so. Not only was Tappan bothering him with his missives, but when they were of no avail, he foisted his gossip on Sheridan, trying to influence one of Sherman's subordinates. Things at Chicago promised to be stormy indeed.

Harney would bear watching, too. In September he had written to Sherman, blandly admitting a violation of certain parts of Order No. 4, which had specified the policy of disbursement to the Indians. He explained that he had great sympathy for the Indians and had given them supplies in excess of his authorization. He had also accepted the "voluntary services of several reliable business men in whom I have the greatest confidence." He was sure, he told Sherman sweetly, that the General would have no objection to such little violations. They were, as brother members of the commission, engaged in a great work of putting "an end to the perfidy and outrage which has generally hitherto characterized the treatment of the Indians by the white men."[32] So Harney was building a little empire of his own up the Missouri. How would he behave at Chicago? Sherman wondered.

As the members gathered for their meeting, Sherman noticed a mounting public support of his recent actions and declarations. The *New York Times,* in an editorial, "Our New Indian Policy," highly praised his "vigorous measures" and predicted an early end to Indian troubles. Admitting that while "the last Indian war" had received the paper's unqualified condemnation, the editor hastened to explain that this time the fault lay with the raiding bands, and they must now be punished. Sherman was the man to do it; he had the *Times's* support.[33] The West was not so optimistic. It had a deep-seated suspicion of all peace commissions and peace efforts. About all that would happen at Chicago, plainsmen told each other, would be apologies for recent Indian depredations. All Sherman could talk about was his unwillingness to be taken in by western clamor. What was wrong with clamor? How could men make their needs known otherwise?[34]

[32] Harney to Sherman, September 27, 1868. William T. Sherman Papers, Volume 24.
[33] October 4, 1868.

226

Sherman did not sound like a fighting man to them. And as these words were handed out, Sherman wrote to headquarters, "It is not improbable that war may obliterate these treaties, and force us to erase the names of Cheyennes, Arapahoes, Kiowas, &c., and unite the fragments of all under some new name at such place as may be to the interest of the Government when the war is over. These Indians doubtless expect to relax their war efforts about December, when the grass will fail them, but that is the very time we propose to begin in earnest, and I hope that by the time the new grass comes a very small reservation will suffice for what is left."[35] The day after he wrote this opinion, he sat down with his colleagues in Chicago.

The meetings began on October 7, with all members present except Senator Henderson. Sherman had long since arranged his hand as he wanted to play it, and while the talk went on, he took trick after trick. A few days earlier he had urged Augur to be on hand to lend his support, promising that he would be prepared to prove his case, step by step. The military had done all it could to maintain peace with the Indians, even to the stretching point, and yet the Indians had gone to war. He would tell the commission that. Liberal treaties had been made with the tribes. They had been given "a fine large Territory in perpetuity," and still they resisted. Now they must go there, or be killed.[36] Reporters noticed the changed atmosphere and commented that Sherman's attitude had been materially altered by recent events. "He is not so much in favor of [the] feeding, and clothing and furnishing ammunition policy, as he was a few months ago," wrote one observer.[37] This was not true. His notions about procedure with regard to the Indians had undergone no change, and he had never approved of giving the Indians ammunition. He had merely tried to co-operate with the commission and keep

[34] An example of such skepticism can be found in the *Cheyenne Leader*, October 6, 1868, published the day before the Chicago meeting convened.

[35] Sherman to Townsend, October 6, 1868. Letters Received 1865–69, Office of the Secretary of War.

[36] Sherman to Augur, September 28, 1868. C. C. Augur Papers.

[37] *New York Times*, October 16, 1868.

still. The outbreak in Kansas merely confirmed what he had believed all along.

Grant, who was in Chicago, also sat with the commission, and his views coincided with Sherman's. Tappan and Taylor saw that they were in the minority, and they struggled fiercely for the softer policy. Grant was reported to have said that the emigrants had to be protected, "even if the extermination of every Indian tribe was necessary to secure such a result."[38] Sherman now pressed his case, while his friend Terry proposed a resolution abrogating the clauses in the Medicine Lodge Treaty that granted to the Indians the right to hunt outside their reservations. Only when peace was restored were they to leave their confinement, and it would then be with written permission from their agents. The resolution closed with the statement that the military would be empowered to force any reluctant Indians onto their assigned lands. Tappan immediately countered with a proposal that the Indian Bureau be made into a separate cabinet department. It was defeated; only Taylor voted with him. The Terry resolution was carried.

When the sessions were concluded, it was revealed that by majority vote the commission had recommended several major changes in policy. The government should cease to recognize the tribes as independent nations, and all Indians should be held individually responsible to federal laws. Terry's resolution, assigning to the military the task of forcibly conveying recalcitrant Indians to their reservations and regulating their right to hunt, was included. As a parting shot, the commission recommended that the Bureau of Indian Affairs be transferred to the War Department.[39] Sherman went back to St. Louis with several scalps, including Taylor's and Tappan's, hanging from his belt.

Three days after the meetings were concluded, Sherman directed General Hazen to go to Fort Cobb, Indian Territory, and make provisions for any Indians who wanted to come there and keep out of war. He warned that even this might not give

[38] *Ibid.*
[39] Report of the Commissioner of Indian Affairs, 1868, *Annual Report of the Secretary of the Interior*, 40 Cong., 3 sess., *House Exec. Doc. No. 1* (Serial 1366), pp. 831–32; *New York Times*, October 11, 1868.

full protection to them, for Sheridan was about to be turned loose, and if it was necessary, he would enter the reservation to catch fleeing hostiles. "I will urge General Sheridan to push his measures for the utter destruction and subjugation of all who are outside in a hostile attitude," he warned. "I propose that [he] shall prosecute the war with vindictive earnestness against all hostile Indians, till they are obliterated or beg for mercy; and therefore all who want peace must get out of the theatre of war, which will not reach the reservation committed to your care, unless absolutely necessary."[40] Meanwhile, humanitarians like Bishop H. B. Whipple of New York pleaded with Sherman to continue the peaceful efforts of the commission.[41] The answer came in a hum of preparations for war.

The die was now cast. After more than two years of waiting, Sherman finally was in position to put his military plans against the Indians into operation. As he awaited developments, he sat down to write his annual report to the War Department. Carefully, he outlined the events of the preceding summer, illustrating how this time the Indians were certainly at fault and how the military, its patience sorely tried, had been obliged to go to war. "It has always been most difficult to discover the exact truth concerning the cause of a rupture with any Indians," he generalized. "They never give notice beforehand of a warlike intention, and the first notice comes after their rifles and lances have done much bloody work. All intercourse then necessarily ceases, and the original cause soon becomes buried in after events." In order to prevent such unforeseen events, the peace commission had spent considerable time studying the matter. It had reported to Congress, in December of 1867, that two large reservations for the Indians would confine them sufficiently to prevent collisions with the whites traveling westward in the strip of land between the two great railroads. But Congress had

---

[40] Sherman to Hazen, October 13, 1868. Nichols, "The Indian: What We Should Do With Him," *Harper's New Monthly Magazine*, Vol. XL (April, 1870), 737.

[41] Whipple pleaded earnestly "for this poor race" and promised Sherman that behind him would be rallied "the Christian sentiment of this nation. You can under God save this poor people." Whipple to Sherman, October 16, 1868. William T. Sherman Papers, Volume 24.

taken no action at that time, and depredations had been renewed in the spring of 1868. Through treaties made during the spring and summer, it had been mutually agreed between the commissioners and the Indians that the reservation plan would be adopted. And then some of the Indians had broken the agreement. Meanwhile, the Senate had confirmed part of the treaties and had not acted upon others by adjournment time.[42]

Sherman then pointed out that many people living in more settled parts of the country were sure that all Indian troubles arose out of wrongs committed by the whites. "I am more than convinced that such is not the case in the present instance, and I hope that I have made it plain," he wrote, in defense of the Westerners. Even so, those who lived near the tribes were incautious, often traveling without protection, and were prone to "run after every wild report of the discovery of gold or other precious metals, thus coming into daily contact and necessary conflict with discontented and hostile Indians." At the same time, the federal government sanctioned the opening of new public lands, approved of locating and building railroads, and established mail routes "as though that region of country were in profound peace, and all danger of occupation and transit had passed away." The confounding part of it all was that while the military had no control over such developments, it was severely criticized for not affording protection for any or all of these projects. They were, in his words, "left in the breach to catch all the kicks and cuffs of a war of races, without the privilege of advising or being consulted beforehand."

To Sherman there was only one answer. Common occupation of these lands was not feasible. The country was "not susceptible of close settlement with farms like Missouri and Iowa, and is solely adapted to grazing." The people, necessarily scattered, could not be protected adequately under the existing conditions.

42 When N. G. Taylor wrote his annual report, three weeks after that of Sherman, the Brûlé Sioux treaty of April 29 had not yet been submitted to the Senate. Sherman's treaty with the Navajos had been proclaimed by then, but Augur's Fort Bridger treaty with the Bannocks and Shoshones had not yet been received. The Medicine Lodge Treaty had been ratified and proclaimed. Report of the Commissioner of Indian Affairs, 1868, *Annual Report of the Secretary of the Interior*, 40 Cong., 3 sess., *House Exec. Doc. No. 1* (Serial 1366), p. 464.

The Indians must yield and go on reservations. They would be fed and cared for, and if they kept their lands "for 50 years [it] will make their descendants rich." Persuasion would not be enough, for "to labor with their own hands, or even to remain in one place, militates with all the hereditary pride of the Indian, and *force* must be used to accomplish this result." And to use that force properly, the affairs of the Indians had to be put solely into the hands of the army. No other branch of government was prepared to act as quickly or as vigorously. He would proceed, until otherwise directed, with the removal of the Indians to their assigned reservations. It was the best thing for the Indians, but "even then there is doubt that the Indians themselves will make the necessary personal efforts to succeed, and I fear that they will at last fall back upon our hands, a mere mass of helpless paupers."[43]

From the West came a general approval of the report, and from the Interior Department, hot words. O. H. Browning expressed doubt, in his annual report, that military guardianship afforded any hope for the tribes or the Treasury. It was the duty of the Interior Department, he said, to improve the moral, intellectual, and material condition of the natives. "There is nothing in the pursuits or the character of the soldier which especially adapts him to this duty," he sneered at Sherman.[44] With that, another war was on, and newspapers once again chose up sides, chewing away at the various arguments for and against the transfer. Meanwhile, the southern tribes paid little attention to the debate. They flocked into Fort Cobb in such numbers that Hazen was soon swamped. Before he knew it, he had over 8,000 hungry, naked Indians, all clamoring for support and asking no questions about who was footing the bill or serving up the goods.

[43] Report of W. T. Sherman, November 1, 1868, *Annual Report of the Secretary of War*, 40 Cong., 3 sess., *House Exec. Doc. No. 1* (Serial 1366).

[44] *Annual Report of the Secretary of the Interior*, 1868, 40 Cong., 3 sess., *House Exec. Doc. No. 1*, Part IV (Serial 1366).

[45] Nichols, "The Indian: What We Should Do With Him," *Harper's New Monthly Magazine*, Vol. XL (April, 1870), 737.

Fourteen

THE DREADED BANISHMENT TO WASHINGTON

IN MANY RESPECTS the fall of 1868 marked the climax of Sherman's career. The war years had made him famous, just as they had made many other men famous. But his appointment to a large military division—one of his own choice—and his successful management of it in peacetime brought him much personal satisfaction. He was fully aware that the drama unfolding in the West was the last act of a historic frontier movement, and his delight at being a part of it shows in every letter he wrote about the region. If the fame he earned at this task was a less quiet kind, attended by knotty problems and harsh criticisms, it was one of permanence and depth. His meteoric rise to fame, in the eyes of the American people, had come from a period of destruction. Sherman was orderly and constructive, in his own mind, and the postwar assignment appealed to him largely because he regarded it as constructive. He was building something.

There were other satisfactions. The friendship with Grant matured and deepened. Sherman's hardheadedness, often annoying to the public, was a comfort to Grant, who appreciated his subordinate's incisive mind. To Sherman's extreme pleasure, Grant had backed his moves, and amid the uproar of armchair strategists, the two had worked away at the solution of the western problems, with the signals being called from St. Louis. The railroads, in which Sherman maintained a deep interest throughout his life, had been guided across the plains by the army, as Grant watched with nodding approval. The quarrelsome Indians, always sniping at the rail tentacles, were being shoved aside. Little by little Sherman had edged his forces into position, and now he was ready to execute some long-planned moves.

There were also rewards of dubious satisfaction. Apparently it had been understood from the time Grant's name came into serious consideration for the presidency that Sherman was the heir apparent to the General of the Army. The public knew of the great friendship between the two men. They noticed that Sherman was high in rank. It seemed so simple. No one asked Sherman if he wanted to go. In answering one of John's letters in June, while at Fort Union, he had said, "Of course I have noticed Grant's acceptance. I take it for granted he will be elected, and I must come to Washington." While he felt that he would have to go if the call came, he did not want it. During the war he had called the place "corrupt as hell" and swore that he would "avoid it like a pest house." Hoping to forestall such a move, he wrote to Grant asking him to put any such notions from his mind. "I shall not ask you to come to Washington until after November and probably not then," was the laconic reply.[1]

As election time drew near, Sherman was still muttering that he did not want to move to the Capital. Grant's promise of "probably not then" was the only thread of hope he could cling to, except for one other grim possibility. His well-known antipathy toward the Radical Republicans and their Reconstruction cause had gained for him many enemies in Congress. Rumors were afloat to the effect that they planned to hurt him by abolishing the office of General of the Army, once Grant was elected. Let them try, he wrote angrily to John. They could strike at him only in a financial way; his reputation as a general was already established. "But if Congress abolishes an office because I don't go it blind on their political theories, it will be as mean an act as a deliberative body ever attempted." If congressmen carried out the threat, he would merely stay on at St. Louis, "which would be much more in accordance with my private inclinations, than the dreaded banishment to Washington."

When the votes were in and Grant had won a smashing victory at the polls, Sherman was panic-stricken about his own fate. The political power his old friend showed in the election quashed any anti-Sherman moves in the party and made it clear that the

[1] Sherman to John Sherman, June 11, 1868. William T. Sherman Papers, Volume 23; Grant to Sherman, June 21, 1868. William T. Sherman Papers, Volume 23.

top army office was safe for the time being. There was now no hope of staying in Missouri. "I do not intend to budge from here until I am ordered," the prospective General of the Army wrote. But even in such stubborn talk he knew that it was only a matter of time, and sorrowfully he expressed the hope that Grant would "hold on until the last moment."[2] During his time at St. Louis, as commander of the western plains, he had done his job faithfully and competently. Now he was to be rewarded— by exile.

As he waited out his remaining weeks of relative freedom, Sherman busied himself with affairs in the Division, trying to forget what lay ahead in his new task. The newspapers, buzzing like bees around his head, would give him no peace. From earlier criticism they now turned to praise and revealed to their readers that no matter what his future capacity might be, he would be very close to Grant. The President-elect opened up for the reporters, calling Sherman "the most brilliant but the least understood of our Generals." Grant, who was as politically naïve as any military man ever elected, confided generously to the press that Sherman was no politician. He was simply too honest to become one. "A more unmanageable man there is not in America," he went on, lauding his friend's integrity and honesty in glowing terms.[3] Miserable in the glare of such laudatory publicity, Sherman buried himself in office routine and counted off the days he could call his own.

He found some comfort in the fact that he was leaving at a time when military matters in the West were more satisfactory to him than at any time since he took command. Tappan was still droning around in the background, firing off volleys of advice, but he could be ignored. The Commissioner complained that Sherman's position was "one of changes" and scolded him for his aggressive action against the Indians. "Upon my honor I do not envy you—better to be the victim than the instrument of oppression," Tappan chattered on. Look out for those volun-

---

[2] Sherman to John Sherman, October 19 and 30 and November 23, 1868. William T. Sherman Papers, Volume 24.

[3] *New York Times*, November 13, 1868.

teers, he warned. They would commit atrocities and make trouble. There would be more Sand Creeks. Then he lectured the General on the abilities of the natives. "Their knowledge of the country, rapidity of attack and flight, their quickness to comprehend the designs of their enemies, facilities of telegraphing information from one to another, and remote locations—render these although few in number a formidable foe to contend with and conquer."[4] Sherman shoved these mouthings aside. He knew something about Indians and had long since decided upon a course of action. He would follow it.

As a kind of valediction, he wrote to his subordinates, encouraging them in their work. Augur had done a fine job in the Department of the Platte, and Sherman praised him, saying, "I think you can take just comfort in the fact that under your care the Pacific Road has met so little difficulty this year that they have actually built over 400 miles without interruption and had only one actual break by Indians." Conditions to the north of Augur's command were not entirely satisfactory, but Sherman was not discouraged. Harney lacked the vigor required for such active duty, but Sherman thought perhaps he would "play out this winter when I can put some younger and better man there." In the meantime he would bear with the old officer's weakness.[5]

Hazen, in charge of the southern reservation, was pulling a full load. "I know we are on the right track now, and I am well satisfied of the part you have acted," Sherman wrote warmly. He promised Hazen all the help available. If more money was required, Sheridan could lend some supplies for the Indians. Sherman himself would bear the responsibility of spending such funds without Congressional authorization.[6] He wrote also to Sheridan, encouraging him to fight when necessary, and promising to fend off anyone who tried to stop him. There was a lot of loose talk, he said, about "extermination." He did not want to exterminate the Indians, or even fight them. "At best it is an

[4] Tappan to Sherman, November 25, 1868. William T. Sherman Papers, Volume 24.

[5] Sherman to Augur, November 23, 1868. C. C. Augur Papers.

[6] Nichols, "The Indian: What We Should Do With Him," *Harper's New Monthly Magazine*, Vol. XL (April, 1870), 737-38.

inglorious war, not apt to add much to our fame or personal comfort, and for our soldiers, to whom we owe our first thoughts, it is all danger and extreme labor, without one single compensating advantage." A dozen years later he was to express the same sentiment, in what would become a classic American expression, when he said that there were those who look "on war as all glory, but boys, it is all hell." Now he told Sheridan that to accuse the military of wanting an Indian war was to accuse it of a want of common sense "and of that regard for order and peace which has ever characterized our regular army." Present hostilities arose out of raids upon white settlements, despite all warnings and entreaties by the commissioners appointed to deal with the tribes. The military accepted the challenge of war "and hereby resolve to make its end final. If it results in the utter annihilation of these Indians, it is but the result of what they have been warned again and again, and for which they seem fully prepared. I will say nothing and do nothing to restrain our troops from doing what they deem proper on the spot, and will allow no more vague charges of cruelty or inhumanity to tie their hands. . . ."[7]

As 1868 drew to a close and Sherman made ready to transfer his office to Washington, signs began to appear that forecast trouble. Early in December the House passed a bill, sponsored by James A. Garfield of Ohio, that proposed to transfer the Indian Bureau to the War Department. Although the proposal passed that body of Congress easily, Sherman was concerned. He and Sheridan had used all their influence, but it was Grant's assistance that guaranteed success. The next hurdle, the Senate, was a much more difficult one, and here, with fewer men to deal with, the Indian ring could exert great influence. Sherman's fears were heightened when he received a letter from Senator E. G. Ross, of Kansas, who predicted a sharp struggle in the upper chamber. The coming session of Congress would be short, said the Senator, so why consume time in inconclusive debate. Why could not "some gentleman having a good military record dur-

---

[7] Sherman to Sheridan, October 14, 1868. Quoted by R. B. Marcy, inspector general of the U. S. Army, in a letter from St. Louis to the editor of the *New York Herald*, November 30, 1868; *Daily Missouri Republican*, December 14, 1868.

ing the war of known intelligence in regard to our Indian affairs, of established personal integrity and one who has the confidence of the army as well as of the Civil Department" be appointed commissioner of Indian affairs? He recommended S. J. Crawford, late governor of Kansas and then colonel of the Nineteenth Kansas Regiment. With such a man in office, the wishes of the War Department would be carried out, and the military would be free of the possibility of further responsibilities being placed upon it.[8] If Sherman read his signs aright, a road block was about to be placed across the army's path. Now was the time to act; he would have to write at length on Indian policy to the frontier solon. He hoped he would not be too late.

From time to time Sherman wrote long, patient letters, outlining his views on western problems and the solution of Indian difficulties. Writing to Senator Ross, he took much the same course, introducing his remarks with the comment that Congress had always been most liberal with the natives, much more so than England, France, or Russia would have been. These people —"a class of savages displaced by the irresistible progress of our race"—were now in danger of extinction, and, in all fairness, they should be given a chance to survive and live alongside the dominant race. In order to receive protection, the Indians had to be localized.

In the process of readjustment and relocation on the plains, conflicts had arisen. When this happened, the army was obliged to act as a police force and take punitive measures. In standing between the settlers and the Indians, the army usually came in for severe criticism. Actually, the army men did not want war, for "Indian wars never bring honors or reward." They did want peace and from time to time had restrained the whites who wanted to annihilate the Indians. "I have never labored harder than I have done the past two years to avoid war," he confessed, "and have been abused therefor by citizens generally, and even my soldiers felt I did not sympathize with them, when I restrained them from resenting insults and murders on them and their comrades, by the Indians."

8 Ross to Sherman, December 12, 1868. William T. Sherman Papers, Volume 24.

Proceeding logically, he now took up the matter of jurisdiction. Only when trouble actually occurred was the army called in and asked to give help. It "is proof in my mind that we should have the corresponding power *beforehand* to prevent trouble, to anticipate and guard against it." Under existing arrangements, the Indian agents had "ministered to the savage wants" more than they had devoted themselves to civilizing the natives. The Sioux, who had been under the control of civil agents since 1849, were just as uncivilized as they had been twenty years earlier. "Instead of teaching civil pursuits, the annuities have gone for paints, feathers, scarlet cloth, guns and powder." While some of the Indians might improve under these conditions, others would not. During such a transitional state, Sherman was convinced that the army was the best medium of control, for the agents were "ridiculously impotent with drunken or warlike savages, whereas we can punish with one hand and caress with the other."

Now, asked Sherman, why did Ross think the establishing of an Independent bureau, or the placing of someone favorable to the military in the old bureau, could solve anything? The machinery and its deficiencies would be the same. Before long, any new bureau would have vested interests and would guard them jealously, ever fearful of interference with its patronage. "I think the greatest objection to an Independent Department is political," he said bluntly. As a constructive suggestion, he advanced the idea of putting the Indians onto a large reservation, like the one west of Arkansas, and giving them territorial government. They would have no agents but would be governed by "laws and an administration on the spot, partially maintained and supervised by Congress direct, adapted to all the wants of the Inhabitants." In the period of readjustment the army should be in control to preserve general order. Within ten or fifteen years every Indian could be so located. Those who did not choose to go into a given territory could be controlled by the laws of any territory or state in which they lived. "Each would then thrive and prosper if he deserved to, or would be restrained or killed if his savage nature would not gradually yield to the humane destiny thus offered him by his Government."

Sherman was convinced that if matters drifted on, with the tribes under the Indian Bureau, they would "remain *forever* a dead charge on the National Treasury." It was an impossible situation, with "fanatics like Tappan" justifying anything the savages might do simply because, as in case of attacks along the Solomon River in Kansas, Congress had not properly ratified the treaties.[9] Sherman's strong feeling about law and order came to the surface when he told Ross that civil society must be protected and that Indian wrongdoers must be punished like any others. They could not hide behind the skirts of a protecting bureau. The agents were frequently far away from their charges, and all too often a state of anarchy obtained in the unsettled regions. "No amount of virtue or intelligence seated in Washington will change the state of facts on the Plains or in the Mountains thousands of miles away, and the men who are to save any part of the wild tribes of America must live among them. Our Army is there and we have the power to keep them there, but nobody in Washington can keep an Indian Agent at his post." Creating a new department would not solve this problem. It would be hard to get anyone to head it who would be any better than Browning of Interior; Taylor, the Indian commissioner, was "as honest and well disposed as any person could be toward Indians." The heart of the matter lay with those who carried on the day-to-day dealings with the Indians, "who tell them what is right, what they should do, and what they should not do, with power to compel when necessary." Then, concluding with much stronger language, Sherman promised that if the Senate adhered to its preconceived opinions, "I am absolved from all responsibility and will simply say 'Farewell Mr. Indian,' for you know he is doomed. You will then need a stronger Army than ever to protect the Indian against the citizens who will rescue their stolen horses, and will avenge on innocent and guilty the loss of their families."[10]

The long discourse to Ross did no good. Not only did the

[9] He refers to treaties with the Arapahoes and Cheyennes of May 10, 1868.

[10] Sherman to Ross, January 7, 1869. Division of the Missouri, Letters Sent, 1868–71. Records of the War Department, U. S. Army Commands, National Archives.

Senate temporize over the transfer of the Indian Bureau, but, even worse, it launched an attack upon the army itself. Senator Henry Wilson of Massachusetts introduced a bill to reduce the military arm, and some Civil War veterans, now in Congress, came to his support. The *Army and Navy Journal* charged that former volunteer generals, like Benjamin Butler, John A. Logan, and Robert C. Schenck, "seemed possessed with an intense hatred against 'West Point' and against the Regular Army."[11] As Sherman looked on with an increasing sense of alarm, Grant moved into the White House. Carefully Sherman studied the inaugural address. Of the problem that so concerned Sherman, Grant, in his usual terse fashion, merely said, "The proper treatment of the original occupants of this land—the Indians—is one deserving of careful study. I will favor any course toward them which tends to their civilization and ultimate citizenship."[12] The enigmatic statement could mean anything. Sherman must have wondered what the course of action tending toward civilization of the Indians would be. It sounded like Indian Bureau language. Clouds of doubt began to eddy in the back of his mind.

On March 5, Sherman was issued his commission as General of the Army; the order contained a stipulation giving the new commander a great deal of power. With delight he read that "the chiefs of staff corps, departments and bureaus will report to and act under the immediate orders of the general commanding the Army. All official business, which by law or regulations requires the action of the President or Secretary of War, will be submitted by the General of the Army to the Secretary of War, and in general, all orders from the President or Secretary of War to any portion of the Army, line or staff, will be transmitted through the General of the Army."[13] It appeared that Sherman was seated firmly in the saddle.

The order of March 5 was a short-lived palliative to the appointee's worries. On March 11, Grant announced that Schofield,

11 February 13, 1869.
12 Grant's Inaugural Address, March 4, 1869. James D. Richardson, *A Compilation of the Messages and Papers of the Presidents, 1789–1908*, VII, 8.
13 Richardson, *Messages and Papers*, VII, 20–21; *Army and Navy Journal*, March 13, 1869.

whom he had asked to "hold over for a while" as secretary of war, was replaced by the President's wartime chief aide and long-time friend, John A. Rawlins. The new cabinet member at once demanded that the order granting Sherman a free hand be revoked. Grant was now faced by one of his first decisions as president, and its solution characterized many of those to come later. Determined to reverse himself, he explained lamely to Sherman that "Rawlins feels badly about it." He said that the tubercular Secretary was not at all well, and the matter would worry him. Sherman argued that Rawlins had understood the wishes of Grant in the matter when he accepted his new post and that he should acquiesce gracefully.

"Yes, it would ordinarily be so," admitted the President, "but I don't like to give him pain now; so, Sherman you'll have to publish the rescinding order."

Sherman objected sharply, pointing out that it was Grant's order, not his. He asked what the public would think of such a sudden change.

"Well," replied Grant, "if its my own order, I can rescind it, can't I?"

Sherman flushed and rose to his feet. Bowing stiffly, he said, "Yes, Mr. President, you have the power to revoke your own order; you shall be obeyed. Good morning, sir."[14]

On March 26 the rescinding order was issued under Rawlins' signature, "By Command of General Sherman." It stated that official business requiring the action of the President or the Secretary of War would be submitted by the chiefs of staff corps, departments, and bureaus directly to the Secretary of War. Orders and instructions relating to military operations, issued by the President or the Secretary, would be released by the General of the Army.[15] Rawlins told his wife that he had received Grant's permission to revoke Schofield's earlier order, "which virtually put the War Department under Sherman," and had done so out of a "sense of duty to my country." Now the War Department

[14] Lewis, *Sherman: Fighting Prophet*, 601.
[15] Richardson, *Messages and Papers*, VII, 22; *Army and Navy Journal*, April 3, 1869.

was again constituted as it had been under Edwin Stanton, with the General of the Army subordinate to the Secretary. "General Sherman felt badly over the revocation of Schofield's order, fearint it would put him in the light of losing Grant's confidence," Rawlins confessed, but added that "he did not seem to think I had any special feelings in the matter, and as to that he was about right."[16]

Sherman had little to say about the difficulty, except to close associates. Grant had been obliged to choose between two old friends, and his sympathy leaned toward the ailing Rawlins, who had declined the chance to take an assignment in the dry climate of Arizona, preferring the honor of high office in Washington. Philosophically, Sherman wrote to Sheridan of the affair. "You must have noticed that the President went back on me in the matter of the Secretary of War. I did not like it at all, but could not help myself. Both he and Schofield had told me more than once that it was easier to be Secretary of War & Genl in Chief rather than to be either separate. I will help keep in mind the End, and try gradually to effect in time which we all want to do and should have done by a single step."[17]

Resolutely the new commanding officer set about his duties, stung by Grant's action but determined to follow orders in the best tradition of his profession. Residents of the Capital were curious about the man from the West, and reporters followed him around, eager for tidbits to feed the hungry readers. They saw a lank, loosely garbed individual with a fine-featured but wrinkle-netted countenance. He was nervous, ever moving, and sometimes impetuous. His new subordinates were amazed at his methods of doing business, and his orders sometimes sent them off muttering to themselves. Just a few days after his appointment, a young officer came to him to talk about the prospect of breaking up near-by Lincoln Barracks. What should be done with the property, he inquired. "Burn it, burn it, sir," Sherman snapped, still deep in thought about his recent difficulties with the War Department.

16 James Harrison Wilson, *The Life of John A. Rawlins,* 354–55.

17 Sherman to Sheridan, April 10, 1869. Sherman-Sheridan Correspondence, Volume 1.

"General," countered the surprised officer, "please put your order in writing and I will obey it."

"Burn it, burn it," Sherman repeated.

Holding his ground, the other insisted that such an order must be reduced to writing. Sherman softened now and asked the value of the barracks. He was told that the establishment was valued at $200,000.

"Well," he concluded, "the fact is this city is a bad place for soldiers, and I want to get them all away from it. You had better put it up for sale and clean the thing out quick."[18]

His contrast with the smartly dressed officers around him caused much comment in a city where the military was literally dressed for parade at all times. When one who knew him well enough to speak of such matters referred to his dress, Sherman told one of his famous stories.

"When I was a second Lieutenant, I was ordered one day to Washington City and went in all the glory of a brand new uniform. I was standing in front of a hotel, sunning myself and quietly smoking a cigar, when I became aware that I had attracted the attention of a number of small boys, who gathered around in such numbers and with such admiring countenances turned up to mine, that I could not but notice them. As I did so, one of the boldest of them spoke out in a loud voice and asked: 'Mister, where is your ingine going to squirt?' "

Sherman confessed that since that time he ceased wearing a completely new uniform. He afterwards bought his uniforms piece by piece and wore them out in installments.[19] The practice, which usually found him in a threadbare garb since he neglected to buy new articles of dress when they were needed, at least kept little boys from asking him about his "ingine," but it led to other complications. When he was in command at Benton Barracks, St. Louis, he neglected even to wear a complete uniform. Most of his men grew accustomed to seeing their commander in an old brown coat and a stovepipe hat. One day, while walking through the grounds, he noticed a soldier vigorously beating a mule.

18 *Omaha Weekly Herald,* March 31, 1869.
19 *Ibid.,* April 28, 1869.

"Stop pounding that mule," he ordered.

"Git out!" growled the soldier.

"I tell you to stop!"

"You mind your business and I will mind mine," the soldier flared, continuing his strokes on the mule's rump.

"I tell you again to stop. Do you know who I am? I am General Sherman."

"That's played out," the soldier answered in bored tones. "Every man who comes along here with an old brown coat and a stovepipe hat on claims to be General Sherman."[20]

Story after story about the gruff, steely-eyed general circulated around the Capital, while puzzled admirers watched him take up his new tasks. The spare Westerner, voluble at times, harsh and defensive at others, contrasted sharply with the solemn, taciturn Grant who now sat in the White House. The public knew of the long and intimate friendship between them, and those interested in military-Indian affairs wondered what would be the turn of events with the two old soldiers in command. Grant, confused by his new duties and mistaking the presidency as a reward for past services rather than a position of great trust, was soon to be in utter confusion. Desperately he would try to placate insistent politicians to escape making hard decisions. Rawlins, in the cabinet, had long since remarked that, of the two, Sherman was the statesman, and time would prove him right, as Grant vacillated and temporized, wriggling futilely in the grip of strange problems.

Sherman, too, would be ill at ease. While his dislike for Washington and the inactivity that characterized administrative duties galled him, the widening breach with Grant burned a deep scar in his sensitive mind. And like sand in the wound, the fawners who hung around him, grasping hungrily at scraps of recognition that might be tossed their way by the nation's highest ranking officer, irritated him. He had often spoken bitterly of the parasites who swelled staff offices and occupied themselves with supplications for favor and advancement. Now he was in a nest of them. As General of the Army, he was subject to endless adora-

[20] Frazar Kirkland, *The Pictorial Book of Anecdotes of the Rebellion*, 438.

tion, some of it real, much of it spurious. The artificiality of the society in which he moved made him think longingly of the West. When people there were critical of him, they said so openly. When they approved, they respectfully called him "the Western Captain." It was their way of signifying that he was the leader, and the use of the word "Captain" was employed in the larger sense. They meant for it to outrank the mere term "General," and he took it that way.

As the Grant administration launched itself, lengthening shadows of discontent reached out for both of the famous generals. One presided uncomfortably over the White House, as graceless as a dirt farmer serving his first term in a legislature. The other sat grimly in the commanding General's office, stripped of real power, serving out the inevitable sentence pronounced by fame. To the man on the street these men stood at the zenith of their careers, but in reality a failing glimmer of twilight revealed the lateness of the hour. Of the two, perhaps only Sherman was aware of it. He saw that he had little more than an increased diversity of responsibility; in depth it had not increased. Instead of dealing only with the Division of the Missouri and problems concerning the land westward to the Rockies, he now had to listen to complaints from all over the nation. Matters in the Northwest were little more than routine, while the South, writhing in the agonies of Reconstruction, saw the military tightly controlled by the radicals in Congress. Sherman, who had shrunk back from politics, was content to let the administration worry about policy for the South. His interest was a western one, and he watched the frontier roll back before the push of population with undiminished attention. While he had no desire for aggrandizement and expansion at the expense of other nations, he was greatly attracted by the process of national growth within the nation's established boundaries. Like a small boy building a house of blocks, he noted with satisfaction each step in the development of the structure. His real worry was that he had been removed from the scene of activity, and there was no promise that he could return to it.

Of the many barriers to western settlement, the American Indian was still the most difficult to circumvent. Without a solution to this problem there could be no orderly progression in peopling the plains. Sherman had come to Washington with high hopes that an office of greater power would lend him more leverage in working out the pacification of such troubled regions. His subordinates, poised for action, felt the same way. But they did not fully reckon with the forces at work in the nation at large, and they badly underestimated the strength of the humanitarian surge, once beamed at the struggling slave, as it now spotlighted the plight of the "noble savage." In 1868 a meeting had been held at New York's Cooper Union to organize a private effort to save the natives from destruction. As a result of the gathering, a group calling itself the "United States Indian Commission" came into being. It was governed by a board of twenty members made up of clergymen and well-known New Yorkers. Peter Cooper, the wealthy glue manufacturer who had founded the Cooper Union back in the fifties, had turned from his antislavery crusade to a postwar interest in Indians. While he was the most prominent member of the new board something of its scope was revealed in the appointment of Henry Bergh, the organizer of the Society for the Prevention of Cruelty to Animals.

The new Indian commission kept its purposes before the public by continually memorializing Congress and publicizing its work in promoting the peaceful civilization of the Indians. Although the *Army and Navy Journal* chided such societies, "who meet annually to deputize clergymen troubled with bronchial complaints" to go at the societies' expense into Indian country, the eastern public seemed fascinated by the idea. Many of the prewar abolitionists, their reforming zeal still at a high pitch, hurled themselves into the task of salvaging this newly discovered minority. Congress seemed willing to listen to "the pipings of these benevolent preachers from Connecticut and Pennsylvania" instead of the advice of army men.[21] General Hazen, in charge of the southern reservation, tried to co-operate with the men of peace in the fall of 1868 by inviting the New York commission to send out one of its representatives to observe conditions. With-

21 *Army and Navy Journal,* July 25, 1868.

in a few months Vincent Colyer, recommended by such important men as Peter Cooper, James A. Roosevelt, and Henry Ward
Beecher, appeared in Indian Territory, where Hazen laid before
him all available records, with permission to use them as he saw
fit. Hazen expressed to Sherman the hope that by this means the
peace commission might better understand the problems.[22]

If Hazen wanted to work with the Indian lovers, Sherman
thought, he could go ahead. He would sooner or later find that
it did little good. If they should ask *him* what he thought about
petting the Indians, he would tell them. Before long, they asked.
The occasion was a convention of peace delegates, called together
by Peter Cooper from all over the country to study the prevention
of war against the Indians. As the group assembled and con-
tentedly listened to Samuel Tappan condemn those who heartlessly called for extermination of the natives, there were nods
of approval among the sixty-odd delegates. There were encouraging letters from various senators and from the Secretary of the
Interior. The pleasant tinkle of compliments contained in them
was suddenly interrupted by the reading of one from Sherman
the terrible. The delegates sat transfixed, as if the General had
pranced across the platform in the buff.

After expressing his regret at not being able to attend, he explained his sentiments about such gatherings. "I doubt not the
generous feelings of the good people interested in the meeting
but it does seem to me that they accomplish little or no good.
The Indian question is a practical one, and not one of mere
feeling; and so far as my observation extends, the wild Indians
are rather harmed than benefitted by the conflict of extreme opinion which the public meetings engender. The real questions can
only be discussed fairly where the Indians are, and if you will
adjourn your meeting to Fort Sully, Fort Rice, or Fort Fetterman,
where you can see the Indians themselves, I will feel strongly
inclined to attend the adjourned meeting."[23]

After a moment of stunned silence, one of the lady delegates
arose and asked that the letter be read again. Then, convinced

[22] Hazen to Sherman, April 6, 1869. William T. Sherman Papers, Volume 26.
[23] *Chicago Tribune*, May 21, 1870.

that she had heard correctly, she unsheathed her forensic scalping knife and commenced. Sherman had "proved himself false to humanity by sending such a contemptuous letter to the convention," she trumpeted. After a few more thrusts of condemnation, she seated herself amidst a storm of applause.[24]

Despite the fact that western papers cheered for Sherman and condemned the philanthropists on these occasions, the men of peace displayed a growing power over the public mind. As Sherman watched the tide of opinion rise and affect Grant's policies, he sensed a major change of policy. Congress, before adjourning, had appropriated two million dollars for Indian matters but characteristically made no provision for expending the money. Urged by Jacob Cox, secretary of the interior, the President appointed a group of philanthropists to advise the government on its Indian policy. Upon the publication of an executive order dated June 3, 1869, the nation learned that Grant had named a number of prominent men to an official commission "to cooperate with the new board."[25] As a part of the new program of peace, two Indian agencies were turned over to the Society of Friends, who pledged themselves to a solution of administrative problems by applications of gentleness and understanding. The new policy, with which Sherman did not agree, thus earned the name "Quaker," because the Quakers were the first of several church groups to participate.

While the President's move gained the approval of many voters along the Atlantic seaboard, it earned him no popularity in the West. For example, when Indians attacked a trading post in central Montana and the defenders brought to bear their "pump thunder" (Henry repeating rifles) with a surprising loss to the assailants, the dead Indians were collected and their remains subdivided in native style. After decapitating them, the whites cut off all the ears, pickling them in whiskey. The heads were then boiled to get all the skin off, and the skulls were inscribed with remarks the victors found suitable. "I am on the Reservation at Last," read one. "Let Harpers Tell of My Virtues" and "Horace

24 *Ibid.*
25 Richardson, *Messages and Papers*, VII, 23.

Greeley Knows I'm Out," said another pair. As a thrust at all peace men, the following words were painted on one: "A good-looking half-breed, the son of a very distinguished Peace Commissioner."[26]

Less grisly but equally vehement complaints came from other sections of the West. Kansans advised the East that if the Quaker agents did not hurry up and get out West, the poor, innocent savages would soon destroy all the small settlements in Kansas and Colorado.[27] "How natural it is," they said, "for even a Quaker, when he becomes connected with that Indian Bureau, to lie in the interests of the worthless murdering Indians of the Plains."[28] There was one solution; just one. Junction City, Kansas sounded the word, loud and clear—extermination. All of the other reports and recommendations were pure hogwash. When Vincent Colyer reported that he had visited thirty-one tribes in Kansas, comprising 66,000 souls, and swore up and down that he had seen no drunkenness or disorder, Kansans said he must be either a liar, a knave, or a confirmed lunatic. "The creature who can manufacture such stuff is truly fit for aiding in carrying out the Quaker policy."[29]

Men in official capacities also wondered at the new departure. General D. S. Stanley, commanding the middle district, the Department of Dakota, doubted the soundness of the Quaker policy and said that the Sioux did not want peace. Writing from Fort Sully, he explained that the more food the Indians received, the more they believed it was given out of the whites' fear of them. They were getting brazen now, threatening to stop river boats ascending the Missouri.[30] Senator John M. Thayer of Nebraska represented western Congressional opposition to Grant's policy. How could one assume that all Quakers were automatically qualified for such tasks? he asked.[31]

Meanwhile, Sherman watched developments, alarmed at

---

[26] *Chicago Tribune,* June 8, 1869, quoting a Helena correspondent.
[27] *Ibid.,* June 2, 1869.
[28] *Junction City Union,* June 12, 1869.
[29] *Ibid.,* June 17, 1869.
[30] *Army and Navy Journal,* May 8, 1869.
[31] *Omaha Weekly Herald,* May 5, 1869.

Grant's sudden swing away from military force as a solution to the Indian problem. He gained some satisfaction out of the fact that even some Easterners thought the new trend was going too far in the direction of peace. Wendell Phillips, the well-known abolitionist, carried the thing too far for New Yorkers by suggesting that the government should even abandon the Pacific railroad to soothe the savages. With the prospect of interocean trade near at hand, residents of the great port city were unwilling to take any such extreme steps. Suddenly a metropolitan paper decided that "we must come back to the old army policy of reservations—peace for the Indian on the reservation, war for his hostilities outside the reservation."[32] Chicago sided in, announcing that it was 900 miles from the Atlantic and 2,350 miles from the Pacific, which made it an eastern city. In its new geographical position, lying at the mouth of a rail cornucopia, commerce was also vital to it. The warlike Phil Sheridan had moved his headquarters of the Division of the Missouri from St. Louis to Chicago, his first official act, and Chicagoans now held that "the first thing that the savages need is so much war and of such kind as shall result in their settlement on reservations. . . . When the War Department has done this, as humanely as possible, its work is done in that line. Then philanthropy can have its turn." Now the commissioners were called "those honest Iagos" who, with their fine talk, were blinding an easygoing Congress that knew nothing of the plains.[33]

These sentiments pleased Sherman, who watched railroad construction carefully, still convinced that the ring of sledges on iron spikes sang a more convincing tune than the gentle "thees" and "thous" of the Quakers. The new line of commerce would not only mean the economic development of a great area of land, but it would also shrink his military problem into one that could be more easily encompassed and solved. On May 10, 1869, Sheridan, Rawlins, and other representatives of the army sat down with him in the War Office, while a telegrapher, hundreds of miles away in Utah, made ready to tell the world of the Pacific

[32] *New York Times,* June 11, 1869.
[33] *Chicago Tribune,* April 17, 1869.

railroad's completion. "All ready now; the spike will be driven. The signal will be three dots for the commencement of the blows," clicked the receiver. In a few moments the electricity pulsed across 2,400 miles to Washington, flashing the news that the long-awaited event had come. Grenville Dodge sent a personal message to his old friend Sherman, saying, "As a steadfast earnest friend of the Pacific Rail Road, I send you greetings the fact at twelve (12) M. today the last connection was made, and you can visit your old friends in California overland, all the way by rail."[34] Sherman wrote out an answer the next day. "In common with millions, I sat yesterday and heard the mystic taps of the telegraph battery announce the nailing of the last spike in the great Pacific road. Indeed, am I its friend? Yea." He reminded Dodge of his part in the California division of the road back in 1854, when he was vice president of a line begun there. He promised to come west just as soon as General George H. Thomas, head of the Division of the Pacific had made some preliminary inspections in his new command. It would be quite a different trip from the one back in 1846, when it took his ship 196 days to round the Horn and struggle north to the Golden Gate.[35]

As the great national engineering project was completed, journals and newspapers throughout the land marked the occasion with fitting comments. The *Army and Navy Journal* came as close as any to assessing the achievement as Sherman himself saw it. It was more than an ocean-to-ocean connection. "It grapples with hooks of steel the widely-distant people, that live under one Government, three thousand miles and more asunder." Then, because of the nature of its reading public, the journal viewed recent engineering events from the military point of view. In former times men and munitions were carried on a journey of sixteen thousand miles—more than half the distance around the world—to reach the Pacific coast. Now the trip would be short and speedy. Not only could soldiers be dispatched quickly across the continent, but the Indian problem itself would be virtually

[34] Dodge to Sherman, May 10, 1869. William T. Sherman Papers, Volume 26.
[35] Dodge, *Union Pacific Railway*, 25.

solved by the railroad. "As to the Indian business," said the editor with finality, "the steady roll of the new tide of emigration will gradually crowd the Indian out of its path; civilization will spread west, as it has east, and the weaker will go to the wall; in the process, the Indian will probably be handled worse than ever hitherto—but it is destiny. Meanwhile army operations against the Indians will be revolutionized by the increased facilities of transportation for troops and supplies."[36]

It was a brisk and unemotional assessment—one that brought cries of heartlessness—but it represented much of the thinking of the time. To the army paper and to men like Sherman, a military problem was at hand. It had either to be solved or avoided completely. In its solution people were going to get hurt. They happened to be Indians. That did not alter the case. The army was going ahead, using all its means, and the railroad promised to be the secret weapon of the day. To the military mind it simply made the job easier and shorter; therefore, it was good.

As the great debate over the fate of the Indians continued throughout the summer of 1869, Sherman remained in the background, saying little. Railroad construction had proceeded apace, while the men of peace had talked earnestly to Grant about the new approach in righting the wrongs toward a minority. In September, Rawlins died, and two days later Sherman was made ad interim secretary of war. Within a month Grant made a permanent appointment. W. W. Belknap, upon Sherman's recommendation, assumed his new post, and with relief the General returned to his regular duties. The shift in cabinet officers, however, did nothing to change the position of the commanding general. Within a matter of days rumors were afloat that he and Belknap were at odds. According to a story going the rounds, Sherman wanted to write the new Secretary's annual report and had been rebuffed. Rumor had it also that the Iowan had, like Rawlins, superseded Sherman's orders. Despite all denials to the contrary, tales of the growing rift would not die. Sherman wrote to Sheridan that the new Secretary was afraid new regulations might be formulated stripping him of his power unless

36 May 15, 1869.

he retained complete control. Life in Washington was not improving for the Westerner. Neither Rawlins nor Belknap had taken kindly to his suggestions about how best to run the army, and with each reverse his gloom deepened.

Biting his lip, Sherman resolved to stick it out and keep still. His promotion had amounted to little more than an exile, without power and devoid of honor. Actually, he had been afforded more real responsibility and a greater sphere of active duty at St. Louis as commander of only part of the army. But his family liked Washington. The new residence—Grant's old home that had been purchased for the Shermans by friends—provided a proper setting for the many social events Ellen enjoyed so much. With the children in school, she turned her energies to entertaining Washington society. The house was always filled with company, and mealtime was never without a guest. As Ellen gaily ladled out the soup from a great tureen, the wrinkled General silently carved the meat and listened to the cascading tinkle of laughter that sounded like those musical streams far away in the stately Rockies. His thoughtful eyes and tight-lipped smile hid the longing deep within him to break and run for the hills. But for the moment he was a hostage to domestic and professional responsibility, and like a good soldier, he would not cry out.

Fifteen

ONE OF THE MEANEST ACTS

Before sherman had been at his new post in Washington a year, he realized that the new assignment was indeed a form of banishment. While the peace commissions had been failures, they had apparently lulled the Plains Indians into silence, and as settlers continued to invade the West, there were few signs that major warfare was imminent. Because there was no war, the American public assumed that none would occur. The army, always cautious, was not so sure, and its leaders urged a constant armed vigilance beyond the Missouri. To Sherman's frustration, Congress listened to the preachments of peace and lashed out at army appropriations with maddening regularity. With each cut, Sherman's prestige dropped.

During February, 1870, Representative John A. Logan sponsored a bill entitled "A Bill to Reduce the Number of Officers in the Army of the United States, and for other purposes." The measure was "full of prejudice," Sherman complained bitterly and admitted to his brother that "Logan will never forgive me for putting Howard in McPherson's place. Both he and Hooker were offended. . . ."[1] John recalled, upon reading the letter, that when General J. B. McPherson was killed in the Atlanta campaign, Sherman, on the advice of General George Thomas, had appointed O. O. Howard to command the Army of the Tennessee. Logan, who had taken temporary command after McPherson's death, had expected to assume the position permanently, as did Hooker, the ranking corps commander. Both were furious in their disappointment that the one-armed Howard had passed over them. Logan's anger continued to burn when he failed in

[1] Sherman to John Sherman, March 21, 1870. William T. Sherman Papers, Volume 27.

his desire to be made a general in the regular army at the end of the war. "For this he feels sore at Grant," Sherman explained. "He wants to force Grant to discharge Halleck and Hancock. If he succeeds Hancock will be the next President." It was politics as usual. Sherman was angered that men like Sheridan, George Meade, George Thomas, and other war heroes should now be looked upon with suspicion by the Republican party.[2]

As the enemies of the army closed in, publicly encouraged by the eastern press that talked loudly about economy, Sherman fought with his back to the wall. Vainly he pleaded with Senator Henry Wilson of Massachusetts, who was chairman of the Senate Committee on Military Affairs. He reminded Wilson that the appropriation bill of March 3, 1869, not only had broken up twenty regiments of infantry but had prohibited all future promotions and appointments in the staff corps until Congress should otherwise decide. The operation of this law would cause the staff corps to wither away, and before long there would be too few quartermasters, paymasters, and surgeons to care for the needs of the army. Now, if Logan's bill should become law, some of the older generals would have to retire at once, making the rate of attrition even faster.[3] Even the General of the Army would be seriously affected. It was true that some friends had purchased Grant's former residence for him, but it had been very expensive to keep. "I have endeavored to entertain my friends, come from what quarter they might, and have given some dinners and some 'receptions,' and hope to do so again, at my own expense, not the people's," Sherman admitted to Wilson. "If my pay is reduced I may not be able to do it to the same extent hereafter, but never will I receive the courtesies or hospitalities of others unless I can reciprocate them."[4]

Logan's bill proposed to do more than reduce the salaries of some high-ranking army officers. It provided that the ranks of general and lieutenant-general would be abolished when vacancies therein occurred. "It involves a very ungracious intimation

2 *Ibid.*
3 *Congressional Globe*, 41 Cong., 2 sess., Part III, pp. 2275–76.
4 *Army and Navy Journal*, April 2, 1870.

to Sherman and Sheridan that they are unnecessary and purely ornamental appendages to our military establishment—which they will be very like to resent, and which the people will not indorse," warned an eastern newspaper.[5] The *Army and Navy Journal* protested bitterly that "our little Army has had a hard fight to make in these times of peace against Congressional jealousy and popular distrust."[6] But expressions of sympathy were not enough, and military men knew they were in a fight against almost impossible odds.

Despite anything Sherman could do, the army bill passed Congress. A conference committee agreed upon a compromise that was not essentially different from Logan's proposal, and the measure was sent to the Senate. "I think it will pass there also," Sherman dispiritedly wrote to Sheridan, "and though I know the President feels opposed to it, I fear he is so placed he will have to approve. I shall make no further efforts to oppose because I see it does no good." Glumly he decided that when salary reductions became effective, he would have to return to St. Louis, resign, or find a less expensive house in Washington. Depressed and near defeat, he admitted to Sheridan that although it would do no good to struggle against Congress, yet "if we submit tamely, the next lick will be to discharge us with a year's pay, or maybe worse. This is a d——d mean treatment, and will not reflect much credit on the party in power, and will do it far more damage than good."[7]

With deep foreboding Sherman watched what he called "this cursed Army Bill" as it was debated in the Senate. To no avail western friends tried to stave off defeat. Senator James W. Nye of Nevada begged his colleagues to consider the effect of the bill upon such a distinguished American as the hero of Atlanta. "General Sherman stands pre-eminently the proudest captain of his age," shouted the "Nevada Nester," as one senator good-naturedly called Nye. "He has written his history upon the mountain tops

5 *New York Times*, April 26, 1870. The *Chicago Tribune* of April 2, 1870, took the same position.

6 May 7, 1870.

7 Sherman to Sheridan, June 13, 1870. Sherman-Sheridan Correspondence, Volume 1.

of the West and upon the plains of the South." The senators listened courteously to a long and impassioned appeal and then, as relentlessly as Sioux warriors, rendered their decision against the army.[8]

The new law was not as stringent as many army men had feared it might be. On or before July 1, 1871, the regular army was to be reduced from over 50,000 enlisted men to not more than 30,000. Sherman's pay was set at $13,500, plus allowances.[9] Charging that the changes made his office little more than a sinecure, Sherman confessed to his brother that he now wanted to sell his home in Washington and return to St. Louis. It was the only realistic course, he reasoned. The next step would surely be "muster out"; why not leave before the final humiliation occurred? All that stood between him and an immediate departure from the Capital was his loyalty to Grant. Despite any disappointments received at the President's hands, Sherman's faithfulness was undiminished, and he knew that the time to leave had not yet come.

The question of his reduced authority burned deeply in Sherman, and after the army bill had passed, he sought once more to clarify his status. Writing of it to Belknap, he referred to a law of July, 1866, which established the peacetime army and fixed the duties of the commanding general. He asked that the Secretary study the matter of divided responsibility. "Under the provisions of this law, my predecessor, General Grant, did not hesitate to command and make orders to all parts of the Army, the Military Academy, and Staff," he argued. "And it was under his advice that the New Regulations were compiled in 1868, that drew the line more clearly between the high and responsible duties of the Secretary of War, and the General Commanding the Army. He assured me many a time before I was called here to succeed him that he wanted me to perfect the distinction, and it was by his express orders that on assuming command of the Army I specifically placed the head of the Staff Corps here in Washington in the exact relation to the Army which they would

[8] *Congressional Globe*, 41 Cong., 2 sess., Part VI, p. 5337.
[9] *New York Times*, July 16, 1870; *Chicago Tribune*, July 18, 1870.

bear to any Army in the field." Now, he said, orders and reports were being made between the Military Academy and the Secretary's office "which the General does not even see, though the Military Academy is specifically named as a part of the Army which he is required to command. Leaves of absence are granted, the stations of officers are changed, and other orders are now made directly to the Army, not through the General, but directly through other officers or the Adjutant General." Did he or did he not have a position of responsibility? Sherman asked. Would the Secretary rule on the matter? It appeared that the General of the Army held high office but was stripped of all his power. "So long as this is the case I surely do not command the Army of the U. S. and am not responsible for it," he tersely concluded.[10]

Belknap ignored the letter. Grant tried to comfort Sherman by telling him that when he commanded the army, it was his view that all orders logically proceeded through the General of the Army's office. However, the President rather dejectedly admitted, Congress had the right to make rules and regulations governing the army, and no matter how irksome they might be, compliance was the only answer.[11] Quickly Sherman answered, assuring Grant that he was quite willing to abide by any decisions the President might make. He had no desire to add to the heavy burdens of the Chief Executive's office; but it did seem that the duties of the Secretary and the commanding general should be defined. Even if such a ruling should be an adverse one, Sherman promised that he would submit without further objection.[12] His loyalty to Grant was still unswerving.

Silently Sherman served at his task in Washington. Only with intimates like Sheridan did he discuss his troubles. It was maddening to see the Secretary of War gradually assume the major duties normally assigned to the General of the Army. When he stooped to appointing individual post commanders, it became

10 Sherman to Belknap, August 17, 1870. William T. Sherman Papers, Volume 28; William T. Sherman, *Memoirs of General William T. Sherman*, II, 446–49; *New York Times*, July 5, 1874.
11 Grant to Sherman, August 18, 1870. Sherman, *Memoirs*, II, 450.
12 Sherman to Grant, September 2, 1870. Sherman, *Memoirs*, II, 451.

almost humiliating. Grant had promised to correct all this, but as Sherman said, "he has his load of troubles, and I do not feel disposed to add to its weight."[13] As he waited, hopeful that his old friend Grant would eventually come to his assistance, Sherman received one of the sharpest cuts of his career. Grant let him down.

The affair arose out of Indian difficulties in northern Texas and the suggestion that this area be included in Phil Sheridan's division, under the immediate care of the experienced C. C. Augur. Such a change would leave the Department of the Platte without a commander, and Sherman recommended that it be joined to the Department of Dakota, with headquarters to remain at Omaha. Instead, Grant ordered that the Platte Department be attached to the Department of Missouri, with headquarters at Leavenworth. Sherman demurred, saying that the people of Omaha would never stand for losing their military establishment. As expected, Omaha protested loudly when the move was ordered. Before long, complaints poured in on Grant from Nebraska and other western localities that opposed consolidation in the face of a still dangerous Indian situation on the plains. Not only was the decision reversed, but the clear implication was left that the order had been one of Sherman's fumbles. The New York *Herald* quickly labeled the move one of Sherman's "ill-considered acts that now and again almost arise to the dignity of blunders," and charged that the change had been slipped in by the wily General and, unnoticed, had been approved.[14]

Infuriated, the accused flatly stated that the charge was absolutely untrue. "The President has backed square down, and though he would not do so mean a thing as to throw off on me . . . he has allowed the inference to be drawn that it was my order he had reversed instead of his own. . . . The order in question was not *my* order but the President's; it was first suggested and ordered by General Grant himself who by law defines the Mili-

[13] Sherman to Sheridan, April 1, 1871. Sherman-Sheridan Correspondence, Volume 1.

[14] *Army and Navy Journal,* December 9, 1871, quoting the *New York Herald.*

tary Departments and appoints the Commanders. I merely executed *his* order."[15] Angrily Sherman confided to Sheridan that it was "one of the meanest acts ever done by persons professing friendship," and not only had Grant promised to stand the brunt of the storm that was bound to arise in Nebraska, but he had cast the whole affair on the shoulders of a good friend when the commotion took place. "I don't like such things at all and I shall not conceal the truth," he promised.[16] Bitterly he repeated that his office was "a nuisance, a sinecure, and one from which I would gladly escape if I could afford."[17] As if this were not bad enough, Grant, in whom he had placed so much trust, had clearly begun to forget his old friends.

As Sherman watched the President drift away from him, he grasped at the consolation that perhaps after Grant's re-election things would get better. Meanwhile, he muttered to Sheridan that some of his subordinates, like Pope, were really better off than he. Pope could at least give an order and enforce its execution. "I can not give an order, nor order a Court, or even review the proceedings of a Court. I am sometimes consulted, but my inferiors in rank can take my advice or not as they please." Since he had "no military Status," he expressed the hope that after Grant was returned to office in November of 1872, "he may feel disposed to give us some of his sympathy and help. But I know that the Leading Politicians are jealous of military fame, and will secretly aid to destroy General Grant, so as to prove that Military men do not make Good Presidents."[18] Late in November, after Grant's election, Sherman again alluded in pessimistic terms to the army's position when he told General B. F. Grierson that the second inaugural would probably be the usual civic procession and ball," for the politicians are most jealous of the Military and seem actually to hate the sight of the uniforms

15 Sherman to Alfred [?], December 20, 1871. William T. Sherman Papers, Volume 31.
16 Sherman to Sheridan, from Gibraltar, December 28, 1871. Sherman-Sheridan Correspondence, Volume 1.
17 Sherman to Sheridan, March 1, 1871. Sherman-Sheridan Correspondence, Volume 1.
18 Sherman to Sheridan, October 7, 1872. Sherman-Sheridan Correspondence, Volume 1.

so much so that I have half a mind to advise such as happen to be here to wear civil dress."[19]

The re-election of Grant proved to be of little benefit to Sherman or the army. The commanding General wrote bitingly in his annual report of 1873 that since no part of the army was under his immediate control and that since the Secretary seemed to be in complete charge, he was not inclined to make any elaborate recommendations. Early in 1874, as the House Committee on Military Affairs renewed its efforts in the direction of economy, Sherman told the members that the army was no more than a "curious compound" of cavalry, artillery, and infantry. He added that Secretary of War Belknap was the real commander of the organization; Sherman was merely a figurehead.[20] However, he strongly urged Congress to refrain from further reducing the army. The vast country west of the Mississippi was of national importance, and it was far from safe from Indian depredations. Urgently he wrote to Sheridan, asking him to apply any influence he might have to the economy-minded legislators. In the scramble for self-preservation he knew that bureau heads in Washington would fight to save themselves, and the best part of the army—the infantry and cavalry—would absorb the worst of the blow.[21]

Struggle as he might, Sherman saw that defeat was inevitable. House committee members were considering a bill to reduce the army to 25,000 men, and if their recommendation went to the floor, passage would surely follow. "I have done my best but they will not listen to the dangers of the Frontier," he said. "They say reduction is demanded by the country, and they must obey."[22] Nothing the General had to offer in the way of army requirements was heard. Congress passed a bill cutting its size to 25,000

[19] Sherman to Grierson, November 29, 1872. Benjamin H. Grierson Papers, Newberry Library, Chicago.

[20] Sherman's testimony of January 6, 7, and 31 can be found in Report to Accompany the Bill (H. R. 2546) to Provide for the Gradual Reduction of the Army of the United States. Reports of the Committees of the House of Representatives, 43 Cong., 1 sess., Report 384 (Serial 1624), II.

[21] Sherman to Sheridan, January 7, 1874. Sherman-Sheridan Correspondence, Volume 1.

[22] Sherman to Sheridan, January 14, 1874. Sherman-Sheridan Correspondence, Volume 1.

men. The reduction was dangerous, Sherman argued; companies were so stripped that their standard of efficiency was seriously impaired. In the more remote stations this created an impossible situation. The legal standard was now so low that by the time the necessary months had elapsed between discharges and the arrival of new recruits at distant posts, there was hardly any effective army left.[23] Writing of his feelings to John, he was far less restrained in his language. "The Republican Party, as a party, without meaning it has been used by these men in Washington, who regard the soldier as a dirty fellow and only fit to lay the foundation for the use of the Fancy Chaps. Without being aware of it you have passed every law that could be devised to put down and oppress the real soldier. So that now, we would regard any party change as of advantage." Even the Democrats were never so mean to the army, he railed at John. While he might never let himself go to the extent of becoming a Democrat, Sherman swore that he had "not the remotest sense of gratitude to the Republicans as a Party."[24]

By the spring of 1874 Sherman had taken enough. Gloomily he accused Secretary of the Interior Delano of trying to throw all the blame on the army if a Sioux war should come. How could the army do anything under existing conditions? While the Interior Department tried to keep its own skirts clean, the Secretary of War "gives orders right over our heads," and such a back-door arrangement would do nothing but demoralize the troops. When Sheridan complained of the situation, Sherman gained a bitter pleasure from the latter's discomfiture. "I rather feel gratified that it has touched you a little on the raw," he confessed to the little cavalryman stationed at Chicago. Then, with more sympathy, he added that "no officer of spirit can act with any confidence if his plans and purposes are undermined by a system of espionage."[25] It was best to slog along from day

---

23 Report of W. T. Sherman, October 24, 1874, *Annual Report of the Secretary of War*, 43 Cong., 2 sess., *House Exec. Doc. No. 1*, Part II (Serial 1635).

24 Sherman to John Sherman, October 23, 1874. William T. Sherman Papers, Volume 37.

25 Sherman to Sheridan, March 6, 1874. Sherman-Sheridan Correspondence, Volume 1.

to day, doing one's duty and not trying anything progressive. If things went on in the present manner, the divisions would soon be wiped out, with departmental commanders receiving their orders directly from the Secretary, "leaving you and me out."[26] Even the press was laying blows on a fallen adversary. A dispatch from the Capital suggested that reports from the Sioux country were gross exaggerations, promoted by those who feared army reductions in an attempt to save their vested interests. "The indications are that the Indian Bureau will be able to prevent any very serious difficulties," was the almost insulting conclusion.[27]

Sherman's cup of forbearance ran over. On May 8, 1874, he applied formally to Belknap for permission to remove his headquarters to St. Louis. "Strong reasons official and personal impel me to this step," he said.[28] With stiff formality, Belknap answered. He had received the request, and it had gone to the President, who assented. However, said the Secretary, in tones of a parent reminding a small boy of his responsibilities, "You will perceive that it does not change the present order of business with this Department. . . . No material change shall be made in the stations of troops or commanders without previous approval by this Department."[29] When Sherman read it, he tried to control himself. His sentence at Washington was nearly up. He could wait it out now.

The announcement that the General of the Army's headquarters would be removed to St. Louis brought a howl of derision from Sherman's critics. One editor, explaining that he was offering the substance of newspaper talk in Washington, said that when an individual wanted the government to follow him around, "he is getting beyond his reach, and by his very request, proves that he has outlived his usefulness to his country—which however much or little, was more the result of an accident than genius—and should ask to be relieved and give way to some one next in rank who will not be troubled with such senseless

[26] Sherman to Sheridan, April 22, 1874. Sherman-Sheridan Correspondence, Volume 1.
[27] *New York Times,* March 2, 1874.
[28] Sherman to Belknap, May 8, 1874. William T. Sherman Papers, Volume 36.
[29] Belknap to Sherman, May 11, 1874. William T. Sherman Papers, Volume 37.

crotchets."[30] The Almighty never created an indispensable man, wrote another critic. Let the General live in Washington or put him on the retired list. That should be the fate of any army officer when he passed beyond his period of usefulness.[31] A Detroit journal saw it as part of a grand scheme to make Sherman president. As a resident of Washington he would have little chance; a western address would be most useful politically.[32] All this talk enraged St. Louis papers. What was all the fuss about? they asked. Since most of the army was on the frontier, why should not the commanding general live in a city adjacent to that region? Washington residents were merely disgruntled at the loss of a fat source of revenue that would result when army headquarters were removed.[33]

In private channels there was also concern. Army men close to Sherman objected strenuously to the move. Sheridan wrote that it was painful for him to differ from his old friend's judgment, but the injury about to be inflicted on both Sherman and the army moved him to speak. "I have not met one single individual either citizen or soldier who has not been astounded at the news and who does not regret it, for your sake, for you have many friends. I assure you my dear General you shake the confidence of the people and the army in the stability and steadiness which they have always attached to your character. You bring a condition on the Army which will ruin it forever by establishing a precedent which places its General in Chief in interment for all time to come." Running away would not solve anything, said Sheridan. It merely turned the General's office over to the Secretary, lock, stock, and barrel. Other generals, stationed in more inaccessible places, would now have no protection at all, with their guardian absent from his post at the door. Sheridan doubted that any army officers would sustain Sherman's move if they were polled on the subject.[34]

30 *Chicago Times*, quoted by the *St. Louis Daily Times*, May 20, 1874.
31 Chicago *Chronicle*, quoted by the *St. Louis Daily Times*, May 20, 1874.
32 Detroit *Free Press*, quoted by *St. Louis Daily Globe*, May 21, 1874.
33 *St. Louis Daily Times*, May 20, 1874.
34 Sheridan to Sherman, May 31, 1874. Sherman-Sheridan Correspondence, Volume 1.

In a letter marked "Private," Sherman gave his answer. He had been humiliated long enough. Grant had specifically asked him to bring the heads of staff bureaus under control of the General of the Army. "He soon backed down, and though I have again and again asked him to define more clearly my field of duty he has not done so—and on my writing to Genl. Belknap to do me this simple act of justice he did not even do me the common courtesy to answer my letter. Could I be of any service to the Army here, I would make any personal sacrifice, but without some recognition on the part of the President it is impossible." He closed with the speculation that if things were as bad as this under a former military man, what could the army expect when a civilian became president?[35] No, this was the time to get out.

As the story of the move got out in Washington, newsmen crowded around Sherman, eager to pry some pithy statement from the outspoken officer. One of them, who managed to gain an audience, found him to be "a tall, angular gentleman. . . . A rough-cast crop of iron gray whiskers about his awkwardly toothed mouth betoken years, but his erect bearing and firm tread are youthful and soldierly."

Did not the General give orders to the army, asked the reporter, casting out his bait.

"The Secretary of War does give all the orders," Sherman answered. "I suppose he thinks it is not necessary to consult me during these times of peace. Anyhow, he does not. He directs every movement of the army, and that without saying a word to me."

"Do you not protest?"

"No, I do not protest. I never protest."

"Is there any warrant of law for the Secretary's course?" persisted the questioner.

"None whatever. The act authorizing the President to appoint a general of the army gave him power, as commander-in-chief, to select some officer to superintend and direct the army. Formerly the general did that work, but of late a practice has grown up

[35] Sherman to Sheridan, June 4, 1874. Sherman-Sheridan Correspondence, Volume 1.

for the President and the Secretary of War to give their orders direct. I suppose that the Secretary thinks the President, the commander-in-chief of the army, is right here, and he might as well take his orders direct from him as to have them come through me."

Had the General decided to move in order to get away from the Secretary? asked the reporter.

"Oh, Well, I've always expected to make St. Louis my home," was the offhand answer. "During the war I thought that I should go to St. Louis and settle down when my military career was ended. Now that congress proposes to cut the army down to nothing, I see a gradual reduction that will bring the command below the dignity of my rank. I think I shall take advantage of the opportunity to do as I have long desired—settle down in St. Louis."

But did the Secretary have anything to do with the move? the newsman repeated.

"Well I think perhaps when I get there, I shall not see so much of this thing," Sherman continued evasively. "It will not be right under my eye and not quite so vexatious."[36] The young man thanked him and gave up.

By the fall of 1874, Sherman and his family were settled in St. Louis. He found a comfortable but comparatively modest house across the street from a rather pretentious mansion owned by a man who had made a fortune in packing pork. Always conscious of his relatively meager financial position, Sherman wryly remarked, upon viewing his neighbor's expensive establishment, that "it is obvious that the pen is mightier than the sword."[37] But despite any such outward inequities in economic status, he took up his new life happily, spending his days at what an Omaha paper jokingly called his "Hindquarters at 10th and Locust, and his evenings in a simple, quiet home far from Washington, D. C."

Life in Missouri proved to be one of near retirement. While Sherman's critics made scathing remarks about his flight from

---

[36] Chicago *Post and Mail,* quoted by *St. Louis Daily Times,* June 6, 1874.
[37] Colonel Isaac H. Hedges to Charles Van Ravenswaay, of the Missouri Historical Society (St. Louis), June 6, 1948.

duty and his friends despaired over what appeared to be a complete withdrawal, the stubborn officer sat out the storm. Those who knew him well realized that both his nervous temperament and years of schooling in military life were incompatible with the situation he had faced. He was a man of decision and action, quick to anger and impatient of delay. He had entered upon his duties in the peacetime army with certain reservations. His one hope was that he could participate actively in the development of a part of America that had long lain dormant. Not until after the war were conditions of transportation favorable to an agricultural assault upon the prairies beyond the Missouri. And as the advance guard of settlers swept forward, flanked by protecting army units, the United States manifested its normal postwar distaste of armed might. The revulsion against the military branch caused Congress to strip the nation of strength it needed. Those in the West knew, if the Easterners did not, that this was no normal time of peace. Sherman's action appeared to be one of surrender and pettiness; it may well have been a move calculated to shock Grant and the administration into a realization that frontier settlement and army activity in the West went hand in hand. The crusty General had made drastic moves before; he thought this one would bear fruit.

Before two years had elapsed, the situation at the nation's capital changed radically. By early 1876, with Grant's administration sinking rapidly into public scandal, the attention of the public was focused upon the sudden resignation of Secretary of War W. W. Belknap. The cabinet officer's first wife had entered into a corrupt bargain with a New Yorker by the name of C. P. Marsh, wherein she was to receive money in return for getting him the position of post trader at Fort Sill. Marsh then made an arrangement with the incumbent at the post to pay him $12,000 annually for not taking the appointment. Half of the money was turned over to Mrs. Belknap. After she died, Marsh continued to pay money to Belknap himself. When the matter came to light, Belknap's hasty explanation was understood by Grant to mean that the Secretary was resigning to protect his wife's name, and Grant, without seeking further details, wrote out a letter accepting the resignation. Although Belknap did not escape impeachment and trial, Grant's letter probably saved him from severe punishment.[38] The Senate voted thirty-five to twenty-five against him; without the necessary two-thirds majority there was no conviction. Moreover, twenty-two of the twenty-five who voted for him stated that his resignation had taken him outside the jurisdiction of the Senate.

Although Sherman had warred unceasingly with Belknap and was delighted to have him banished from office, he did not hold Grant blameless in the matter. He did not regard the Iowan, who had served under him at Shiloh and whom he had later recommended for brigadier general, as naturally dishonest. Belknap was a victim of legislation put together by Congress that "has almost invited this very system." There would be repercussions from the affair, and Sherman knew that people might think he had had some knowledge of the situation before the scandal broke. "You may answer positively that I had no knowledge except what Congress and the President had," he wrote to John. He then remarked that if Grant had brought Belknap and himself together, as he had repeatedly promised to do, things might have been better.[39] But Grant had temporized, as always, and matters drifted too long.

With the fall of Belknap's star, that of Sherman rose. Alphonso Taft, a judge from Cincinnati, was chosen to be the new secretary of war, and he at once turned to Sherman for help. "I have been with the new Secretary who is a man of good policy and an excellent lawyer and judge but utterly innocent of Army knowledge," Sherman told Sheridan shortly after the appointment. "I have just parted with him and he said emphatically, 'I must have you here.' I told him repeatedly that I wanted nothing for myself, would rather return to St. Louis as President of the 5th Street Road than remain in W. on any terms—but that if he would define what was the Army of the U. S. and leave me to command it, of course my duty was to conform. He says he is

38 William B. Hesseltine, *Ulysses S. Grant: Politician*, 395–96.
39 Sherman to John Sherman, March 4 and 10, 1876. William T. Sherman Papers, Volume 42.

more than willing to concede that the Line and Adjt Genls Dept entire shall be subject to my orders and that no order shall go to the Army except through me."[40]

After a long slump, Sherman's spirits began to rise. Not only had the unhappy situation in the War Department turned more favorable, but Grant's coolness had disappeared. Although the President had not been well and had denied all others admission to his room, "he admitted me, and I sat and gossiped with him nearly two hours," Sherman exultantly told Phil Sheridan. It was more like old times. Sheridan answered, by a letter marked "confidential." Like a schoolboy plotting a sneak day from classes with a fellow conspirator, he talked about the happy days ahead. Get your status fixed the way you want it, he told Sherman, but then take things quietly "and gradually make such changes as seem best and proper for the public service." For example, he agreed with Sherman's notion that the Platte and Dakota departments should be combined, but cautioned his friend to tread lightly, for it would cause "much ill-will on the part of the people of the Northwest if Headquarters should go to Omaha. This ill-will will be sure to follow you and the Army." Why not wait awhile, he suggested. The departmental commanders were working closely under him anyway, accomplishing the same desired result. Sheridan saw "no use of raising a storm at the present time."[41] Little by little they would work things out their own way.

By April, 1876, Sherman had made preparations to return to Washington. Despite his dislike of the place, the matter had now taken a refreshing turn, and he was willing to comply with Taft's wishes. "I find the new Secretary in every way agreeable, and he co-operates admirably," he wrote delightedly to Sheridan. "He wants to do right. . . ."[42] Further gratification came in the many letters written by subordinates in the field. "I congratulate you on having at last been placed in your proper position, the Army can now feel that it has a head," wrote General J. J. Reynolds

[40] Sherman to Sheridan, April 1, 1876. Sherman-Sheridan Correspondence, Volume 1.

[41] Sheridan to Sherman, April 3, 1876. William T. Sherman Papers, Volume 43.

[42] Sherman to Sheridan, April 8, 1876. Sherman-Sheridan Correspondence, Volume 1.

from Fort D. A. Russell in Wyoming.[43] From San Francisco came a message from General John M. Schofield. "We were all delighted at the news of your return to Washington. . . . We want our general where he can best look after all the interests of the military service, with power to command the army in fact as well as in name."[44] Nelson Miles, at Fort Leavenworth, saw a more practical side to the development. "You have an opportunity now of clearing Washington of your enemies and that corps of lobbyists that have controlled legislation for years." Anticipating action, now that Sherman was back at the helm, General Miles offered some advice. "I think if you would explode the Black Hills humbug, and clear out those lawbreakers from the Sioux Reservation and send word yourself to Red Cloud and Spotted Tail to bring in their outlaws you would settle that Indian war in three weeks."[45]

Rejoicing among army officers was general. After some troublous years, fraught with hamstringing attacks by ambitious congressmen and near neglect from Grant, the federal army appeared to be moving toward happier days. Peace commissions to the Indians had brought nothing but delay and misunderstanding; Grant's Quaker policy was no panacea; the Interior Department had tried its hand, and still the western tribes were powerful and arrogant. Sherman and his generals felt that they had been held in leash long enough; the day had come for a showdown with the adversaries of white progress on the High Plains. What better year for it could there be? America was celebrating its centennial; the army would go into the Dakotas and, with strokes of the sword, give the people real reason to commemorate a century of progress.

43 Reynolds to Sherman, April 11, 1876. William T. Sherman Papers, Volume 43.
44 Schofield to Sherman, March 30, 1876. John M. Schofield, *Forty-Six Years in the Army*, 440–41.
45 Miles to Sherman, April 14, 1876. William T. Sherman Papers, Volume 43.

Sixteen

━━━━━━━━

WE ARE PLACED BETWEEN TWO FIRES

As GRANT'S ADMINISTRATION drew to a close, Sherman could look back upon it with a sense of disappointment. Ever since he had been returned to Washington, at Grant's pleasure, his position had amounted to a sinecure and his policies ignored. Meanwhile, the important Indian question was no nearer a final solution. Time after time troops had sallied into Indian country; when they were defeated, Westerners complained, and when they won, Easterners protested at the bloodshed. The administration watched, almost helplessly, and let matters drift.

In the fall of 1868, as Sherman readied himself for his new post, his men initiated what was hoped would be the final campaign. Phil Sheridan, ignoring the advice of such old hands as Jim Bridger, commenced midwinter movements against the tribes south of the Platte, bent upon punishing those who had continued to raid on white commerce. Using the Nineteenth Kansas Volunteer Cavalry, along with eleven troops of the Seventh Cavalry and five companies of infantry, he marched southwestward. S. J. Crawford, commanding the Kansas troops, agreed to meet Sheridan at a designated point in hostile country. Resolutely "Little Phil" set off, and the very first day he ran into a blinding blizzard. After a miserable night, he admitted that "the gloomy predictions of old man Bridger and others rose up before me with great increased force," but he plunged ahead despite the initial discouragement.[1]

At Camp Supply, set up at the confluence of Beaver and Wolf creeks, about two hundred miles south of Fort Dodge, Sheridan halted to await the arrival of reinforcements. Crawford's regi-

---

[1] Sheridan, *Personal Memoirs*, II, 311; Carl Coke Rister, *Border Command: General Phil Sheridan in the West*, Chaps. VIII and IX.

ment was "unaccountably absent," and after a few days of waiting, Sheridan decided to send the Seventh Cavalry out on a scout. On November 23, in biting cold weather, General Custer left camp, and at dawn, four days later, his scouts peered over a rise on the line of march to behold Black Kettle's camp along the Washita. To the blare of "Garry Owen," the Seventh struck, and by nine that morning Black Kettle and over one hundred of his warriors were dead. Approximately fifty women and children were huddled together as prisoners of war.

Within forty-eight hours the wrinkled old scout California Joe, astride his mule, came plodding into Sheridan's camp with the news. Phil at once notified Sherman of the successful strike along the Washita, and the latter immediately approved of the move. "I congratulate all the parties for their great success which I regard as decisive and conclusive," Sherman telegraphed. He thought that by Christmas the hostile southern tribes would be begging for their lives. Sheridan could then turn them over to General Hazen, after having executed all those guilty of commencing hostilities.[2]

Sheridan agreed that "one month more will let us out of this country with a fair settlement of the Indian troubles on the condition that punishment should always follow crime." Despite the fact that Crawford's Volunteers had become lost and had to be brought in by a searching party, Sheridan was in a charitable mood. " 'The Boys,' I mean the 19th Kansas are doing pretty well, better a great deal than could have been expected," he told his superior. At least, having missed the battle, the Volunteers would not "gratify 'Old Stick in the Mud Taylor' in the realization of his anticipated massacres." Sheridan did not care whether Crawford had been lost; he had been "trapped by the Indian Ring just before coming out, with the promise of Old Taylor's place and without doubt took the bate & swallowed it."[3] Perhaps

2 Sherman to Commanding Officer, Fort Hays, December 2, 1868. Division of the Missouri, Letters Sent, 1868–71.

3 Sheridan to Sherman, December 2, 1868. William T. Sherman Papers, Volume 24. For a close look at the opinions of the Kansas boys see David L. Spotts, *Campaigning With Custer and the Nineteenth Kansas Volunteer Cavalry on the Washita Campaign, 1868–69,* ed. by E. A. Brininstool (Los Angeles, Wetzel Publishing Company, 1928).

after the abortive military venture, Crawford would be ready for a less violent assignment with the tribes. Seven hundred of his horses had died of starvation and exposure, thus effectively dismounting the Kansas cavalry. Now what would the western editors say about the ability of the local boys to go out and bring in the savages?

Tappan was wild with anger when he heard the news of Washita. Hurling himself at his inkstand, he splashed out a violent letter to Taylor, in which he charged that this latest aggression on the part of the army would cause a general Indian war in the West. See the President, call on the Secretary of the Interior, he bayed. This war policy must be abandoned; all volunteers should be immediately recalled.[4] With the latter sentiment a good many dispirited Kansas farm boys agreed; as they shivered in Sheridan's snow-swept camp, the fireside at home looked good.

The western press answered Tappan's letter with a prediction that if the army was left unhindered, "the Indian of the Western prairies will be as much a curiosity as the Indians who once inhabited the Atlantic slope, and disputed the advance of our Revolutionary forefathers."[5] Tauntingly the papers asked Tappan what the peace commissions had accomplished. "He has made a treaty of peace with seventy thousand Indians that were at peace, while those who were hostile are still on the warpath," an Omaha editor said of him. Had not Sherman already charged the Indians with responsibility for the hostilities? Then let the soldiers fight; let the guilty be punished.[6]

Sherman had his own answer to Tappan's outcry. Privately he wrote to Sheridan and Hazen of the charges made by "Tappan, Taylor & Co. to the effect that Black Kettle's was a friendly camp, and that Custer's battle was a second Sand Creek affair." He had furnished the President with sufficient facts to counteract the

[4] Tappan to Taylor, December 4, 1868. Report of the Commissioner of Indian Affairs, *Annual Report of the Secretary of the Interior*, 40 Cong., 3 sess., *House Exec. Doc. No. 1* (Serial 1366), p. 834.
[5] *Chicago Republican*, quoted by *Omaha Weekly Republican*, December 2, 1868.
[6] *Omaha Weekly Republican*, December 2, 1868.

effect of "their bald and naked assertions." Pay no attention to the furor raised, he told his officers. "This you know is a free country, and people have the lawful right to misrepresent as much as they please, and to print them, but the great mass of our people cannot be humbugged into the belief that Black Kettle's camp was friendly with its captive women and children, its herds of stolen horses and its stolen mail, arms, powder, &c., trophies of war. I am well satisfied with Custer's attack, and would not have wept if he could have served Satanta's and Bull Bear's band in the same style. I want you all to go ahead; kill and punish the hostile, rescue the captive white women and children, capture and destroy the ponies, lances, carbines &c &c of the Cheyennes, Arapahoes and Kiowas; mark out the spots where they must stay, and then systematize the whole (friendly and hostile) into camps with a view to economical support until we can try to get them to be self supporting like the Cherokees and Choctaws."[7]

Stung by a barrage of charges from the peace faction, Sherman sent one of his aides, J. C. Audenried, to Fort Cobb for talks with Hazen and Sheridan. He wanted all the information he could get about the country known as Indian Territory. Was it a suitable place for colonization? What had been the effect of recent military operations upon the wilder as well as the more peaceful tribes? Get at the heart of the matter, he told Audenried, and bring back all the facts he could, so that "I can adopt them as my own." Note distances, modes of travel, where white settlements ceased and peaceful Indians were encountered, where wild Indians ranged, he requested. Typically, Sherman was in search of all the facts.[8] Matters were reaching a head with the Indian Bureau, sparked by the Washita campaign, and he wanted to be armed with all the arguments he could muster when the showdown came.

Meanwhile, he sought to soothe his subordinates, particularly

[7] Sherman to Sheridan, Hazen, and Grierson, December 23, 1868. Division of the Missouri, Letters Sent, 1868–71. Hazen challenged the assertion that Black Kettle's camp was a peaceful one, quoting a conversation with the Chief a few days earlier when he admitted that many of his young men were on the warpath. Hazen to Sherman, December 31, 1868. *Cheyenne Leader*, January 30, 1869.

[8] Sherman to Audenried, January 11, 1869. Division of the Missouri, Letters Sent, 1868–71.

Sheridan, by standing firmly behind the recent strikes in Indian country. "I feel certain that the great mass of our people sustain us fully, but we cannot silence those who have an interest in keeping up an eternal war on the Plains, for 'none are so blind as those who will not see,' " he advised the man who would succeed him. Go ahead, he told Sheridan, and do what was necessary; Sherman would back him up.[9] Then, turning upon army headquarters, he wrote scoldingly that it was out of place for Colonel E. W. Wynkoop, agent for the Cheyennes and Arapahoes, to refer officially to the chief who lost his life at Washita as "the murdered Black Kettle." If he was so concerned about his charges, why had he gone "two thousand miles away to lecture on the perfidy of our people and the innocence of the Indian," when he should have been with his charges as their lawful agent?[10]

Sheridan answered Sherman's reassuring letters, reporting that the southern Indians were now coming in slowly, "but I believe as fast as they can, they are utterly broken down in horse flesh and even the runners who came in are on foot leading their horses." He related that Custer was champing at the bit, begging for permission to "go out and hurry them up"; to this request he had consented.[11] Meanwhile, from the northern reservation Sherman learned that affairs were less satisfactory. Expressing concern to the Secretary of War, he said that Harney had spent more money than had been allotted. Now merchants were writing in, asking if the orders for additional purchases of goods were valid. Harney, "who never reads anything," had exceeded his authority; parties having claims for goods would simply have to turn to Congress.[12] At the next opportunity he would get rid of the troublesome old warrior.

While army men were relatively satisfied with the start made

[9] Sherman to Sheridan, January 18, 1869. Division of the Missouri, Letters Sent, 1868–71.

[10] Sherman to Townsend, January 28, 1869. Division of the Missouri, Letters Sent, 1868–71.

[11] Sheridan to Sherman, January 20, 1869. William T. Sherman Papers, Volume 25.

[12] Sherman to Townsend, January 28, 1869. Division of the Missouri, Letters Sent, 1868–71.

at Washita, convinced that many Indians who now thought about fighting would reconsider, Westerners in general did not feel such a sense of security. From Wyoming came warnings of further conflict; in Montana mass meetings organized to beg for more troops; Arizonians pleaded openly for extermination of the Indians, root and branch. People living near the Union Pacific Railroad were somewhat less excited. Even those living as far west as Utah, yet near the rails, commenced to wonder openly if might made right, while Omaha now sounded almost eastern in its attitudes.[13] An atmosphere of safety, hence tolerance, was slowly permeating the region along the new road. It was not yet a wide area of understanding, but it would spread as time went on.

As one went north or south of the Union Pacific, he heard increasingly loud cries that the West was being abandoned to its fate and that even the army did not care. Kansans were afraid of their tribes, who seemed unhappy about their new reservation homes. In the Upper Missouri country steamboats were still being fired upon, and settlers were continually losing stock to raiding bands. In New Mexico, Governor Robert B. Mitchell, discouraged by the lack of army activity in his territory, told the people to go ahead and organize for their own defense. He called the Navajos "outlaws," and Vincent Colyer moaned in anguish at the prospect of things to come. A correspondent traveling through New Mexico told his readers that the hand of industry there was absolutely paralyzed by the Indians and that neither Sherman nor the Quakers had made a move to alleviate the condition. In fact, "General Sherman had the impudence to tell the people of this place when he was here, that 'if he were an Indian he would behave worse than the Indians do, and that white men had no business in this country.'" Sherman, he said, had virtually passed a death sentence on the territory. All its precious metals would now remain forever hidden, simply because twelve thousand Apache savages had decreed it so and Sherman had agreed with them! The newsman thought Mitchell

[13] *Cheyenne Leader*, March 24, 1869; *Montana Post*, April 2, 1869; *Deseret News*, March 31, 1869; *Omaha Weekly Herald*, April 14, 1869.

had done his best, under the circumstances, but he feared Sherman would disavow his actions.[14]

Such fears were not without foundation. Sherman did not approve of territorial volunteers and would comfort Westerners no more than to say that he would call them when and if necessary. Late in 1869, Montanans had again tried to solve their own problems by organizing a local force, but merchants who were still trying to collect money for supplies they had advanced two years earlier showed little enthusiasm for war at their own expense. At a meeting, attended by such well-known Montanans as Nathaniel Langford, Martin Maginnis, and Samuel Hauser, there was talk of organizing for war. William Burmeister, the chief of police at Helena, offered to raise a company for six months' service. When the inevitable question of funds arose, he proposed that a reward be given for each Indian scalp taken and that he and his men be allowed to keep all the property they might capture from the enemy.[15] It was an old idea, one that had been much discussed in the West, but there was little enthusiasm for it now. Recalling earlier attempts at military organization on a local level, one of the newspapers guessed that there were more colonels in Montana than any other portion of the Union. To illustrate his point, the editor revealed that recently a well-known colonel had gone to the stage office to see a friend off. When the departing traveler said, "Good-bye, Colonel," twenty-two men were said to have arisen from near-by benches and responded, "Good-bye, Sir!"

The volunteer business, like gold panning, was beginning to play out in Montana. No one wanted to involve the territory in further debt, and any proposals to raise troops locally were little more than threats made with the hope of putting pressure on the regular army. The government's notion of peace without war was beyond the comprehension of Montanans, and they tilted their chairs back against the false-fronted business houses and philosophically shook their heads at the weak-mindedness of those

[14] *Chicago Tribune*, August 5 and 13, 1869. Report of traveling correspondent.
[15] *Helena Weekly Herald*, September 30, 1869.

in Washington. When mass meetings and resolutions failed to stir the army, a United States grand jury officially complained about depredations wrought upon helpless and scattered mining communities. The move may have had some effect, for Sheridan shortly reminded Sherman of his desire to campaign against the Piegans during the winter. On November 4, 1869, Sherman cautiously gave his permission to proceed.[16] His hesitancy did not arise out of desire to avoid conflict; experience had taught him to be wary of territorial politicians. "I regard the clamor in Montana as identically the same as occurred two years ago, the same Indians the same men and the same stories," he warned Sheridan. Go ahead, however. But watch Alfred Sully; he was apt to fall in with local politicians, and before the army knew it, someone else, perhaps the Interior Department, would be running the show.[17]

Sheridan lost no time in ordering an attack. In January, 1870, Colonel E. M. Baker of the Second Cavalry hit a camp of Piegans, killing 173 and destroying 41 lodges. With satisfaction, Sheridan reported to his superior, "I think this will end Indian troubles in Montana and will do away with the necessity of sending additional troops there in the spring as contemplated."[18] In revealing what he regarded simply as a successful and legitimate military operation, Sheridan stirred up a hornet's nest that was more damaging to the army than defeat on the field of battle. While the Baker affair might have alleviated Indian pressure in Montana, it touched off a blaze of sympathy in the East that spread all over the country. Vincent Colyer at once unsheathed his pen and hit the warpath. Writing to a fellow peace commissioner, Felix R. Brunot, he charged that Baker's attack of January 23 had killed but 15 fighting men, the remainder of the 173 being women and children, or old, helpless men. According to his figures, 90 women and 50 children had died at the hands of Baker's heroes. Most damning of all, Colyer stated his source of

16 Sheridan to Sherman, October 21, 1869; Sherman to Sheridan, November 4, 1869. *Chicago Tribune*, February 3, 1870.
17 Sherman to Sheridan, December 30, 1869. Sherman-Sheridan Correspondence, Volume 1.
18 *Chicago Tribune*, February 3, 1870.

information to be Lieutenant W. B. Pease, an agent for the Black-feet. General Sully, about whom Sherman had warned Sheridan, had obligingly endorsed the report and sent it to Colyer.[19]

Sheridan was furious. "I see that Mr. Vincent Colyer is out again in a sensation letter," he said to Sherman. "Why did he not mention that Col. Baker had captured over one hundred women and children? This he suppressed, in order to do injustice to that officer, by deceiving the kind hearted public, and to further the end of the Indian ring, doubtless in whose interest he is writing."[20] Sherman came back in a roaring rage. "*The Piegans were attacked on the application of General Sully and the Interior Department,* and that these should now be shocked at the result of their own requisition and endeavor to cast blame on you and Colonel Baker is unfair. General Sully, by communicating by telegraph for the use of Mr. Collyer [*sic*], did an unofficerlike and wrong act, and this will, in the end, stand to his discredit."[21] Sully, true to Sherman's prediction, had thrown in with "the enemy"—the Interior Department.

Baker quickly explained to Sheridan that of the 173 killed at the Piegan village, 120 were able-bodied men, while the remaining 53 were women and children. After the battle, 140 women and children were captured and then released. "I believe that every effort was made by the officers and men to save the non-combatants, and that such women and children as were killed were accidentally killed. The report published in the Eastern newspapers is wholly and maliciously false."[22] Sherman agreed, and asked, "Did we cease to throw shells into Vicksburg or Atlanta because women and children were there?"[23] It was simply an incident of war. If people wanted to believe the reports of those living at Fort Benton, more than one hundred miles from the site of the battle, he could do nothing about it. The campaign had been planned for months, and the Indian Bureau knew all

[19] *New York Times,* February 23, 1870.
[20] Sheridan to Sherman, February 28, 1870. *Cheyenne Daily Leader,* March 11, 1870.
[21] Sherman to Sheridan, March 7, 1870. *Helena Daily Herald,* March 23, 1870.
[22] Baker to Sheridan from Fort Ellis, Montana, March 23, 1870. *Army and Navy Journal,* April 2, 1870.
[23] *Boulder County News,* April 20, 1870.

about it. There had been no complaints whatsoever from that organization when it was informed about the proposed strike. What he had said before he now told Sheridan: That in trying to protect both settlers and Indians the army's lot was a sorry one. "We are placed between two fires, a most unpleasant dilemma from which we cannot escape, and we must sustain the officers on the spot who fulfil their orders."[24] He would stand behind Colonel Baker.

The newspapers changed alliances now, as a result of what quickly became known as the "Baker Affair." The East, which, in mistaking army restraint on the plains for moderation, had come to support Sherman, was now thrown into a state of horrified excitement, and words of hot condemnation rang on editorial anvils. The *New York Times* demanded an investigation and called the battle brutality, a needless barbarity, a crime, and a blunder. The editor confessed that his paper had defended Custer when he moved against Black Kettle a year earlier and had approved of General E. A. Carr's cavalry raids in Kansas, holding that in both cases the Indians received just punishment. But this was slaughter in the Chivington manner. While 173 Indians had died, only one soldier had been killed and one injured as he fell from his horse. That made it a massacre.[25]

Montanans, on the other hand, suddenly found a friend in General Sherman. They forgot their recent animosities toward him and had nothing but praise for the Baker attack. Some of the territory's important men memorialized their Congressional delegate, publicly thanking Sherman and Sheridan "for the humane desire they have manifested in the protection of the lives of the people in this Territory."[26] Montana newspapers, in much less formal language, gave their unstinted approval. Said one, in mock tribute to the dead Piegan leader, "O, Mountain Chief, last and most distinguished horsethief, most chivalrous scalper of all, we will think of you when we travel in Montana; we will try to regret that you were cut off from your skull practice by

24 Sherman to Sheridan, March 24, 1870. *Army and Navy Journal*, April 2, 1870.
25 *New York Times*, February 24 and March 10, 1870.
26 *Chicago Tribune*, March 29, 1870.

Colonel Baker before you had any opportunity to cast your ballot in our particular poll. . . . We are philanthropists. We would not kill you—at least, so long as you didn't try to kill us. But now that you are dead, 170 of you, more or less, we congratulate you."[27]

The pros and cons of warfare with the tribes had been battled over many times in the press, but few affairs produced such a devastating effect upon the army as the Baker incident. It was not that this latest bloodletting was any more horrifying in its details; it was simply a matter of timing. During the early months of 1870 the army was particularly hopeful of seeing the long-desired transfer of the Indian Bureau into its hands finally consummated. Just as it appeared likely that such a bill would pass Congress, Baker swept down upon the Piegans, guns ablaze. And like the shot heard around the world in colonial times, the echo reverberated back and forth across an America already deeply touched by the humanitarian sentiments of Grant's "Quaker Policy." The army organ readily confessed that "had the late grand explosion and uproar of the Indian Ring been regulated by a patent fuse, it could not have been timed more accurately than it was to the looked-for event." The army bill, at a critical point of near passage in the House, was shot dead center by Baker's men. The clause containing a provision for the Indian Bureau transfer flew out like a shattered clay pigeon. "It seems to have been stricken out by general consent, and it had no friends to say a word for it," lamented a friendly editor.[28] The *New York Times* scolded the army and told its readers that surely this was no way to keep peace on the plains. With satisfaction it reported the failure of the transfer and said, in loud tones of righteousness, that this was no time to turn Indian affairs over to so reckless a crowd as the military men.[29] The army had won a battle and lost a campaign.

While Colonel Baker's attack upon the Piegans was a partial attempt to satisfy the demands of Westerners for more living

[27] *Army and Navy Journal,* March 12, 1870.
[28] *Ibid.,* March 26, 1870.
[29] March 10, 1870.

room, it illustrated the fact that the Indians and whites were daily edging closer together and that ultimately a mighty clash would result. During the same time the Montana campaign had been planned and executed, events southward in Wyoming indicated that the same irritants were at work. That they did not result in bloodshed was only a matter of luck.

During the winter of 1869–70, an organization calling itself "The Big Horn Mining Association" made its appearance in the nation's newspapers. It was organized at Cheyenne for the purpose of sending a body of armed men into the Big Horn Mountains on a mass gold-mining expedition. Wyoming businessmen called for support from cities like Omaha and Chicago, promising that they would reap large profits from supplying such a venture and predicting a large emigration to the new bonanza when spring came. Four companies of eighty men each were proposed. Each man would pay $65.00 into a general fund and would provide his own horse and gun. The money collected was to be used for wagons, supplies, and the hiring of a competent surgeon.[30] With predictions that the expedition would cause one of the greatest Indian wars ever known ringing in their ears, the Association leaders made ready to leave for Sioux country. Such warnings were brushed aside by Cheyenne residents, as they hungrily looked forward to sudden wealth in the mountains. "The Indians must stand aside or be overwhelmed by the ever advancing and ever increasing tide of emigration," wrote a Wyoming editor bravely. "The destiny of the aborigines is written in characters not to be mistaken. The same inscrutable Arbiter that decreed the downfall of Rome, has pronounced the doom of extinction upon the red men of America. To attempt to defer this result by mawkish sentimentalism in favor of the savages is unworthy of the spirit of our age." As he worked himself into a rationalization for the invasion of Indian land, the writer defied the government and challenged it to prevent an expedition of such economic merit.[31]

30 *Cheyenne Leader,* January 3 and 6, 1870; *Omaha Weekly Herald,* February 16, 1870. For further comments on the Big Horn expedition see Raymond L. Welty, "The Policing of the Frontier Army, 1860–1870," *The Kansas Historical Quarterly,* Vol. III, No. 3 (August, 1938), 248–49.

When General C. C. Augur informed Governor John A. Campbell of Wyoming Territory that the proposed movement would conflict with federal treaty obligations in the Big Horn country, the Governor complained loudly to Washington. Judge J. H. Howe, chief justice of the Territorial Court, agreed to go to the Capital himself to use his influence with old friends like General John Logan, with whom he had once served. Before long, he telegraphed triumphantly from the East, "A great struggle but finally successful. Expedition permitted. Instructions sent to Augur."[32]

As Cheyenne celebrated, Sherman sat in silent defeat. Grant had succumbed to entreaty and persuasion. Orders went out to Sheridan to countermand Augur's order of refusal. Wyoming learned from Sherman that Grant had now authorized the expedition provided that the leader would sign an agreement with General Augur promising not to trespass on the reservation of the Shoshone or Snake Indians. Nor would the army go north of the Wyoming line or east of the Big Horns into Sioux country. It was further stipulated that the Big Horners were on their own. The army disclaimed its intention to give protection either to the men involved or to any communities they might establish during the mining venture.[33] Grimly Sherman told Howe that before the miners got back, they would have to fight Sioux, despite all precautions. In that case, he said crisply, "I hope the boys will whip them."

Toward the end of May, 1870, the main party got off, and for the next three months reports dribbled back to Cheyenne of its fruitless efforts to find gold. By August the group had broken up into disappointed fragments, and one by one they straggled back to civilization. Residents of Cheyenne bitterly attributed the failure to the army's refusal to allow the men into a country they regarded as the best gold-bearing part of the whole region. As an epitaph to the dead venture, a Cheyenne newsman dismally concluded that "the tedious process of Indian extinction must

31 *Cheyenne Daily Leader*, March 3, 1870.
32 Augur to Campbell, March 21, 1870. *Cheyenne Daily Leader*, March 23, 1870. See also issues for March 25 and April 14.
33 *Cheyenne Daily Leader*, April 19, 1870.

go on, perhaps for years," before honest white men could extract their just due from Wyoming's golden hills.[34] The pick and pan assault had ended without an Indian war, and officials in Washington heaved a sigh of relief. General E. S. Parker, commissioner of Indian affairs, said that "considering the provocation given . . . by an ill-timed, if not injudicious movement on the part of certain citizens," the nation was fortunate indeed not to have been involved in serious difficulty.[35] He admitted frankly that political pressure had been so great that Grant overrode Sherman in the matter.[36] For once, however, the army had been lucky; no violence had ensued. But its commanding officer had suffered another rebuff.

During the months that followed Colonel Baker's attack in Montana, and while the Big Horn gold hunters plunged northward across Wyoming, the Sioux chief Red Cloud watched anxiously the intensifying white pressure. As summer approached, he sent word that he would like to accept earlier offers of an opportunity to talk with the leaders in Washington. Sherman did not approve of the idea and said that he was sure the President would oppose it. He thought such visits usually resulted in more harm than good; but General Parker and the peace men thought otherwise, and before long some of the chiefs were on their way east. Once more Sherman had guessed wrong about Grant.

In June, Red Cloud of the Oglala band and Spotted Tail of the Brûlés showed up in Washington, eyeing each other suspiciously, yet driven together momentarily in common defense against the swirl of Washington society. After visiting the Indian Bureau, they were hustled off to the Navy Yard to be impressed by the big guns of the white man. To the surprise of the hosts, the Indian women put their hands over their ears before the cannons were fired, showing that they already knew about the "big thunder."

34 *Ibid.*, August 23, 1870.
35 Report of E. S. Parker, commissioner of Indian affairs, *Annual Report of the Secretary of the Interior*, 1870, 41 Cong., 3 sess., *House Exec. Doc. No. 1* (Serial 1449), p. 468.
36 *Army and Navy Journal*, May 7, 1870.

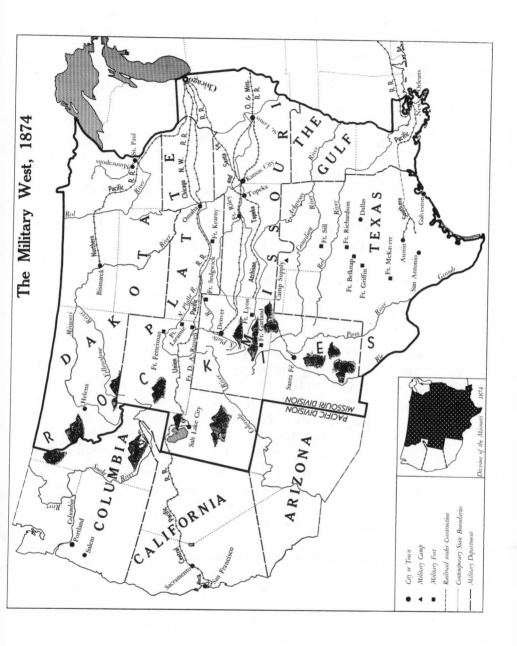

The Military West, 1874

When councils were later held, the chiefs also proved disappointing to the enthusiasts who had invited them. Stoically Red Cloud told Secretary Cox and others that the white man must get out of the Powder River country. Although Forts Reno, Phil Kearney and C. F. Smith had been removed, Fort Fetterman still stood. Nor did the Chief want to go on a reservation along the Missouri River. Putting officials on the defensive, he said, "You are the people who should keep the peace. For the railroads you are passing through my country I have not even received so much as a brass ring for the land they occupy." Grant, upon hearing the request, answered that Fort Fetterman would stay. It was a supply base for the army and offered protection not only to the whites but also to the Indians. When he was reminded of the treaty of 1867, Red Cloud solemnly said he had never heard of it. Secretary Cox explained that Sherman, Sanborn, Harney, Tappan, Augur, Taylor, and Terry had made it, and it had been signed by two hundred different Sioux of the various bands. Why did not Red Cloud take back a printed copy to show his friends? Scornfully the Indian refused, saying it was "all lies," and charging that at the time of the signing the interpreters told a different story about its provisions from the one they now gave him. Trying another tack, Commissioner Parker turned to Little Swan, asking him if he would keep the peace. The shift in tactics proved to be abortive, for the Indian gravely related that he had just visited Congress, where he had found no agreement among the whites themselves. Quickly changing the subject, the Commissioner asked Little Swan how he had become a great chief. Was it by killing people? "Yes, the same as the Great White Father in the White House," he answered sagely, referring to Grant's claim to fame. Checkmated, the interrogator gave up.[37]

Sherman must have been amused when he heard of the turn of events. He refused to see Red Cloud, believing it would do no good. "We can make no promises because Congress don't enable us to fulfil even our provisions already made and contained in Treaties ratified by the Senate. I did not think it worth while

[37] Accounts of the visit are found in the *New York Times*, June 4, 5, 8, 10, 11 and July 9, 1870.

to bring these Indians here unless they came as petitioners to Congress. We can do nothing here that we have not already done out at Laramie." He felt that it was useless to bring the Indians east just to impress them. It had been done before, and when the emissaries returned home they lost their influence with the tribe, because "they have tasted the white man's medicine, and are deposed, to be replaced by young men who represent the feelings and habits of their enterprising bucks. I regard all this as a mere concession to the popular sympathy felt in the East for the oppressed Indians."[38] Subordinates agreed with their General. Officers out on the plains knew that men like Red Cloud could not control their young braves any more than the government could contain the whites who surged toward tribal holdings.[39]

But the opinions of high military officers did not deter those whose tearful sentimentality toward the Indians made them crowd around the colorful savages from the western wilds. Red Cloud was hauled off to New York's Cooper Institute, garbed uncomfortably in a white starched shirt, a new waistcoat, and a high hat, to make a speech before a sweltering but fascinated audience of metropolitans. When he told the audience that "my father [the President] has a great many children out West with no ear, brains, or heart," New York approved, and "extermination" became a dirty word.[40] Red Dog was next shoved out on the stage before staring eyes. Tongue in cheek, he explained to his attentive listeners that the reason he was so fat was because he was stuffed full of lies. The white men thought he was trying to be funny, and reporters called him the wag of the tribe. Easterners nudged each other in delight and confessed it was quite a show. And the United States Indian Commission did not have to go to Fort Sully after all, as Sherman had acidly suggested to them. The Indians had come to see them.

The West watched the side show in silent contempt and decided that it had been wrong about Sherman all along. A reporter, visiting Cheyenne, wrote of the army in terms as senti-

---

[38] Sherman to Augur, June 9, 1870. C. C. Augur Papers.
[39] Hancock to Sherman, June 17, 1870. William T. Sherman Papers, Volume 28.
[40] *New York Times,* June 13 and 17, 1870.

mental as those appearing in the New York papers about the visiting Indians. "The West and the army are inseparable," he said. "If you write about the country west of the Missouri, you must also write about the army; for no sooner do you leave the States than the blue coats begin to appear, and the further you go toward the setting sun the more numerous they become." The East knew little of these men, confessed the visitor. Rarely did they come back across the Missouri, and when they did, it was usually for just a short visit. Meanwhile, in Congress "legislation is steadily against them, and on the frontier they are hated and despised by the settlers and sojourners. It is said they cannot catch an Indian, and that every savage killed or captured by the regular army costs the United States $115,000 each." It was all so unfair. The army was the pioneer of civilization in the West, yet it was caught between the Easterner who wanted to civilize the Indian and the Westerner who wanted to kill him. The result was that both sides were perpetually unhappy.[41]

"It is safe to say that the West now has one friend in high official position," agreed a western editor. While the Quakers talked of peace in the West, Sherman, its true friend, knew that the Indians intended to continue their course of warfare. "We have some confidence that the naturally perverse head of General Sherman will lead him to persist that there is no peace, and after while, humanity may be beaten into the heads of the Indian agents, ring-speculators, and pseudo-philanthropists of the East."[42] Gradually it began to dawn on peevish Westerners that Sherman had been working in their interest during the days they excitedly had condemned him for his lethargy.

Quietly, somewhat contemptuously, Sherman had watched the Indian performance in Washington and New York. When it had run its course, he decided to do what the philanthropic Indian commission would not do—go out and examine the Indian problem at its source. During the spring of 1870, Texas was readmitted to the Union under the Reconstruction plan of the

41 *Chicago Tribune,* January 11, 1870, by a correspondent signing himself "Aaron About," written from Cheyenne.
42 *Cheyenne Daily Leader,* July 8, 1870.

Radical Republicans, and what had been known as the Fifth Military District of the South ceased to exist. A Department of Texas, commanded by General J. J. Reynolds, was now erected; it included the states of Texas and Louisiana. With the addition of Texas to the western command there were cries for help against the raiding Indians in that sector. That these people were advocates of direct action is suggested in a letter signed "Texas," written from Sherman, Texas, wherein the writer begged, "Give us Phil Sheridan, and send Phil-anthropy to the devil."[43] In May, 1871, Sherman visited the Southwest, determined personally to assess the problems in another part of the West where Indians and whites rubbed each other with increasing friction.

Accompanied by Inspector General Randolph B. Marcy, he first visited General Reynolds at San Antonio. Then moving northwestward to the source of the San Saba River, he inspected Fort McKavett, remarking that it was a surprisingly well-constructed post. Its location seemed to him to be at the westernmost point of white habitation in Texas, a section of country suited only for the raising of livestock," as the Indians are gradually killed off, or domesticated." Fort Concho lay a day's travel to the north. Although the area of the two forts was subject to some raiding by horse-stealing bands of Indians, he was glad to report that the people were not particularly alarmed about their safety.[44]

A few more days' travel to the north and slightly eastward to Fort Griffin did nothing to change Sherman's opinion that in general the region was quiet. "I have seen not a trace of an Indian thus far and only hear the stories of people, which indicates that whatever Indians there be, only come to Texas to steal horses," he reported to General Reynolds. These bands of thieves were so scattered that it was useless to send troops out to hunt them. The people should organize for their own defense and "take precautions such as all people do against all sorts of thieves." He thought Texas was a fine grazing country, with a climate far

[43] *Chicago Tribune*, April 25, 1870.
[44] Sherman to Reynolds, May 10, 1871. William T. Sherman Papers, Volume 30.

more agreeable than he had been led to expect. People would come, and the Indians would be shoved aside. Despite any talk to the contrary, he saw no reason why in time "it may not become a prosperous and rich State."[45]

As Sherman and his party headed for Fort Richardson, still traveling in a northeasterly direction, Texas seemed quiet and pastoral. No Indians showed themselves to disturb the tour or the General's thesis that this talk of Indian troubles was somewhat exaggerated. However, as his party made its way past Fort Belknap, between Forts Griffin and Richardson, and passed across an open prairie near Salt Creek, it barely avoided a local demonstration of Indian misconduct. A band of Kiowas, led by Satanta, Big Tree, Satank, and Eagle Heart, swooped down upon the wagon train of Henry Warren as it toiled toward Fort Griffin, loaded with shelled corn. After a brief but violent encounter, the Indians captured the twelve wagons and killed seven teamsters, including the wagon master. That night five survivors crept into Fort Richardson and reported the affair to Sherman, who had only hours before passed over the battleground, within twenty miles of the fort.[46] For years afterward a story circulated in the Southwest that upon hearing of the attack from Thomas Brazeale, one of the survivors, Sherman kicked and cursed the man, saying he did not believe a word of what he had to say, and refused to send out soldiers to investigate the matter. Contrary to the vicious tale, of which kind Sherman was so often the victim, the surprised and angry General at once ordered Colonel R. S. MacKenzie, commanding Fort Richardson, to take 150 cavalrymen with thirty days' rations and hunt down the marauders.[47]

The next day a crowd of from two to three hundred border people from around Jacksboro waited upon the General and lodged a vigorous protest with him. These Indians, they said,

[45] Sherman to Reynolds, May 15, 1871. William T. Sherman Papers, Volume 30.
[46] Sherman to Colonel William H. Wood, commanding officer at Fort Griffin, May 19, 1871. William T. Sherman Papers, Volume 30; Carl Coke Rister, "Documents Relating to General W. T. Sherman's Southern Plains Indian Policy, 1871–1875," *Panhandle-Plains Historical Review*, Vol. IX (1936), 19 (extracts from General R. B. Marcy's journal); Rister, *Border Command*, 174–76.
[47] The false story is found in Dudley G. Wooten (ed.), *A Comprehensive History of Texas, 1685–1897* (2 vols. Dallas, W. B. Scarff, 1898).

were reservation Indians. Could they go to Fort Sill and recover stock recently stolen by this band? They could, said Sherman. If the stock could be identified, its recovery was promised. "It is all important that this case be followed up with extreme vigor, and principally that we find out whether or no, the impression be well founded that the numerous robberies and murders on this Frontier have been done by the Fort Sill Reservation Indians," he wrote to Colonel William Wood at Fort Griffin. That officer was ordered out with instructions to search the region along the Little Washita and to "attack any party of Indians there found."[48]

Eager to follow up this latest case of Indian depredations, Sherman hastened on to Fort Sill. In four days his mule-drawn ambulances arrived there, and he was greeted by his old wartime friend General Benjamin H. Grierson, now in command at the post. He at once sought out the Indian agent, Lawrie Tatum, whom he called "a good honest man," and learned that both the Kiowas and Comanches under his charge were completely out of control, ranging far off the reservation on raids. To Sherman, it was the same old story. The Indian Bureau fed and supplied these Indians regularly, but had no power to keep them from sallying forth for the recreational purpose of killing settlers. "I do think the people of Texas have a right to complain," he confessed. "Only their complaints are now against the troops who are powerless, but should be against the Department that feeds and harbors these Indians when their hands are yet red with blood." He advised Tatum to feed only those who stayed at home, and when the truant ones were caught raiding and killing, they should be turned over to Texas authorities for trial and punishment. "A few examples would have a salutary effect," he remarked bluntly.

Meanwhile, Sherman talked at length with Texans who had come to Fort Sill for the purpose of regaining any stock stolen by the Indians. He explained once again that Indians like the Kiowas were under the supervision of the Interior Department, and he was, therefore, "unable to apply a remedy" to their im-

[48] Sherman to Wood, May 19, 1871. William T. Sherman Papers, Volume 30.

mediate troubles. So far as the culprits of the recent raid were concerned, he hoped that they were caught and punished before they got back on the reservation. Writing of the affair to Pope, he went further and said that these raiders should be hurt even to the extent of denying their families food on the reservation. "Now these Indians openly boast of their deeds of bravery in Texas, and even show scalps taken in their raids," he continued. The Indians were well armed with Sharps, Spencer, and Henry rifles and fully supplied with ammunition. Sherman believed that the source of supply was a highly organized trade in stolen horses and mules carried on in near-by Kansas and New Mexico. The whole business ought to be stopped at once.[49] One of the purposes of the reservation system was to keep the Indians localized while some attempt was made to tame them. But apparently the aims of the philanthropists had not been realized here. The young Kiowas and Comanches preferred the feel of a scalp lock to that of a textbook. Although they had been corralled for two years, their education had progressed but little. "I hear of none engaged in agriculture and Mr. Tatum told me today that not a single child of these two tribes was now at his school," Sherman reported to headquarters. "Their progress in Civilization is a farce."[50]

Rather than expand his forces and call for more military establishments in the region, Sherman decided that the progress of events called for consolidation. Writing to Reynolds, at department headquarters in San Antonio, he defined the over-all problem. "Looking back on the frontier of Texas it reminds me of the line of battle of some of our Corps Commanders, who regardless of their neighbors would refuse their flanks."[51] Some changes had to be made, and he would recommend them. The whole line of defense needed tightening. He at once wrote to Washington, expressing the opinion that forts like McKavett and Concho

[49] Sherman to Pope, May 24, 1871. Rister, "Documents Relating to General W. T. Sherman's Southern Plains Indian Policy, 1871–1875," *Panhandle-Plains Historical Review*, Vol. X (1937), 50–52.

[50] Sherman to Townsend, May 24, 1871. Rister, "Documents Relating to General W. T. Sherman's Southern Plains Indian Policy, 1871–1875," *Panhandle-Plains Historical Review*, Vol. X (1937), 53–55.

[51] Sherman to Reynolds, May 24, 1871. William T. Sherman Papers, Volume 30.

were well located but that Griffin and Richardson were not. The latter two were placed as though the army proposed to retreat from the Indians. A straighter, bolder line of defense was needed.

Even as he laid out his plans for future protection, Sherman saw the latest Indian difficulties terminated before he left Fort Sill. On the afternoon of May 27, 1871, Satanta, Kicking Bird, Satank, Lone Wolf, and several others turned up at the post and blandly asked for their rations. When Tatum inquired about the recent wagon-train attack, Satanta spoke up and freely admitted that he and the others had committed the crime. In fact, said the Chief, so meritorious was the act that if any other claimed credit for it, he was a liar. It was Satanta and none other who had led the group. Tatum at once sent word to Sherman that he wanted the Indians arrested. When they were brought before the visiting army officers, they proudly repeated the story they had told Tatum, whereupon Sherman ordered his men to place the Kiowas under arrest.

Satanta now began to show concern. He said that although he had been present, he had not killed anyone, nor had he even blown a bugle. His young men had insisted upon a little fight, and he merely accompanied them. That was all. Sherman angrily scolded the Chief, telling him that the attack by one hundred warriors upon twelve poor teamsters was a cowardly thing. Why had not Satanta fought with the soldiers if he enjoyed combat? Now, he said, the Indians would have to go to Texas for trial. The promise of Lone Star justice agitated Satanta considerably, and he was not long in expressing his opinion about it. With a great show of emotion, he begged Sherman to have him shot on the spot.

About this time Kicking Bird arrived at the parley. As a powerful member of his tribe and one whose conduct had been somewhat more above reproach than that of the others, he tried to intercede in Satanta's behalf. He explained that it had been his policy to restrain the young braves as much as possible and that for the sake of any good he might have accomplished, he asked consideration. More than that, he would even return the stolen mules.

Sherman replied that he appreciated all that had been done and that Kicking Bird would be treated in a kindly way as long as his conduct remained above suspicion, but the three Indians—Satanta, Big Tree, and Satank—must be sent to Texas. The Indian pressed his case, suggesting that war might result if the General carried out his threat. As he made his threat, about twenty soldiers pressed forward, ready to execute Sherman's command.

Just as the situation reached its climax, Lone Wolf rode up on a splendid horse and, dramatically swinging down from his mount, laid two Spencer carbines and a bow and quiver of arrows on the ground. Carefully tying his horse to a fence, he dropped a blanket from his shoulders and tied it to his waist. As Sherman and the soldiers watched him curiously, he picked up his arms and strode casually up to the piazza where the General sat and, without a word, handed a carbine to an unarmed Indian and a bow and arrows to another. Then resolutely he seated himself and cocked his carbine, amidst clicks from the guns of the soldiers.

It was too much for Satanta. He and some of the others cried out "No! No!" The soldiers were ordered to hold their fire, but almost the instant the order was given, shots were heard just outside the fort. The commotion resulted from the attempt of some Indians to leave the post against orders, and in the melee a guard was wounded and one of the fleeing Indians killed. When the excitement subsided, Sherman, who had been watching the immobile Lone Wolf and his cocked carbine, told the group around the piazza that the forty-one mules Kicking Bird had promised to return must be given up at once. This eased the situation momentarily, but when Kicking Bird reached his near-by camp, he discovered that the women had been so frightened that they had run off with all the animals but eight. Discouraged by this act of feminine duplicity, the Indian returned disconsolately to the fort, bringing the remaining mules. The meeting then broke up, with Satanta, Big Tree, and Satank in irons and the remaining Indians stalking off angrily, free for the time being.[52]

[52] Rister, "Documents Relating to General W. T. Sherman's Southern Plains Policy, 1871–1875," *Panhandle-Plains Historical Review*, Vol. IX (1936), 22–24;

Texans did not seem unhappy about the outcome of the affair with the Kiowa raiders. Although they talked of raising volunteers and eighty men presented themselves to the military authorities at Fort Richardson, ready for action, no occasion arose for taking the field. Satanta, Big Tree, and Satank, heavily manacled, were loaded into a wagon and hauled from Fort Sill to Jacksboro. If there was to be no fighting, the residents decided that a legal hanging would fulfill any deficiencies in the way of justice. By the time the culprits reached the little Texas town, the Indians, as in the nursery rhyme of the "Ten Little Indians," were fewer. Satank momentarily freed himself en route and tried to attack his guard. Two shots from a sergeant's rifle ended the struggle, and Satank's body was dumped unceremoniously out of the wagon beside the road.

The trial was brief and quite satisfactory to all concerned, except Satanta and Big Tree, who were quickly found guilty and sentenced to death by hanging. The prediction of an army officer who said, "I feel assured that a civil court in Texas will do them full justice and that on Texas soil they will find an early grave," seemed about to be borne out.[53] However, before frontiersmen could hammer together a scaffold, howls of protest were heard from humanitarians all over the country. Great pressure was put on Grant, who, along with the others, used his influence on the governor of Texas. The sentence was commuted to life imprisonment.[54] By 1873 the two Kiowas were free, and the next year a trail of blood in Texas led right to their doors. Sherman was not surprised. If he had been given his choice, they would have stretched hemp in the spring of 1871. He must have regretted his insistence upon civil justice in Texas; it had fallen short of his expectations.

Despite all the army wanted to do, it seemed to be tightly held by the checkrein of public sympathy for the Indians. The Baker affair in Montana had brought howls from those who supported

Tatum to Grierson, May 27, 1871. William T. Sherman Papers, Volume 30; *Chicago Tribune*, June 7, 1871.

[53] Mizner to Sherman from Fort Richardson, June 9, 1871. William T. Sherman Papers, Volume 30.

[54] Rister, *Border Command*, 182–85.

the Indians' cause, and the Big Horn Mining Association incident drew caustic remarks from the advocates of free enterprise who wanted to exploit western resources without restraint. Even the army's attempt here, to protect Indian treaty rights, gained it no praise. The Indians won even when their misconduct was as flagrant as that revealed near Fort Sill, where military men had leaned over backward in seeking civil justice for the criminals. Bitterly Sherman wrote, "If I ever come to Fort Sill, and any of those Indians come about bragging of killing people in Texas, I won't bother their courts, but will have the graves dug at once. It does seem to me these Indian loving christians have abundant faith, for I hear of more Indian murders now than ever before."[55] He wondered how long sniping at the flanks of white settlement would go on before major warfare occurred. Probably until the army was so weakened and reduced that it could be of no real use. Then it would really hear criticisms from a fickle public.

[55] Sherman to Grierson, September 28, 1872. Benjamin H. Grierson Papers.

███████████████

Seventeen

DEATH MUST BE METED OUT

As the american republic neared its centennial year there was increasing indication that its people could look back over the first hundred years with the knowledge that at last the continent had been subdued. During the earlier seventies, rail lines, fanning out from the original trunk, carried farmers and their tools westward. Occasional depredations by small raiding Indian bands still disturbed the peace, but despite continual warnings to the contrary, there had been no major war. Slowly the public mind began to believe that the silent Grant was right and final quiet on the plains was in sight.

The opiate of peace deadened all vigilance, and each passing month saw the army in more straitened circumstances. Faced by dwindling rosters, post commanders were hard pressed to furnish men at points of possible emergency, and vainly Sheridan warned that he was obliged to contain a large and hostile Indian population with insufficient forces. With but seventy-two military posts, garrisoned by only seven regiments of cavalry and fifteen of infantry, he could muster little more than eleven thousand men to defend an area extending from Canada to Mexico and from the Missouri River westward to the Division of the Pacific. Should any serious outbreak occur, a force of this size would be wanted for just one of the four departments within his vast command.

But there would be no difficulty. The advocates of the Quaker policy said so. The Interior Department and Grant, who also believed it, said so. The public agreed. There were practically no stories in the press now about depredations. They seemed to have passed out of the picture to make room for accounts of economic progress, settlement, and agricultural expansion. Indians who drifted in and out of western towns were beginning to be regarded as sources of amusement, and more than one resident already looked upon them as positively quaint.

When fighting suddenly broke out with the Indians in 1873, it was not with any from whom real trouble had been anticipated. The American reading public was somewhat surprised to hear of violence from the Modocs. Many people did not know of their existence, and within a few days the region along the Oregon-California border became something of a geographical discovery in more than one eastern home. Back in 1864, the Klamaths, Modocs, and Yahooskin Snakes had agreed to reservations. Two years later some amendments were made to the agreements, but, as was often the case, ratification dragged on and was not finally effected until December, 1869. The long delay made some of the Indians suspicious, and there were complaints that the final draft did not represent what they believed they had earlier consented to. One of the Modoc leaders named Kientpoos, dubbed "Captain Jack" by the whites on account of some military ornaments he liked to wear, was outspoken in his objections, and it was with the greatest reluctance that in late 1869 he led his people to an assigned reservation.

Swallowing their disappointment, the Indians went to work building new homes and laying out plots of ground for future cultivation. Before long they complained that the Klamaths were bothering them. The Modocs were now relocated, but again they were dissatisfied. Once more they were given fresh lands, but by now they were considerably upset and said that the most recent location designated for them was only a trap to put them in the power of their enemies, the Klamaths, and with that they fled the reservation.[1]

In 1870, Captain Jack made formal application for land on either side of the Oregon-California line, near the head of Tule

1 General E. R. S. Canby to Division Headquarters, February 7, 1872. Official copies of correspondence relative to the war with the Modoc Indians in 1872–73, 43 Cong., 1 sess., *House Exec. Doc. No. 122* (Serial 1607), p. 84. Hereinafter cited as "Official Modoc War Correspondence." See also Hubert Howe Bancroft, *History of Oregon*, II, chap. XXII; A. B. Meacham, *Wigwam and War-Path; or the Royal Chief in Chains;* Doris Palmer Payne, *Captain Jack: Modoc Renegade.*

Lake. Indian Superintendent A. B. Meacham, as powerless as any other agent to coerce the Indians, recommended to the Secretary of the Interior that the request be granted. As restless settlers watched the Indians take over land of their own choosing, signs of trouble began to appear. Captain Jack, who boasted that he could go anywhere he pleased and appeared to be defiant in general, heightened the nervousness in near-by white homes. In 1871 suspicions about him grew when he killed an Indian "doctor" who was living on the near-by reservation. Since the treaty promised that those Indians living on government reserves would be protected against violence by anyone, Jack's arrest was in order. He refused to come in, putting off Indian agency representatives with a number of excuses. In the meantime, during November, 1871, settlers in the Tule and Clear lakes district petitioned General E. R. S. Canby and Agent Meacham to move the Modocs away, saying that their families could not live in safety under existing conditions. After nearly a year of delay and fruitless negotiation with the Modocs, a small military force was sent to bring them in. On November 29, 1872, the first shots of the Modoc war were fired as the Indians resisted the attempts of the military authorities. Within a few days eighteen white settlers died at the hands of Captain Jack's men.

After a swift thrust at neighboring ranches, where his men captured both arms and ammunition, Jack led his warriors into the rugged lava beds south of Tule Lake. In a perfect defensive position, he now defied both federal troops and volunteers from Oregon to dislodge him. During the winter months that followed there was desultory fighting, but the troops were able to accomplish little against the well-entrenched Modocs. Attacks availed them nothing but alarmingly high casualties and a sinking morale. By January 30, 1873, the Secretary of War directed Sherman to give up all offensive operations and order Canby to confine his efforts to repelling attacks against the troops and citizens. Within twenty-four hours orders went out to "let all defensive measures proceed, but order no attack on the Indians till the former orders are modified or changed by the President, who seems disposed to allow the peace men to try their hands on

Captain Jack."[2] It was not Sherman's idea of appropriate procedure, but then he was not running the army.

While negotiations dragged on, Grant talked about the "benign influences of education and civilization" for the natives. He saw no other proper course. It was either peace or extermination, and the latter was both expensive and wicked. "Our superiority of strength and advantage of civilization should make us lenient toward the Indian," he told the public. Americans listened to the President's reaffirmation of his policy, while men near Tule Lake tried to carry out his wishes. All during the spring of 1873 the peace commissioners and Canby maneuvered, trying to get an agreement from Captain Jack on a time and place of meeting. Sherman urged Canby to be patient, for the administration very much wanted the whole matter settled amicably. However, he said, should the Modocs "resort to deceit and treachery, I trust you will make such use of the military force that no other Indian tribe will imitate their example, and that no other reservation for them will be necessary except graves among their chosen lava beds."[3] With this in mind, Canby pressed for a final discussion and at last succeeded in setting a date, April 11, that was agreeable to both sides.

On the morning of April 12 the nation read the astounding news that the peace parley had backfired with violence and bloodshed. The Modocs, quietly smoking Canby's cigars as they listened, had tensed themselves for a pre-arranged signal from Jack. When it was given, they drew revolvers and started shooting. Canby fell, shot through the head, without a chance to follow Sherman's recent advice. The Reverend Elezar Thomas, a Methodist preacher who had agreed to serve as a peace commissioner, was also killed. Agent Meacham was shot five times, knifed, stripped of his clothes, and left for dead. When troops arrived, he was still alive and recovered to write his version of the proceedings in a widely read volume. There was another casualty at the conference in the lava rocks. It was Grant's peace

2 Sherman to Canby, January 31, 1873. "Official Modoc War Correspondence," 65.

3 Sherman to Canby, March 13, 1873. "Official Modoc War Correspondence," 70–71.

policy. Although not mortally wounded, the program was forced to the sidelines for the time being.

Sherman's reaction was swift. As soon as he heard the news, he telegraphed orders to General Alvan C. Gillem, who had succeeded Canby. The field officer was ordered to make an attack against the Modocs "so strong and persistent that their fate may be commensurate with their crime. You will be fully justified in their utter extermination."[4] Newspaper reports indicated that for the moment there was a unanimity of feeling about what had to be done. Leading officials and the entire cabinet were said to be of a single mind in their desire to punish the treacherous Indians.[5] Sherman's views suddenly became popular again, and reporters flocked to his office for words they knew they were sure to hear. Was not this act of duplicity unparalleled? one of them asked him.

"No, Sir," he answered in his characteristically quick, nervous way. "Treachery is inherent in the Indian character. I know of a case where the Indians murdered the man who not two hours before had given them food and clothing."

Then came more questions. How did Grant feel about the affair? Sherman answered that the President was deeply affected by Canby's death and fully concurred in the belief that no mercy should be shown the murderers.[6]

As the immediate excitement subsided, newspapers throughout the country began to take divergent stands. In New York it was admitted that Grant's peace policy had been given a severe blow, but that did not mean extermination was the answer. From the West came the expected reaction. Governor Austin, of Minnesota, openly criticized the missionary policy. Chicago papers asked that Jack's band be wiped from the face of the earth and expressed the belief that all through the West there was discontent with the existing Indian policy.[7] Denver headlines read, "A General Indian Outbreak Feared in Eastern Oregon," and the familiar subheading announced that "Settlers Ask that Arms be

[4] *New York Times,* April 16, 1873.
[5] *Ibid.,* April 14, 1873, quoting a Washington dispatch.
[6] *New York Times,* April 15, 1873.
[7] Quoted by the *New York Times,* April 15, 1873.

Furnished them."[8] Sherman himself defended the policy of violent retribution against the Modocs. Writing to the Society of Friends in Washington, he maintained that since the whole band had participated in the outbreak, every one of them should be punished, "and if all be swept from the earth they themselves have invited it." To him there was no other course. He promised that as long as resistance was offered, "death must be meted out, but the moment resistance ceases firing will stop, and the survivors will be turned over to the proper Indian agents." Already anticipating the aftermath of the affair, he asked for "shelter against such a howl as followed Major Baker after the Piegan attack, or General Custer after his attack on Black Kettle's camp." [9]

Before long, press accounts dwindled in quantity, and proponents of either course began to argue about minor items. Sherman again became a small storm center, as the newsmen quarreled over whether he had advocated offering a bounty for Indian scalps.[10] It was a sign that real news on the Modoc affair was getting scarce. Meanwhile, the army lumbered into action, opposed as always by distance, rugged terrain, and a wily enemy. The usual pieces of advice were cast from the side lines, while armchair strategists unlimbered their pens. Humanitarians in the East asserted that this little instance of Indian misconduct could not be counted as a failure of Grant's peace policy. Westerners hooted at this and complained that the army was sitting on its hands, doing nothing. "The blunders in carrying on the Modoc war are growing more plain every day, and would be laughable, if they weren't so pitiful," said a Colorado paper. "It makes the frontiersmen mad to read of mortars laboriously hauled into position to shell the possible hiding places of scattered savages." Indians never fight according to the rules of war, explained the editor, and the officer who sent his men against them "dress parade like" was guilty of little less than murder. Why not solve all the difficulty by offering a scalp bounty? In a month the Mo-

8 *Daily Rocky Mountain News,* April 27, 1873.
9 *Sacramento Daily Record,* April 22, 1873.
10 *New York Times,* May 2, 1873.

docs would all be bald-headed![11] Promises, promises, promises, cried Denver. The army was always promising action. Where was it? Why not turn the trappers and hunters loose on the savages? It would be better than listening to Mr. Beecher pray for the "poor children of the forest." Westerners were willing to pray for the red man too. They would say, "Lord, save the soul of that poor Indian," and then promptly put a bullet through him.[12] Meanwhile, one Samuel Roberts of Denver wrote to Sherman, offering sixty local hardies for service in the field. The government had only to furnish arms, horses, and rations, and Roberts promised to "finish up any tribe against whom we may be sent in a short time."[13] Another Coloradan, with the familiar name of Boone, made an even better proposition. If furnished with only rations and free transportation to and from the scene of fighting, he would collect from one to five hundred men and lead them into battle, in Oregon or any other place. All he asked was permission to "fight on our own hook, untrammelled."[14] For the moment, Westerners forgot their amusement at the antics of the quaint red men who occasionally drifted into town and picked up rubbish in the alleys.

Despite all criticisms and gratuitous offers of help, the army corralled Jack and his followers by the first of June. Then came the struggle Sherman dreaded—obtaining just punishment for the criminals. He told Schofield that some should "be tried by court martial and shot," others delivered to the civil authorities, and the balance "dispersed so that the name of Modoc should cease."[15] He urged the Secretary of War to act promptly with court-martial proceedings, "before some Indian agent makes a fatal promise." He had seen Satanta wriggle out of civil proceedings and return to his savage pursuits. "I'm sorry that Jack & most of the Modocs were not killed in the taking," he told Sheridan, "for I fear they will be petted and finally turned loose like Satanta, ready to repeat the same old Game."[16]

[11] *Boulder County News*, May 9, 1873.
[12] *Daily Denver Times*, May 6, 7, and 9, 1873.
[13] *Daily Rocky Mountain News*, May 10, 1873.
[14] Boone to Sherman, May 3, 1873. *Boulder County News*, May 9, 1873.
[15] Sherman to Schofield, June 3, 1873. "Official Modoc War Correspondence," 86.
[16] Sherman to Sheridan, June 3, 1873. Sherman-Sheridan Correspondence, Volume 1.

While Sherman fretted and again expressed his opinion that army men should have taken no prisoners, so that there "would have been no complications," his fears about Jack's escaping punishment were not realized.[17] A military commission was appointed on the last day of June, and within a few days the trial began. After hearing testimony from Indians with such interesting names as Shacknasty Jim, Steamboat Frank, Bogus Charley, and Hooker Jim, four of the Modocs, including Captain Jack, were pronounced guilty and sentenced to death. On October 3, 1873, they were hanged at Fort Klamath, and Sherman had his wish. When the remnants of the band were taken to Indian Territory to live out their days in exile, he saw another of his desires realized.

To Sherman the Modoc war was little more than a case study of the whole problem as he saw it. It was another example of the Indians' misunderstanding and dissatisfaction with the reservation system. When the Modocs first left their assigned land and took up new ones of their own choice near Tule Lake, the Interior Department dallied and considered their request for a reservation in that location. Then the trouble commenced with near-by settlers. It was the old story of not being able to keep the Indians on reservations once they were placed there. And only when the shooting began, and blood had been shed, was the army called in to try to subdue the Indians, who had passed out of Interior Department control. Sherman believed in this case, as in others, that if at the beginning enough force had been employed to allow no room for misunderstanding on the part of the Indians, unnecessary bloodshed would have been avoided. But with split jurisdiction, the Indians were able to run from one parent to the other, demanding and getting concessions that finally resulted in a major disciplinary problem.

During the months the nation's attention was focused on the small patch of land along Oregon's southern boundary, Sherman watched the whole military-Indian picture with increasing con-

17 Sherman to Sheridan, June 6, 1873. William T. Sherman Papers, Volume 35. Sherman also expressed this opinion publicly. See *Daily Denver Times*, June 14, 1873.

cern. In the larger view, the Modoc "war" was only a minor disturbance, characterized by treachery and the spectacular murder of Canby. Of much more significance was the uneasy truce with the powerful Sioux, who were being slowly cornered in Dakota. Early in 1873, Sherman urged Sheridan to nurse the wandering members of that tribe back to their assigned lands. Many of them were drifting south of the Platte, on the hunt. Get them back north, Sherman counseled. But do it without force if possible. The situation was delicate, for the Indians claimed the right to hunt in the Republican River country, south of the Platte, by virtue of their treaty of 1868. Sherman recalled his membership on that commission and said he had been bitterly opposed to such an arrangement. The whites had thought it only temporary, since the buffalo were nearly extinct in that region, but the Indians still clung to their right to hunt, and only a new treaty could persuade them otherwise.[18] While the question stood perched upon that legal point, settlers continued to shove forward, cursing the army for not getting the Indians out of their way.

What complicated the army's problem particularly was the fact that over five thousand settlers had taken up surveyed lands under the Homestead Act but were discovered to be on the reservation created by the earlier treaty. Despite objections by the Sioux, homesteaders resolutely refused to give up their farms and complained loudly that they were within their rights under the land law.[19] Again, government agencies had worked at crosspurposes to complicate the larger problem.

Meanwhile, the Northern Pacific Railroad stabbed at the Sioux from the east. Sherman watched the process, convinced that a clash was inevitable. "Find out if you can if the North[ern] Pacific Road contemplates any work west of the Missouri this year," he instructed Sheridan. He hoped that the section crossing Sioux country could be built last. The panic of 1873 stepped in to help satisfy this desire, and a fight with the Sioux was delayed

[18] Sherman to Sheridan, January 16 and May 2, 1872. Sherman-Sheridan Correspondence, Volume 1.
[19] *New York Times,* May 2 and 19, 1873.

when railroad-building came to a halt. Sherman knew the delay would be only temporary.

By the spring of 1875, as travel once again flowed heavily along western trails, the military-Indian situation became unusually tense. Coupled with the annual spate of rumors about prospective war on the plains was the story that gold-hungry miners were making ready to invade Sioux lands in the Black Hills. Sherman at once said publicly that the white men would be prevented from doing any such thing. If they entered the reservation, they would be driven out by the force of arms. Sarcastically he remarked that it was all right for the frontier people to complain about Indian law breaking, yet they did not seem to see the injustice of rushing across lands that were not theirs, acquiring property in the Indian mode. When Indians at the Red Cloud agency heard about the condition of things, they approved of the General's desire to protect Sioux rights. Recalling the strident demands of Indian-fighting volunteers in previous years and the hunger of the whites for loot, Red Cloud's braves now gravely inquired if they could have all the horses, wagons, and equipment they might capture from the miners. It was a kind of humor that appealed enormously to Sherman.[20]

Anxiously the miners eyed the Black Hills, wondering if Sherman would make his word good, and as they paused, some of the Sioux warriors began to anticipate hostilities by engaging in the usual spring raids in lands adjacent to their reserve. Sheridan complained about this, insisting that the Indians should be punished for harassing the near-by settlements, but the army held its men in check. In June, Red Cloud, Spotted Tail, Little Wound, and some other Sioux went to Washington to air their grievances. Grant tried to buy them out, offering $25,000 for any residual rights of the hunt along the Platte, but the Sioux declined, and another peace parley failed. About all that resulted was a Congressional complaint that the administration had too long made treaties right and left with the Indians, obliging the legislators to dig up the money promised. A Constitutional ques-

20 *Ibid.*, January 3, March 13 and 15, 1875.

tion, to raise its head again in the next century, had some interesting roots in Indian relations.

Although warnings came from the West that there would be war in 1875, the summer months proved to be singularly uneventful. Unnoticed, but much more significant, was a note in an Omaha paper to the effect that settlers were passing through that city in unprecedented numbers, bound for new homes on the plains.[21] As these hundreds filtered silently westward, unknown and undistinguished, they were gradually weighting the scales against the natives, who could not enlist immigration on their side but had to rely solely on natural increase. In that small notice, and in others like it, lay the answer to the Indian problem. It was not found in the noisier events of cavalry charges, the brassy cry of bugles, or the now romanticized notes of "Garry Owen." Such sounds were heard only by a public whose ear could not pick up the crump of Nebraska sod as it was ripped out and turned grass-side down. The Indians, who watched the corrugation of their hunting grounds, knew that the furrows spelled out words they could not erase.

Sherman talked with his subordinates about Indian affairs. "We could settle them in an hour," he said, "but Congress wants the patronage of the Indian Bureau and the Bureau wants the appropriation without any of the trouble of the Indians themselves." It was the most palpable waste of money in the history of the world, he told his brother. The government was sinking deeper and deeper into debt by both fighting and feeding the Indians.[22] But its course seemed firmly fixed, and nothing he could do or say would change it. He could but wait until the final eruption took place and then hope to handle the conflagration as best he could.

By the close of 1875 the American people, readying themselves for a centennial celebration, could say that finally a condition of peace prevailed on the plains. The Secretary of the Interior was pleased with the nonwarlike attitude of most Indians, but

[21] *Omaha Republican*, quoted by the *New York Times*, April 15, 1875.
[22] Sherman to John Sherman, March 18, 1875. William T. Sherman Papers, Volume 38.

cast a worried eye in the direction of the restless Sioux. He was annoyed at the persistence of miners who slipped back into the Black Hills as fast as they were evicted, and he wondered whether they understood that the government was trying to protect them, not punish them.[23] The Commissioner of Indian Affairs tried to comfort him with the knowledge that even though the Sioux appeared hostile, there had been no major depredations that year. "This fact is significant," he said with an air of finality.[24] Sherman was not so sure. The Black Hills situation was a powder keg, and he predicted accurately that "in the spring it may result in collision and trouble."[25]

During the early months of 1876 there was increasing feeling in the West, and among the army officers generally, that this year perhaps the usual talk about an Indian war would result in something more than wasted verbiage. One day in January, Lieutenant Colonel George A. Custer happened to meet Colonel Henry Carrington at the New York Historical Society. In talking over the possibility of trouble, Custer recalled Carrington's part in the grisly Fetterman massacre on the Bozeman Trail nearly ten years earlier, and said significantly, "It will take another Phil Kearney massacre to bring Congress up to a generous support of the Army."[26] Although his words were prophetic, his hope that it might result in a more enlightened view on the part of Congress toward the army was not to be realized.

As eastern papers fussed about the prospect of trouble with Sitting Bull, who was "behaving in a very unhandsome manner," Sherman thought in terms of the entire body of Sioux as his primary target. He correctly told Sheridan that a showdown with those Indians was near, and he was anxious to "finish this Sioux business, which is about the last of the Indians."[27] Army officers

---

23 *Annual Report of the Secretary of the Interior,* 1875, 44 Cong., 1 sess., *House Exec. Doc. No. 1,* Part IV (Serial 1680), p. 9.
24 Report of Edward P. Smith, commissioner of Indian Affairs, *Annual Report of the Secretary of the Interior,* 1875, 44 Cong., 1 sess., *House Exec. Doc. No. 1,* Part IV (Serial 1680).
25 Sherman to Sheridan, November 20, 1875. Sherman-Sheridan Correspondence, Volume 1.
26 *New York Times,* July 12, 1876.
27 Sherman to Sheridan, April 1, 1876. William T. Sherman Papers, Volume 43.

throughout the West, tired of continual administrative restraint and eager for action that might mean promotion, tingled with anticipation. At long last it appeared that the hounds of war were to be unleashed.

One of the younger cavalrymen, George A. Custer, was almost wild with anguish at the turn of events. Just when bugles were about to blow, it appeared that he would be denied a chance to be in on the kill. The well-known victor of the Washita battle had come on bended knee to Sherman, begging for permission to join his command at Fort Abraham Lincoln, near Bismarck, Dakota Territory. Grant, however, was displeased with Custer for his unfavorable testimony in the Belknap investigation and was in no mood to give him any favors, and Sherman's hands were tied. The impetuous cavalryman then started off for Chicago on his own hook, and when Sherman heard of it, he directed Sheridan to stop him there to await further action or orders. As far as Sherman was concerned, "Custer is now subject to any measure of discipline which the President may require."[28] Nor did Sheridan show much sympathy for the eager warrior. "I am sorry Lieutenant Colonel Custer did not manifest as much interest by staying at his post to organize & get ready his regiment & the expedition as he does now to accompany it; on a previous occasion in eighteen sixty-eight (1868) I asked Executive Clemency for Colonel Custer to enable him to accompany his regiment against the Indians & I sincerely hope, if granted this time, it will have sufficient effect to prevent him from again attempting to throw discredit on his profession and his brother officers."[29] Despite the unfriendly attitude of his superiors, Custer managed to have his way, and before long he was at Fort Abraham Lincoln, preparing for a summer campaign.

By the end of May a three-pronged movement against the Sioux was under way. "I suppose now the Indians will lead our troops a will-o-the-wisp circle, until some lucky turn may give one of

[28] Sherman to U. S. Grant, Jr., secretary to the President, May 4, 1876. William T. Sherman Papers, Volume 43; Stewart, *Custer's Luck*, chap. VI.

[29] Sheridan to Townsend, May 7, 1876. William T. Sherman Papers, Accession 6131.

the columns a chance," Sherman wrote without enthusiasm.[30] By June 25 the "lucky turn" came, but good fortune rode with the enemy that day. Custer fell upon a large encampment of Sioux along the Little Big Horn River and was promptly engulfed by Indians. It was like pounding a maul into a bin of wheat. Where Sioux warriors fell, others appeared to take their place. By evening the cavalryman's prediction of the Fetterman massacre had been fulfilled, and he had taken his place beside the rash young Captain in death. While the corpses of the "boy general" and his command stiffened on a lonely Montana hill, another indestructible American legend was born. Beside the troopers lay a correspondent of the New York *Herald,* whose paper had only days before warned that the army underrated the power of the Sioux. For once an eastern paper had been prophetic about the course of Indian affairs in the West—but to no avail.

Sherman was right about one thing. He did not hear much of events in Montana until July. It was not until after Independence Day that word of the disaster reached the East, and even then the press was to tell the War Department of it. Sherman was furious about the embarrassment of being kept in the dark and said that perhaps "some enterprising newspaper correspondent bought up the messenger," thus keeping headquarters in ignorance of the tragedy. Sheridan was plunged into gloom when the story came out and called the slaughter an unnecessary sacrifice, "due to misapprehension and superabundance of courage, the latter being extraordinarily developed in Custer."[31]

As the army settled down to the complex problems ahead, the whole country rocked from a wave of horror at the massacre. Eastern papers thought in terms of defensive tactics and a careful containment of the wild tribes, while Westerners took up the throaty cry of "extermination." There were the expected demands for volunteers and much large talk from plainsmen about their unusual fighting abilities. Congress responded with elec-

30 Sherman to Sheridan, May 22, 1876. Sherman-Sheridan Correspondence, Volume 1.
31 Sheridan to Sherman, July 7, 1876. *Cheyenne Daily Leader,* July 9, 1876.

trifying suddenness. Senator Algernon S. Paddock, of Nebraska, at once introduced a bill authorizing the President to call for volunteers from western localities to act with the regular army. Eastern men swallowed their standing dislike of this idea and decided that the breed of men on the frontier, "who can live, like the Indians, two or three weeks at a time on jerked beef and water, with now and then a piece of hard tack," might be just the thing for Indian fighting.[32]

Sherman did not agree. He did not want the sudden public enthusiasm for Indian blood to get beyond control and result in a grand, final, and disorganized Indian hunt in Sioux country. To him a reverse at the Little Big Horn did not mean that the situation was out of hand. Far from it. It was a sharp reminder that he was dealing with a determined, capable adversary; but then, he had never lacked respect for those Indians. He was confident that, by shifting more regular troops to the north, the whole matter could be handled quite capably. If Congress wanted to respond to the emergency with additional funds and more regulars, even if only on a temporary basis, that was fine. Shortly, the gentlemen on Capitol Hill opened their purse strings and voted the army $200,000 and authorization for an additional 2,500 enlisted men. The volunteer plan died aborning.

As orders began to pour out to the various commands, preparatory to shifting sufficient troops northward for the coming campaign, there was the usual discontent among professional letter writers who never failed to express their dissatisfaction with the course of military-Indian affairs. Wendell Phillips, displaying his "title to inquire" as a private citizen, fell upon Sherman among the printed columns and clawed at him with sharpened pen. He sang the old refrain about army brutality toward the poor natives and mournfully lamented that matters were in the hands of violent, headstrong men. At the same time, Westerners roared their disapproval at the commander for declining their services in the field. "That attempt to make Sitting Bull out a West Pointer has been exploded," fumed a Denver paper. "There is no use

[32] *New York Times,* July 6–9, 1876.

in trying to establish the conviction that a man can't fight unless he graduated at that school."[33] Men who lived along the Rockies could understand neither humanitarian sentiments regarding the Indian nor army conservatism in treating him.

"If I wuz the govern'ment, I'd buy lots of barrels of whisky, and lots of big knives, and I'd put 'em out somewhar in the West, an' invite every devilish redskins in the hull land to what they call a conf'rence," wrote a frontier journalist as he caressed an imaginary buckskin fringe along his trouser leg. "After they'd got thar I'd knock in the heads of the barrels, and scatter the knives round loose, so they'd be handy. Then I'd go away and leave the Injuns to themselves. Of course they'd take the whisky and the knives, and before sundown thar wouldn't be more than one redskin left, and then I'd go and knock his brains out afore he could do any more damage. That sir's, the only reel way to settle the Injun question. I've been among 'em, an' I know. Plenty of whisky an' long knives'll fix 'em out, an' nothing else will."[34]

With gratuitous advice pelting him like hailstones, Sherman turned his back and let it bounce away. He knew what he had to do, and he did not need any help at the moment. If the Westerners were angry because he had said the volunteers were a class of men more successful at bragging than fighting, they would have to get over it. He was not going into the volunteer matter again. It was all finished. He was perfectly aware that a a volunteer army had won the Civil War, but those men had served in the federal army at regular pay. If Westerners did not want to fight under those terms, they could stand on the side lines. Terry and Crook, who would work under Sheridan, were experienced Indian fighters. With troops pulled in from other assignments they would be able to do the job. There would, of course, be criticism and carping in the press, but that was only normal. Fortunately the men in the field did not have time to hear or read much of it. That was Sherman's task.

Immediately after the Custer affair, Sherman ordered Nelson

33 *Denver Daily Times*, August 24, 1876.
34 *Ibid.*, August 23, 1876.

Miles, with six companies of the Fifth Infantry, and Colonel E. S. Otis, with six companies of the Twenty-second Infantry, to Montana. They joined Terry's command at the mouth of the Rosebud in a summer campaign against the triumphant Sioux and diligently scoured the country from the Big Horns eastward without tangible results. The Indians had fought their pitched battle. They would not engage the troops again until there was a time and place of their own choosing.

Relentlessly Miles crisscrossed the snow-swept plains during the winter of 1876-77, vainly searching for Sitting Bull, whom he very much wanted to take. The ambitious General was much like Custer in his eagerness to make a name for himself, and as the winter passed, he drove his men mercilessly in search of those Indians who had been so successful at the Little Big Horn in June. Even before that tragedy Miles had watched the Sioux with interest and had offered to "go up into their country and stay with them until they are worn out or subjugated. The one who has the last chance at them will be likely to render the best results." He got his wish and, Custer-like, soon demanded of Sherman the command of the whole region so that he could "soon end this Sioux war." Impatiently he sought promotion and threatened that if he was not put in charge of at least a department, Sherman could order the Fifth Infantry out of Montana, for all he cared. But "if you will give me this command & *one half the troops now in it, I will end this Sioux war once & forever in four months,*" he promised.[35]

Neither Sherman nor Sheridan was so sanguine of success as the impatient Miles. Sheridan wrote that it was an almost impossible task to satisfy the public in an Indian campaign. The Indians would not stand still long enough to receive a blow sufficient to end it all, "therefore it has to peter out, as the saying is."[36] Sherman felt the same way and answered that not only were the Indians an unorthodox enemy, but in the recent cam-

---

[35] Miles to Sherman, June 15, 1876. William T. Sherman Papers, Volume 44; Miles to Sherman, November 18, 1876, and January 20, 1877. William T. Sherman Papers, Volume 45.

[36] Sheridan to Sherman, February 10, 1877. William T. Sherman Papers, Volume 45.

paign they had even beaten the army at the game of strategy. He was sharply critical of George Crook for not having put continuous pressure on the Sioux he had encountered before the Little Big Horn battle. Had he done so, perhaps Custer would not have lost his life. "This in my judgment was a terrible mistake and I cannot shut my eyes and understanding to it. Surely in Grand Strategy we ought not to allow savages to beat us, but in this instance they did." Even worse, Crook was still making errors. For example, his habit of taking along newspaper correspondents meant that the reporters naturally wrote glowing accounts of the troops they accompanied and by inference minimized the work of other units in the field. By their praise of Crook, Terry suffered.[37]

Nor was Sherman the only one who sensed the harm being done. Angrily Nelson Miles wrote, "I would suppose that a General officer could find some other employment than questioning a lying Indian and giving his statements to the press in such a way as to reflect discredit upon the honest efforts of a small part of the army not under his command. It will be remembered that with all the resources of a Dept. this same officer [Crook] started with the great 'Powder River Expedition' of twenty-two hundred men to subjugate or destroy this same body of Indians and that after the engagement of Mackenzie with the Cheyennes, and when within a few days march of Crazy Horse's camp he turned round and marched back to [Fort] Reno & then down toward Bell Fourche where there has not been a camp of hostile Indians in two years, camped fourteen days on a sage brush plain & returned to winter quarters, having accomplished nothing, but given the Indians renewed confidence. These insinuations come with very poor grace from a man who was a failure during the war and has been ever since."

During the closing days of winter Sherman and Sheridan continued to discuss Indian matters in their correspondence. Sheridan promised that when spring came he would push matters in hostile country to the fullest extent of his means. With Miles

37 Sherman to Sheridan, February 17, 1877. Sherman-Sheridan Correspondence, Volume 1.

working along the Yellowstone and Crook pressing north from bases at Forts Fetterman and Reno, the Sioux would be caught in a giant vise. Sherman hoped that the two field officers could force a showdown soon, for the emergency troops were due to muster out. As Crook waited and Miles fussed, accusing the former of stealing Indians from his bailiwick, large numbers of hostiles drifted into army camps, ready to surrender. Finally, on May 6, Crazy Horse and his entire following gave up, and to all intents and purposes the war was over.[38] Crook and Miles, vying with each other for military glory, were thus denied their supreme moment.

Scarcely had the Sioux been driven from the field in eastern Montana when the western part of that territory was thrown into an uproar by yet another Indian scare. This time it was Chief Joseph and his Nez Percé followers, bent on fleeing their home in Idaho for refuge in Canada. Montana was their avenue of escape. The story was the old one of vacillation on the part of the government and misunderstanding among the Indians. The Nez Percés believed that the Wallowa Valley in eastern Oregon was undisputably a part of their reservation, but on June 10, 1875, President Grant had suddenly thrown open the valley to white settlement. The angry Indians were told, as were the Modocs a few years earlier, that the government would move them to a new reservation.

Typically, the Indians were slow to move and matters drifted on until the spring of 1877. Joseph, their young and capable leader, was anxious to avoid trouble, and patiently he urged his followers to accede to the order from Washington. Some of the more warlike braves were unwilling to acquiesce, and on the afternoon of June 13 three of them murdered an old settler who lived about twenty miles from Fort Lapwai. They followed up this triumph by killing three more men the next morning and then exultantly rode back into their camp. General O. O. Howard, commanding the Department of the Columbia, happened

[38] *General George Crook: His Autobiography* (ed. by Martin F. Schmitt), 216. Interestingly enough, Miles does not even mention Crook's name when discussing the final phases of the campaign in his *Serving the Republic* (New York, Harper and Brothers, 1911).

to be at Fort Lapwai at the time, and by the next morning troops were on the march. After several pitched battles, the Nez Percés, led by Joseph, who had reluctantly joined his people on the battleground, began a long and tortuous retreat eastward over the old Lolo Trail once used by Lewis and Clark in crossing the mountains.[39] Their immediate destination was Montana, where they had gone in former years to hunt buffalo.

Howard gave futile chase to the fleeing Indians, while the territories of Montana and Idaho fumed at Sherman for failing to call out volunteers and cursed their own empty treasuries that rendered them helpless. Montanans, who watched their neighbors in Idaho put a few citizen soldiers in the field, regardless of territorial insolvency, loudly appealed to Sherman, then in Montana on an inspection tour. Their disappointment turned to rage when they heard that one of General Irvin McDowell's aides had remarked that the volunteers who tagged along with Howard were worse than useless.[40] To Sherman the refrain was familiar; he had listened to clamors for local employment since he had come to St. Louis in 1865. And he had an answer for Montanans. On August 2, he wrote to Governor B. F. Potts, telling him that if volunteers were called out, they must serve under regular army officers at army pay. "I am sure Congress will pay for the necessary stores for their maintenance; also pay them in time," he said cautiously. "I know it is the office of the General Government to protect its citizens, but you know the extent of our territory, the great diversity of local dangers, and the fewness of soldiers allowed by law." It was a softening explanation, and he always added it when denying such requests, never forgetting that he was dealing with a federally appointed governor whose authority stemmed from the same source as his. There were more troops on the way, he told Potts. Howard was in the field, as was Colonel John Gibbon. Terry was sending reinforcements. He had done

---

39 Helen Addison Howard and Dan L. McGrath, *War Chief Joseph*. See chapters VIII–XVI for a more complete account of the difficulties that led to the Nez Percé war.

40 *Helena Weekly Independent*, July 26, 1877. This paper, on August 2, expressed the conviction that surely, with Montana actually invaded, Sherman would call for volunteers.

what he could, and now there was no other course but to await results from the regular army.[41]

Sherman was not excited about the Nez Percé entrance into Montana. Early in August he reported to Secretary of War George McCrary that the Indians were about three hundred miles to the west, heading for buffalo country north of Fort Ellis. As he understood it, they had been for years, along with the Blackfeet, accustomed to hunting in the Yellowstone country and "traversing the whole of Montana, doing little or no damage." But the great herds were no longer there. The whites had slaughtered them so efficiently that they were becoming quite scarce. On his recent travels in the region Sherman's party had seen but four animals and had killed two of them. He guessed that ten years earlier he would have seen one million. But now, with hunting so poor, the Indians should be prevented from ranging the land in search of game. There were a number of scattered settlements in Montana, and they would be endangered by Indian hunters who were perfectly willing to shoot cattle and steal horses in lieu of buffalo. The inevitable result was murder and war. Now that the troops were in the field, the soldiers would "change their proposed buffalo hunt into a fight." If they successfully evaded the army, "I see no alternative but to drive them across the British border to join Sitting Bull." Gibbon and Howard were prepared to cope satisfactorily with the fleeing Indians, and Sherman did not propose to interfere. "Too many heads are worse than *one,*" he admitted.[42]

[41] *New North-West* (Deer Lodge, Montana), August 10, 1877; *Helena Weekly Independent*, August 16, 1877.

[42] Sherman to George McCrary, secretary of war, August 3, 1877. *Reports of Inspection Made in the Summer of 1877 by Generals P. H. Sheridan and W. T. Sherman of Country North of the Union Pacific Railroad,* 31–33. Hereinafter cited as *Reports of Inspection Made in the Summer of 1877.* This publication contains a number of letters written by Sherman to George McCrary, secretary of war under Rutherford B. Hayes. Don Cameron, who was married to one of Sherman's nieces, held the office for only a year before being replaced by McCrary. The new Secretary, only forty-one years old, had already had quite a political career representing Iowa in Congress. It was he who proposed a joint committee to settle the election dispute in 1876, and he was one of the members of that committee. As soon as the dispute was settled in favor of Hayes, McCrary was appointed secretary of war. L. D. Ingersoll, *A History of the War Department of the United States,* 578–88. For further information about Sherman's inspection tour of 1877 see Robert

With that Sherman left for Yellowstone, determined to keep out of the field of operations and away from his subordinates. Howard's troops trailed Joseph's people as they neared Montana, while Gibbon quickly moved 150 men to intercept them. Contact was made at a place known as the Big Hole, in western Montana, on August 9, and after a sharp but indecisive engagement, Joseph broke away and moved toward Yellowstone. As the western press stridently cried out about the "miserable policy" of the government and asked how long it proposed to sacrifice its gallant officers and poorly paid men against better-armed Indians, Sherman emerged from Yellowstone.[43] He had just missed a head-on collision with Chief Joseph.

Ignoring the journalists' barbs, Sherman explained to Washington that in the battle of the Big Hole, Gibbon had done his best, inflicting a heavy loss on Joseph's followers but sustaining a corresponding loss himself. The company of cavalry that had accompanied Sherman across Montana was now turned over to Gibbon, and as a part of Howard's main force, it was presently in pursuit of the hostiles. Then, in defense of his profession, Sherman contended that Montana had for years been the home of powerful tribes, subject to sudden hostilities, but normally had been protected by no more than a regiment of infantry and four companies of cavalry. Thanks to Congress, even these units were far below strength. "Our little army is overworked," he wrote heatedly, "and I do not believe the officers and soldiers of any army on earth, in peace or war, work as hard or take as many risks of life as this little army of ours. In what we call peace I am proud of them."[44]

Like gnats, the newsmen hummed around Howard. When he failed to catch up with Joseph, they heaped criticism and jeeringly called his force the Indians' best supply line. McDowell had earlier written to Sherman, from division headquarters in San Francisco, that he was sorry about the way the papers were

---

Vaughn, *Then and Now; or, Thirty-Six Years in the Rockies,* 331–33; Hanson, *Conquest,* 372–74.

43 *Daily Alta California* (San Francisco), August 8 and 12, 1877.
44 Sherman to McCrary from Fort Ellis, August 19, 1877. *Reports of Inspection Made in the Summer of 1877,* 33–34; Vaughn, *Then and Now,* 342–43.

picking on Howard. It would be better, he said, if the General would concentrate on Indians instead of trying to fight back at the newsmen. "His orders seem addressed to another audience as well as his own troops and he cannot quite confine himself rigidly to his mere soldier work," McDowell complained. "I think it is to this, in dealing with Joseph's case in the beginning that largely caused the attacks on him in the papers when the effort to put Joseph back on the reservation failed! Both your orders and mine required this work to be left absolutely to the Indian Dept., he merely aiding with his military force in case of need. But he could not keep in the background and hence received the stings of the press when the effort failed."[45] Now, as August neared its close, McDowell remarked that he understood Miles to be on his way to help Howard in the attack. "I have many times wished he could have had Howard's right column, or his command . . . , as I am sure the whole affair would have been closed up a month ago." "Despite his feelings about Howard, McDowell confessed that soldiering was a hard enough profession these days without "the abuse from the hounds and whores of the press."[46]

Although Sherman had promised to stay out of the Nez Percé affair and let his field officers carry out their assignments, he knew that McDowell and others expected him to prod Howard into action. "I don't want to give orders, as this may confuse Sheridan and Terry," he wrote to the slow-moving officer, "but that force of yours should pursue the Nez Percés to death, lead where they may. Miles is too far off, and I fear Sturgis is too slow. If you are tired, give the command to some young energetic officer, and let him follow them, go where they may. . . . For a stern chase infantry are as good as cavalry."[47] From Virginia City came a quick answer from Howard. He was not tired, he said indignantly. "I never flag." Sherman acknowledged the reply,

[45] McDowell to Sherman, July 31, 1877. William T. Sherman Papers, Volume 46.
[46] McDowell to Sherman, August 24, 1877. William T. Sherman Papers, Volume 46.

[47] Sherman to Howard from Fort Shaw, August 24, 1877. Report of W. T. Sherman, November 7, 1877, *Annual Report of the Secretary of War*, 45 Cong., 2 sess., *House Exec. Doc. No. 1*, Part II (Serial 1794), p. 13.

saying, "Glad to find you so plucky. Have every possible faith in your intense energy, but thought it probable you were worn out, and I sometimes think men of less age and rank are best for Indian warfare. They have more to make."[48] Howard declined to yield to a younger man, and Sherman resolved to say no more about it. He would not force his wartime comrade to yield. While he hoped that his urging would bring some action, he was not overly sanguine about sudden results. "I don't think Howard's troops will catch Joseph but they will follow trusting to your troops heading them off when they come out on the East of the mountains," he advised Sheridan at Division headquarters in Chicago.[49]

Leaving Montana, certain that Joseph's band would soon be cornered, Sherman visited the Pacific coast states. While at San Francisco he learned that on October 5 the Indian leader had surrendered to Generals Howard and Miles. The victory gave him an opportunity to vindicate Howard, who had suffered severely at the hands of the reporters during the entire campaign. In an after-dinner speech he said that "the one-armed soldier-chief," as the Indians called him, had pursued Joseph in obedience to orders, ignoring the adverse criticism "by comfortably-housed newspaper writers, who perhaps knew nothing of the country over which the chase was made, or who would not undergo the hardships endured by each member of the pursuing party for $500 per day."[50] Sherman knew full well that Howard had not ignored adverse criticism, but, conscious that Congress was once more tugging at its purse strings, he took advantage of the situation to praise the regular army, using the eulogy of Howard as his vehicle.

When the nation heard of Joseph's final stand in the Montana Bear Paw Mountains and learned that another Indian campaign was concluded, the burning question of the day revolved around the future of the captives. Before he left San Francisco, Sherman

48 *Ibid.*
49 Sherman to Sheridan, August 26, 1877. Division of the Missouri, Letters Received, 1877–79. Records of the War Department, U. S. Army Commands, National Archives.
50 *Daily Alta California*, October 10, 1877.

telegraphed to Sheridan that the Indians should never be allowed to return to their old homes. Other western tribes were watching the course of events, and they must learn the penalty for revolt. March Joseph and his people to Fort Buford and send them down river by boat, where they could be taken by train to Indian Territory, he said.[51] Accordingly, in November the order was carried out, and four hundred Nez Percés were moved to Fort Leavenworth, later to be placed upon a reservation.

Joseph's able leadership and his masterly retreat into Montana aroused an unusual amount of admiration on the part of his opponents. En route to exile, he and his people passed through Bismarck, Dakota Territory, and even that place, still close to hostile Indian country, had to doff its cap to the fallen leader. Joseph was invited to a banquet tendered by the ladies of the city, who wanted to "show you our kind feelings and the admiration we have for your bravery and humanity." After weeks of near starvation, the Chief sat down to his favorite dish, salmon, amidst the admiring glances of those who knew something of Indian warfare and recognized him as a "good Indian."[52] Had Sherman been at Bismarck, undoubtedly he would have joined the party, for he, too, held the young Chief in high regard. In his annual report he called the Nez Percé war "one of the most extraordinary Indian wars of which there is any record. The Indians thoroughly displayed a courage and skill that elicited universal praise; they abstained from scalping, let captive women go free, did not commit indiscriminate murder of peaceful families which is unusual, and fought with almost scientific skill, using advance and rear guards, skirmish-lines and field-fortifications."[53] The ambitious Nelson Miles, who had eagerly pitted his forces against the Nez Percés, admitted that Joseph was by far the ablest Indian on the continent.[54] To the military mind Joseph's inclination to "play the game" put him a cut above the

[51] Sherman to Sheridan, October 10, 1877. Division of the Missouri, Letters Received, 1877–79.

[52] Howard and McGrath, *War Chief Joseph*, 294.

[53] Report of W. T. Sherman, November 7, 1877, *Annual Report of the Secretary of War*, 45 Cong., 2 sess., *House Exec. Doc. No. 1*, Part II (Serial 1794).

[54] Miles to Sherman, October 28, 1877. William T. Sherman Papers, Volume 46.

average Indian. However, his opponents were glad to see him relegated to a reservation and out of any future contest.

The events of 1876 and 1877 proved to be the real climax of Indian difficulties in the American West. With the Sioux dispersed and the railroads laden with settlers who would soon penetrate their country, final quiet on the northern plains was in sight. The Nez Percé outbreak in Idaho was followed there in 1878 by a short revolt of the Bannocks, a disturbance that was promptly put down by the army. The next year saw an affair of no greater magnitude unfold in Colorado when the Utes ran amuck, only to be cornered almost at once. These were the last twitches of a dying race that had once ruled a continent. They would be in evidence for a few more years, rapidly decreasing in significance. Meanwhile, the rising tide of immigration of the seventies rose to full flood in the eighties, and the Indians were engulfed in a swirl of people so enormous that almost overnight they were nearly as rare as the once plentiful buffalo. Scandinavian, Russian, and German farmers, armed with plows, windmills, and barbed wire, followed the army as a clean-up corps that accomplished the final obliteration of a proud and courageous race. When they had divided the land into artificial squares and turned the sod face down, civilization was said to have arrived. Personally, Sherman was as sympathetic to the majority of the Indians as anyone; professionally, their containment was simply part of his job.

████████████

Eighteen

TO RING DOWN THE CURTAIN

THE SETTLEMENT of the High Plains was accomplished under somewhat more difficult circumstances than that of earlier frontiers. Not only were its distances more vast and its horse Indians more fierce, but such important natural resources as wood and water were scarce and in some instances nonexistent. Americans in general had edged forward across the Appalachians and down along the Ohio and Mississippi rivers, but when they moved beyond the Missouri, they leapfrogged their little colonies over great stretches of land. The problem of defense posed by such widely scattered settlements was tremendous, and the post–Civil War army, constantly shrinking, was faced with almost impossible odds in answering calls for help.

Besides the great natural barriers—distance, drought, and difficult terrain—Westerners were faced by constant opposition from the American Indians, who stubbornly contested every foot of land. General Sherman's interest in the postwar West was not that of fighting Indians. He was fascinated by the nation's growth and was eager to participate in its completion. His contribution was to aid settlement wherever he could by pushing aside the barriers facing it. That of distance was solved by the railroad, and in the construction of the roads the army played a material part, lending every assistance possible. Removal of the Indian barrier was even more a part of the army's task. While Sherman participated in this work for nearly two decades after the Civil War, it was not an occupation that gave him any enjoyment. Removing Indians to reservations and containing them was, at best, a thankless task, and the army found that it involved dealing with not only the recalcitrant natives but the Interior Department, the peace societies, and a sentimental public as well.

Rewards for guarding the railroad construction crews or chasing Indian raiders back to the reservation came as the American people moved their families into a new land and settled on farms or in fresh little towns. As the railroads moved out across barren lands, like tree trunks rising skyward, settlements clustered along them, gradually spreading out until branch lines appeared to serve the growing communities. Sherman had envisioned this development in 1865, when he first saw the little stub that was the Union Pacific Railroad jutting west from Omaha. The Secretary of the Interior made the discovery four years later, after the main line was completed. He said that the new road had "totally changed the conditions under which the civilized populations of the country come in contact with the wild tribes. Instead of a slowly advancing tide of migration, making its gradual inroads upon the circumference of the great interior wilderness, the very center of the desert has been pierced. Every station upon the railway has become a nucleus for a civilized settlement, and a base from which lines of exploration for both mineral and agricultural wealth are pushed in every direction. Daily trains are carrying thousands of our citizens and untold values of merchandise across the continent, and must be protected from the danger of having hostile tribes on either side of the route."[1]

Western reactions to the new type of settlement were equally interesting. Earlier frontiers had emphasized individual labor, a hand-hewn kind of culture, but now there was more talk about the necessity of capital. In Cheyenne, a town sired by the railroad, an editor warned newcomers that the new road made pioneering so easy that many might forget there were still hardships in the new land. Do not expect Turkish baths, streetcars, or luxuries in Cheyenne, he wrote. His concern arose from a realization that the old pioneer process had changed. Railroads and telegraph lines now preceded population, "thus reversing the usual order of things." As he elaborated he tipped his hat inferentially to Sherman. "The iron horse, the advance guard of empire, in his resistless 'march to the sea,' surprises the aborigines upon

1 Report of J. D. Cox, 1869, *Annual Report of the Secretary of the Interior*, 41 Cong., 2 sess., *House Exec. Docs.* (Serial 1414).

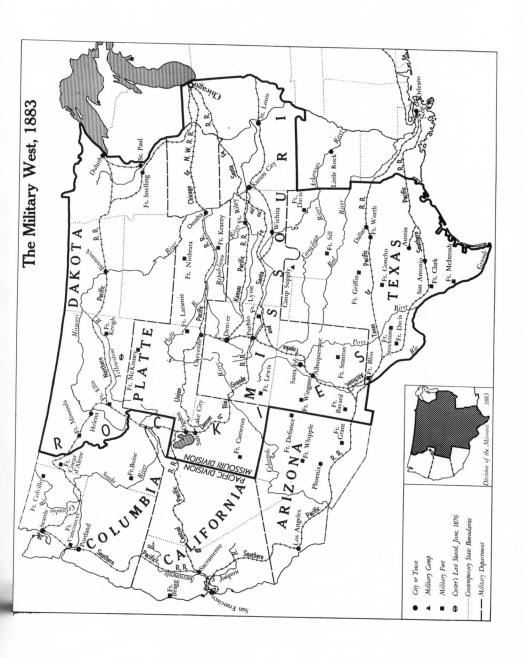

The Military West, 1883

their distant hunting grounds and frightens the buffalo from the plains where, for untold ages, his race has grazed in the eternal solitudes. The march of empire no longer proceeds with stately, measured strides, but has the wings of morning, and flies with the speed of lightning."[2]

To this end Sherman had worked ever since he took command at St. Louis. Doggedly he had maintained his position, insisting that the railroad was the paramount consideration, and all other things were, as he said, side issues. Amidst catcalls and insults concerning the details of his plan, he had protected the road builders, and no one had been louder in complaint than the western editors, who now began to discover that something important had happened. By the time he was promoted to General of the Army the main line of the Union Pacific had been completed, and very shortly the Kansas Pacific would reach Denver. His task of protecting the construction of these roads was finished, and his interest now turned toward the further development of rail lines in the broad West.

In the fall of 1870 he went over the new road to San Francisco and noted that it lay generally in a yet unsettled land. His words to Westerners on that trip were those of encouragement and hope. At Portland he told his listeners to work hard at the development of their region; the roads were coming. A few days later at Boise, Idaho, he followed the same theme, saying he hoped the next time he visited that place it would be by rail. The mention of such transportation facilities excited his listeners, for they had come to associate the western army with railroad-building, and the General's words held a promise. At Salt Lake City, where townsmen called their fellow Westerner "the Great Captain," there was more rejoicing over the new railroad and a full realization by both Sherman and the people of Utah what it meant to the West and the nation.

With the completion of the Union Pacific and the Kansas Pacific, the central High Plains were fenced off by railroads all the way to the mountains. In the vast region lying between the lines, settlers commenced to take up farms, and soon all Indians

2 *Cheyenne Leader,* September 28 and October 25, 1869.

would be driven out. Meanwhile, a new line called the Northern Pacific was commenced, and as it worked across Minnesota and headed into Dakota Territory, it became obvious that a new stretch of land was being blocked out for white settlement. The Northern Pacific was aimed straight at the heart of Sioux country. As it approached, the young bucks became nervous, and even the old men wondered whether the time for a showdown had not come.

Sherman had the same feeling. "That Northern Pacific Road is going to give you a great deal of trouble, and I expect to stand back and do the halooing whilst you or younger men go in," he wrote Sheridan in the fall of 1872. "My notion is that all the way from the Missouri River about [Fort] Stevenson till you enter Montana about Fort Ellis the land is miserable, and the Indians will be hostile in an extensive degree. Yet I think our interest is to favor the undertaking of the Road, as it will help to bring the Indian problem to a final solution."[3] He predicted that along this road there would be a real conflict, because, as he correctly said, the Sioux regarded the coming struggle as their last-ditch stand.[4]

The president of the Northern Pacific realized that his road was headed for an area of possible warfare. He said it was almost impossible to hire Swedes and Norwegians to work on the line between the Red River and the Missouri, so fearful were they of Indian attacks. Francis Walker, the commissioner of Indian affairs, was annoyed at this complaint. He maintained that the road itself would be the solution to the Sioux problem and would leave ninety thousand Indians ranging between the two transcontinental lines, incapable of resisting the United States government. "Columns moving north from the Union Pacific, and south from the Northern Pacific would crush the Sioux and their confederates as between the upper and nether millstone," he wrote in his annual report.

Walker, whose ideas sounded very much like those of Sherman,

[3] Sherman to Sheridan, September 26, 1872. Sherman-Sheridan Correspondence, Volume 1.

[4] Sherman to Sheridan, October 7, 1872. Sherman-Sheridan Correspondence, Volume 1.

further held that soon other railroads would corral Indians in Colorado, Utah, Arizona, and New Mexico. Those already built, combined with those projected, would "multiply fourfold the striking force of the Army in that section; the little rifts of mining settlement, now found all through the mountains of the southern Territories will have become self-protecting communities; the feeble, wavering line of agricultural occupation, now sensitive to the faintest breath of Indian hostility, will then have grown to be the powerful 'reserve' to lines still more closely advanced upon the last range of the intractable tribes."[5]

Sherman agreed with the Commissioner's theory that the nature of western immigration had changed and that because of it, alterations in policy were necessary. If a cordon of troops had been thrown out, behind which the settlers could have worked in safety, at least one hundred thousand soldiers would have been required. As Walker said, "Men of adventurous cast will live and work behind a line of troops with, it is possible, some exhilaration of feeling on that account; but, as a rule, men will not place women and children in situations of even possible peril, nor will they put money into permanent improvements under such circumstances."[6] Traditionally, Americans had regarded danger as one of the features of pioneer life, and many of them did not now comprehend the reluctance of thousands coming over from Europe, where the people were accustomed to absolute safety and security. The Swedes and Norwegians, whom the Secretary had mentioned when referring to their reluctance to work on the Northern Pacific, were good examples. They were quite willing to till the Dakota soil or work on the railroad, but they did not like to hold a rifle in the crook of the arm at the same time.

Sherman knew all this. It had long been his contention that the impact of settlement and density of population would offer the ultimate solution to the Indian problem. His part in western development had been more concerned with controlling the Indians during the time that settlement was edging forward. He

[5] Report of the Commissioner of Indian Affairs, *Annual Report of the Secretary of the Interior*, 1872, 42 Cong., 3 sess., *House Exec. Doc. No. 1* (Serial 1560), pp. 393–97.
[6] *Ibid.*

did not object to feeding them on the reservations. What he did not like was the fact that the Interior Department did not sufficiently feed or control them once they were on their reservations. And when the restless braves strayed off to hunt or raid, they knew they could find sanctuary by running across the reservation boundary lines, mocking the troops who stood helplessly outside. Sherman was a conservative and a lover of law and order. His main aim was to preserve peace on the plains and to punish men—red or white—for crime. Slowly he had discovered that the American public would let him do neither.

The latter half of the sixties had been a period of preparation and initial attack so far as settlement by small farmers was concerned. They edged forward cautiously, still somewhat suspicious of the land before them, but by the decade of the seventies, the rush of homesteaders westward approached flood tide. A rash of railroad-building broke out, and the American promoter came into his own as he preached to the world about the glories of the High Plains. In the remaining years of the century, men and women would come from all corners of the earth to participate in the West's final land rush. During the seventies Sherman watched the area's growth with interest and surprise. So persistent were the land seekers, so reckless were they in their choice of the remotest corners of the land, that the General constantly revised his opinions about regions he had previously felt would never be settled.

The Southwest was the most frequent source of surprise to him, for he refused to believe that any homeseeker in his right mind would consider that part of the country. As late as 1874 he seriously doubted that western Texas would ever amount to much, but he was willing to admit that the eastern part of the state had some promise. "In due time it will fill up with a good population; and although this process is very slow, it is bound to come." West of Texas there was no hope. He called Arizona "an immense, miserable country full of Apache Indians." He was quite serious when he said that both Arizona and New Mexico should be given back to old Mexico. He was willing to make the statement before a Congressional committee.[7] But within three years he had commenced to alter his opinion. The railroad forced the change. As steel rails penetrated the parched Southwest, commerce mysteriously thrived, and after a visit in 1878, the crusty old officer was forced to admit that he had earlier underestimated the region's potential.

Curiously the southwestern people watched their General as he scanned the country, made notes of his findings, and painstakingly gathered up nearly two hundred pounds of ore specimens to take home with him. Those who knew him noticed that he was now quite gray and even more grizzled looking than before. The younger Westerners were surprised to see such a dignitary dressed in a brown alpaca duster, linen vest, "Quaker" pants, straw hat, and a checked shirt with a white collar. He seemed quite an unmilitary figure. Between himself and his aide there were but four small handbags. It was "less baggage than would have sufficed a Second Lieutenant over night," wrote an admiring reporter at Yuma, Arizona.[8]

A few days later, in cool San Francisco, he wrote of his impressions to David D. Colton, vice president of the Southern Pacific Railroad, thanking him personally and officially for having put a first-class line across the California desert to the Colorado River. To anyone who had been hauled across barren Arizona behind a span of plodding mules, the sight of gleaming steel rails was as welcome as an oasis in the desert. Now, from sweltering Yuma to Los Angeles the dusty miles were no longer a barrier.

With great earnestness Sherman wrote, "The public convenience is so great, especially to the troops who garrison the Arizona posts, that I, as their head, venture to offer you thanks, and to express an earnest hope that in due time your labors and enterprise will be duly rewarded." With the construction of roads from the East, a junction with the Southern Pacific would be effected, giving the nation another transcontinental road. "A railroad east and west through Arizona, apart from its importance as a com-

7 Sherman's testimony of January 6, 7, and 31 can be found in *Report to Accompany the Bill* (H.R. 2546) to Provide for the Gradual Reduction of the Army of the United States. 43 Cong., 1 sess., *House Report 384* (Serial 1624), II.

mercial route from the Pacific to the Atlantic, is a 'great civilizer,' and will enable the military authorities to maintain peace and order among Indians as well as the equally dangerous class of robbers who of late have so much increased in numbers and boldness." Aside from purely military benefits to be derived from a railroad, Sherman was willing to admit that Arizona had some economic attractions for the Southern Pacific. "I do not entertain a high opinion of Arizona as an agricultural Territory," he said frankly, "but there seems to be no doubt about its minerals—gold, silver and copper." There was also a prospect of some trade with Mexico that would at once aid the road and "cause friendly relations and secure peace on that national border."[9]

About the Northwest he had never entertained any doubts. In the early seventies he had called Montana one of the most promising territories in the land. It was even then filling rapidly with a fine population, perhaps as many as thirty thousand, engaged in mining and cattle raising. Despite their constant applications for troops, he felt those people had "managed to keep the peace very well indeed, and the Territory is now prospering." During the summer of 1877 he had an opportunity to see some of Montana and near-by territories, and as his party moved up the Yellowstone Valley, the General took notes on the agricultural and mining possibilities, as well as the terrain and its tactical problems. Anticipating renewed construction activity on the Northern Pacific Railroad, he spoke of the beautiful farming country, whose thousands of productive acres, capable of raising oats, corn, barley, garden vegetables, and livestock, would soon be opened to homeseekers. Ranches were already springing up, and he guessed that in a few years the land along the valley would be as safe as the Platte or the Arkansas.[10] Its settlement would

---

[8] *Arizona Sentinel* (Yuma), September 28, 1878.

[9] Sherman to Colton, September 26, 1878. *Daily Alta California*, October, 1878. See also Neill C. Wilson and Frank J. Taylor, *Southern Pacific: The Roaring Story of a Fighting Railroad*, 65.

[10] During the preceding winter an officer of the Twenty-second Infantry remarked with similar optimism about the opening of the Yellowstone Valley. "Within a few years all this country will change; it will be occupied by cattle raisers, and domestic cattle instead of buffalo will roam the grassy hills. I have never before been any length of time in entirely *new* country, and it is interesting

331

force the Indians to break up into small and harmless parties, as the coming of the homesteader had done in other sections of the West. Iron rails would bring all these changes. "I do not know a single enterprise in which the United States has more interest than in the extension of the Northern Pacific railroad . . . ," he wrote enthusiastically. With a railroad running through such promising farm regions, he estimated that not over ten years could elapse before a community as strong and capable of self-defense as Colorado would emerge.[11]

Sherman watched new areas like the Yellowstone region open to settlement and recognized that such developments were closely related to military operations. All through the postwar years the thousands of settlers who moved westward had caused innumerable problems for the army, but their presence meant economic growth and ultimate stability for a new land. While he thought that the population rush was somewhat disorderly and the individualistic tendencies of the frontiersmen made his task more difficult, he did not at any time believe that the course of empire should be hindered, even when it trickled into the more remote and dangerous places. The army merely acted as outriders for this unprecedented invasion, and its work was primarily that of clearing the way.

Montana was simply a Nebraska or a Kansas of a later day. The pattern of settlement was similar; so were its problems. Sherman was fascinated when he visited little towns like Helena, isolated and far from "the States." Here, nestled in a mountain gulch, lay a small city boasting many comforts expected only in more settled places. "It contains good hotels, stores, shops, and United States assay-office, courthouse, and many most excellent houses, some of brick, but mostly frame, and not a few would

---

to watch the gradual change, but still every man carries his rifle, no one can go a mile without one." Major Alfred Lacey Hough to Mary Hough, December 1, 1876. Alfred Lacey Hough Papers, in possession of John N. Hough, University of Colorado, Boulder, Colorado. See also Robert G. Athearn (ed.), "A Winter Campaign Against the Sioux," *The Mississippi Valley Historical Review*, Vol. XXXV, No. 2 (September, 1948), 272–85.

11 Sherman to McCrary, July 25, 1877. *Reports of Inspection Made in the Summer of 1877*, 29–30.

be good dwelling houses in Washington. There must be three or four thousand people here, who seem to live as comfortably as they would in Iowa."[12] Despite the existence of powerful Indian tribes between such a community and the outer world, the region seemed prosperous and safe. Somehow Americans had a genius for transporting their civilization into a virgin land and successfully planting it.

Turning to a general assessment of what he had seen, Sherman described Montana to the Secretary of War, taking a long look at its future. "I still retain a high opinion of this Territory, and think it merits the fostering care of the general government, especially of the military. Its extent is an empire, the greater part of which is exclusively adapted to the rearing of cattle, horses and sheep." The vast expanse of land was capable of raising all kinds of crops and enough for one million people, he thought. He was impressed by the timber and mineral deposits, and correctly stated that considerable capital would be necessary for thorough extraction, particularly with regard to silver and gold. He viewed the Montana Rockies as "the real backbone of the continent, whose gulches right and left all contain more or less gold and silver, so that the matrix is here, and sooner or later will be found, when machinery will accomplish what the naked hand cannot—the reduction of the ore." However, it was his judgment that "the day is gone when men in England and New York will venture their money in such speculations." Here he seriously underestimated the speculative impulses of eastern and foreign capital.

Although it seemed to him that Montana, with its promising agricultural and mining possibilities, would be a most valuable state for the Union, he knew that the burning necessity was transportation and saw little prospect of immediate improvement in that field. "All dream of a railroad, but I discourage the thought, and believe for many years the people must content themselves with the Missouri River, navigable as high as Benton; the Yellowstone as high as Bighorn, with teams to haul thence and from

[12] Sherman to McCrary from Fort Ellis, August 19, 1877. *Reports of Inspection Made in the Summer of 1877*, 33–34.

the Pacific Railroad, 400 miles distant." While he seemed to think that the Northern Pacific would move west as far as Tongue River, he somehow imagined that it would stop here, at least for some years to come. Yet, within a half-dozen years that railroad was to span Montana, and Sherman himself would ride over the newly completed road. As always, he would express amazement at such progress and admit ruefully that he just did not see how it all had been accomplished.[13]

After visiting the Northwest and the Pacific coast states in 1877, Sherman expressed the opinion that in the years ahead very little military assistance would be required by California, Oregon, and Washington. However, inland along the slopes of the Rockies there might still be minor collisions, and it was on that final frontier that the presence of the army would be required for a little longer. He had said a few years earlier that even at that time there were, in a land where troops had once fought for their very existence, a number of settlements strong enough to defend themselves. "You may now see ranches with cattle with little adobe houses strung along as far out as the Omaha." By 1877 the line of settlement had advanced deep into the Rockies.

South of the Union Pacific lay the Kansas Pacific line, serving Kansas and Colorado. Sherman estimated in 1874 that already fifty thousand settlers had made homes along that road, and more were coming. "When I passed over that country in 1865–'66–'67 there was no population in it or near it," he reminisced.

---

13 Residents of Fort Benton, whose existence depended upon river travel, eyed the coming of the railroad along the Yellowstone with considerable trepidation. In the fall of 1877 the *Benton Record* criticized Sherman for recommending to McCrary that the Northern Pacific be extended up the Yellowstone Valley. Accusing him of narrowness, the editor said he was worried only about the military posts in that region and charged that the General's opinions were "merely expressions of the well known prejudices, favoritism and weak conclusions of some of the army officers and moneyed citizens of the Territory." As anybody knew, the Yellowstone Valley was not a good place for a railroad, said the paper; instead, the north side of the Missouri, "along what is known as Governor Stevens' route, a region of unredeemed fertility, but which is destined at no distant day to become the most populous section of the Northwest," was the best location. *Benton Record*, November 2, 1877.

"No man could go west of the Little Blue without running one chance in three of having his scalp taken. Now there are counties laid out; there are county courts and roads. I have no doubt that from one to two millions of acres of public lands have been entered since 1866."

By 1878, Sherman had, in the preceding two years, covered most of the American West. It was his conclusion that with the Sioux and Nez Percé wars ended and the brief uprising of the Bannocks that summer crushed, the impact of settlement was gradually resolving the major problem of the army. He had not changed his mind about the inability of red and white men to live peacefully together, but he readily acknowledged that the enormous growth of white population was rapidly reducing the complexities of defense. Soon the settlers would require little protection from the army, which could then turn more men to the task of running down small bands of raiding Indians.[14]

Each time the General looked back over the changes wrought in the past few years he was amazed. "The game is nearly all gone, the Indian has been forced onto small reservations; farms and herds of neat-cattle are fast taking the place of the buffalo, and every ox and steer has an owner who will fight for his property," he reported to the Secretary of War. Most of the Indian treaties had been made on the theory that these developments would occur slowly and that the government would have to furnish only a part of the Indians' subsistence, since they could partially support themselves from the hunt. "I know that such was the belief of the commission, of which I was a member, which negotiated the treaties of 1868, and, having traversed the plains ten or fifteen times since that date, I can bear personal testimony that where in 1868 millions of buffalo could be found, not a single one is now seen." People who had not visited the West were simply unable to understand the rapidity of settlement and the enormity of change effected in a mere decade. Looking at the High Plains, now dotted with farms and interlaced with rail lines, Sherman wrote that "this vast region has undergone in the

[14] Sherman to Sheridan, October 13, 1878. Sherman-Sheridan Correspondence, Volume 2.

past ten years a more violent and radical change than any like space of the earth's surface during any previous fifty years."[15]

During the late seventies and early eighties, as western growth astounded the rest of the nation and the world, Sherman continued to comment on the phenomenon. At Laramie, Wyoming, in the fall of 1880, while on a tour with President Rutherford B. Hayes, he told townsmen that he could remember when only God greeted travelers at that place. "If anybody had told me then that within a hundred years a single house of your city would be built, I would have told him he was a fool. I did not believe anybody would live out here of his own choice. Soldiers had to come here because they could not help themselves." He thought it was well that his predictions had not been fulfilled, for Wyoming was a wealthy land. There were minerals in quantity, and occasionally people could raise a garden. His listeners thought this was carrying praise too far, and a laugh went up. Well, not much of a garden, Sherman ruefully admitted. But they had a railroad, and it could bring all the comforts of life right to their door. "I do not think that in the whole world there is a more important connection than this Pacific Railroad, which joins Asia with Europe through America. We are not yet done, boys; you are just barely on the threshold of the future, and if we can keep together—the north and south, east and west—there is no man wise enough to tell what America is to become."

There were many changes since the day Sherman had first seen Wyoming. And the white man had brought them. The Indians had been shoved aside, some to the north, some to the south, and "some have gone into the ground." The settlers had "built up here what the Indians could not have done in ten thousand years. You have corn growing where the Indians never made

15 Report of W. T. Sherman, November 7, 1878, *Annual Report of the Secretary of War*, 45 Cong., 3 sess., *House Exec. Doc. No. 1*, Part II (Serial 1843), p. 5. Secretary McCrary agreed that much progress had been made and commended the effort shown to educate the Indians. However, while teaching them the ways of the white man, he recommended that the government "confront them with such military force as will teach them the futility of any attempt to resist the power of the United States." Like Sherman, he felt that the government was lax in feeding the Indians it held prisoner on reservations, and he stated that he was in full agreement with the General of the Army on this point.

corn grow; you have made wheat grow where wheat never grew before. If the Indian had remained here to the end of time he would never have accomplished this. . . . You are just as good as the emigrants in Massachusetts and when they talk about your being cruel and inhuman to the Indian I tell them you are no more so to them than to the emigrant." This was the kind of talk Westerners liked to hear, and they roared their approval. "It becomes the fashion now-a-days to denounce our frontier people," he continued. "Now in Montana and in Idaho some of you boys probably know that in the valleys where Indians have been for ten thousand years nearly, there are fine wheat fields, and homes, and cattle, and everything that maintains civilization."

Mentally scanning the westward sweep, Sherman told the crowd that "we used to call this the west. You are no longer in the west, boys; you are in the middle." This notion delighted the residents of the Wyoming prairies, and a ripple of self-conscious guffaws interrupted the speaker. "That is where you are," he insisted. "If they do not behave themselves east, you make them; and if they do not behave themselves west, you turn west and make them behave themselves. . . . I have faith in you in the future, and whenever you want an advocate here or elsewhere call on Uncle Billy." His closing remarks would have puzzled an eastern crowd, but to a scattered population, perched precariously in a new and untried western community, they were words of encouragement. The men and women of Cheyenne knew perfectly well that they were not going to make anyone do anything, and they were aware that Sherman knew it. The phrases were simply a verbal pat on the back and were taken as such. It took courage to plant a community on the raw, uninviting prairies, and residents there were glad someone from east of the Missouri recognized the fact.[16]

A few days later, in California, Sherman continued the enunciation of his thesis. The new railroads were links binding together not only the United States but the many scattered western settlements. He was angered that some of his fellow passen-

[16] *Cheyenne Daily Leader*, September 5, 1880.

337

gers had growled about the alkali desert over which they had just passed. "If I had my way I would put you out, and make you drive a fine yoke of oxen," he snapped at them. Only those who had been obliged to cross the plains under sterner conditions could have appreciated the benefits of modern travel. The Pacific Railroad was more than parallel strips of steel; it was "a link in the chain which binds all mankind together. We are simply a part of the whole world, although favored among nations, grand in territory, magnificent in one people, with a history of which we are all proud, and a future beyond the speculation of the wisest man on earth."

In 1880, Sherman called the progress of settlement west of the Mississippi during the preceding fifteen years "simply prodigious." Prospectors had combed the mountains for their treasures, and ranches now stood where a decade earlier no man had dared to venture. What was the explanation? It was due to the presence of troops, "but in equal, if not greater measure, to the adventurous pioneers themselves, and to that new and greatest of civilizers, the railroad." The rail lines "have completely revolutionized our country in the past few years, and impose on the military an entire change of policy." The numerous small posts, necessary as stopping points along stage and wagon routes, were now useless. Not only had the railroads contracted the great distances, but they had attracted thousands of farmers who in themselves afforded security to the countryside.[17] He agreed with Sheridan that development was almost too fast for the mind to grasp. "Under the stimulus of our present general prosperity, emigrants are so rapidly taking up land everywhere in the West, and towns and hamlets are so quickly springing up that almost constant additions have to be made to our military maps to enable us to keep posted regarding the spread of our frontiers," were Sheridan's words.[18]

The enormous change deeply impressed Sherman, but at the same time it somewhat puzzled him. He found it hard to fathom

[17] Report of W. T. Sherman, November 10, 1880, *Annual Report of the Secretary of War*, 46 Cong., 3 sess., *House Exec. Doc. No. 1*, Part II (Serial 1952), pp. 4–5.
[18] Report of Philip H. Sheridan, 1880, *Annual Report of the Secretary of War*, 46 Cong., 3 sess., *House Exec. Doc. No. 1*, Part II (Serial 1952), p. 55.

the reason for the onrush. Certainly, the West had many attractions and was very large, but it was not without some disadvantages. A year earlier he had said to an old friend, "When I think of the naked plains of Nebraska, Kansas, & Dakota, westward to which go annually a half million of Emigrants, I do not think I was wrong in advising some to go to North Georgia & Alabama, where you have at least water and firewood. But each Emigrant must choose for himself."[19] Now, as he pondered over his annual report for 1880, he reiterated his wonder to a correspondent. "The trains go out loaded with Emigrants—to Nebraska, Dakota, and Kansas, Colorado—New Mexico &c. &c.— where water is scarce where fuel is dear if not absolutely beyond price—and where the soil is often barren for want of the necessary rain fall. Yet the Alleghany Range with innumerable valleys abounding in rushing streams, boundless forests of timber, and good soil remain in a state of nature." Somehow the fascination of the West for the settler seemed to him to have progressed beyond reason. He predicted that the tide would surely turn in the other direction before long. The rush to the plains must have a point of diminishing returns.[20] He thought it had been reached, but again he had miscalculated or had failed fully to understand the mysterious force of the westward movement. Men would drive on, long after 1880, into the most barren recesses of the plains, blindly convinced that here was Eldorado, and no one, not even nature itself, could convince them otherwise. They would cling perilously to their little toe holds through drought, hail, blizzards, and grasshopper invasions, stubbornly refusing to yield, ever hopeful that this was the promised land—because it was west of the place from which they had come.

The phenomenon continued to fascinate him, and he again alluded to it in his official writings. "Heretofore the officers of cavalry and infantry have been doomed to everlasting service in the very remotest parts of what was known as the 'West,' always in advance of civilization. No sooner than the settlements reached their post, which they had built of sod, or stone, or wood, they

---

[19] Sherman to Warner, March 9, 1879. Letters of Major Willard Warner.
[20] Sherman to Warner, November 18, 1880. Letters of Major Willard Warner.

had to pull up stakes, move two or three hundred miles ahead, till the same game was repeated, and so on, *ad infinitum;* but this is also changed. Railroads traverse the continent east and west in the interest of trade and commerce, and these troops are shoved to the right and left to guard the embryo settlements against the Indians, or the Indians against the intrusive settlers. ..."[21] Texas was a good example. Within ten years defense problems there had been completely altered. The building of railroads, to an extent almost unforeseeable, had made life in most of the state as safe as in Georgia or Alabama. "The Western part is proportionately safe, but from its arid nature can never admit of dense settlement, and may be subject to individual casualties incident to such a country against which soldiers cannot guard." The Kiowas and Comanches, who used to raid from the north, could never again terrorize Texans, for the railroad stood ready to pour in troops at a moment's notice.

The same was true of Arizona, where a number of posts, thanks to the railroad, could now be abandoned. In fact, Sherman was quite surprised at the appearance of security and order there. At Tombstone, for example, a place of low reputation, Sherman found "a live American town of seven thousand people, as much like the old California towns of 1849 as possible." There had been much talk of lawlessness and shooting there, but he saw none. "The habits of the people evinced no more signs of danger than would be common in Denver or Omaha," he wrote in 1882. "There are millions of spots in Arizona as like Tombstone as possible, and as the country is not fit for agriculture or grazing, and as the inference is that God did not make a country good for nothing, I am encouraged to believe that Arizona will be the permanent mine of silver to the United States."

By 1882, Sherman's time for retirement was near, and his writings reveal a tone of summary as he looked back over his career

21 Report of W. T. Sherman, November 3, 1881, *Annual Report of the Secretary of War*, 47 Cong., 1 sess., *House Exec. Doc. No. 1*, Part II (Serial 2010), p. 32. The thirty-eight-year-old cabinet officer was Abraham Lincoln's eldest and only living child. Active in politics and married to the daughter of Senator James Harlan of Iowa, Robert Lincoln was Garfield's choice for the War Department.

in the postwar West. Stressing the importance of that region in his official reports, he said, "For a hundred years we have been sweeping across the continent with a skirmish line, building a post here and another there, to be abandoned next year for another line, and so on. Now we are across and have railroads everywhere, so that the whole problem is changed. . . ."[22] He regarded the frontier line as having vanished, and he believed that, so far as the army was concerned, its ever moving job was nearly finished. Go to Congress with a plan "that will approximate permanency," instead of one which, as before, merely met temporary wants along a continually shifting line of settlement, he advised the War Department. Indian disturbances, once so important, were now negligible. The reason was the "unexampled development of the railroads in that region, and the consequent rapidity of settlement by farmers and grazers, who are generally prepared to defend their own property. No person, who has not been across the continent by the several routes, can possibly comprehend the changes now in progress there. Nearly two-thirds of the domain of the United States lies west of the Mississippi, and at the close of the civil war (1865) the greater part of it was occupied by wild beasts, buffalo, elk, antelope, and deer, and by wilder Indians. Now, by the indomitable courage, industry, and thrift of our people, this vast region has become reduced to a condition of comparative civilization."[23]

On February 8, 1884, Sherman would be sixty-four years old, and by the operation of law he would on that date terminate his military career. Early in 1883, he decided to retire in November, after he had written his annual report. Since the "official year" terminated then, and because Congress would be in session by

[22] Sherman to John Sherman, February 28, 1882. Letters Sent, 1882, Headquarters of the Army. Records of the War Department, National Archives. In one of his speeches Beck remarked, "If $1,000 or $10,000 is to be expended by General Sherman to carry his whole staff all over the country under the pretense of making inspections, to hire steamboats, palace cars, and everything else, and then call for a deficiency, because they see fit to do that, it is not a legitimate expenditure." *Congressional Record,* February 24, 1882, 47 Cong., 1 sess., Vol. XIII, 1421.

[23] Report of W. T. Sherman, November 6, 1882, *Annual Report of the Secretary of War,* 47 Cong., 2 sess., *House Exec. Doc. No. 1,* Part II (Serial 2091), p. 5.

February and the army's chief needed to be present to protect his department, Sherman elected to turn over the reins of office to Sheridan a few months early. It would be better that way.

But before he handed over the reins of power, there was one more thing he wanted to do: take another lingering look at the West, where he had worked so actively for the past eighteen years. Here was an opportunity to see, perhaps for the last time, some of the land over which he had watched like a father. Henry Villard, president of the Northern Pacific Railroad, wrote him that travel facilities would be available; no man had done more for the road than Sherman.[24] In a party that included two justices of the Supreme Court, Colonel Richard Irving Dodge and General Alfred Terry, Sherman set out for the West in June, 1883.

Already the Montana region, so recently the scene of the Sioux war, had changed. New towns had sprung up, farms flourished where only buffalo chips had dotted the land a few years before, and the white men apparently had come to stay. At Portland, Oregon, Sherman told listeners, "We old men, who are passing from the stage of life commit to you the grand task of building up the northwest and making it equal, if not superior, to the sister cities of the east and to those of the greater valley of the Mississippi, and connected to you by iron rails, which like a tube placed between two barrels of water, will soon make the two equal in contents."[25]

San Francisco welcomed its former resident with its usual enthusiasm and thought about changes wrought during his command of the army. Because he talked now about recent progress, or perhaps by coincidence, a leading paper editorialized on the passing of the frontier. Conditions in the West had been radically altered in the past few years, and the type of people filtering into its many still undeveloped corners pointed up that fact to the editor. "The frontiersman is no longer a person who shoulders his rifle and his axe and drives an ox team off into the forest. He rides to his destination in a railroad car, and more than likely instead of being a farmer's boy, reared on the frontier, he

24 Villard to Sherman, June 5, 1882. William T. Sherman Papers, Volume 57.
25 *Daily Oregonian* (Portland), August 24 and 27, 1883.

is a tenderfoot, from far East, perhaps a professor of geology, wandering through the hills and chipping rocks with a hammer. The invaluable rifle no longer leans against the fire-place in every settler's cabin, or if it does, the gun is kept to shoot squirrels and not bears or Indians. The modern frontiersman would not be so much of an Indian fighter as his predecessor even if given a chance. The Indian-fighting pioneer is gone with the era of home-spun clothing and log cabins."[26]

Already, in 1883, while Indians were yet a potential danger in some western spots, a California editor could look back upon "the old West" with a nostalgia that was shortly to fashion an important segment of American folklore. The raw, homespun individual—who so frequently squatted in defiance on some lonely spot, shot at Indians indiscriminately, both peaceful and warlike, swindled his neighbor in trade when he could, cried out stridently for the federal government to fulfill its obligations to protect him, sneered at the efforts of the troops when they tried, and often unnecessarily took justice into his own hands—was not even an extinct species before the American people deified him and placed him prominently in its hall of national saints. Sherman had watched the pendulum-like qualities of his countrymen for years. He was probably not surprised that some of those who had so recently cursed the aggressive pioneer for his rowdy conduct now suddenly decided that he represented the individualism of which Americans were inordinately proud.

When Sherman sat down to write his final report, his thoughts turned to the future of his own men. The western soldiers had served long and well, and the day was now at hand when the privations they had been obliged to undergo were no longer necessary. There was no reason why the modern soldier should be content to live in a dugout on his pound of bread, pound of meat, and gill of whiskey a day. Not now, when the farmers who lived near by had all the coffee, vegetables, and sugar they wanted on their well-stocked tables. The West had changed. The day of isolation in a sea of aborigines was no more. There was no longer an Indian threat. Sherman said he regarded it as "sub-

[26] *Daily Alta California*, September 17, 1883.

stantially eliminated from the problem of the Army." There might, of course, be temporary alarms, but no serious outbreak was possible. A condition of general peace prevailed, and he took pains to point out the reasons for such a development. "The Army has been a large factor in producing this result, but it is not the only one. Immigration and the occupation by industrious farmers and miners of lands vacated by the aborigines have been largely instrumental to that end, but the *railroad* which used to follow in the rear now goes forward with the picket-line in the great battle of civilization with barbarism, and has become the *greater* cause."

Casting his eye in the direction of the railroads in particular, the writer dwelled for a moment upon their progress. "I regard the building of these railroads as the most important event of modern times, and believe that they account fully for the peace and good order which now prevail throughout the country, and for the extraordinary prosperity which now prevails in this land. A vast domain, equal to two-thirds of the whole surface of the United States, has thus been made accessible to the immigrant, and, in a military sense, our troops may be assembled at strategic points and sent promptly to the places of disturbance, checking disorders in the bud." These roads, he cautioned, were the "instrumentalities rather than the substantial causes" of the great economic development, and they were not an infallible touchstone of success. A single man, out of malice or enmity, could cripple a railroad seriously, by merely pulling a switch or burning a bridge. The soldier must protect and foster them, for they were capable of sending troops to any given point of danger at a speed of five hundred miles a day, a distance that formerly took a full month of marching.

Looking at the entire West, an area he had for years watched grow toward economic maturity, Sherman declared that the vast land was "now completely open to the immigrant in regions where a few years ago no single man could go with safety." There were no Indian wars in progress. The land was largely plotted out into farmsteads, and the course toward final peace with the Indians was irrevocably set.[27] As he had earlier written, "The country is now generally prosperous, and the army is in reasonably good condition considering the fact that peace and politics are always more damaging than war."[28] His job was finished, the challenge had been met, and now the best thing he could do was to settle down at St. Louis and watch his people enjoy the fruits of their struggle.

Perhaps, in addition to his own findings, Sherman gleaned something of the change from reading western newspapers. There was a definite shift in opinion, and, typically American, hardly had the enemy been rendered harmless when his problems were being viewed sympathetically by those who had so recently fought him. For example, during the fall of 1883 a California paper talked about the "abatement of that feeling of intense hostility among the people of the new States and Territories" toward the Indians.[29] Even more revealing was the comment of an Idaho paper, written by an editor who undoubtedly had seen much of the problem firsthand. He complained that the natives "should not be treated in a niggardly and parsimonious manner by the government; but liberally, and in a spirit of justice and equity."[30] Colonel Richard Irving Dodge, for whose book, *Our Wild Indians*, Sherman had written an introduction, wondered why the changed conditions were not more clearly recognized by the entire American public. "This whole Indian business is now so easy of solution that it seems strange that no statesman can be found to place it in its proper light before the people," he wrote to Sherman. "Every Senator seems to regard the Indian from the standpoint he gained while a boy at school." He called for "a little common sense, fair dealing & courage enough to fight the Indian Ring" as all that was needed for a final solution to a problem as old as America.[31] From edi-

[27] Report of W. T. Sherman, October 27, 1883, *Annual Report of the Secretary of War*, 48 Cong., 1 sess., *House Exec. Doc. No. 1*, Part II (Serial 2182), p. 46. Appended is Colonel O. M. Poe's Report on Transcontinental Railways, 255–318.

[28] Sherman to John Sherman, June 7, 1883. William T. Sherman Papers, Volume 60.

[29] *Daily Alta California*, December 14, 1883.

[30] *Idaho World*, November 20, 1883, quoting the *Nez Percé News*.

[31] Richard Irving Dodge to Sherman, October 7, 1882. William T. Sherman Papers, Volume 58.

tors to army officers there was a growing feeling that what had once been a burning issue was now merely a glowing ember in the blaze of western settlement.

Sherman looked back over the years and considered his part in the mighty movement that was still under way. To his annoyance he had been fixed in the American mind as a man who rose to fame as a destroyer. His legendary march through Georgia marked him as a hard, ruthless, vindictive individual who heartlessly burned a swath across his own land. Although his judgments were crisp and his methods often blunt, he was sensitive and even artistic in temperament. His mind was an orderly one, and his constitutional leanings guided him unerringly and without deviation in the direction of just ends. He sought the western command in 1865 because he saw an opportunity to participate in the final stages of nation-building. There was not an ounce of desire in him for further fame except as a contributor to national development. The vast reaches of land that tilted gently upward west of the Missouri were challenging in that they were the scenes of western growth, and it was there he wanted to work. It must have pained him to visit proudly places in whose behalf he had labored to be welcomed by the strains of "Marching Through Georgia." Americans could not visualize years of patient, methodical planning, or the lackluster duties connected with protecting the most extensive military fronts and the longest supply lines in their army's history, beyond the Missouri. They understood only the more spectacular events, and so they sang of Sherman's past glories in the Georgia cotton fields.

Silently he had worked, speaking out frankly of his feelings when asked, but seldom complaining publicly of his troubles. That his was a thankless task soon became apparent to him. The westward rush, as it had been from the beginning, was a disorderly scramble for land, with men fighting first the original claimants and then each other for its possession. Sherman, in command of the only disciplinary arm of government available to the extensive regions, was frequently forced to permit developments he felt were wrong, because the American citizen, standing before the trough of economic gain, was the most vocal human on the surface of the earth, and the slightest move to halt him brought forth cries that easily reached legislative halls in Washington. Vainly the military commander sought justice, equity, and a more orderly progression of events, but his words were lost in a thunderous symphony of laissez faire. The years following 1865 constituted a period of international peace, so far as the United States was concerned, and all Americans focused their eyes upon the spectacle unfolding in the golden West. Typically, each was his own strategist, and no matter what was done there were complaints that it should have been done otherwise. Vainly army men tried to keep red and white men separated on the High Plains and did a remarkable job, considering the numbers involved and the aggressiveness of the invaders. Congress contributed its bit to the difficulty by continually reducing the armed forces in times of peace (Indian wars being considered mere disturbances) and by interfering with Indian control by sponsoring policies it was often unwilling to implement fully. In the middle of the political vortex Sherman worked, struggling to patch a thousand leaks in the settlement dikes, while at his back lurked the legislators impishly hiding his shovels.

That the settlement of the Trans-Mississippi West was accomplished with unparalleled rapidity and characterized by wasteful duplication of human and physical resources, most historians agree. By what method it could have been better effected, they disagree. With even a man of Sherman's courage and conviction in command of the army, much of the story is a sordid one. What it would have been with a weaker personality at the military helm is not a source of pleasant speculation. The region under consideration bloomed economically in a postwar expansion that paradoxically saw the army shunned by appropriations committees, while its services were sorely needed in a part of the nation that was technically at peace but actually at war. Perhaps never in American history were army men asked to solve such widespread military problems with so few men. That they succeeded as well as they did is surprising and something for which little credit has been given.

Despite the absence of appreciation for his complicated postwar accomplishments, Sherman's affection for the West and its people was deep. As he reviewed recent years, his sentimental nature showed through the tough, protective outer skin. He would like to see the Westerners once again, he said in his memoirs. "Still more would I like to go over again the many magnificent trips made across the interior plains, mountains, and deserts before the days of the completed Pacific Railroad, with regular 'Doughertys' drawn by four small mules, one soldier with carbine or loaded musket in hand seated alongside the driver; two in the back seat with loaded rifles swung in the loops made for them; the lightest kind of baggage, and generally a bag of oats to supplement the grass, and to attach the mules to their camp. With an outfit of two, three, or four of such, I have made journeys of as much as eighteen hundred miles in a single season, usually from post to post, averaging in distance about two hundred miles a week, with as much regularity as its done to-day by the steam-cars its five hundred miles a day; but those days are gone, and, though I recognize the great national advantage of more rapid locomotion, I cannot help occasionally regretting the change."[32]

Sherman, like many a Westerner, had worked diligently toward the settlement of a raw and unexploited region. But no sooner had towns come, with rails to serve them and windmills to dot the countryside, than he began to regret that the excitement of the moment had passed. As retirement faced him, he talked in terms of days gone by and his near regret about modern changes. There was no way to look but back. In his own hardheaded, realistic way, he summed up his life, saying that "I have done many things I should not have done, and have left undone still more which ought to have been done. . . . . I can see where hundreds of opportunities have been neglected, but on the whole I am content; and feel sure that I can travel this broad country of ours, and be each night the welcome guest in palace or cabin; and as 'all the world's a stage, And all the men and women merely players' I claim the privilege to ring down the curtain."

Lowering the curtain, he knew that he had lived at a time of

32 Sherman, *Memoirs*, 457.

348

great national events and that fate had made him a leading participant. Perhaps his fellow men, their eyes fixed upon even greater economic glories in the West, did not share his nostalgia for the days gone by, when it was America's last unsettled region. After its submission, there were no new worlds to conquer. Now, nearly one hundred years after Sherman first commanded it in post–Civil War years, the West is not only crisscrossed by rails and its every secluded nook available by highway, but its last secrets are daily bared to a dozing public that languidly watches it from the air. Today a growing fraternity shares Sherman's lingering doubts about America's plunging progress in the nineteenth century, and its members would be quick to join him in a jouncing Dougherty far from mankind and faced only by a raw and beautiful western landscape. They realize what he knew seventy-five years ago and join him in his regret that America's last frontier is gone.

BIBLIOGRAPHY

THE PRINCIPAL unpublished sources for this volume are found in the Library of Congress and the National Archives.

Sherman's postwar career is well documented in Volumes 17–61 of the William T. Sherman Papers, Library of Congress. They contain his letters from June 29, 1865, to November 24, 1883. In the Philip H. Sheridan Papers are two volumes of letters from Sherman to Sheridan, covering part of the same period.

In the War Records Division of the National Archives are the reports of officers serving in the Military Division of the Missouri, commanded by Sherman from 1865 to 1869. Valuable also is the correspondence from the Adjutant General's Office. The Records of the Bureau of Indian Affairs in the Interior Department files, National Archives, are indispensable in treating the army's western problems.

No existing biography of Sherman does more than touch upon his eighteen years of service after the Civil War. None credits him with his part in the building of the West. In many ways the Sherman story really began in 1865.

I. UNPUBLISHED MATERIALS

1. *Library of Congress*

David Dixon Porter Papers.

Endorsements and Memoranda. Volume 1, dating from March 29, 1876, to September 8, 1882, contains copies of Sherman's endorsements on letters sent to him. There are many caustic and succinct comments on Indian policy to be found here.

Letter Books. Copies of Sherman's correspondence from 1866 to 1883. Volume 1 covers 1866–71. Letters from 1872 to 1883 are found in Volumes 6–10.

Philip H. Sheridan Papers (Sherman-Sheridan Correspondence. 2 vols.).

Semiofficial Letters Sent by William T. Sherman, February 11, 1866, to February 10, 1881. 2 vols.

William T. Sherman Papers.

2. *National Archives*

a. Bureau of Indian Affairs

Letters Received, 1865–70.

Letters Received, Kiowa, 1867. M 597.

b. Department of State

Territorial Papers of Montana. 2 vols.

c. War Records Division

Division of the Mississippi, Letters and Telegrams Sent, October 19, 1863, to September 26, 1865. Book 1.

Division of the Mississippi, Letters Sent, July 5, 1865, to August 10, 1866.

Division of the Missouri, General Orders, 1865–82.

Division of the Missouri, Letters Received, 1877–79.

Division of the Missouri, Letters Sent, November 30, 1868, to December 24, 1871. Volume 41.

Division of the Missouri. Special File. Record Group 98. Nineteen boxes of papers relating to Indian wars contain field reports and letters sent and received by the Division Headquarters, 1866–69.

Headquarters of the Army, Document File. Boxes 85 and 93 contain telegrams and letters sent by Sherman in 1866 and 1868.

Headquarters of the Army, Letters and Telegrams Received, 1866–68.

Headquarters of the Army, Letters Sent, 1882.

Headquarters of the Army, Telegrams Received, January 3, 1867, to July 31, 1867. Volume 173.

Office of the Adjutant General, Post Returns, Fort Buford, 1867.

Office of the Secretary of War, Letters Received, 1865–69.

Office of the Secretary of War, Telegrams Received, 1866–67.

Office of the Secretary of War, Telegrams Sent, 1866–67.

3. *Other Depositories*

Alfred Lacey Hough Papers, in the possession of John N. Hough, Boulder, Colorado.

Benjamin H. Grierson Papers, Newberry Library, Chicago.

C. C. Augur Papers, Illinois State Historical Library, Springfield, Illinois.

Bibliography

Grenville M. Dodge Papers, Iowa State Department of History and Archives, Des Moines, Iowa. Also found in this depository is a set of typed volumes entitled "Data, Chronologically Arranged for Ready Reference in the Preparation of a Biography of Grenville Mellen Dodge." "Dodge Records" in the footnotes refers to this.

Letters of Major Willard Warner, Illinois State Historical Library, Springfield, Illinois.

Rutherford B. Hayes Papers, The Hayes Memorial Library, Fremont, Ohio.

Sherman-Ewing Correspondence, Ohio State Archaeological and Historical Society, Columbus, Ohio.

II. Published Materials

1. Congressional Documents

Annual Report of the Secretary of the Interior, 1866–83.

Annual Report of the Secretary of War, 1866–83.

Inspection by Generals Rusling and Hazen, 39 Cong., 2 sess., *House Exec. Doc. No. 45* (Serial 1289), 1867.

Letter from the Secretary of the Interior, communicating, in obedience to a resolution of the Senate of the 30th of January, information in relation to the late massacre of United States troops by Indians at or near Fort Phil. Kearney, in Dakota Territory. 39 Cong., 2 sess., *Senate Exec. Doc. No. 16* (Serial 1277), 1867.

Letter of General W. T. Sherman in letter of the Secretary of War, communicating, in compliance with a resolution of February 5, 1867, information in relation to an order issued by Lieutenant General Sherman in regard to the protection of trains on the overland route. 40 Cong., 1 sess., *Senate Exec. Doc. No. 2* (Serial 1308), 1867.

Letter of the Secretary of War, 41 Cong., 2 sess., *House Exec. Doc. No. 121* (Serial 1417).

Letter of the Secretary of War, communicating, in compliance with a resolution of the Senate of the 11th instant, further information respecting armed expeditions against the western Indians, 40 Cong., 1 sess., *Senate Exec. Doc. No. 1* (Serial 1308).

Letter of the Secretary of War, in compliance with a resolution of the Senate of the 30th ultimo, the official reports, papers, and other facts in relation to the causes and extent of the late massacre of United States troops by Indians at Fort Phil. Kearney. 39 Cong., 2 sess., *Senate Exec. Doc. No. 15* (Serial 1277), 1867.

Letter of the Secretary of War, transmitting a communication from Lieutenant General Sherman, relative to the subsistence of certain Indian tribes by the War Department, etc. 40 Cong., 2 sess., *House Exec. Doc. No. 239* (Serial 1341), XV, 1868.

Official copies of correspondence relative to the war with the Modoc Indians in 1872–73. "Official Modoc War Correspondence." 43 Cong., 1 sess., *House Exec. Doc. No. 122* (Serial 1607).

"Protection Across the Continent." Letter from the Secretary of War in answer to a resolution of the House of December 6, 1866, transmitting information respecting the protection of the route across the continent to the Pacific from molestation by the hostile Indians. 39 Cong., 2 sess., *House Exec. Doc. No. 23* (Serial 1288).

Reduction of Army Officers' Pay, Reorganization of the Army, and Transfer of the Indian Bureau. 44 Cong., 1 sess., *House Report No. 354* (Serial 1709), II, 1875–76.

Removal of Navajo and Ute Indians. Letter from the Secretary of the Interior, transmitting telegram from Lieutenant General Sherman, relative to the removal of the Navajo and Ute Indians. 40 Cong., 2 sess., *House Exec. Doc. No. 308* (Serial 1345), XIX, 1867–68.

Report of four members of the joint committee appointed by the two houses of Congress, at its last session, to take into consideration the expediency of transferring the management of Indian affairs from the Interior to the War Department. 45 Cong., 3 sess., *House Report Nos. 92 and 93* (Serial 1866), January 31, 1879.

Reports of Inspection Made in the Summer of 1877 by Generals P. H. Sheridan and W. T. Sherman of Country North of the Union Pacific Railroad. Washington, Government Printing Office, 1878.

Report to Accompany the Bill (H. R. 2546) to Provide for the Gradual Reduction of the Army of the United States. 43 Cong., 1 sess., *House Report No. 384* (Serial 1624), II.

Report to the President by the Indian Peace Commission, January 7, 1868, in *Annual Report of the Secretary of the Interior*. 40 Cong., 3 sess., *House Exec. Docs.* (Serial 1366), 1868–69.

Testimony in relation to Indian war claims of the territory of Montana. 42 Cong., 2 sess., *House Misc. Doc. No. 215* (Serial 1527).

Testimony taken by the Committee on Military Affairs in relation to the Texas Border Troubles. 45 Cong., 2 sess., *House Misc. Doc. No. 64* (Serial 1820), 1878.

Bibliography

Transfer of the Bureau of Indian Affairs to the War Department.
46 Cong., 2 sess., *House Report No. 1393* (Serial 1937), 1880.

2. *General Government Documents*

Congressional Globe.

Congressional Record.

Richardson, James D. *A Compilation of the Messages and Papers of the Presidents, 1789-1902.* 10 vols. Washington, Government Printing Office, 1903.

United States Statutes at Large.

3. *Newspapers*

Arizona Sentinel, Yuma.

Army and Navy Journal, New York.

Benton Record, Montana.

Boulder County News, Colorado.

Cheyenne Leader, Wyoming. On January 13, 1870, the paper's name was changed to *Cheyenne Daily Leader.*

Chicago Daily Times.

Chicago Tribune.

Cleveland Plain Dealer.

Daily Alta California, San Francisco.

Daily Denver Times. On October 11, 1875, the paper became the *Denver Daily Times.*

Daily Missouri Republican, St. Louis.

Daily Oregonian, Portland.

Daily Rocky Mountain News, Denver.

Daily Times, Leavenworth, Kansas. On January 1, 1866, the paper became the *Leavenworth Daily Times.*

Daily Union Vedette, Salt Lake City.

Deseret News, Salt Lake City.

Helena Daily Herald, Montana.

Helena Herald, Montana.

Helena Weekly Herald, Montana.

Helena Weekly Independent, Montana.

Idaho Tri-Weekly Statesman, Boise.

Idaho Weekly Statesman, Boise.

Idaho World, Idaho City.

Junction City Union, Kansas. Before November 17, 1867, the paper was called the *Junction City Weekly Union.*

Leavenworth Daily Conservative, Kansas.
Montana Post, Virginia City.
Morning Call, San Francisco.
Morning Oregonian, Portland.
Nebraska Advertiser, Brownsville.
Nebraska City News, Nebraska.
Nebraska Republican, Omaha.
Nebraska Statesman, Nebraska City.
New North-West, Deer Lodge, Montana.
New York Daily Tribune.
New York Herald.
New York Times.
Nonpareil, Council Bluffs, Iowa.
Omaha Daily Herald, Nebraska.
Omaha Weekly Herald, Nebraska.
Omaha Weekly Republican, Nebraska.
Owyhee Avalanche, Ruby City, Idaho. On August 18, 1866, the name of the location changed to Silver City, Idaho.
Sacramento Daily Record, California.
St. Louis Daily Globe.
St. Louis Daily Times.
San Francisco Chronicle.
Santa Fe Weekly Gazette, New Mexico.

4. *Articles*

Athearn, Robert G. "Early Territorial Montana: A Problem in Colonial Administration," *The Montana Magazine of History,* Vol. I, No. 3 (July, 1951), 15–22.

———. "The Fort Buford 'Massacre,'" *The Mississippi Valley Historical Review,* Vol. XLI, No. 4 (March, 1955), 675–85.

———. (ed.). "From Illinois to Montana in 1866: The Diary of Perry A. Burgess," *The Pacific Northwest Quarterly,* Vol. XLI, No. 1 (January, 1950), 51–52.

———. "General Sherman and the Montana Frontier," *The Montana Magazine of History,* Vol. III, No. 1 (January, 1953), 55–65.

———. "The Montana Volunteers of 1867," *The Pacific Historical Review,* Vol. XIX, No. 2 (May, 1950), 127–37.

———. (ed.). "A Winter Campaign Against the Sioux," *The Mississippi Valley Historical Review,* Vol. XXXV, No. 2 (September, 1948), 272–85.

Bibliography

Ayres, Mary C. "History of Fort Lewis, Colorado," *The Colorado Magazine,* Vol. VIII (May, 1931).

Burgess, Henderson L. "The Eighteenth Kansas Volunteer Cavalry, and Some Incidents Connected with Its Service on the Plains," *Collections of the Kansas State Historical Society,* Vol. XIII (1913–14), 534–38.

Davis, Theodore R. "A Stage Ride to Colorado," *Harper's New Monthly Magazine,* Vol. XXXV (July, 1867), 137–50.

———. "With Sherman in His Army Home," *Cosmopolitan,* Vol. XII (December, 1891), 165–205.

Fenton, W. D. "Political History of Oregon from 1865 to 1876," *The Quarterly of the Oregon Historical Society,* Vol. II, No. 4 (December, 1901), 357–58.

Forbes, Archibald. "The United States Army," *North American Review,* Vol. CXXXV (August, 1882), 127–46.

Garfield, James A. "The Army of the United States," *North American Review,* Vol. CXXVI, Part I (March–April, 1878), 193–216; Part II (May–June, 1878), 442–66.

Lummis, Charles F. "Pioneer Transportation in America," *McClure's Magazine,* Vol. XXVI (November, 1905), 84–85.

Moore, Miles C. "A Pioneer Railroad Builder," *The Quarterly of the Oregon Historical Society,* Vol. IV, No. 3 (September, 1903), 200.

Nave, Orville J. "The Status of Army Chaplains," in T. G. Steward, *Active Service.* New York, no date.

Nichols, George Ward. "The Indian: What We Should Do With Him," *Harper's New Monthly Magazine,* Vol. XL (December, 1869–May, 1870), 372–79.

Price, W. E. "Major and Mrs. Price's American Tour," in M. Philips Price, *America After Sixty Years.* London, 1936.

Rister, Carl Coke. "Documents Relating to General W. T. Sherman's Southern Plains Indian Policy, 1871–1875," *Panhandle-Plains Historical Review,* Vol. IX (1936), 7–28; Vol. X (1937), 50–60.

Sanford, A. B. "Reminiscences of Kit Carson, Jr.," *The Colorado Magazine,* Vol. VI (September, 1929), 183.

Shanks, W. F. G. "Gossip About Our Generals," *Harper's New Monthly Magazine,* Vol. XXXV (July, 1867), 210–16.

Sherman, Minnie Ewing. "My Father's Letters," *Cosmopolitan,* Vol. XII (November–December, 1891), 64–69, 187–94.

Utley, Robert M. "The Celebrated Peace Policy of General Grant," *North Dakota History,* Vol. XX (July, 1953), 121–43.

Thompson, Albert W. "The Death and Last Will of Kit Carson," *The Colorado Magazine,* Vol. V (October, 1928), 190.

Weller, Ella Fraser. "Stranger than Fiction. A true short story told mainly in a series of unpublished letters by General Sherman," *McClure's Magazine,* Vol. VIII (April, 1897), 546–50.

Welty, Raymond L. "The Frontier Army on the Missouri River, 1860–1870," *North Dakota Historical Quarterly* (1928), 85–99.

———. "The Policing of the Frontier Army, 1860–1870," *The Kansas Historical Quarterly,* Vol. III, No. 3 (August, 1938).

———. "Supplying the Frontier Military Posts," *The Kansas Historical Quarterly,* Vol. VII, No. 2 (May, 1938), 154–69.

5. *Books*

Athearn, Robert G. *Thomas Francis Meagher: An Irish Revolutionary in America.* Boulder, Colo., 1949.

Bancroft, Hubert Howe. *History of Oregon.* 2 vols. San Francisco, 1888.

———. *History of Washington, Idaho and Montana.* San Francisco, 1890.

Biddle, Ellen McGowan. *Reminiscences of a Soldier's Wife.* Philadelphia, 1907.

Boyd, James P. *The Life of General William T. Sherman.* Philadelphia, 1891.

Brockett, L. P. *Men of Our Day.* Philadelphia, 1872.

Browning, Orville Hickman. *The Diary of Orville Hickman Browning.* Edited by James G. Randall. 2 vols. Springfield, 1933.

Burlingame, Merrill. *The Montana Frontier.* Helena, 1942.

Byers, S. H. M. *Twenty Years in Europe.* Chicago, 1900.

Byrne, P. E. *Soldiers of the Plains.* New York, 1926.

Chase, Edward. *The Memorial Life of General William Tecumseh Sherman.* Chicago, 1891.

Crawford, Samuel J. *Kansas in the Sixties.* Chicago, 1911.

Crook, General George. *His Autobiography.* Edited by Martin F. Schmitt. Norman, 1946 and 1947.

Davis, E. O. *The First Five Years of the Railroad Era in Colorado.* Denver, 1948.

Dodge, Grenville M. *How We Built the Union Pacific Railway.* 61 Cong., 2 sess. (1909–10), *Senate Doc. No. 447* (Serial 5658).

———. *Personal Recollections of President Abraham Lincoln, Gen-*

eral Ulysses S. Grant and General William T. Sherman. Council Bluffs, 1914.

Dodge, Richard Irving. *Our Wild Indians.* Hartford, 1884. (Sherman wrote the introduction.)

Downey, Fairfax. *Indian Fighting Army.* New York, 1941.

Force, Manning Ferguson. *General Sherman.* New York, 1899.

Ganoe, William Addleman. *The History of the United States Army.* New York, 1924.

Hall, Frank. *History of the State of Colorado.* 4 vols. Chicago, 1899.

Hanson, Joseph Mills. *The Conquest of the Missouri.* New York, 1909 and 1946.

Hesseltine, William B. *Ulysses S. Grant: Politician.* New York, 1935.

Hitchcock, Ethan Allen. *Fifty Years in Camp and Field: The Diary of Major General Ethan Allen Hitchcock.* New York, 1909.

Howard, Helen Addison, and Dan L. McGrath. *War Chief Joseph.* Caldwell, 1941.

Howbert, Irving. *Memories of a Lifetime in the Pike's Peak Region.* New York, 1925.

Hunt, Elvid, and Walter E. Lorence. *History of Fort Leavenworth, 1827–1937.* Fort Leavenworth, 1937.

Hyde, George E. *Red Cloud's Folk: A History of the Oglala Sioux Indians.* Norman, 1937.

Ingersoll, L. D. *A History of the War Department of the United States.* Washington, 1880.

Johnson, Willis Fletcher. *Life of William Tecumseh Sherman.* Philadelphia, 1891. (Introduction by General O. O. Howard.)

Keleher, William A. *Turmoil in New Mexico, 1846–1868.* Santa Fé, 1952.

Kimball, James P. *A Soldier-Doctor of Our Army.* Edited by Maria Brace Kimball. Boston and New York, 1917.

Kingsburg, George W. *History of Dakota Territory.* 2 vols. Chicago, 1915.

Kirkland, Frazar. *The Pictorial Book of Anecdotes of the Rebellion.* St. Louis, 1889.

Leonard, Levi O., and Jack T. Johnson. *A Railroad to the Sea.* Iowa City, 1939.

Lewis, Lloyd. *Sherman: Fighting Prophet.* New York, 1932. (The best biography of Sherman.)

Liddell Hart, B. H. *Sherman: Soldier, Realist, American.* New York, 1929.

Ludeke, Henry. *Frank Buchser's Amerikanische Sendung: 1861–1871.* Basel, Switzerland, 1941. (One chapter describes Sherman's western trip of 1866. Buchser went along to paint western scenes in Wyoming and Colorado.)

McAllister, Anna. *Ellen Ewing: Wife of General Sherman.* New York, 1936.

Northrop, Henry Davenport. *Life and Deeds of General Sherman.* Boston, 1891.

Payne, Doris Palmer. *Captain Jack: Modoc Renegade.* Portland, 1938.

Perkins, J. R. *Trails, Rails and War; Life of General G. M. Dodge.* Indianapolis, 1929.

Richardson, Rupert Norval. *The Comanche Barrier to South Plains Settlement.* Glendale, 1933.

Rister, Carl Coke. *Border Command: General Phil Sheridan in the West.* Norman, 1944.

Robins, Edward. *William T. Sherman.* Philadelphia, 1905.

Rodenbough, Theo. F., and William L. Haskin. *The Army of the United States.* New York, 1896.

Rogers, Fred B. *Soldiers of the Overland.* San Francisco, 1938.

Root, Frank A., and William E. Connelley. *The Overland Stage to California.* Topeka, 1901.

Rusling, James Fowler. *Across America: or, the Great West and the Pacific Coast.* New York, 1874.

————. *Men and Things I saw in Civil War Days.* New York, 1899.

Sabin, Edwin L. *Building the Pacific Railway.* Philadelphia, 1919.

Shelton, Mason Bradford. *Rocky Mountain Adventures.* Boston, 1920.

Sheridan, Philip H. *Personal Memoirs of P. H. Sheridan.* 2 vols. New York, 1888.

Sherman, William Tecumseh. *Memoirs of General William T. Sherman,* 4th ed. 2 vols. New York, 1891.

Schmeckebier, Laurence F. *The Office of Indian Affairs, Its History, Activity, and Organization.* Baltimore, 1927.

Schofield, John M. *Forty-Six Years in the Army.* New York, 1897.

Stanley, Henry Morton. *My Early Travels and Adventures in America and Asia.* 2 vols. New York, 1895.

Stewart, Edgar I. *Custer's Luck.* Norman, 1955.

Taylor, Joseph Henry. *Sketches of Frontier and Indian Life on the Upper Missouri and Great Plains.* Bismarck, 1897.

Bibliography

Thorndike, Rachel Sherman (ed.). *The Sherman Letters*. New York, 1894.

Trobriand, Philipe Régis de. *Military Life in Dakota*. Translated and edited by Lucile M. Kane. St. Paul, 1951.

Turner, Katharine C. *Red Men Calling on the Great White Father*. Norman, 1951.

Vaughan, Robert. *Then and Now: or, Thirty-Six Years in the Rockies*. Minneapolis, 1900.

Wharton, Clarence. *Satanta: The Great Chief of the Kiowas and His People*. Dallas, 1935.

White, Henry Kirke. *History of the Union Pacific Railway*. Chicago, 1895.

Wilson, James Harrison. *The Life of John A. Rawlins*. New York, 1916.

Wilson, Neill C., and Frank J. Taylor. *Southern Pacific: The Roaring Story of a Fighting Railroad*. New York, 1952.

Wright, Robert M. *Dodge City: The Cowboy Capital of the Great Southwest*. Wichita, 1913.

UNIVERSITY OF OKLAHOMA PRESS

NORMAN